Helping Skills

Helping Skills

Facilitating Exploration, Insight, and Action

Third Edition

Clara E. Hill

American Psychological Association

Washington, DC

First Printing March 2009
Second Printing October 2009

Published by
American Psychological Association
750 First Street, NE
Washington, DC 20002
www.apa.org

To order
APA Order Department
P.O. Box 92984
Washington, DC 20090-2984
Tel: (800) 374-2721; Direct: (202) 336-5510
Fax: (202) 336-5502; TDD/TTY: (202) 336-6123
Online: www.apa.org/books/
E-mail: order@apa.org

In the U.K., Europe, Africa, and the Middle East, copies may be ordered from
American Psychological Association
3 Henrietta Street
Covent Garden, London
WC2E 8LU England

Typeset in Meridien by Circle Graphics, Inc. Columbia, MD

Printer: United Book Press, Inc., Baltimore, MD
Cover Designer: Minker Design, Bethesda, MD
Technical/Production Editor: Dan Brachtesende
Cover art: Paul Gauguin, *Breton Girls Dancing, Pont-Aven*, Collection of Mr. and Mrs. Paul Mellon, Image © 2003 Board of Trustees, National Gallery of Art, Washington, DC, 1888, oil on canvas.

The opinions and statements published are the responsibility of the authors, and such opinions and statements do not necessarily represent the policies of the American Psychological Association.

Library of Congress Cataloging-in-Publication Data

Hill, Clara E., 1948-
  Helping skills : facilitating exploration, insight, and action / Clara E. Hill. — 3rd ed.
      p. cm.
  Includes bibliographical references and index.
  ISBN-13: 978-1-4338-0451-9
  ISBN-10: 1-4338-0451-4
  1. Counseling—Textbooks. 2. Helping behavior—Textbooks. I. Title.

  BF637.C6H46 2009
  158'.3—dc22
                                        2008047812
British Library Cataloguing-in-Publication Data
A CIP record is available from the British Library.

Printed in the United States of America
Third Edition

To my husband, Jim Gormally, my fellow traveler in the process of learning helping skills; to my children, Kevin and Katie, who have tested my helping skills; and to my students, who have taught me how to teach helping skills.

Contents

V

Preface

My interest in training helpers has developed from teaching helping skills classes to undergraduate and graduate students for about 35 years. When I first taught these courses, I felt frustrated in trying to find the right textbook that would embody my philosophy of helping and address the needs of my students. Few, if any, helping skills texts integrate the importance of affect, cognition, and behavior in the process of change. Some concentrate on feelings while disregarding the role of challenge and action in facilitating critical life changes, whereas others highlight insight at the expense of affective exploration and behavior change. Several popular texts focus solely on a problem-solving approach, which neglects the critical role of affect in helping clients express, understand, and alter that with which they are dissatisfied in their lives. Other books do not provide the crucial theoretical and empirical foundation for the helping skills. To address these limitations, I used the knowledge garnered from my experiences as a student, teacher, counselor, supervisor, and researcher to write a book that teaches helpers to assist clients in exploring their feelings and thoughts, gaining new insights about their problems, and moving toward positive behavior changes.

My Philosophy of Helping

This text introduces an integrated model that is grounded in practice, theory, and research. Grounding the model in practice and theory is important to take advantage of the work of accomplished clinicians and theoreticians who have articulated a rich theoretical knowledge base. Rogers, Freud,

Erikson, Mahler, Skinner, Ellis, Beck, and others have provided brilliant insights into the nature of human beings, the mechanisms of change in counseling and therapy, and the techniques for assisting individuals to achieve their potential and accomplish their goals. The three-stage model is grounded in the contributions of these sage theorists, and readers are introduced to the salient aspects of their work.

Grounding the model in research is also important. Research educates helpers about the effective (and ineffective) use of helping skills. Our confidence in promoting the helping skills is strengthened by the knowledge that these skills have been tested empirically and found to be useful to clients. Of course, research on helping skills is still in its infancy, so there is much that is not known. I hope that by providing a clear model of the helping process, more people will take on the task of doing empirical research to test the model (see also the companion text; Hill, 2001, on empirical foundations).

The model involves three stages: exploration, insight, and action. The exploration stage is based on client-centered theory (e.g., Rogers, 1942, 1951, 1957, 1959). Psychoanalytic and interpersonal theories (e.g., Freud, 1940/1949; Teyber, 2006; Yalom, 1980) form the foundation for the insight stage. The action stage is based on behavioral (e.g., Goldfried & Davison, 1994; Kazdin, 2001; Watson & Tharp, 2006) theories. These major theories are integrated in this three-stage model because all have proven to be effective in helping clients (see Wampold, 2001).

The helping process can be conceptualized as involving moment-by-moment interaction sequences (Hill, 1992). Helpers develop intentions for how they want to help clients. These intentions are based on what they know about clients and what they hope to accomplish with clients at a given time. With these intentions in mind, helpers select verbal and nonverbal skills with which to intervene. In turn, clients react to the interventions in ways that influence how they then choose to behave with helpers. Thus, helping involves not only the overt behaviors but also the cognitive processes of helpers (i.e., intentions) and clients (i.e., reactions). Awareness of intentions assists helpers in selecting effective interventions. In addition, attention to the clients' reactions to the interventions can aid helpers in planning future interventions.

Finally, I sought to write a book that both supports students' development as helpers and provides challenges to facilitate the development of helping skills. Becoming an effective helper is an exciting and challenging process. For some, this undertaking can be life changing. Many students are fascinated by the process of becoming helpers, and they pose thoughtful questions as they struggle to learn the skills and develop confidence in their ability to assist others. Because the focus of this book is on helpers (not clients), I pose many questions that relate to the helpers' development and concomitant feelings and thoughts.

What This Text Does Not Provide

It seems necessary to clarify the focus of this book by also indicating what this text does not provide. It is beyond the scope of this book to provide information about counseling children, families, or clients who have serious emotional or psychological difficulties. Although the helping skills taught in this book are crucial and form the foundation for work with all these groups, helpers will need much more extensive and specialized training before they will be qualified to work with these groups.

Furthermore, I do not address the diagnosis of psychological problems or identify characteristics of psychopathology, which are two important topics that require extensive additional training. I encourage helpers to pursue further training in assessment and psychopathology after developing a working knowledge of basic helping skills. I believe that all helpers, even those working with healthy populations, should be able to recognize serious psychological disorders. This level of knowledge aids helpers in making appropriate referrals and working only with clients they have been trained to assist.

In addition, this book touches only briefly on cultural issues related to helping. The influence of culture is pervasive and is reflected in the helping process through the client's and helper's worldviews and the interaction between them. Clients need to be viewed in the context of the multitude of influences that have an impact on their lives (e.g., family and friends, support systems, racial and cultural background, work experiences, life transitions, socioeconomic status). I strongly encourage helpers to educate themselves about multicultural theory and research (e.g., D. R. Atkinson, Morten, & Sue, 1993; Helms & Cook, 1999; Pedersen, Draguns, Lonner, & Trimble, 2002; Ponterotto, Casas, Suzuki, & Alexander, 1995; D. W. Sue & Sue, 1999).

Goals for This Book

I have several goals for this book. Readers should be able to articulate the principles of the integrated three-stage model of helping as well as the theoretical and research foundations underlying this model. They should demonstrate an understanding of the interactional sequences of helping, including the intentions that helpers have for interventions with clients, the helping skills that are commensurate with these intentions, the possible reactions and behaviors demonstrated by clients, and the means by which helpers evaluate the interventions used. In addition, readers should gain a better understanding of themselves in relation to becoming helpers, including their thoughts about helping as well as their strengths and areas for continued growth. Finally, I hope to instill enthusiasm for the process of learning to help others—an enterprise that is certain to provide countless challenges and rewards throughout a lifetime.

Changes in the Third Edition

I continue to modify the model as I teach and do research on helping skills. The model feels like a living thing because of how I continually find ways to improve it on the basis of on my experiences with teaching it. The third edition of this book differs from the first and second editions in several ways:

- The skills are organized within goals for each of the stages, as opposed to previously having just presented the skills within the stages. This change is because I have come to believe that goals are more important than skills and that more than one skill can be used to implement each of the goals.
- The chapter on attending, listening, and observing skills (chap. 5) has been extensively rewritten.
- The challenges chapter (chap. 10) has been changed to make it clearer conceptually.
- Open questions has been dropped as a separate chapter and, rather, open questions have been added into other chapters (open questions for thoughts in chap. 6; open questions for feelings in chap. 7; open questions for insight in chap. 11; and open questions for action in chap. 15).
- New steps have been added in the insight stage.
- Self-disclosure has been dropped as a separate chapter and, rather, disclosures of different types have been added into other chapters (disclosures about feelings into chap. 7, disclosures about insight into chap. 11, and disclosures about strategies into chap. 15).
- The action stage has been changed to focus on steps for accomplishing four types of action (relaxation, behavior change, behavioral rehearsal, and decision making).
- There is more discussion of culture.
- A DVD—*Helping Skills in Practice: A Three-Stage Model*—has been created to illustrate the three stages. It is available from the American Psychological Association.

i Web Resources

As with the previous edition, this third edition of *Helping Skills* offers a Web-based "Instructor and Student Resource Guide" (http://www.apa .org/books/resources/Hill3), the student portion of which features a dozen Web Forms (in downloadable PDFs) that are referred to throughout this text to assist students in evaluating their helping skills and helper–client sessions:

Web Form A
Session Review Form

Web Form B
Supervisor Rating Form

Web Form C
Sample Transcript

Web Form D
Helper Intentions List

Web Form E
Helping Skills System

Web Form F
Using the Helping Skills System for Research

Web Form G
Client Reactions System

Web Form H
Client Behavior System

Web Form I
Session Process and Outcome Measures

Web Form J
Self-Awareness and Management Strategies Survey

Web Form K
Counselor Activity Self-Efficacy Scales

Web Form L
Process Notes

Emotion Words Checklist

The Web Forms page also includes an Emotion Words Checklist—a downloadable version of this edition's Exhibit 7.2 (see chap. 7)—which students have found helpful to have handy in a printed format for easy reference during the exploration stage of a helper–client relationship. In addition, the student resources of the *Helping Skills* Web area includes downloadable versions of the Labs at the end of various chapters, and of the Practice Exercises featured at the end of the skills chapters of the book.

Acknowledgments

I am very grateful for the many people who have read selected chapters or all of the book and provided valuable feedback of one or all editions: Margaret Barott, Jennifer Dahne, Elizabeth Doschek, Lisa Flores, Suzanne Friedman, Melissa Goates, Julie Goldberg, Jim Gormally, Allison Grolnick, Kelly Hennessey, Beth Haverkamp, Jeff Hayes, Debby Herbenick, Pamela Highlen, Merris Hollingworth, Jennifer Jeffery, Ian Kellems, Sarah Knox, Misty Kolchakian, Jim Lichtenberg, Rayna Markin, John Norcross, Karen O'Brien, Sheetal Patel, David Petersen, Missy Roffman, Eric Spiegel, Jessica Stahl, Nicole Taylor, Barbara Thompson, Linda Tipton, Terry Tracey, Jonathan Walker, Heather Walton, and Elizabeth Nutt Williams. I have profited considerably from the editorial feedback, guidance, and encouragement of Beth Beisel, Dan Brachtesende, Amy Clarke, Phuong Huynh, Linda McCarter, Peter Pavilionis, Susan Reynolds, and Shenyun Wu all from the American Psychological Association Books program, on the different editions of the book.

I am most indebted to the many students in my undergraduate course in helping skills and graduate course in theories and strategies of counseling over the last several years. They have taught me a tremendous amount about how to teach helping skills with their willingness to challenge my ideas, offering thoughtful perspectives on the process of becoming helpers and providing examples for the text. I tried out all the chapters and the lab exercises on many classes before including them in the book. Finally, and with much gratitude, I recognize and acknowledge my therapists, professors, and supervisors, who served as wonderful models for how to use helping skills and who provided much encouragement throughout my process of becoming a helper. I particularly want to acknowledge Bill Anthony (who studied with Robert Carkhuff), from whom I first learned helping skills many years ago in graduate school. I clearly recall the heady times of coming to believe that I could help clients if I applied the helping skills.

OVERVIEW

Introduction to Helping

1

Nothing in life is achieved without effort, daring to take risks, and often some suffering.

—*Erich Fromm*

Angeli was a stellar student and athlete. She was president of her high school class and had been accepted into an elite eastern university. By any standard, she was an exceptional and talented individual with much promise. However, after arriving at college, Angeli began to feel sad. Much to the dismay of her family, teachers, and friends, she lost interest in interacting with others, studying for her classes, and attending track practice. Angeli's track coach encouraged her to meet with a helper, who helped Angeli explore her feelings and gain understanding of the issues underlying her sadness and inactivity. Angeli felt supported by, cared for, and challenged by her helper. The helping relationship enabled her to express, understand, struggle with, and overcome the feelings of inadequacy, loneliness, and loss that emerged when she left home for college.

As you read about Angeli and think about what it would be like to be her helper, you may have contradictory thoughts and feelings. You may feel confident that you could help someone like Angeli because you have listened to and advised friends and family members about their problems. But you may also feel anxiety about knowing how to help her explore her feelings and gain understanding.

If you are interested in learning more about the skills that would help you work with someone like Angeli, you have come to the right place. The first purpose of this book is to provide you with a theoretical framework that you can use to approach the helping process. The second purpose is to teach you specific skills to use in sessions with clients to help them explore, gain insight, and make changes in their lives. The third purpose is to get you started in the process of coming to think of yourself as a helper.

This chapter provides an introduction to the helping process, defines helping, and reviews facilitative and problematic aspects of helping. I talk about what makes people seek out professional helpers, and that leads naturally to a discussion about the effectiveness of helping. Next, I introduce the idea of becoming a helper, specifically exploring the healthy and unhealthy motivators for helping other people. Finally, I describe the organization of the book and discuss how it can best be used.

Welcome aboard! I hope you enjoy learning helping skills as much as I have.

What Is Helping?

Helping is a broad and generic term that includes the assistance provided by a variety of individuals, such as friends, family, counselors, psychotherapists, and human service providers. I use this broad term (rather than the more specific terms *counseling* and *psychotherapy*) because not everyone learning these skills is in a program that offers training and credentialing to become a mental health professional. Of course, these same skills are used by counselors and psychotherapists, but you cannot call yourself a counselor or psychotherapist until you have had further training, practice, and supervision and pass a credentialing examination.

Throughout this book, then, the term *helper* refers to the individual providing assistance, and the term *client* refers to the person receiving support. *Helping* can be defined as one person assisting another in exploring feelings, gaining insight, and making changes in his or her life. Helpers and clients work together to achieve these outcomes, with helpers guiding the process and clients deciding what, when, and how they want to change.

When I talk in this book about trainees who are learning helping skills practicing with each other or with volunteer clients, I refer to the process as *helping*. In contrast, when I talk about clients seeking help from professionals, I use instead the terms *counseling* (or counselor) and *psychotherapy* (or therapist or psychotherapist).

I am often asked about the differences between counseling and psychotherapy. At times, the two are differentiated by length of treatment (counseling may have fewer sessions than psychotherapy); clientele (counseling is more often used with relatively "healthy" individuals who have issues with adjustment, whereas psychotherapy serves those with more serious pathology); qualifications of the provider (counselors may have master's or doctoral degrees, whereas psychotherapists tend to be doctoral-level practitioners); and types of problems presented in sessions (counseling may deal with development and life transition issues, whereas psychotherapy may address more serious psychological disturbances). However, this book is written from the perspective that counseling and psychotherapy are very similar, that helping skills form the foundation for both counseling and psychotherapy, and that most individuals can benefit from learning basic helping skills.

Facilitative Aspects of Helping

There are a number of ways in which helping can be facilitative. For people in emotional pain, helping can provide support and relief. For example, Jillian and Jesse went to couples counseling because Jillian had been involved in a sexual relationship with a colleague. Both Jillian and Jesse were extremely hurt and felt angry with each other. Positive changes in their relationship came after months of working on communication skills, receiving assistance in exploring feelings, understanding the factors related to the affair, and learning how to work proactively to improve their relationship. After several sessions, Jillian and Jesse were able to communicate their feelings more openly, grieve the loss of trust in their relationship, and move toward rebuilding their lives as a cohesive and caring couple. They felt that their therapist had been supportive and they felt relief from the problems for which they sought therapy.

Through the process of helping, clients can also gain insight, such that they come to understand themselves in new ways. For example, in her recent book about serving as a psychologist in Iraq, Kraft (2007) described the process of therapy working with a soldier who could not walk even though the medical doctors found no physiological reason for this inability. After establishing a good relationship with the soldier, Kraft talked about how the soldier was finally able to tell her about losing a friend who died trying to shield him from danger. Once the soldier gained insight into the reason for his symptom, he was able to walk again. It is interesting to note that many of Freud's first patients similarly had conversion hysteria and were healed through catharsis and insight.

In addition, helping can assist individuals in dealing with existential concerns (i.e., who am I, where am I going, and what do I want out of life?). As Socrates said, "The unexamined life is not worth living." Helping can promote proactive involvement in life when these questions are asked, reflected on, and answered. For example, Max was referred for helping because of failing grades, poor peer relationships, and generalized sadness. After several sessions, Max began to address critical questions regarding how he might live his life, the fears he often confronts within himself, and the salience of his relationships with others. Helping provided him with an opportunity to look within himself, discover what was important, and then make decisions about how to change his unhealthy behaviors.

Moreover, clients can learn skills needed to live more effectively and reach their potential. These skills may include learning how to communicate with others, practicing ways to resolve conflicts, becoming more assertive, identifying decision-making strategies, studying more effectively, learning to relax, or changing unhealthy habits (e.g., rarely exercising; having unprotected, anonymous sex). Often, these skills can alleviate the powerlessness that individuals feel when they are unable to communicate their emotions directly and can assist clients in engaging more fully in their lives.

Helping can also assist individuals in making decisions about the direction of their lives. The most effective helpers have the ability to assist individuals in determining goals that are consistent with their dreams, values, and abilities. For example, Mai Lin came to counseling because she was uncertain about whether she should move far away from her family and end her relationship with her live-in boyfriend. She described her current situation and asked the helper to tell her what the best path for her would be. After dealing with her anger and frustration at the helper for not providing the answers, Mai Lin was able to explore her unwillingness to take responsibility for the direction of her life and her reluctance to address the questions that plagued her. She contemplated her fear of taking action and of making wrong decisions and connected this with feelings of helplessness she had experienced as a child of a battered woman. Further exploration of thoughts, feelings, and behaviors provided her with the desire to make small decisions (with the support and encouragement of her helper). Soon, Mai Lin was able to progress to more challenging decisions (e.g., ending her romantic relationship, moving across the country alone to explore her independence and to understand herself better).

An additional facilitative aspect of helping involves helpers providing feedback about how clients appear to others, information that others might hesitate to provide. For example, a client who is having difficulty maintaining relationships may be able to hear (from the helper) that he appears dependent and needy in sessions and may want to examine whether these behaviors are present in other relationships. Although helpers should phrase their comments in a gentle manner, honest feedback can be extremely helpful in motivating individuals to change.

Helping also can enable a client to experience a healthy, non-damaging, intimate relationship with another person. Sometimes the helping process involves a corrective relational experience (something like reparenting) in that a caring relationship with a helper alleviates some of the hurtful and unhealthy interactions experienced with important figures early in life. For example, Kondja came to helping because she felt depressed and lacked direction in her life. She believed that her mother did not want her as a child, and she cried when she saw mothers and daughters who were connected and loving with one another. Kondja had been in a series of relationships in which she felt ignored, alone, uncared for, and discounted. During the helping process, Kondja experienced the helper as unconditionally accepting, actively listening, and genuinely caring. The development of a supportive relationship with a helper assisted Kondja in healing past wounds, drinking less alcohol to numb her feelings, and developing healthy relationships in which she valued herself enough to ensure that her needs were met.

Finally, effective helping teaches clients to function on their own. Similar to the way children grow up and leave their parents, clients also need to leave their helpers. Perhaps some of you have tried to teach another person to skate: You hold the person up, and she or he hangs on while making a first attempt at skating. In time, the person begins to skate alone. The steps that the learner makes on his or her own are rewarding not only for the learner but also for you as the teacher. The same is true with helping: Providing the initial support and teaching the skills are most effective when individuals internalize the messages and take off on their own.

Problematic Aspects of Helping

Although helping is usually beneficial, there are a few potentially problematic aspects. Sometimes helping can provide just enough relief to enable people to stay in maladaptive situations or relationships. For example, battered women's shelters provide needed safety and security to abused women and their children. However, some shelter workers have observed that occasionally they provide just enough assistance to enable women to return to the abusive situation. When the workers in one shelter confronted this "enabling" in themselves and discussed these behaviors with the residents, some of the battered women were able to identify their pattern of seeking shelter during the abusive periods and returning home in the honeymoon period. Without this insight, helping could have enabled some of the women to continue in a potentially deadly cycle.

Another potential problem is that helping can create dependency if clients rely too much on their helpers for support and feel unable to explore feelings or make changes in their lives without assistance from the helper. For example, Kathleen might decline a spontaneous invitation to join her new partner's family on Cape Cod for a week because her helper is on vacation and unavailable for consultation. Helpers sometimes facilitate dependency by providing clients with "the answers" to their problems (e.g., if her helper told Kathleen not to go to Cape Cod). Effective helpers understand that providing the answers does not typically help clients; rather, most clients need to participate actively in a process whereby they uncover new insights and discover which actions feel best for themselves. This strategy works because only clients fully know the situations, experience the associated feelings, and have the best answers to the presenting problems. In addition, advising others may be problematic when the solution that is provided does not fit with their needs. Many of us have made suggestions to family members or friends about how to handle difficult situations, only to find that our advice was not exactly what they wanted to hear. For example, a helper advised a client to stay away from her boyfriend who broke up with her because he was not good enough for her. Although the client was eager at the time to hear about how rotten the boyfriend was, she resented the helper's critical words about her sweetheart when they later got back together.

In addition, helpers' personal issues sometimes place them at risk for encouraging dependency in those they assist. For helpers who are lonely and isolated, their clients' dependency may fulfill personal needs that are not being met elsewhere. Helpers who have not developed a network of social support and personal relationships may be at special risk of encouraging their clients to rely extensively on them.

Another problematic aspect of helping emerges when helpers unduly impose personal or societal values on their clients (McWhirter, 1994). Although all of us have values that shape who we are, the goal of helping is to encourage clients to explore and decide on their own values. Examples of undue influence are when a helping professional attempts to alter the sexual orientation of people who are lesbian, gay, or bisexual (Haldeman, 2002); advises parents to raise their children in a certain religion because the helper believes that problems in families result from children not having a strong religious foundation; or states that women should not work outside the home because they take jobs away from qualified men who have families to raise. These examples all involve the helper attempting to force his or her values on the client.

Values can also be imposed at a more subtle level. In an investigation of Carl Rogers providing therapy, Truax (1966) found that in fact Rogers was more reinforcing of some client behaviors than others. For example, Rogers responded with more empathy and warmth when the client expressed insight, but with less empathy and warmth when the client was ambiguous. In other words, even Rogers, who worked hard to be accepting and empathic, demonstrated that he valued certain client behaviors over others. These results show that it is difficult to leave our biases behind.

It can also be problematic when helpers work outside their areas of competence (e.g., working with someone who has substance abuse but not having knowledge about that area). Similarly, helpers sometimes try to force clients to explore difficult topics, such as sexual abuse, without making sure that clients feel safe and have the necessary emotional regulation skills to explore such topics. Finally, it can be difficult when helpers are paired with clients with whom they do not "click." As in friendships, one needs to have a certain "clicking" with one's helper to feel comfortable enough to talk about one's problems. Without that matching, clients can become discouraged and actually feel more distressed because they might feel that no one can understand and help them.

When Do People Seek Help From Others?

Two factors seem to be necessary for people to seek help (Gross & McMullen, 1983). First, a person must become aware that she or he is in pain or is facing a difficult situation and then must perceive her or his feelings or situation as being problematic. Obviously, the perception of pain varies from person to person, such that what is unbearable for one person is easily tolerated or ignored by another person.

Second, the pain must be greater than the perceived barriers to seeking help. Sometimes the barriers involve practical considerations, such as the time or money required to obtain help; but often the obstacles are emotional and can include fears about exploring problems deeply or concerns about the opinions of others regarding people who seek therapy.

Many people hesitate to seek professional help (Gross & McMullen, 1983) because they feel embarrassed or ashamed about asking for assistance or believe that seeking help constitutes emotional weakness or inadequacy (Shapiro, 1984). Many Americans, for example, believe that individuals should rely solely on themselves and that all problems should be solved individually. Given these beliefs, it is not surprising that researchers have found that people seek help first from friends and family members and only last from professionals (Snyder, Hill, & Derksen, 1972; Tinsley, de St. Aubin, & Brown, 1982; Webster & Fretz, 1978).

Some people are concerned about talking with others because they feel that no one else can possibly understand their situation (e.g., Thomas thought that no one could understand his experience growing up in a religious cult). Others fear a punitive response or a value judgment regarding their thoughts, feelings, or actions (e.g., Candace felt that she would be judged for having had two abortions). Furthermore, some people may be concerned that they will be labeled *mentally ill* and thus be subject to the many negative stereotypes and stigma associated with this label (D. Sue, Sue, & Sue, 1994). Some clients may be hesitant to seek therapy because they rely on their insurance companies to pay for therapy: They may be concerned that the stigma associated with receiving therapy could have negative ramifications for obtaining insurance or employment in the future.

For example, Conchita came to her first session of psychotherapy because she was experiencing multiple stressors: Her mother had committed suicide 3 years earlier, her sister had been diagnosed with depression, she was failing all of her courses (previously she had been an "A" student), her first serious boyfriend had broken up with her, and she was pregnant. For some time, Conchita had felt that she should handle her problems by herself because she feared what others might think of her if they knew that she needed to see a therapist. Moreover, she was on a limited budget and was reluctant to pay for therapy. However, Conchita had begun to feel that she could no longer cope with her problems by herself. Her brother had gone to a therapist and felt better, so she thought that going to a therapist might work for her. Thus, Conchita sought help because she perceived herself as having problems and she believed that the potential benefits associated with therapy (e.g., emotional support, assistance with coping) outweighed the costs (e.g., financial expense, perceived stigma).

Individuals in considerable pain who are able to admit their need for psychological assistance have made significant progress toward obtaining the help they need. Support from friends and family can provide the encouragement these individuals need to contact trained helpers (Gourash, 1978). For example, Joe was reluctant to seek help after his wife of 40 years died. His friends and children encouraged him to attend a support group for adults who had lost their partner. Although initially reluctant, Joe was so upset about his loss that he agreed to participate in the group sessions if his daughters would accompany him. The support his family and friends provided enabled Joe to access the help that he needed.

Helpers need to work to change negative attitudes about seeking professional psychological assistance in our society. We helpers can begin by seeking help ourselves and encouraging others to seek help when needed. We can also work to initiate and support legislation for additional mental health benefits. In addition, we can work to educate the public by publicizing information about mental health treatments. Finally, we can do research to discover more about the process and outcome of helping endeavors and disseminate these research findings to the public.

Is Helping Effective?

Investigators have overwhelmingly concluded that psychotherapy is generally helpful. Most clients improve by the end of psychotherapy. Specifically, Wampold (2001), in his review of the literature, found that the average client who was in psychotherapy was psychologically healthier than 79% of untreated individuals. Wampold concluded that "psychotherapy is remarkably efficacious" (p. 71).

Once researchers established conclusively that psychotherapy in general is indeed helpful, they began to examine the relative effectiveness of different types of therapy. To date, hundreds of studies have compared different types of treatment (e.g., client-centered, psychodynamic, cognitive–behavioral, experiential), but no one type of therapy has been found to be more effective than others (Wampold, 2001; Wampold et al., 1997). Wampold noted, however, that the treatments studied were all sanctioned forms of treatment rather than fringe or quack forms of treatment, so these results may not hold for nonmainstream treatments. Similarly, no differences have been found between individual and group treatments (Piper, 2008; M. L. Smith, Glass, & Miller, 1980). The findings from this area of research have been humorously summarized using the dodo bird verdict from *Alice in Wonderland:* "Everyone has won and all must have prizes" (Carroll, 1865/1962, p. 412).

It is probably hard to understand how therapies that are so different can all lead to the same outcomes. Many different reasons have been proposed for the lack of differences across approaches. The most currently popular explanation is that factors involved in all types of mainstream approaches (i.e., common factors) lead to positive outcomes. Frank and Frank (1991) discussed six factors that are common across psychotherapies: the therapeutic relationship, instillation of hope, new learning experiences, emotional arousal, enhancement of mastery or self-efficacy, and opportunities for practice. Another explanation for the lack of differences among psychotherapeutic approaches is that client and therapist factors explain more of the variance than treatment types (again see Wampold, 2001). Yet another explanation (and one that I personally prefer) is that our research is still at a rather primitive state and that our tools for examining the process and outcome of therapy are not sophisticated enough to pick up the differences between approaches. It is quite possible that all approaches can be helpful and lead to similar outcomes but do so through different mechanisms. For example, experiential therapy might heal through allowing deep immersion into feelings, which then leads the client to change thoughts and behaviors. By contrast, cognitive–behavioral therapy might begin with changes in thoughts and behaviors, which in turn lead to a change in emotions. Furthermore, different therapists and clients may prefer approaches that fit with their worldviews and personality styles.

Another interesting line of research has examined how many psychotherapy sessions are needed to reduce psychological distress and return the client to normal psychological functioning (e.g., Grissom, Lyons, & Lutz, 2002; Howard, Lueger, Maling, & Martinovich, 1993; Kopta, Howard, Lowry, & Beutler, 1994). In their reviews of a large number of studies, these researchers proposed three phases of the psychotherapeutic recovery process. In the first phase, clients change rapidly in terms of feeling subjectively better. In the second, slower phase, there is a remediation of symptoms such as depression and anxiety. In the third and slowest phase, there is rehabilitation of troublesome, maladaptive behaviors that interfere with life functioning in areas such as family and work. Clients with minimal distress improve fairly quickly, whereas clients with chronic characterological problems (i.e., innate, severe, ongoing, and difficult-to-treat disorders) require the greatest number of sessions to return to normal functioning.

Cultural Issues in Helping

Culture has been defined as the customs, values, attitudes, beliefs, characteristics, and behaviors shared by a group of people at a particular time in history (Skovholt & Rivers, 2003). In addition, culture can be considered the "shared constraints that limit the behavior repertoire available to members of a certain sociocultural group in a way different from individuals belonging to some other group" (Poortinga, 1990, p. 6). It can also be thought of as "a convenient label for knowledge, skills, and attitudes that are learned and passed on from one generation to the next. Accordingly, this transmission of culture occurs in a physical environment in which certain places, times, and stimuli have acquired special meanings" (Segall, 1979, p. 91). An even broader definition of a cultural group is "any group of people who identify or associate with one another on the basis of some common purpose, need, or similarity of background" (Axelson, 1999, p. 3).

Culture includes such things as race/ethnicity, gender, age, ideology, religion, socioeconomic status, sexual orientation, disability status, occupation, and dietary preferences (Pedersen, 1991, 1997). Each of us belongs to many cultures, any one of which may become salient depending on the time, place, or situation (Pedersen & Ivey, 1993). Some cultural groups require admission (e.g., one has to attend school and pass tests to become a psychologist). Others are biologically determined (e.g., age, gender). And still others are a person's choices, although they are influenced by environmental factors (e.g., religion, vegetarianism).

Even the definitions of human development seem to be culturally determined. For example, McGoldrick, Giordano, and Garcia-Preto (2005b) suggested that

> Eastern cultures define the person as a social being and categorize development by growth in the capacity for empathy and connection. Many Western cultures, in contrast, begin by positing the individual as a psychological being and define development as growth in the capacity for autonomous functioning. (p. 3)

Although it is important to learn about general characteristics of a culture because there are usually some grains of truth about general trends (and there are some excellent books that review this area, e.g., D. R. Atkinson & Hackett, 1998; McGoldrick, Giordano, & Garcia-Preto, 2005a; Muran, 2007; Pedersen, Draguns, Lonner, & Trimble, 2002; Ponterotto, Casas, Suzuki, & Alexander, 1995; D. W. Sue & Sue, 1999), it is important not to assume that everyone within a given group is the same. In fact, there are generally more differences within groups than there are between groups (D. R. Atkinson, Morten, & Sue, 1998; Pedersen, 1997). For example, although Irish people might be characterized as being jokers, storytellers, and dreamers (see McGoldrick, 2005), an individual Irish person might be quite the opposite.

Individuals within groups also vary in terms of racial identity, or how much they identify with their racial or ethnic culture (Fouad & Brown, 2000; Helms, 1990; Helms & Cook, 1999). Of course, people can develop over time in their sense of racial identity (Helms & Cook, 1999). For example, in the United States, racial and ethnic minority group members (e.g., African Americans) often move from a depreciative perspective of their own race or culture to a more appreciative perspective, whereas European Americans, it is hoped, move from a perspective of ignorance and entitlement to understanding the privilege inherent in their status and thus begin to work for social justice.

Enculturation and *acculturation* are also key constructs to consider for people who have moved from one culture to another (e.g., when a person emigrates from Vietnam to the United States). Enculturation refers to retaining the norms of one's indigenous culture, whereas acculturation refers to adapting to the norms of the dominant culture (Kim & Abreu, 2001). Adults who come to the United States from another country often remain closely aligned with their culture of origin, whereas their children quickly acculturate to American ways. This difference in cultural values often causes rifts and strains in the family, with parents being upset that their children are not retaining the traditional cultural values and dress but are behaving according to different cultural norms. It also can cause strain in the family and upset the lines of authority when children acculturate faster than the parents and know the new language better than the parents. Children often have to serve as interpreters with teachers and cannot receive help with their homework, which upsets the traditional hierarchies of families.

It is clear that the helping process differs for both clients and helpers at different levels of racial identity and enculturation–acculturation. Helpers need to be aware of and sensitive to cultural differences in the helping process. Skovholt and Rivers (2003) suggested that helpers need to consider (a) the general experiences, characteristics, and needs of the client's cultural groups; (b) the client's individual experiences, characteristics, and needs; and (c) basic human needs—those common to all people (e.g., food, shelter, dignity, respect). Hence, knowledge of general cultural characteristics can provide some background information about societal forces impinging on clients, but helpers also need to learn about the individual from the individual. Thus, helpers work to determine which helping skills are most effective with different clients.

On Becoming a Helper

Helping seems to be a natural tendency in many people who have an innate desire to assist others (Stahl & Hill, 2008). Such individuals may recognize a special talent in themselves for listening and supporting others. Many students in helping skills classes indicate that friends and family talk with them when hurt or upset. Contrast these natural helpers with the stereotypical engineer who prefers things to people.

Helpers tend to have several characteristics in common. They listen carefully and empathically, are nonjudgmental, encourage exploration of thoughts and feelings, assist others in gaining new perspectives on problems, and motivate others to take actions to improve their lives. Another important characteristic for helpers that has recently been identified is tolerance for ambiguity (see also Ladany, Walker, Pate-Carolan, & Gray Evans, 2008), or the ability to perceive and process information about ambiguous situations. Given that helpers are bombarded with a lot of confusing stimuli in a helping situation, it is crucial to be able to sort these stimuli out and make sense of them.

For most of us, our natural inclination toward helping must be complemented by learning and practicing helping skills until they become an integral part of who we are, even when those behaviors initially feel awkward and forced. Many effective helpers have stories about their initial attempts at assisting others. For example, when one person first started studying helping behaviors, her father was undergoing heart surgery. She spoke with him every day and asked him how he was feeling. After weeks of this, he asked her whether she really wanted to know how he was feeling. "Finally!" she thought, "he'll share his innermost feelings with me." Her father said he was feeling that he liked her a lot more before she began studying helping skills.

Many of your friends and family may have similar reactions as you begin to learn helping skills. This may initially be discouraging, but it may help to know that most effective helpers practice these behaviors for many years before comfortably integrating them into their interactions with clients. In fact, some helpers discover that during the process of becoming a helper, their helping skills and confidence get worse before they get better. This down-and-up pattern makes sense given that trainees learn that not all of their old communication styles work and they feel temporarily awkward until the new patterns become integrated into their own personal style.

The process of becoming a helper might begin profitably with helpers trying to understand what motivates them to want to help others. Typically, beginning helpers have a variety of positive and negative reasons for wanting to be helpers.

One positive reason is altruism and wanting to make a difference in people's lives. For example, helpers might want to provide support to those in need by volunteering to work in a shelter for homeless women or by becoming a buddy to a gerontology patient confined to a nursing home. People who are motivated to use helping skills in situations like these provide others with supportive relationships in which clients feel listened to, cared for, and understood. Some helpers also choose to make a difference in children's lives by mentoring or tutoring young students, using the foundation of helping skills to develop encouraging relationships. Others hope to make life less painful for those in troubled situations. For example, helpers can provide an important function by assisting teens who think they might be gay or lesbian and fear retribution from family and friends.

Some people view helping as consistent with their cultural values and thus seek careers that enable them to assist others. These people are often natural helpers and have had role models (e.g., parents, aunts or uncles, cousins) who have dedicated their lives to the service of others (e.g., were counselors, ministers, or social workers).

Furthermore, some people aspire to be helpers because they experienced therapy as helpful when they were struggling with painful issues. For example, Kendra was 12 years old when she lost her mother and had to assume the role of mother to her five siblings. She received therapy to help her cope with her loss and her new responsibilities. Kendra now aspires to help children who have experienced loss in their lives. Another example involves rape survivors who become crisis counselors after receiving supportive counseling that helped them resolve disturbing issues related to the rape. Similarly, some people who overcome substance abuse want to help others both as a way of helping others with similar problems and as a way to help themselves stay sober.

For many individuals, the helping environment is attractive because it allows them to work with clients who are striving toward actualization of their potential. Furthermore, helpers are often excited by their contribution to the process of change in clients' lives and are energized by their clients' hard work and striving toward personal growth. One therapist told me that there was no better job in the world than being able to be a witness to the growth of people in their journeys to understanding themselves.

Another aspect of the helping environment that may appeal to many people is the opportunity to interact with smart, capable colleagues who value personal growth and helping others. They may receive support from their colleagues to actively examine their own issues and improve themselves to ensure their continued success in the helping role.

Finally, people may enter helping fields to work for social change. Helping affords a unique opportunity to make a difference in the lives of individuals and, sometimes, to influence social policies. Helpers who work with adolescents in at-risk environments may provide them with skills, hope, and encouragement to overcome obstacles and graduate from high school and college. Other helpers may draft legislation or testify on behalf of policies that fight discrimination (e.g., sexual harassment) or encourage funding for social services (e.g., child care). Contributions to social change can also occur through research that helpers undertake to evaluate the effectiveness of helping interventions (e.g., studying the efficacy of training undergraduate students to be effective helpers for battered women who have entered the criminal justice system).

Most of us are also motivated toward becoming helpers for less healthy reasons (Bugental, 1965). Most of you have probably heard the jokes about how students major in psychology to figure themselves out. Indeed, many people enter helping fields to work through unresolved personal issues or to change situations that they found painful in the past (e.g., an unhappy childhood). Furthermore, some people may want to help others because they are needy themselves and view helping as a way to develop relationships. These people might have difficulty with intimacy and so seek a safe way of getting close to others.

Individuals sometimes envision themselves as saviors for the less fortunate or as wise distributors of knowledge and advice. These people want to go into the helping profession as a mission. However, such motivations can be dangerous. When helpers need to make clients change to build their own self-esteem, they often cannot allow clients to explore and make their own choices. Others may use helping as a way to feel better about what they have by comparing themselves with those who are less fortunate. For some people, helping others enables them to feel superior to those whom they are attempting to help.

So how can you assess your reasons for wanting to help? The third exercise in Lab 1 about mindfulness is a place to start. Imagine yourself in a helping situation and think whatever thoughts come up. Later, as you begin to see clients, you can examine your reactions to them and to the helping process.

Benefits to Helpers of Seeking Help

The key to becoming a good helper is to understand your motivations and to monitor them in the helping process. I heartily recommend that people who want to become helpers seek therapy to learn more about themselves and their motivation for becoming helpers and to resolve personal problems. For an account of my own, very valuable experiences in therapy, see Hill (2005a).

Getting into their own personal therapy can enable helpers to recognize personal issues that could interfere with their ability to help if they are preoccupied with themselves and their problems or are unaware of negative personal behaviors. Furthermore, therapy can enable helpers to work on their own growth and self-understanding. An occupational hazard of being a helper is that the helping process stirs up personal issues that might otherwise lay dormant. For example, if a client talks about problems with alcoholism and the helper has not resolved similar problems, it might be difficult for the helper to attend to the client's pain instead of focusing on his or her own. Although people learn a great deal about themselves through the process of being helpers, their personal therapy gives them the opportunity to work on themselves in an appropriate setting rather than taking time away from clients who have come for help and deserve full attention.

Being in therapy themselves as clients can also teach helpers about the process of helping. Being a client allows helpers to learn what it is like to be on the receiving end of helping, to see what is and is not helpful, and to experience how difficult it is to open up and reveal painful material about oneself. Being in therapy also provides a model for helpers about how they would (or would not) want to act in sessions with their clients. In other words, the firsthand experience of what it is like to be on the receiving end of helping is invaluable.

It is troublesome when helpers-in-need refuse to seek help themselves but are willing to be helpers for others. One worries about the motivations of such persons for wanting to be helpers. Helpers who have the attitude that helping is only for weak or defective people may inadvertently communicate that attitude and cause clients to feel ashamed for seeking help.

To give you some idea of what outcomes you might gain from learning helping skills, let me describe two recent studies. The first study involved undergraduate helping skills classes (Hill, Roffman, et al., 2008). The classes lasted for 15 weeks and met 4 hours a week (2 hours in lecture/discussion about the skills and about research related to the skills, 2 hours in lab practicing the skills in small groups). Students did brief (20 minute) helping sessions at the beginning of the semester and then again midway through the semester after they had learned the exploration skills. As helpers, students conducted better sessions, used more exploration skills, were more empathic, and talked less in the second session compared with the first, so it appeared that they were able to use the exploration skills in sessions with clients talking about real problems. In addition, students gained substantially in terms of self-efficacy about being helpers. Interestingly, we were not able to predict (using self-report measures of empathy, perfectionism, and overall grade point average assessed at the beginning of the semester) which students gain the most in the course. We speculated that what was more important than these predictions was that students became involved and excited about learning the helping skills.

The second study was a qualitative study of the journals kept by five students throughout their first semester in a counseling psychology doctoral program (Hill, Sullivan, Knox, & Schlosser, 2007). Students discussed challenges related to becoming therapists, such as being too self-critical, having a number of troubling reactions to their clients, and learning how to use the helping skills effectively. They also reported many gains across the course of the semester, particularly in terms of using the helping skills more effectively, becoming less self-critical, and being more able to connect with clients. These two studies show clearly that undergraduate and graduate students profit considerably from helping skills training and provide a lot of richness into the experience of what it is like to learn the skills.

Overview of This Book

ORGANIZATION OF THE BOOK

The second chapter in Part I of this book provides an overview of the helping process in terms of the three-stage model and a description of the components of helping. Chapter 3 provides an overview of ethical issues involved in helping. Parts II, III, and IV present more description of the exploration, insight, and action stages, respectively. In each part, an overview chapter highlights the theoretical foundation and the goals of the stage. The chapters that follow the overview chapter focus on skills that can be used to accomplish specific goals within the stage. At the end of each part, a chapter addresses the integration of the skills taught for that stage and presents clinical issues that arise in implementing the stage. Finally, Part V involves integrating the skills into ideas for how to conduct sessions with clients.

Please note that a lot of examples are used throughout the book to make the points come more to life. Some examples are based on real people (names have been changed to protect the identities of those involved); other examples are completely fictitious, created to illustrate a given point.

EXPERIENTIAL COMPONENT OF THE BOOK

Reading about helping skills is important, but reading alone will not make you an effective helper. Many students have said that when they did the reading the skills sounded easy, but when they tried to actually practice doing the skills they came to realize how difficult it is to use them and use them effectively.

Acquiring extensive knowledge about helping, although important, is only the first step in your journey toward helping others. Probably the best way for you to learn the skills is first to read and study the text and then try to apply what you have learned by answering questions about the material and by participating in practice helping exercises and lab experiences. The following sections describe the ways in which you can use this book to maximize your growth as a helper.

What Do You Think?

Several questions are provided at the end of each chapter to stimulate your thinking about the text material. I strongly feel that it is important for students to debate the issues raised in this book rather than slavishly accepting everything written here. There are few hard-and-fast "truths" related to helping skills; rather, many of the issues are matters of taste, style, or art, and trainees need to think for themselves about how they want to be as helpers. I encourage you to contemplate each question and discuss your responses with your classmates.

Practice Exercises

At the end of each skills chapter, practice exercises provide readers with the opportunity to think about and formulate responses to hypothetical client situations before practicing the skills in the lab setting. You can practice by downloading the PDF of the exercise from the student resources area of the *Helping Skills, Third Edition* Web site (http://www.apa.org/book/resources/Hill3), writing down an intervention for each client situation on the Practice Exercise sheet, and then comparing your answers with the suggestions for possible responses (remembering that these are just suggestions).

Laboratories

Throughout this book, labs are provided so that beginning helpers can practice helping skills in dyads or small groups. These labs are ones that I have used over the years in both my undergraduate- and graduate-level helping skills classes, so they have been tested and seem to work (although, of course, instructors should feel fee to modify these labs to fit their own preferences and situations).

During labs, helpers are asked to practice the skills with peers who act as clients presenting real or role-played problems. Observers take careful notes and attend to the helper's ability to deliver a particular skill, so that they can provide feedback to the helper. Thus, everyone has an opportunity to experience the roles of helper, client, and observer for each skill. At the end of each lab in the personal reflections section, students are asked to think about their ongoing development as helpers.

Disclosure During Lab Exercises

The success of the lab experiences depends partly on the participants' willingness to reveal information about personal topics. It is preferable for participants to discuss personal topics for two reasons. First, helpers have difficulty learning what is effective when "clients" are not responding genuinely. Second, "clients" often are unable to provide useful feedback to helpers about what is helpful and how the interventions feel if they are not discussing real problems. When role-playing, "clients" are often more involved in trying to think of how the person they are pretending to be might feel or behave than immersing themselves in the immediate experience.

As clients, however, students should only disclose about easy, safe topics. Students should never disclose about deep topics, even if they are comfortable disclosing, because their classmates will not be comfortable trying to help them and it takes the focus too much off the helper learning helping skills to the helper trying to help the client. At times, students might start talking about an issue they think is safe but then become uncomfortable, either because of the depth of the topic or because they do not feel comfortable with the helper. I stress that students always have the right (without jeopardy or prejudice) to indicate that they choose not to explore a particular issue further.

At this point, it may be helpful to note that the "Ethical Principles of Psychologists and Code of Conduct" (American Psychological Association, 2002, Section 7.04) indicates that

> Psychologists do not require students or supervisees to disclose personal information in course- or program-related activities,

either orally or in writing, regarding sexual history, history of abuse and neglect, psychological treatment, and relationships with parents, peers, and spouses or significant others except if (1) the program or training facility has clearly identified this requirement in its admissions and program materials or (2) the information is necessary to evaluate or obtain assistance for students whose personal problems could reasonably be judged to be preventing them from performing their training- or professionally related activities in a competent manner or posing a threat to the students or others. (p. 9)

This guideline was established to educate people about the perils of requiring disclosure. Thus, although I recommend easy, safe, nondeep disclosure because it typically facilitates the training process, I urge both instructors and students to be alert for possible negative effects.

If students are not willing to disclose personal information, they can role-play a hypothetical client. In such cases, they should not reveal whether the problem is role-played or real—in this way no one ever knows whether the person is actually disclosing or whether the problem is role-played, thus preserving confidentiality.

Exhibit 1.1 provides topics that students in our courses have discussed. Although a topic may be "safe" for many people, it may not be comfortable for an individual student, so trainees must think about what they want to discuss. Students may want to refer to this list throughout the semester when a topic is needed for the lab exercises.

Confidentiality During Lab Exercises

Although practice sessions might seem somewhat artificial, the information shared is personal and should be treated in a confidential manner. Helpers should not disclose information shared in practice sessions without the permission of the client. Specifically, helpers should only discuss the material presented in helping sessions with their supervisors and classmates, and then only when it relates to developing their helping skills. When one respects clients, they respond by sharing personal information and delving into their thoughts and feelings. Confidentiality of shared information provides a foundation for respectful interactions with others (see extended discussion of ethical issues related to confidentiality in chap. 3).

Benefits of Being a Volunteer Client

The primary focus of the lab experiences is on the helper learning the helping skills. However, students often report that it is beneficial to talk about their concerns when they participate in the client role and that the experience of being a client provided them with firsthand exposure to how

---

EXHIBIT 1.1

Topics for Volunteer Clients to Talk About in the Labs

Ideal Topics
  Anxieties about learning helping skills
  Worries about performance of helping skills
  Academic issues (e.g., studying, test anxiety)
  Career; future plans
  Choosing a major or graduate program
  Pets
  Problems at work
  Public-speaking anxiety
  Roommate issues
  Romantic relationships
  Feelings about technology
  Happy childhood memories
  Hobbies and extracurricular activities
  Problems with health
Relatively Safe Topics Depending on Client
  Minor family issues
  Autonomy–independence struggles
  Minor relationship concerns
  High school experiences
  Personal views on alcohol and drugs
  Existential concerns (e.g., Who am I? What is the meaning of life, death?)
  Financial difficulties
  Problems with physical appearance
  Moral dilemmas
Topics to Be Avoided
  Substance abuse
  Fears about going crazy
  Traumas (e.g., sexual or physical abuse, rape, victimization, child abuse, serious medical condition)
  Serious problems in romantic relationships
  Shameful feelings
  Serious family disputes
  Sex
  Sexual abuse
  Suicidal thoughts
  Murderous thoughts

---

it feels to receive the various helping skills. Moreover, students often develop empathy with their clients after having experienced what is involved in being a client. Being a participant in counseling allows students to experience "the other side" of helping and to gain respect for the courage clients exhibit when they share their concerns with their helpers. In addition, beginning helpers often report that watching their helpers provide helping skills can teach them about effective (and ineffective) helping techniques.

I stress, though, that being a client in practice helping sessions should not be used as a substitute for seeking counseling or therapy. Students experiencing personal distress should seek help from a trained and qualified counselor or therapist. University counseling centers or health services often provide counseling services for college students at little or no cost and offer an excellent opportunity for students to learn more about themselves and address salient issues.

Problems Related to Practicing Skills With Friends

Another issue to discuss in this section involves the recognition that problems can occur when practicing helping skills with classmates who are friends or acquaintances. During helping sessions with friends, it is a good idea for helpers to pretend that they know nothing about their friend and respond only to what the "client" actually reveals during the helping session. Although it is challenging to discount relevant information, students in my classes have found the lab exercises easier to perform if they consider only information provided in the practice helping session. For example, Nancy was practicing her helping skills with her friend, Katrina, who was bemoaning the fact that her partner had not called her in 2 weeks. Although Nancy knew that Katrina's partner had not called because Katrina had dated someone else, she focused only on Katrina's expressed feelings related to not having contact with her partner.

Providing Feedback to Peers

Providing feedback is an essential component of training. Helpers appreciate positive feedback because learning helping skills is challenging, and they appreciate encouragement when they are on the right track. However, they also need and want feedback that helps them change and improve their helping skills. It is enjoyable to have people tell us that we are doing a terrific job as helpers, but we also need observers to provide concrete recommendations for how we might improve our skills. Students often feel cheated if they consistently receive only positive feedback yet also feel wounded if they receive too many critical comments.

Claiborn, Goodyear, and Horner (2002) recommended providing positive feedback first and then providing only one piece of constructive feedback. It is less overwhelming and more feasible to focus on making one change in a given lab experience rather than trying to fix everything at once. For example, the observer might say,

> You used good attending and listening skills; I particularly liked
> that you had good steady eye contact, leaned forward while you

were listening, and did not interrupt. One thing I noticed though that you might think about is that you asked a lot of questions in one speaking turn, making it hard for the client to know which one to respond to.

Note that the feedback should be stated in behavioral terms (e.g., "You were looking away a lot and playing with your hair") rather than in broad and nonspecific terms (e.g., "You did not connect with the client"). Having clear, concrete feedback gives the helper specific ideas for how to change.

The best source of feedback is the client who experienced the helper's interventions firsthand and experienced whether or not these interventions were helpful. The next best source of feedback is from observers who have watched the practice session and see from the outside what was happening. It can be beneficial for helpers to hear that different people have different responses to the same intervention, thus emphasizing that there is no one right way to intervene.

DVD

A new feature of this edition of the book is an accompanying DVD—*Helping Skills in Practice: A Three-Stage Model*—that can be used to illustrate the three stages of the helping skills model. Modeling has been shown to be an effective training tool (see review in Hill & Lent, 2006), probably because it brings the written word to life. It is important to remember though that the DVD provides only one example of how to do the three stages. How you implement the three stages will depend on your style and the needs of the particular client.

Continued Practice

To become a good helper, you will need to continue practicing after this course. It takes many years to become an expert counselor or therapist (see also Orlinsky & Ronnestad, 2005; Skovholt & Jennings, 2004), so I encourage you to pursue professional training and practice, practice, practice.

Is This Book Right for You?

The material presented in this book can be applied to countless helping situations involving both professional and lay helpers. Perhaps the most obvious audience for this book is students who are training to become mental health professionals. Individuals who plan to provide psychological services to others benefit from learning the helping skills because they serve as the foundation for most psychological interventions. Specifically, students enrolled in counseling classes at the undergraduate, master's, and doctoral level in counseling psychology, clinical psychology, social work, and psychiatry could use this text to learn helping skills that they can apply to their work with clients. Of course, counselors/psychotherapists who plan to work with specific types of clients (e.g., those who abuse alcohol and drugs, those who are physically disabled, children, older people, couples) will need to learn additional, more specialized knowledge to work effectively with their clients. But by first learning the basic skills, students will have a strong foundation for learning the more specialized skills of working with specific populations. Similarly, having a strong foundation in helping skills may enable students to learn other approaches to therapy (e.g., cognitive–behavioral therapy, psychodynamic therapy).

The helping skills taught in this book are also applicable to people who assist clients in helping professions other than psychology. For example, volunteers and staff members in nonprofit agencies often are required to practice effective helping skills. Hotline volunteers benefit from applying basic helping skills to communicate empathy and understanding to the clients with diverse problems whom they encounter over the phone. Crisis workers assisting battered women and their children use basic helping skills to ensure the safety of their clients. Hospice workers can learn how to respond empathically to individuals struggling with despair, loss, loneliness, and pain. Furthermore, hospice workers often use basic helping skills when interacting with patients' family members and close friends. Being able to listen empathically and reflect feelings appropriately can assist patients' significant others in resolving issues related to illness and death.

Another application of helping skills in professional interactions involves other health professionals. Recently, a physician inquired whether the university provided basic helping skills courses. She explained that about 60% of her clients presented with emotional concerns as well as physical complaints. She felt that her medical training did not prepare her to deal effectively with the personal problems presented by her patients. Many medical professionals and health service providers could enhance their effectiveness by using helping skills. Doctors, dentists, and nurses could learn to respond effectively to clients who fear invasive procedures or want additional information about loved ones who are ill. In fact, researchers have found that patients with breast cancer who interacted with a surgeon trained either to use basic helping skills or to chat with them on the night before surgery evidenced less anxiety and depression a year after their operation (Burton, Parker, & Wollner, 1991). Furthermore, there is probably no time when effective helping skills are needed more by medical professionals than when they must notify a patient's significant others of a death. The use of the skills taught in this book could enable helpers to respond empathically toward the families and significant others in these situations. Finally, volunteers in medical settings encounter many instances in which the use of helping skills is warranted (e.g., when worried families are frustrated with waiting to hear about the results of surgery, when visiting with a patient who has been unable to leave the hospital for weeks).

In addition, training in helping skills could assist nuns, priests, rabbis, ministers, and lay clergy in working with individuals who question their faith, celebrate important events, or struggle with loss and grief. Given that people often turn to religious leaders rather than professional helpers, training in basic helping skills could prepare these leaders for responding empathically at critical moments in people's lives.

Professionals pursuing business and law careers that involve working with others also could benefit from learning to communicate effectively. Many people would rather do business with, and make referrals to, an accountant who listens patiently and understands their fears related to paying taxes. Helping skills also can be useful to attorneys when confronting hostile couples filing for divorce or when helping personal injury clients make decisions about whether to accept a settlement. The ability to listen effectively and understand nonverbal behavior could assist lawyers in uncovering important material in depositions to further positive outcomes for their clients. The importance of helping skills in the legal profession is demonstrated by the inclusion of a basic counseling skills course in the curriculum of some law schools. One can also argue the benefits of bartenders and hairstylists learning helping skills because many customers tell these people their problems.

Some students have suggested that professors be required to learn basic helping skills. Imagine if every teacher were trained to be an effective helper! Although professors would probably still not believe some of the outrageous excuses for late assignments, they might be able to listen empathically and also respond positively to questions posed or personal struggles faced by students.

A less obvious (but equally important) reason for learning helping skills involves improving relationships with friends, significant others, and family members. After learning the attending and listening skills, students often report that they now realize how often they have not really listened to the people they love. Although difficult, using listening skills when a significant other is complaining about one of your irritating behaviors could help in resolving the issue. Improvements in listening often result in more open and healthy communication with significant others.

Helping skills can also be used to assist friends and family members who are struggling with important choices or painful issues. At times, friends may ask for help when they experience significant losses (e.g., the ending of a relationship, the death of a family member). Family members may request assistance when they encounter an important decision (e.g., which job to pursue, whether to relocate for a romantic relationship). In addition, helping skills are used when people experience a crisis in their significant relationships (e.g., close friends strongly disagree about an important topic, two members of a couple feel differently about having children).

Although using some of the basic helping skills in relationships is appropriate (especially the exploration skills of listening carefully to the feelings of others), I caution students against becoming too involved in being in the helper role with friends and family members and delving too deeply into issues with them because it is not usually possible to be objective with loved ones. Furthermore, relationships may be less satisfying and less mutual when one person is always the helper and the other is always the client. It is usually best for the other person to seek therapeutic help from a professional who is not personally involved (see also chap. 7 about the ethical issues involved in dual relationships) and for you to remain as the interested, loyal friend who listens and provides emotional support as well as being listened to in an equal relationship.

Concluding Comments

You are about to embark on an exciting and challenging journey toward becoming a helper. Although learning helping skills takes time, knowledge, and a lot of practice, the rewards for integrating helping skills in your personal and professional repertoire are plentiful. I hope to help you reach your destination of learning helping skills by focusing on the development of these skills while providing a theoretical and research foundation for helping behaviors, as well as by providing exercises to practice these skills. Effective helping requires practice, and even experienced helpers often return to the basics to review and refresh skills. I hope this book assists you in learning helping skills and exploring your potential for, and interest in, becoming an effective helper. Bon voyage!

What Do You Think?

- Think of a time when you felt helped by someone. What did that person do that was helpful to you?
- Now remember a time when you needed help and the person you turned to was not at all helpful. What did she or he do to make this experience unhelpful?

- Describe how society perceives those who seek professional help.
- How could you help decrease the stigma attached to help seeking in our society?
- Write a brief job description for a helper. Include personal characteristics, required training, and job responsibilities. Now, evaluate yourself in comparison with the description that you developed.
- What would it take for you to seek professional help? Address the benefits and costs you associate with seeking assistance.
- Debate why people want to become helpers.
- Identify several current situations in your life where helping skills could be used.
- In your opinion, what are the top three characteristics of an effective helper?
- What is your definition of culture?
- Debate the role of culture in functioning.

i LAB 1. Self-Awareness

A downloadable PDF of this Lab is available in the student resources area of Helping Skills, *3rd ed. Web site: http://www.apa.org/books/resources/Hill3.*

Goal: To help beginning helpers become aware of their own cultural values, begin to appreciate other cultures, and begin to be more mindful.

Exercise 1: Cultural Awareness

1. Get in a dyad with someone who is culturally different from you in terms of race/ethnicity, socioeconomic status, sexual orientation, gender, or religion. Each person should talk for at least 5 minutes about some aspect of culture that she or he experienced as a child (e.g., holiday customs, a time when one was sharply aware of one's culture). The other person should listen without interrupting except to encourage the person to keep talking.
2. Get back together in the large group. Each person can introduce the other person and say something he or she learned about the person's culture.

Exercise 2: Hot Buttons

1. Take a minute to visualize yourself sitting across from a client in each of the following categories and think about how you would feel and react. What "hot buttons" (intense inner reactions) would get elicited? On each line, circle the category of person you would be most comfortable working with and put an X through the category of person you would be least comfortable working with (e.g., you might circle lesbian but put an X through heterosexual clients). Be honest with yourself—awareness is the first step to understanding and changing.

   - race/ethnicity (African, Asian, Caucasian, Hispanic, Native American)
   - sex (female, male)
   - sexual orientation (bisexual, gay, heterosexual, lesbian, transsexual, questioning)
   - religion (atheist/agnostic, Buddhist, Christian, Hindu, Islamic, Jewish)

- age (6 to 17 years, 18 to 30 years, 31 to 60 years, 61 to 100+ years)
- socioeconomic class (poor, middle class, wealthy)
- psychological status (substance abusing, depressed, anxious, actively psychotic, mildly distressed)

2. Get together with another person and talk about what you think your list reveals about you. What are you most proud of? What is your edge that you want to work on?

Exercise 3: Mindfulness

The purpose of this exercise is to begin to learn to look at your thoughts and examine them—but not beat yourself up about them. This is a first step toward self-awareness, which we will be talking about throughout the book.

1. Get comfortable in your chair with feet on the floor and nothing on your lap. Close your eyes. Take several deep breaths and relax. Clear your mind of anything outside the present moment.
2. Think about being a helper. Let a thought come into your mind, think about it, and then let it go. For example, you think that you will be anxious when you try to be a helper. Think about that for a minute. What would it feel like to feel anxious? Where would you feel that in your body? Imagine the experience of sitting across from a client. And then let that thought go. Take a deep breath. And let another thought come. Perhaps you think about how helping is something you've always wanted to do. Experience that thought completely. Think about the pride of feeling like you can help others. Think about a life where you gain meaning by helping others. And then let the thought go. Again, take a deep breath. And let some other thought come into your mind. Do this exercise for about 5 minutes.
3. Practice mindfulness on your own throughout the semester.

Personal Reflections

- What did you learn that is new about yourself?
- What did you learn that is new about a different culture?
- What reactions did you have to thinking about your hot buttons?
- What could you do to work on your hot buttons?
- What were your feelings during the mindfulness exercise? Were you able to let the feelings go?

An Overview of Helping 2

We ought to respect the effect we have on others. We know by our own experience how much others affect our lives, and we must remember that we in turn must have the same effect on others.

—*George Eliot*

t is important to have a theoretical foundation for helping because this helps you make decisions about how to conduct the helping process. Furthermore, given that (as reviewed in chap. 1) no differences have been found among the major theoretical orientations in terms of their effects on outcome (see Wampold, 2001), it makes sense to integrate the best of the approaches in a philosophically consistent way. Thus, the three-stage model moves from exploration (based on client-centered therapy) to insight (based on psychoanalytic therapy) to action (based on behavioral therapy). The first section of the chapter presents my assumptions and then presents the three-stage model.

Beyond the theoretical approach is the process of helping in the moment—what the helper and client intend to do to move the process forward. I break the process down to make sense of it in the second part of the chapter.

Assumptions Underlying the Three-Stage Model

Assumptions about human nature form the philosophical foundation for any model, so it is important to explicate my assumptions before presenting the model. I discuss these assumptions only briefly because my focus is on describing the helping model rather than creating a theory of personality development.

I believe that people are born with varied potential in the psychological, intellectual, physical, and interpersonal domains. Thus, some people are genetically more intelligent, attractive, physically strong, active, verbally articulate, and mechanically adept than other people. Temperamental differences among infants at birth (e.g., some children are active, whereas others are phlegmatic) carry over to adulthood. These potentials unfold as children develop, and there is a strong biological pull toward growing and developing one's potential. I do not believe that people are either inherently good (as Carl Rogers postulated) or inherently governed by instinctual urges (as Sigmund Freud postulated) at birth. Instead, once again, I believe that people have certain biological predispositions at birth and have a tendency toward fulfilling these potentials. How they are developed depends largely on the environment, to which I turn next.

The environment can enhance or thwart the innate movement toward survival and development. Healthy environments provide basic biological needs (e.g., food, shelter) and emotional needs (e.g., relationships characterized by acceptance, love, support, encouragement, recognition, and appropriate challenges). When infants and children are provided with a "good enough" environment that meets their basic needs, their potential unfolds naturally. No environment is perfect, but the environment needs to be at least adequate to allow children to grow and develop. In contrast, when negative things happen in a child's environment, the child's development is thwarted. A child growing up in the midst of war and terrorist attacks has a different view of life than a child growing up during peace. Furthermore, either too much gratification or too much deprivation stunts children's growth, but an adequate amount of support allows children to develop naturally to fulfill their potential. So resiliency, or the ability to adapt, is both biologically and environmentally determined.

Early experiences, particularly in terms of attachment and self-esteem, are crucial in laying the foundation for personality. Infants need to be nurtured by caretakers to have a firm foundation for interpersonal relationships and self-esteem. If these attachment needs are not met, children become anxious or avoidant of human contact (Bowlby, 1969,

1988). People continue to change and adapt throughout their lives, of course, within the limits of their biological predispositions and early experiences. Thus, although a foundation is laid, there is still a wide range within which people can grow and develop. They cannot transform their personalities completely, but they can come to accept who they are and make the most of their potential.

People develop defenses to cope with anxiety, particularly during childhood, when they tend to have less control over their personal destinies (e.g., a child might learn to withdraw to defend against dominating parents). A moderate level of defenses is adaptive because one needs strategies to cope with life. These defenses become problematic, however, when the individual cannot discriminate when it is appropriate to use defenses. For example, if a child who was abused avoids all adults, she or he cannot form benevolent relationships with caring people.

Although people are influenced by genetics, past learning, and external circumstances, I believe that they have some degree of control over their lives and over their choices about how they behave. Within limits of what is available, one makes choices that alter the course of one's life. For example, although friendliness is influenced by personality (e.g., introversion vs. extroversion) and previous experiences with meeting people, a person still has some range of choices about how she or he acts with others in a new situation. Thus, determinism is balanced by free will.

Free will is enhanced if individuals gain insight into their background, needs, and desires. Understanding enables one to have more control over one's fate. One can never have complete control over fate, but one can have some influence through awareness and conscious effort.

I also propose that emotions, cognitions, and behaviors are all key components of personality. All are intertwined and operate in combination with one another—mind and body cannot be separated. How people think influences how they feel and behave (e.g., if a person thinks that others are out to get him, he will feel afraid when another person approaches). How people feel has an impact on how they think and behave (e.g., if a person feels happy, she is likely to seek out other people and think that they will like her). Finally, how people behave affects how they think about themselves and how they feel (e.g., if a person studies hard and gets good grades, he or she is likely to feel efficacious). Thus, any treatment approach must focus on all three aspects of human existence (emotions, cognitions, and behaviors) to help people change.

In summary, I believe that people are influenced by both their biology and their environment, particularly early experiences that contribute to the development of attachment to others and self-esteem. Furthermore, although people are influenced by past experiences, they have some choice and free will. It is also important to recognize that people develop defenses as strategies for coping with the demands of the world.

I believe that people can change within limits. They cannot discard past learning or biological predispositions, but they can come to understand themselves more, live with themselves, and accept themselves. They can develop more adaptive behaviors, thoughts, and feelings. People can adjust to their inner potential, make the best of what they have, and make choices about how they want to live their life within the limits imposed by biology, early experiences, and external circumstances. These assumptions lead to an optimistic, but cautious, view about the possibility of change.

The Three-Stage Model

The helping process involves taking clients "down and into" understanding themselves more and then "up and out" into the world, better able to cope with problems (Carkhuff, 1969; Carkhuff & Anthony, 1979). The three-stage model for helping is a framework for using helping skills to lead clients through the process of exploring concerns, coming to greater understanding of problems, and making changes in their lives. Thus, as Figure 2.1 illustrates, the helping process involves beginning with exploration, moving to insight, and then to action. To accomplish this, helpers act as collaborators and facilitators. Although they have no special knowledge or wisdom about how clients ought to live their lives, helpers can be empathic and use specific helping skills to guide clients in exploring their feelings and values, understanding their problems, making choices, and implementing changes in thoughts, affect, and behaviors.

EXPLORATION STAGE

In the exploration stage, helpers seek to establish rapport, develop a therapeutic relationship, encourage clients to tell their stories, help clients explore thoughts and feelings, facilitate the arousal of emotions, and learn about clients. Exploration is crucial to give clients an opportunity to express their emotions and to think through the complexity of

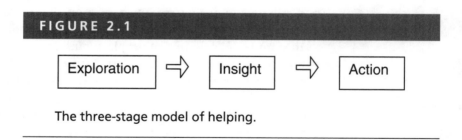

FIGURE 2.1

The three-stage model of helping.

their problems. Having another person act as a sounding board or mirror is often helpful because it allows clients to open up; it is much easier to examine one's concerns when another person is actively listening. When clients think about issues by themselves, they often become blocked by their defenses and anxieties. Being blocked can make clients feel that they are going around in circles rather than gaining insight and making changes.

The exploration stage also provides helpers with an opportunity to learn more about their clients. Helpers cannot assume that they know clients' feelings or problems, even when they are similar in age, race, gender, religion, and sexual orientation. Helpers might be imposing their own standards and values on clients if they assume that they know how clients feel about problems or what solutions clients should choose. For example, Jennifer, who was similar in age, race, and gender to her helper, disclosed that she had just become engaged. The helper had just recently gotten married and was very happy in her relationship, so she assumed that Jennifer felt similarly and started congratulating her. Jennifer, however, broke down in tears and ran out of the room. Fortunately, the helper realized her mistake, called Jennifer and apologized, and asked her to return for another session. It turned out that Jennifer felt pressured to get engaged and, in fact, felt quite ambivalent about the relationship. When the helper could listen without assumptions, she was able to learn how Jennifer truly felt.

INSIGHT STAGE

In the insight stage, helpers collaborate with clients to help them achieve new understandings about themselves, their thoughts, their feelings, and their behaviors. They also work to help clients attain new awareness of their role in perpetuating their problems. Insight is important because it helps clients see things in a new light and enables them to take appropriate responsibility and control over problems.

When clients have some understanding, it is usually easier for them to change. For example, it was easier for Jacques to take a chance on getting involved in another relationship once he understood that he became scared of getting close to others because of his punitive relationship with his mother. Thus, understanding, however imperfect, guides future behavior. Insight may also lead to long-lasting change because it provides clients with a template for making sense out of events and helps them make better choices. Having an explanation seems to be important for helping people make choices.

Although people can and certainly do attain insight on their own, hearing new ideas and receiving feedback from a caring helper who has a different perspective can enable them to develop a deeper level of awareness and understanding. In contrast to the purely client-centered stance in the exploration stage, helpers work more actively with clients in the insight stage to construct meanings together. Helpers not only maintain an empathic and collaborative stance but also occasionally challenge client perspectives, tentatively offer their own ideas, and use their own experiences in helping clients see things in a new way. Clients sometimes need the helper's external perspective to give them new ideas and feedback, especially when they are stuck or blocked. Of course, helpers do not necessarily have the "right" perspective, but they may have alternative perspectives that clients can consider.

In addition, helpers provide clients with feedback about their behaviors in sessions and assist clients in understanding how these behaviors have developed and what function they now serve. By understanding how they are perceived by their helpers, clients are often better able to understand how other people react to them.

In addition, helpers and clients sometimes work through problems that arise in the therapeutic relationship, helping clients have a corrective relational experience, modeling how to interact with others more effectively, and working together to attain insight into relationships. Thus, the relationship itself can be a focus of learning in the insight stage.

ACTION STAGE

In the action stage, helpers help clients think about changes that reflect their new understandings. Helpers and clients together explore the idea of changing. They try to determine whether clients want to change and explore the meaning of change in clients' lives. They brainstorm possible changes and help clients make decisions about which changes to pursue. In some cases, helpers teach clients skills needed to make changes. They also might help clients develop strategies for trying new behaviors and asking for feedback from others outside the helping relationship. In addition, helpers and clients continually evaluate the outcome of action plans and make modifications to assist clients in obtaining the desired outcomes. As in the first two stages, the process is collaborative. Helpers continue to ask clients to talk about their feelings related to changing. Again, helpers are not experts but guides who assist clients in exploring thoughts and feelings about action and about making positive changes in their lives.

Psychoanalytic theorists have often assumed that insight naturally leads to action and thus that helpers do not have to be concerned with encouraging clients to think about making specific changes. For some clients, this may be true. However, clients often do not have the skills to behave differently, have defenses that block them from making changes, or have obstacles in the real world that make it hard to change, so they need help to make the changes occur. By putting their new ways of thinking into practice, clients are able to consolidate the changes in their thinking that occurred in the exploration and insight stages. Without action, changes in thinking (insights) are typically short-lived.

RELATIONSHIP AMONG THE THREE STAGES

The exploration stage lays the foundation for clients to understand their motivations and take responsibility for changing. Both helpers and clients need an adequate understanding of the scope and dynamics of the clients' problem before developing an action plan. Unlike radio and television talk show psychologists who listen for three sentences and then advise clients, helpers rely on careful, thoughtful listening and probing to help clients fully explore their problems and gain new insights for themselves.

Thus, each of the stages in the model is important in the helping process. Thorough exploration sets the stage for the client to gain insight, and deep insight prepares the path for the client to make good decisions about action. Furthermore, making changes encourages the client to come back for exploration of other problems. Hence, helpers need to give due attention to all three stages.

Although it sounds straightforward to move from exploration to insight to action, things rarely flow so smoothly with real clients, and stages are not always as differentiated and sequential as they appear when reading about them (Figure 2.2 shows some of the variations on the basic model). Within sessions, helpers and clients sometimes move back and forth among the stages. For example, helpers often have to

FIGURE 2.2

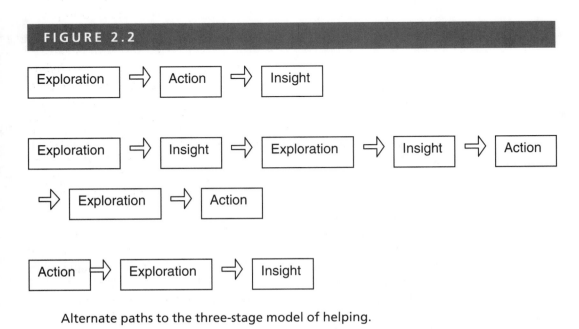

Alternate paths to the three-stage model of helping.

return to exploring new facets of a client's problem during the insight and action stages. In addition, attaining insight often forces a client to explore newly recognized feelings and thoughts. Realizing that a client is reluctant to change in the action stage might necessitate more exploration and insight about obstacles. Sometimes action needs to be taken before much exploration has taken place, such as when a client is in crisis and needs help immediately. For example, a client who has medical problems caused by anorexia might first need to learn to eat in a healthy manner and only later might be ready and able to explore motives underlying her eating disorder. In other cases, clients cannot really explore until they have been taught to relax. Other clients cannot handle insight and are resistant to having anyone "poke around in their heads"; they only want guidance about specific problems. With such clients, helpers may need to move more quickly to the action stage. However, I caution helpers to explore enough to make sure they know what is going on, what actions have been tried, and what help is needed before they rush to generate possible actions.

In summary, the three-stage model provides an overall roadmap for the helping process, but helpers must attend to individual needs of clients and environmental pressures before determining how to respond at any given moment. This book is not meant to be a simplistic "cookbook" or manual of what to do at every specific moment in helping. That would not be possible, given the infinite number of situations that could arise with different helpers and clients. Instead, helpers need to think about what they are trying to accomplish at each point in the helping process, become skilled at delivering the various possible skills, and then observe the client's reactions to help devise better interventions for the particular client.

STAGES, GOALS, AND SKILLS

In this model, there are three stages, which are overall strategies. For each stage, there are midlevel goals that helpers are trying to accomplish. For each goal, there are different specific skills that can be used. See Exhibit 2.1 for an overview of the stages, goals, and skills.

In the exploration stage, the first goal is to attend nonverbally to clients and listen carefully to everything they say, verbally and nonverbally, which helpers implement through nonverbal behaviors. The second goal is to encourage clients to explore thoughts, which helpers implement through probes for thoughts and restatements. The third goal is to encourage exploration of feelings, which helpers do through probes for feelings, reflections of feelings, and disclosures of feelings.

The first goal of the insight stage is to foster awareness, which helpers do primarily through challenges. The second goal is to facilitate insight, which helpers do through probes for insight, interpretations, and dis-

EXHIBIT 2.1

Goals and Skills for the Three Stages

Stage	Goals	Associated skills
Exploration	Attend, observe, listen	Nonverbal behaviors, minimal verbal behaviors
	Explore thoughts	Restatements, open questions for thoughts
	Explore feelings	Reflections of feelings, disclosures of feelings, open questions for feelings
Insight	Foster awareness	Challenge
	Facilitate insight	Open questions for insight, interpretation, disclosures of insight
	Facilitate insight into relationships	Immediacy
Action	Facilitate action	Open questions for action, giving information, process advisement, direct guidance, disclosures of strategies

closures of insights. The final goal is to work on the therapeutic relationship, which helpers do through immediacy. In addition, because insight attainment is more complicated than exploration, there are a number of recommended steps for implementing the skills that will be presented in Part III of the book.

The overall goal of the action stage is to help clients explore the idea of changing and then implement action plans that are chosen by clients. The major skills for this stage are open questions for action, giving information, process advisement, direct guidance, and disclosure of strategies. More important, there are four major types of action plans (relaxation, behavior change, behavioral rehearsal, and decision making), each of which is implemented through several steps and several skills. These steps are covered thoroughly in Part IV of this book.

Empathic Collaboration

Empathic collaboration is a major feature of all three stages of the model. Helpers need to try to understand their clients as much as possible, while at the same time recognizing that it is never possible to fully understand another person. Empathy implies understanding clients at both a cognitive level (what they are thinking and saying) and an affective level (what they are feeling; Duan & Hill, 1996). Empathy also involves genuinely caring about the client, nonjudgmentally accepting the client, being able to predict the client's reactions, and communicating one's experience to the client in a sensitive and accurate manner.

Although helpers sometimes feel the same emotions as their clients, empathy requires that they recognize that the pain, anger, frustration, joy, or other emotions belong to the client and not the helper. Empathy is sometimes confused with a certain way of responding to clients (e.g., using reflections of feelings), but empathy is not a specific response type or skill; rather, it is an attitude or manner of responding with genuine caring and a lack of judgment. Empathy involves a deep respect for clients and for the clients' willingness and courage to explore their problems, gain insights, and make changes. This empathic attitude is experienced and also implemented through a variety of helping skills, depending on what helpers perceive clients as needing at specific times.

No one can fully understand another person. We can try to empathize and imagine how the other person feels, but we can never fully remove ourselves from our own experiences to understand another person completely. Similarly, although we might try to have unconditional positive regard (i.e., caring about, understanding, and appreciating clients for who they are, regardless of how they behave), our regard for clients usually has some conditions (e.g., that they allow us to help them, that they talk openly about their problems, that they not get angry at us). Unfortunately, we are not always fully aware of all of our personal issues and the conditions that we place on clients. As helpers, we need to do our best to form positive therapeutic relationships with clients; but when we are not able to establish good relationships, we need to examine our own issues as well as think about how client dynamics might be influencing the interaction.

Furthermore, the whole helping process is collaborative in that helpers guide or coach clients in working through problems. Helpers are not experts in how clients ought to live their lives, but helpers can be experts at facilitating the process of helping clients explore feelings and values, achieve understanding, and make choices and changes. Rather than giving answers to clients, helpers try to teach clients how to think through problems, make decisions, and implement changes. This whole model is essentially client centered in that helpers work with clients to choose their solutions to the problems they face. A good metaphor is the parable about teaching a hungry person to fish: Giving someone a fish feeds the person for one meal, whereas teaching her or him to fish enables the person to eat for a lifetime.

Although both empathy and collaboration are crucial components of the helping process, they are not specific skills that can be taught directly. Rather, they are outcomes of the successful implementation of helping skills and a reflection of an attitude that the helper feels toward the client. As helpers, we can be knowledgeable about our implementation of verbal and nonverbal behaviors, aware of how we come across when using these interventions, aware of our intentions for using different interventions, and aware of client reactions to these interventions. However, we cannot always control the outcome of the helping session. We can strive toward empathy and collaboration, but we cannot always attain these goals because much depends on clients and how well we "match" or "click" with them. Even so, through knowledge, self-awareness, and a genuine desire to understand, respect, and work with another person, empathic collaboration is likely to emerge and to be experienced by clients.

A Model for the Process and Outcome of Helping

Much of what happens in helping situations is so complex that it is often difficult for helpers, especially beginning helpers, to have a full awareness of the process. Furthermore, the helping process occurs at lightning speed, which does not give helpers much time to give conscious thought to every component and decision that accompanies interactions. Helpers must learn to react quickly because clients constantly present new needs and challenges.

By looking at the individual components of the process and outcome, helpers can begin to understand their reactions and responses in different situations and learn about clients' reactions to their interventions. Greater self-awareness allows helpers to be more psychologically available for clients and more intentional in their behaviors.

Analyzing each part of the helping process and outcome initially feels uncomfortable and cumbersome because beginning helpers are not used to breaking down their interactions and examining them so carefully. Furthermore, most beginning helpers are not used to thinking about their reasons for doing things and are not used to examining the reactions of others. As most beginning helpers continue with it, they become more comfortable taking apart and analyzing the process and then are able to put it all together to function more effectively in sessions. So let's turn to some of the variables that go into the moment-by-moment process.

HELPER BACKGROUND VARIABLES

Helpers bring unique ways of viewing the world to the helping process. They contribute their personalities, beliefs, assumptions about the world, values, experiences, and cultural and demographic characteristics. In addition, helpers bring their theoretical orientation (beliefs about how to help) and their previous experiences in helping (both informal and formal). For example, one could imagine that an introverted, young, European American female helper with a psychodynamic theoretical orientation would have a very different impact on the helping process than an extroverted, middle-aged, Iranian American male helper with a cognitive–behavioral theoretical orientation.

CLIENT BACKGROUND VARIABLES

Similarly, client background variables influence the process. A young, bright, attractive college student who is away from home for the first time and is feeling lonely and homesick is very different from a substance-abusing, older man who has been ordered by the court to attend counseling sessions because he batters his wife. As with helpers, clients bring unique ways of viewing the world to the helping process in terms of their individual personalities, beliefs, assumptions about the world, values, experiences, and cultural and demographic characteristics.

Clients are at various stages of readiness for change. Some are reluctant to participate in any form of helping; others are eager to learn more about themselves; and yet others are ready to make changes in their behaviors. Prochaska, Norcross, and DiClemente (1994, 2005) identified five stages of change:

- In the *precontemplation stage,* clients are unaware of the need to change or have no desire to change. Precontemplators lack information about their problems, engage in denial about their problems, and often blame other people or society for their problems. Other people are typically more bothered by the precontemplator's behavior than is the precontemplator.
- In the *contemplation stage,* clients are aware of and accept responsibility for their problems. They are beginning to think about changing but have not yet actively decided to change. Fear of failure often keeps clients stuck in this stage. Clients in this stage spend time thinking about the causes of their problems and ponder what it would be like to change.
- In the *preparation stage,* clients have made a commitment to change and are preparing themselves to begin the change process. Some clients make public announcements that they plan to change (e.g., "I plan to lose 30 pounds"). Some clients prepare themselves mentally for how their lives will be different (e.g., "When I lose weight, I will feel healthier and be more attractive and it will be easier to exercise").
- In the *action stage,* clients actively begin to modify their behaviors and their surroundings. They might stop smoking cigarettes, begin studying at regularly specified times, start taking more time for themselves, or decide to get married. The commitment and preparation done in the contemplation and preparation stages seem to be crucial for success in this stage, in that prepared clients are more aware of what they are striving for and why.

■ In the *maintenance stage,* clients have changed and are trying to consolidate their changes and deal with lapses. The process of change does not end, then, with the action stage. It takes several weeks or years for change to become incorporated into one's lifestyle, and people often recycle back to earlier stages in the process of change, suggesting that it is not easy to make changes that stick. This stage is very challenging because permanent change is difficult and often requires major lifestyle alterations.

Our goal as helpers is to assist clients in moving through the stages so that they become aware of problems, take responsibility for their behaviors, make decisions about whether and how to change, make the actual changes, and then work on consolidating their changes. Movement through the stages can often take considerable time; thus, a client might be in one of the stages for a given problem for several months or even years. Furthermore, clients can be at different stages of change for different problems (e.g., a client could be in the maintenance stage for stopping smoking but at a precontemplation stage for resolving spiritual issues in his life).

Working with precontemplative clients can be difficult (but not impossible) because they often come to helping under duress (e.g., court referral) rather than because they genuinely want to change. One can compare working with precontemplative clients to trying to push carts with square wheels: It is more difficult to push a cart with square wheels than to push a cart with round wheels. In contrast, working with clients in the later stages tends to be easier because these clients are more eager to work on themselves. The process works better when clients are interested in, rather than resistant to, change.

THERAPEUTIC RELATIONSHIP

Researchers have consistently found that the therapeutic relationship is a major predictor of the outcome of therapy (Gelso & Carter, 1985, 1994; Horvath & Bedi, 2002). Clients typically report that the most helpful aspect of therapy is feeling understood and supported. For some people, the relationship itself is curative, and they need nothing else from the helper (although others may need more in the way of helper skills).

Gelso and Carter (1985, 1994) theorized that the therapeutic relationship is made up of the real relationship, the working alliance, transference, and countertransference. The real relationship is the genuine, nondistorted connection between the helper and client. The working (or therapeutic) alliance is the part of the relationship focused on the therapeutic work and consists of the bond (i.e., the connection between the helper and client), an agreement on goals (a consensus about changes the client needs to make), and an agreement on tasks (a consensus about what is to take place during the helping process to meet the goals). A strong working alliance might involve a helper and client genuinely liking and respecting each other, deciding together to work on exploration and insight in the sessions, and agreeing about their goals to help the client develop better interpersonal relationships. Note that different types of working alliances may fit better for different types of clients. For example, Bachelor (1995) found that some clients prefer helpers who are warm and supportive, whereas others are put off by too much warmth and prefer helpers who are objective and businesslike.

In contrast to the straightforward concepts of the real relationship and the working alliance, transference and countertransference involve distortions in the relationship. Transference involves client distortions of the helper, and countertransference involves helper distortions of the client, both on the basis of experiences in previous significant relationships. Transference and countertransference are thus like lenses or filters through which one views the world. For example, a female client may expect that the helper will be bored with her because her parents ignored her (transference). Likewise, the helper may react poorly to client anger because anger was not an acceptable emotion in her or his family (countertransference).

Although most researchers agree that a good therapeutic relationship facilitates the helping process, they are much less clear about how to establish good relationships with clients. I postulate that helpers establish good therapeutic relationships by attending and listening carefully to clients, using the appropriate helping skills at the right times, treating clients according to their individual needs, being aware of feelings and limitations, being aware of clients' reactions to their interventions, and being open to feedback from clients (see also Hill, 2005b).

I propose that the therapeutic relationship works as follows. Clients often come to helpers feeling that no one listens to them or cares about them. Helpers attend to their clients and communicate an understanding of clients' feelings and experiences. Helpers are empathic and nonjudgmental and accept clients as they are, which allows the clients to feel safe enough to express deep feelings. Finally, helpers are skilled in their interventions, helping clients explore, gain insight, and make decisions about action and building clients' confidence that they can be helped. Within the context of the helping relationship, clients begin to feel that if their helpers accept them for who they are, they must be okay. It also allows them to see that not all people are like the others with whom they experience difficulty. Furthermore, working with helpers facilitates clients in reducing their anxiety and thus increases their capacity for facing interpersonal pain and anxiety. Clients slowly begin to build self-esteem and gain hope that they can change, which is the foundation for change. They also feel it is safe to explore thoughts and feelings, come to new understandings, and make changes. It is clear, then, that the relationship and skills are interrelated in influencing the therapeutic process.

Helpers cannot establish relationships with all clients, especially those who are not motivated or ready to be helped. For example, an adolescent girl might be forced by her parents to go for helping but not want to be there. Moreover, some clients have been so hurt and their capacity to trust so seriously impaired that they cannot benefit from a facilitative relationship. One therapist suggested that such clients are like leaky gas tanks—you can never fill them up. Clients who have been seriously damaged in relationships often have difficulty attaching to therapists.

The fault sometimes lies with the helpers, however. All helpers have limitations related to their backgrounds (e.g., dysfunctional families) and personal problems. In essence, helpers are wounded healers who have personal issues that they have not resolved completely. All of us have issues, and if these issues are not too overwhelming and all-encompassing, we can set them aside when we are helpers. If the personal issues are too salient, however, helpers are more likely to focus on their own rather than on the client's needs. For example, a helper who just had a major fight with his or her parent (or child) may not be able to concentrate on listening to a client's problems about fighting with her parents. This does not mean that helpers must have all their problems resolved (which would be impossible); but problems must be resolved enough so that they do not interfere with the work.

Some matches between helpers and clients are not ideal and do not result in positive therapeutic relationships. For example, a female client who was raped recently might not be able to talk to a male helper no matter how kind he is because she is terrified of all men. An alcoholic client might not want to see a helper who has never had problems with alcoholism because he fears that such a helper could not understand his struggle to stay sober. Similarly, helpers who have not resolved their own experiences of traumatic sexual or physical abuse might not be able to hear a client's story of abuse without having strong emotional reactions or being distracted by their own pain.

MOMENT-BY-MOMENT INTERACTIONAL SEQUENCE

Given the background variables and the specific context, the helper needs to act at a given moment in the session. Helpers formulate intentions on the basis of their assessment of the current situation. These intentions lead to the choice of specific helping skills. In turn, clients react to the helpers' interventions, which lead them to reevaluate their needs and goals and decide how to behave with the helpers. Helpers then assess clients' reactions and reevaluate what they need to do for their next intervention. The process thus continues with each person reacting both overtly and covertly, trying to determine the intentions of the other and deciding how to interact. The process thus changes depending on the perceptions, needs, and intentions of the moment. So let's slow down the process and look at each piece. See Figure 2.3.

Helper Intentions

Helpers think about what can be accomplished with the next intervention on the basis of everything they know at the time (Hill & O'Grady, 1985). Helpers develop intentions (e.g., give information, identify feelings) for how to work with the client (see the Helper Intentions List, Web Form D). These intentions guide the helper's choice of verbal and nonverbal interventions. Thus, the helper's intention is the reason behind the intervention.

Intentions are covert and are not necessarily apparent to clients or helpers (Fuller & Hill, 1985). In fact, helpers are not always aware of their intentions at the time of delivery. For example, helpers sometimes inadvertently self-disclose to make themselves feel better rather than to be helpful to clients. Reviewing audio- or videotapes after sessions (alone or with a supervisor) and thinking about or writing down intentions for each intervention is an excellent way to increase awareness of what one was trying to accomplish. Helpers are typically able to identify intentions pretty easily when they review tapes within 24 hours of the session and recall how they were feeling and reacting at a given moment in the session (rather than indicating how they currently feel about their interventions). By slowing down the process and examining it piece by piece, helpers can discover the different layers of feelings, thoughts, and actions. After gaining experience with examining intentions during videotape replays, helpers are often able to obtain an awareness of intentions while they are in sessions with clients. I encourage beginning helpers to become intentional in their interventions and to think about what they are trying to accomplish during each intervention.

Helper Helping Skills

For each intention, the helper could use a few different helping skills (see the Helping Skills System, Web Form E). For example, to facilitate the client talking about feelings, the helper might reflect feelings, self-disclose about feelings, or ask open questions about feelings. All of these might be quite appropriate but subtly move the client in different directions. It is also typically helpful to use a variety of skills so that the process does not become too stilted (e.g., clients might become annoyed if helpers continually say, "How does that make you feel?").

In addition to matching the skill to the intention, helpers should bear in mind that there are verbal and nonverbal components to the skills and that the same intervention can have a different impact depending on the manner of delivery. If the helper says "You seem to be feeling anxious"

FIGURE 2.3

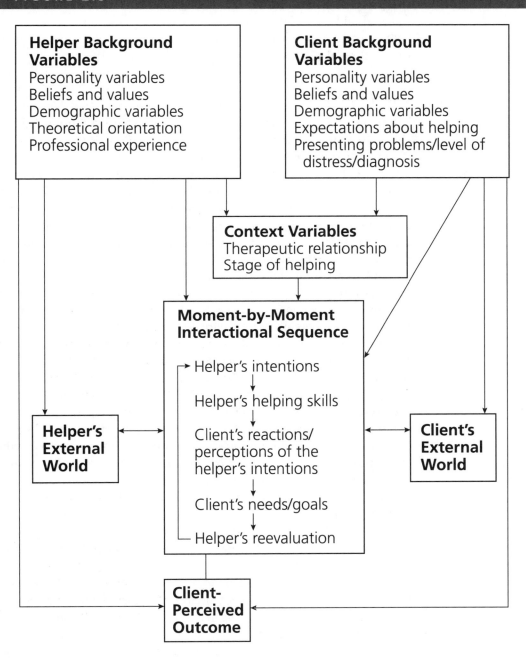

Factors influencing the helping process.

in a supportive, gentle tone and makes appropriate eye contact, the client will probably have a different reaction than if the helper uses a critical, judgmental tone and does not make eye contact. Appropriate nonverbal behaviors vary across clients and situations (see chap. 4), so helpers need to use nonverbal behaviors carefully and intentionally.

Client's Reactions

A helper intervention is met by one or more client reactions (see the Client Reactions System, Web Form G). When a helper is successful, the client's reactions match the helper's intentions and helping skills. For example, if the helper's intention is to provide emotional support and the helping skill used is an encourager such as "I understand what you're going through," the client's reaction might be to feel understood and supported. However, if the intervention is not successful, the client might feel that the helper did not really hear what was being expressed or that the helper made incorrect assumptions.

Clients are sometimes consciously aware of their reactions, although at other times they might be unaware of their reactions to helpers. In addition, clients sometimes have difficulty admitting to reactions that are not socially acceptable (e.g., feeling angry at a helper's intervention). Admitting negative feelings about helpers can be difficult if clients respect and depend on the helpers or if clients cannot allow themselves to have negative emotions. For example, a client might react negatively to something a helper says because it is similar to something her parents said, but the client might not allow herself to express these negative feelings for fear of hurting the helper. Instead, the client might smile politely but feel somewhat distant and unengaged, not understanding consciously why she withdrew from the interaction. Research suggests that clients often hide negative reactions from their therapists out of fear of retaliation or out of deference to the helper's authority (e.g., Hill, Thompson, Cogar, & Denman, 1993; Hill, Thompson, & Corbett, 1992; Rennie, 1994). For example, clients who feel angry at or misunderstood by their helpers are not likely to reveal those feelings if they feel unsafe in the therapeutic relationship.

In addition to hiding negative reactions during sessions, research indicates that clients often do not disclose important material in sessions (Hill et al., 1993; Kelly, 1998; Regan & Hill, 1992). Clients in these studies indicated that they left things unsaid because the emotions felt overwhelming, they were ashamed or embarrassed, they wanted to avoid dealing with the disclosure, they feared that the helpers would not understand, or they thought that either they or the helpers could not handle the disclosure. In one interesting study (not involving therapy), Bonanno et al. (2002) found that people who voluntarily disclosed having been sexually abused as children had facial expressions of disgust, whereas people who chose not to disclose had facial expressions of shame and did more polite smiling. The implication of these findings for the helping process is that clients might not disclose because of deep feelings of shame. These results remind us that helpers cannot "read" clients' minds and cannot assume that they know how clients are reacting.

A number of factors influence the reactions clients have to helper interventions. First, clients' reactions are influenced by their needs at the time. For example, clients in severe crisis might tolerate almost any intervention because they are desperately in need of help. In contrast, high-functioning clients might be more demanding that helpers be competent and knowledgeable about how to help them.

Second, client reactions are moderated by the therapeutic relationship. In generally positive relationships, clients might tolerate some mistakes from helpers without an adverse reaction because they feel that helpers are genuinely trying to be helpful. If the relationship is problematic or rocky, however, anything helpers do might elicit negative reactions from disgruntled clients.

In addition, clients' reactions seem to be influenced by their impressions of the helper's intentions. For example, if clients think that their helpers were acting out of their own personal needs rather than in the best interest of the clients (regardless of what the helpers' actual intentions were), they might have negative reactions. If clients think that therapists want to extend therapy to make more money rather than because their clients need help, clients might become angry and uncooperative. In contrast, if clients think that their helpers are beginners who are struggling to be helpful (perhaps with limited success), they might feel sympathetic and have positive reactions. Clients' perceptions, then, even though they might not match the "reality" of helpers' intentions, seem to influence clients' reactions.

Clients' Needs or Goals

Clients decide what they need and want from the interaction and determine what is possible to obtain from helpers at a particular time. Clients are not passive recipients of helpers' interventions but are actively involved in getting what they need from interactions. For example, one client might feel a need to retreat to avoid further confrontation. Another client might decide that he wants to reveal more because his helper is accurate in understanding him and can be trusted with secrets.

Clients also want to have an impact on their helpers. They might want to impress or please their helpers by doing whatever the helpers suggest. For example, Sam wanted to please his helper and so kept telling her what a good job she was doing. Other clients might decide not to reveal shameful secrets because they do not want to tarnish the helper's opinion of them.

Clients do not typically consciously plot the reactions they want to elicit from their helpers. Rather, they act on the basis of their past experiences in ways that maximize the probability of getting their needs met (e.g., to feel close to or distant from the helper). Most of this decision process about what they need from the interaction and what impact they want to have on helpers is intuitive rather than consciously planned. Some of these client goals are influenced by transference, which occurs when clients project how significant people in their lives (e.g., parents) behaved onto how they expect their helpers to behave (see Gelso & Hayes, 1998; Gelso, Hill, Mohr, Rochlen, & Zack, 1999). For example, if a client feels that no one listened to her as a child, she might not be able to believe that anyone could possibly want to listen to her now. Hence, even though the helper is attentive, the client might want the helper to "prove" that he really wants to listen to her or she will not talk in the session. Rather than recognizing that the helper is silent because he does not know what to say, this client might perceive the silence as occurring because the helper is bored by her. In another example, a client with a critical father may have difficulty believing that an older male helper is genuinely supportive.

Clients' Behaviors

Clients engage in specific behaviors (e.g., resist, agree, make an appropriate request, recount, engage in cognitive–behavioral or affective exploration, come to insight, or discuss therapeutic changes; see Client Behavior System, Web Form H) on the basis of their reactions, feelings about the therapeutic relationship, needs in the interaction, and goals for a desired impact. Clients' behaviors are determined not only by the interaction but also by their communication ability, awareness of needs, level of pathology, and personality structure. Hence, one client might be very articulate and insightful about describing the causes of his pain, whereas another client might be unskilled at communicating feelings and be unaware of what she is feeling in the moment.

Helpers' Assessment of Client Reactions and Reevaluation of Goals

Helpers, in turn, try to assess clients' reactions to their interventions. For example, they observe the client's behavior to determine what the client's reaction was to the intervention (e.g., whether the client felt supported and understood or confused and misunderstood). Unfortunately, helpers are not always accurate in determining clients' reactions. A popular perception is that helpers can read clients' minds. In fact, my research suggests that helpers are not particularly adept at perceiving negative client reactions to their interventions, although they are more

An Overview of Helping

accurate at perceiving positive than negative client reactions (Hill et al., 1992). The lesser ability to perceive negative client reactions might occur because, as noted earlier, clients hide negative reactions from helpers. People often learn as young children not to show negative reactions for fear of evoking displeasure or being punished (e.g., imagine what would happen if an elementary school student told her teacher that she did not like what the teacher said). Hence, helpers cannot assume that clients feel positively just because the clients are not displaying negative reactions.

In addition, helpers might be reluctant to recognize when clients have negative reactions. For example, many helpers have a hard time with clients' anger directed at them (Hill, Kellems, et al., 2003). They want everyone to like them, and having clients get angry at them feels scary and upsetting. When clients are angry, these helpers might misinterpret the anger as a rejection of them personally, rather than appreciating that clients are able to express their anger (as they might other feelings). Other helpers might have difficulty allowing clients to become upset and cry, because they feel obligated to make everything better and have all clients be happy.

Unfortunately, not all helpers have received skills training or have learned to examine the effects of their interventions on clients, so they use interventions that feel comfortable (e.g., giving advice) rather than ones that match the client's needs in the specific situation. In addition, there is a danger that over time helpers can become insensitive to the influence of their behavior on clients and assume that they know how the clients are reacting internally. Helpers, even when they are experienced, must strive to be aware of their reactions and the impact of their interventions on clients.

On the basis of their perceptions of the client's reactions (whether accurate or not) and observation of the overt behaviors, helpers reevaluate what they are trying to accomplish and thus come up with new intentions and accompanying skills for the next intervention. If a helper perceives that the last intervention was successful and thinks that a similar intervention would be appropriate, she might continue with the same intention–skill combination. For example, if a reflection resulted in the client talking about sadness, the helper might use another reflection to help the client delve even deeper into these feelings. If a helper perceives that the last intervention was helpful but that something new is needed, he might choose a different intention–skill combination. For example, if a helper had reflected feelings and the client responded by talking about deep feelings but seemed to have a sense of completion, the helper might decide to use an open question to find out more about other aspects of problems.

If, in contrast, a helper perceives that the last intervention was not received well by the client, the helper would, one hopes, try to determine why the intervention was not successful. If the timing was poor, the helper might decide not to continue that intervention but to go back to a more exploratory intervention to learn more about the problem. If the helper decides that the intentions were on target but the wrong skill was used, the helper might use a different skill to implement the same intention. For example, a beginning helper might implement the intention of encouraging the client to talk about feelings by asking a closed question, such as "Did you have any feelings about that?" If the client responds, "No," and adds nothing further, the helper might realize that the closed question stopped rather than facilitated exploration. The helper might then use a reflection of feeling (e.g., "Perhaps you feel scared right now") in the next intervention and observe how the client responds. Thus, by paying attention to client reactions, helpers can devise new interventions to fit the immediate need.

Given that the most important criterion for the effectiveness of the helper's intervention is the client's response, helpers need to monitor client reactions to determine whether their interventions are helpful and make adjustments when clients respond negatively. I like to think of helpers as personal scientists, investigating the effects of each intervention, testing what works and what does not work, and then deciding what needs to be done next. Helpers thus have to be very attentive to what works with individual clients. Even if a helper finds that certain helping skills work well with one client, those same skills might not work with the next client.

Of course, such constant awareness demands that helpers be open to feedback, have the skills in their repertoires to try something different, and have a good enough relationship with their clients to allow for misunderstandings. Unfortunately, many helper issues can interrupt this process: a bad day, a lack of openness and awareness, a lack of skills, or a lack of a good enough relationship with the client. No helper can ever be perfect because there is no such concept as perfection in helping. In fact, one could argue that being a perfect helper would not be helpful for clients because it would not present a realistic relationship—everyone makes mistakes, and learning how to deal with mistakes can be very therapeutic. Helpers who recognize their mistakes, apologize, and process the event can provide a powerful example for clients about how to deal with problems in relationships. Thus, the best advice is that helpers should relax, do the best they can, and try to learn from their experiences. Furthermore, helpers should seek out therapy, training, and supervision to help them deal with obstacles to their effectiveness.

EXTERNAL WORLD

Many external forces influence the helping process. We can look at these forces for both clients and helpers.

Clients

Typically, helping sessions last only 1 hour or so a week, whereas clients live the rest of their lives outside of the helping sessions. As helpers, we hope that clients take what they have learned from helping sessions and try to apply it to "real life." In one case of brief psychotherapy presented in Hill (1989), the therapist confronted the client with the fact that the client did not seem to need him or listen to anything he said. The client was very surprised because she had never viewed herself this way. She thought that she was working hard on her issues both within and outside of therapy. She discussed this with her friends, who agreed with the therapist's assessment that she seemed self-possessed and did not appear to need anything from them. Hearing this feedback from both the therapist and her friends forced the client to look at her behavior; she used the feedback from her friends to validate what she was learning in therapy.

In intensive psychotherapy, clients sometimes form images, or what have been called *internal representations,* of their therapists to remind them of their helpers in between sessions (Farber & Geller, 1994; Geller, Cooley, & Hartley, 1981; Geller & Farber, 1993; Knox, Goldberg, Woodhouse, & Hill, 1999; Orlinsky & Geller, 1993). For example, some clients might hold imaginary discussions with their helpers to figure out what the helpers would suggest they do in difficult situations. Others might imagine their helper comforting them in difficult situations. These internal representations often help clients cope between sessions.

Another important influence in the external world is social support, which has been documented extensively (e.g., Cobb, 1976). More specifically, clients who have social support tend to do better in therapy (Mallinckrodt, 2000). Clients with friends are less likely to become overly dependent on their therapists. They have other people to talk to, and they obviously have enough social skills to form friendships.

However, relationships in the external world can sometimes present obstacles to progress in therapy. Perhaps the clearest example is when a client's changes threaten the status quo of family life, causing family members to undermine the client's progress. For example, a severely overweight man's weight loss may threaten his marital relationship. The wife may fear that the husband is now attractive to other women and might lose interest in her. She may begin to cook tasty, fattening desserts to tempt the man to regain the weight and thus stabilize the relationship. These behaviors are not necessarily performed consciously but often are desperate attempts to maintain stability in relationships (see Watzlawick, Weakland, & Fisch, 1974).

Thus, events in the external world can both help and hinder the therapeutic work. Helpers cannot just attend to what goes on in session;

rather, they need to be aware of how external events influence the help-ing process. They can also encourage clients to talk in the helping setting about issues that come up outside of helping, and they can encourage clients to take responsibility for making changes in their lives.

Helpers

Many of the same external forces that influence clients also influence how helpers feel and behave in helping sessions with clients. If helpers have a lot of stress and conflict in their personal lives, it is difficult for them to put these aside (bracket them) so that they can focus on their clients. A particular stress that affects beginning helpers is anxiety: The more anxious helpers are about their ability to perform in helping ses-sions, the less able they are to focus on and be empathic with clients. It is hoped that helpers seek personal therapy to work on their personal issues and supervision to work on the professional issues so that they can be available to clients in sessions.

OUTCOMES OF HELPING FOR CLIENTS

All of the variables discussed to this point (helper and client background variables, context variables, moment-by-moment interactional sequences, and the external world) interact to determine the outcome of the helping process for the client. Thus, the outcome is influenced by many factors, and individuals react idiosyncratically to different aspects of the process.

One way to categorize outcomes is in terms of three areas: (a) *remor-alization,* or the enhancement of well-being; (b) *remediation,* or the achieve-ment of symptomatic relief; and (c) *rehabilitation,* or the reduction of troublesome, maladaptive behaviors that interfere with functioning in areas such as family relationships and work. Outcome research indi-cates that remoralization happens first and is the easiest thing to change in therapy; remediation follows at a slower pace; and rehabil-itation takes the longest time to accomplish (Grissom, Lyons, & Lutz, 2002; Howard, Lueger, Maling, & Martinovich, 1993). Hence, a client may feel more hopeful after a few sessions of therapy, but it may take longer for the client to feel less depressed and anxious, and even longer for the client to make changes in terms of new ways of behaving in rela-tionships and work.

Another way to talk about outcome is in terms of *intrapersonal, inter-personal,* and *social role performance* (Lambert & Hill, 1994). Intrapersonal changes refer to outcomes that occur within the client (e.g., decreased symptoms, increased self-esteem, improved problem-solving abilities, new behavioral skills such as assertiveness, increased subjective feelings of well-being). Interpersonal changes take place in the client's intimate relationships (e.g., improved communication, increased marital satisfaction, healthier relationships). Social role performance refers to the client's ability to carry out responsibilities in the community (e.g., improved job performance, increased participation in community activities, greater involvement in school, reduced antisocial behaviors). For example, a client with good outcomes in all three areas may feel better about herself, have a clearer sense of who she is and the meaning of her life, have an improved relationship with her husband, and have fewer days of absence at work related to illness.

It is important to note that therapy does not result in "cures," such that clients are functioning perfectly after therapy. In my view, there is no such thing as functioning perfectly because the human condition involves inherent feelings of existential issues such as isolation, fears of responsibility and freedom, and death anxiety. Rather, helpers can expect that clients begin to function more effectively, feel better about themselves, and become more acceptant about their condition in life. Sometimes, however, therapy can actually make clients more anxious as they grapple with existential issues (Yalom, 1980); becoming more anxious is thus appropriate.

Helpers, clients, and clients' significant others often have different perceptions of the outcome of the helping process (see Strupp & Hadley, 1977). For example, a helper might feel pleased with her performance as a helper with Jack and believe that Jack benefited a great deal from the helping because he said he was going to change his major. In contrast, Jack might feel that he only participated in counseling to please his parents and that he listened politely and responded compliantly in the session to appease the helper but dismissed all the helper's advice as soon as he left. Jack's parents might feel sad because their son is not choosing the career they want for him and resigned that even helping did not improve their relationship with their son. Thus, the outcomes of helping can be quite different depending on the individual's perspective.

Concluding Comments

The whole helping process undoubtedly seems incredibly complex, especially to the beginning trainee. Similarly, all the components of driving at first seem overwhelming to a person learning to drive, but later driving becomes so familiar that the driver often does not even think about the separate steps (e.g., turning the wheel to make a turn). At this point, having a broad overview of the model can provide you with a framework for understanding the individual intentions and skills.

What Do You Think?

- What are your assumptions about human nature and the possibility of change?
- How do your assumptions compare with those presented in this chapter?
- Debate whether all three stages are needed for a complete helping process or whether another model might be better.
- Discuss the role of empathic collaboration in helping.
- Discuss whether empathy is an attitude or a skill.
- The helping process was described as being very complicated. Do you agree? What components were left out of the helping process, and what components were not necessary?
- What parts of the helping process are unconscious (i.e., not open to awareness)?
- How might helpers increase awareness of their intentions and of client reactions?
- Why do you think that helpers and clients experience the same interaction differently?
- How important do you think helping skills are to the therapeutic relationship in terms of leading to client change?

i LAB 2. Initial Session

A downloadable PDF of this Lab is available in the student resources area of Helping Skills, *3rd ed. Web site: http://www.apa.org/books/resources/Hill3.*

Goal: To get a baseline of what skills are used in a 20-minute session prior to training. Having this baseline will allow you to examine changes over the course of training.

Helper's and Client's Tasks During the Helping Interchange

1. Students take turns being helper, client, and observer for 20-minute sessions.
2. Helpers bring copies of the Session Review Form (Web Form A), Helper Intentions List (Web Form D), Client Reactions System (Web Form G), and Session Process and Outcome Measures (Web Form I) to the session. Observers bring copies of the Supervisor Rating Form (Web Form B).
3. Helpers bring an audio- or videotape recorder (tested ahead of time to ensure it works) and a tape, and turn the recorder on at the beginning of the session.
4. Helpers introduce themselves and assure clients of confidentiality.
5. Each helper conducts a 20-minute session with his or her client, being as helpful as possible. Clients talk about an easy topic (see Exhibit 1.1 in chap. 1). Observers record what they thought was the most and least helpful thing the helper did.
6. While watching the session, the observer completes the Supervisor Rating Form.
7. Helper and client complete the Session Process and Outcome Measures.
8. The observer and client give feedback to the helper.

Helper's and Client's Tasks During the Postsession Review of the Tape

1. After the session, the helper and client review the tape (takes about 40–60 minutes). Helpers stop the tape after each helper intervention (except minimal utterances such as "um-hmm" and "yeah") and write the key words on the Session Review Form (so the exact spot on the tape can be located later for transcribing the session).
2. Helpers rate the helpfulness and record the numbers of up to three intentions (using the Helper Intentions List) for each intervention, responding according to how they felt *during* the session rather than while listening to the tape. Helpers should try to use the whole range of the Helpfulness Scale and as many intentions as possible. Do not complete these ratings in collaboration with clients.
3. Clients rate the helpfulness of each intervention and record the numbers of up to three reactions, responding according to how they felt *during* the session. Clients should try to use the whole range of the Helpfulness Scale and as many reactions as possible (helpers learn more from honest feedback than from "nice" statements that are not genuine). Clients should not collaborate with helpers in doing the ratings.

Lab Report

1. Helpers should type a transcript of their 20-minute session (see the sample transcript in Web Form C). Skip minimal utterances (e.g., "okay," "you know," "er," "uh").
2. Divide the helper speech into response units (see Web Form F).
3. Using the Helping Skills System (Web Form E), determine which skill was used for each response unit (i.e., grammatical sentence) in your transcript.
4. Erase the tape. Make sure no identifying information is on the transcript.
5. Compare the helper and client scores on the Helping Skills Measure, Relationship Scale, and Session Evaluation Scale with those of other students (see Web Form I, Session Process and Outcome Measures), where all these measures are included.

Personal Reflections

- What did you learn about yourself from this experience?
- What was it like for you to be a helper?
- What was it like for you to be a client?

Ethical Issues in Helping 3

Intellectual integrity, courage, and kindness are still the
virtues I admire most.

—*Gerti Cori*

E thics are principles and standards that ensure that professionals provide quality services and are respectful of the rights of
the people with whom they work. Acting in an ethical manner also involves following the laws and rules governing one's
profession. Hence, a mental health organization's or association's principles are aspirational guidelines that people in the
profession have agreed on by consensus, whereas the profession's standards (its bylaws and rules) are enforceable through
sanctions or professional censure as stipulated by the relevant
organization or association. Furthermore, principles and standards can be differentiated from personal morality (e.g., being
for or against abortion rights).

Although beginning helpers are not yet professionals
and as such are not obligated to follow the professional principles and standards, they should aspire to the extent possible to the ethical principles and standards of the profession.
They should model their conduct in a helping session in a
professional, therapeutic way.

The instructor of the class (or the instructor's supervisor,
if the instructor is a graduate student), in contrast, is a professional, and is responsible for what goes on in the classroom
and in required helping sessions. Thus, the instructor has a
responsibility to be aware of the ethical issues and educate his

other students about these issues. It would be advisable for instructors to have conversations with students early in training as well as throughout training about what topics should be disclosed in helping sessions (see Exhibit 1.1), informed consent (Exhibit 3.2, later in this chapter), confidentiality (see more detail later in this chapter), and other potential ethical issues. In addition, because laws, statutes, and legal decisions vary in different jurisdictions and states, instructors should be aware of and educate students about local requirements.

Ethical Codes of Conduct

Most helping professions (e.g., counseling, medicine, nursing, psychology, social work) have developed ethical codes that are intended to protect both the practitioners and the clients. These codes describe the underlying ethical principles to which professionals aspire in making their decisions. These principles encourage professionals to act in a responsible manner, ensure quality client care, and contribute to society through their work. Rather than providing "the right answer," the principles provide guidelines to helpers for behaving in a responsible manner and resolving ethical dilemmas. The codes also involve specific standards of conduct for what professionals should do (e.g., talk about confidentiality) and should not do (e.g., have sexual relations with clients). Exhibit 3.1 provides a list of several professional organizations and their Web sites for their ethical codes.

EXHIBIT 3.1

List of Professional Organizations and Web Sites for Ethical Codes

- American Association for Marriage and Family Therapy (2002)
  http://www.AAMFT.org
- American Counseling Association (1995)
  http://www.counseling.org
- American Psychological Association (2002)
  http://www.apa.org/ethics/code2002.html
- American School Counselor Association (1998)
  http://www.schoolcounselor.org
- National Association for Social Workers (1996)
  http://www.naswdc.org

General Ethical Principles

Many ethical codes stress the importance of six basic ethical principles (Beauchamp & Childress, 1994; Kitchener, 1984; Meara, Schmidt, & Day, 1996):

- *Autonomy* refers to the right (of both the consumer and the provider) to make choices and take actions, provided the results do not adversely affect others. This principle grants individuals the opportunity to determine their actions on the basis of their belief systems. For example, a helper may be working with a client about career decisions, independent of the client's parents' hopes for her to pursue law school. Suddenly, the client announces that she is ending counseling and giving up her scholarship to pursue a career as a country music singer. The helper might suggest that the client reevaluate this decision and consider the pros and cons of life as a country music singer. However, the principle of autonomy allows the client the right to make her own decisions, provided these decisions are not harmful to others. In this example, the helper supported the client's decision to attend college and simultaneously pursue her dream of becoming a musician.

- *Beneficence* refers to the intent "to do good" by helping and promoting growth in others. This principle clearly states that helpers should be committed to the growth and development of their clients. Helpers who strive to provide the most comprehensive, empirically supported services to their clients are embodying the principle of beneficence, whereas helpers who see clients solely to make money violate this important principle.

- *Nonmaleficence* can be described with the phrase "above all, do no harm." Professionals are asked to ensure that their interventions and actions do not inadvertently harm their clients. Thus, neglect on the part of the helper (even if unintentional) would be problematic. For example, a student in a helping class might be out drinking margaritas with friends and telling them about the practice helping session he had in class that day. Later, he might notice that his practice client is in the booth next to him and had probably overheard him telling his friends about her issues. Although the helper may not have used the client's name or intended to harm her, he would be responsible for the unintentional harm that results from having disclosed confidential information about his practice client.

- *Justice* can be defined as fairness or ensuring equality of opportunities and resources for all people. One could interpret this to mean that helpers have an ethical responsibility to rectify the unequal distribution of helping services by making their services more accessible to those who are unable to pay. For example, helpers can contribute to building a just society by volunteering at not-for-profit agencies (e.g., shelters for battered women, clinics for people with AIDS). An additional method of promoting justice involves attempts to influence public policy or legislation to ensure that mental health services are available to those in need, regardless of their ability to pay, location, language preference, or disability status.

- *Fidelity* refers to keeping promises and being trustworthy in relationships with others. Fidelity is a critical component of the relationship between helpers and clients. Without confidence in the helper's ability to be faithful to the agreements articulated in the helping session, minimal progress can be made. For example, the agreement between helpers and clients typically involves both parties meeting at a certain time for a specified number of sessions. If helpers are consistently 20 minutes late for each session, they are breaking the promise to be available to clients at an arranged time. Violations like these can have a detrimental impact on the development of the helping relationship.

- *Veracity*, which refers to telling the truth, is a powerful and necessary principle in helping settings. Clients often rely on their helpers to provide honest feedback about their interactions in the helping sessions. One example involves a 21-year-old client who worked with a helper for many months. Takiesha had not made much progress in the last few sessions and asked the counselor for some direct feedback about her work in the helping sessions. The helper provided several positive remarks and also indicated that at times, Takiesha appeared to place responsibility for her problems on others instead of empowering herself. Although Takiesha was upset about hearing this feedback, she was grateful to the helper for being honest and was able to understand how her reluctance to take responsibility prevented her from making necessary changes in her life.

Ethical Issues for Beginning Helpers

Professional therapists and counselors deal with many ethical issues. Here I focus on a few of the ethical issues that beginning helpers will encounter.

CONFIDENTIALITY

Beginning students learning helping skills may encounter confidentiality issues when they practice with classmates or volunteer clients who present real problems. It is important that helpers respect a client's confidentiality by not divulging information shared in the helping session, except in limited circumstances (see next paragraph). Sometimes, maintaining confidentiality can be challenging if students interact with clients outside of the sessions or if they have friends in common. However, the success of the helping relationship is due in part to a client's ability to trust that information shared with a helper in sessions will be held in confidence.

There are a few limits to confidentiality (recall as mentioned earlier in this chapter that requirements often vary by jurisdiction or state and so you need to be aware of local requirements). First, you need to be able to talk about your clients with supervisors so that you can learn from your errors and grow as a helper. Second, if the client reveals to you harm (or intent to harm) to self or other, you (and/or the responsible instructor or supervisor) may be legally obligated to report this threat to the appropriate authorities. Third, if the client reveals abuse to children, elderly persons, or disabled persons, you (and/or again the responsible instructor or supervisor) may be legally obligated to report such abuse to the appropriate authorities. It is important to inform clients about the general principle of confidentiality at the beginning of the first session and then have the client sign an informed-consent form similar to the one shown in Exhibit 3.2. In addition, helpers have to deal with issues related to confidentiality as they arise in sessions, by first reminding clients about the limits of confidentiality as they begin to disclose issues related to harm or abuse and second by consulting immediately with supervisors and legal authorities and then carrying out the recommended procedures.

RECOGNIZING LIMITS

It is critical that helpers recognize and practice only within the areas for which they have been trained and are competent. For example, after going through this course, you will probably be able to use the exploration skills (e.g., listening and reflecting feelings) with classmates but you will not have expertise in such areas as working with children, facilitating personality change, doing crisis intervention, or working with patients with severe mental illness. As an example, a friend who discovers that you are learning helping skills may ask you to speak with her cousin who has been acting in a strange manner and hearing voices that tell him to destroy the psychology building at the university. Appropriate ethical behavior in this case would involve telling your

---

EXHIBIT 3.2

Informed Consent Form

I understand that my helper is a student-in-training.

I understand that my helping session(s) may be audio- or videotaped for training and supervisory purposes; that only my helper and those involved in the course will review any tapes; and that confidentiality will be strictly maintained in accordance with the law. Recordings will be destroyed in a timely manner.

I understand that all information shared in this session will be kept confidential, with a few key exceptions:
   a. supervisors may listen to the session or read transcripts of sessions (transcripts will have no identifying information);
   b. harm or intention to harm self or others (as required by law);
   c. reasonable suspicion of current or previous abuse of children, elderly, or disabled individuals, as required by law;
   d. court orders.

With the understanding that I may withdraw my consent to the above conditions at any time, I grant my permission to participate in the session(s) and to be audio/videotaped by the helper whose signature appears below.

Signature of Client: _____   Date: _____

Signature of Helper: _____   Date: _____

---

friend that meeting with her cousin is outside of your area of competence. You might, however, offer to speak with your professor to obtain a referral to a competent practitioner who has training and expertise in working with people who hear voices.

In a related vein, as a helper, you need to be honest about your qualifications—that you are a beginning trainee. Helpers who describe themselves as counselors or advertise that they provide psychological interventions they have not been trained to use are not acting ethically. For example, a practice client may refer to you as his "psychologist." Given that *psychologist* is a legal term associated with obtaining a doctoral degree and passing a major national examination, ethical behavior would involve telling the client that you are in training to learn helping skills and do not yet have a degree or license to practice psychology.

Furthermore, beginning helpers should consult with supervisors to enable them to best serve their clients. In one helping class, a student met with a client who mentioned that she had considered suicide because of all of the stressors in her life. The student immediately contacted her lab leader who consulted with the instructor, who then intervened with the client to provide the necessary assistance. Furthermore, when one's own issues threaten to interfere with the helping process, helpers need to consult supervisors. For example, at the same time John was struggling with his decision to marry his long-term girlfriend, his client was also considering whether to make a lifelong commitment to his partner. John realized the potential for harm in this situation and discussed with his supervisor how to ensure that his personal issues related to commitment would not have a negative impact on the helping sessions with his client.

EDUCATING CLIENTS ABOUT THE HELPING PROCESS

Clients have a right to understand the nature of the helping relationship. Many clients have never experienced a formal helping relationship and are uncertain about what to expect. Helpers can explain their theoretical orientation in simple, clear terms so that clients can make an informed decision about whether to participate in the process. For example, helpers should provide information about fees, length of the helping relationship, techniques used, whether anyone will be observing or supervising, and whether the sessions will be audio- or videotaped. As noted previously, beginning helpers must also inform clients about the limits of confidentiality and their status as helpers (e.g., that they are not professionals). It is a good idea for helpers to ask clients to sign an informed consent that explains the process (see Exhibit 3.2). In fact, it is good practice to do so given that all health care professionals are now required by the Health Insurance Portability and Accountability Act (HIPAA) of 1996 to have their patients sign statements related to privacy and security of health care information.

Furthermore, clients have the right to understand what outcomes can be expected. Here it is important not to promise something that you cannot be sure that you can deliver. Thus, for example, it is appropriate to say that helping involves an opportunity for clients to explore themselves, but you cannot guarantee that they will be "cured" or even that they will feel better.

Furthermore, when providing services to families or couples, helpers must clarify their roles and the relationships that occur during the time of service. For example, a helper was seeing an adolescent client whose parents were divorcing. The mother was struggling during this time and asked if she could talk privately with the helper to discuss some of her issues related to the divorce. The helper gently reminded her of the importance of having a special relationship with the client (the daughter) and indicated that this relationship might be jeopardized by even one helping session with the mother. The mother was given referrals to other qualified helpers.

FOCUSING ON THE NEEDS OF THE CLIENT

At times, the best interests of clients may conflict with the needs of helpers. For example, Jim may be preoccupied during a session because he needs to study for an exam. Jim may have a difficult time focusing on the client (e.g., listening, giving eye contact), and he may hope to end the session early to go home and study. However, it is critical that the helper focus on listening carefully to the concerns of the client and be as present as possible in the helping session.

An interesting situation results when the client's unresolved issues result in behaviors that benefit the helper. For example, Himee noticed that her helper often had a soft drink on his desk. Himee then began to give the helper a soft drink at the beginning of each helping session. Although it might be in the best interest of the helper to accept his favorite drink, ethical behavior requires that the helper try to understand the meaning of Himee's behavior and act in a manner that places her needs first. In this case, the helper might assist Himee in uncovering her desire to please the helper and her fear that the helper might abandon her if she did not bring gifts to the sessions. Perhaps it would be in the best interest of the client to assist her in viewing herself as valuable in relationships, independent of the gifts she presents to others.

AVOID HARMFUL DUAL RELATIONSHIPS

A potentially harmful dual relationship occurs when someone in power (e.g., a helper, professor, supervisor) adds another role to his or her interaction with a less powerful individual (e.g., a client, student, supervisee) because the dual relationship may lead to the harm or exploitation of the less powerful person. For example, it would not be unusual or problematic for a supervisor also to be a student's professor and evaluator; however, if the supervisor–professor also took on the role of therapist, the dual relationship could be harmful because confidential information disclosed in therapy could potentially be used to the student's detriment. Helpers need to be aware of the power differential when working with others and ensure that clients are not harmed by their interactions. For example, if a beginning helper is assigned a client for whom she or he is also a teaching assistant, harm might occur if the client-student felt that disclosures could be used against him or her when the helper was grading exams. Hence, helpers should not take on clients with whom they have other relationships if that would interfere with the helping process.

Helpers also should not provide helping sessions to friends or family members. Although helping skills can be used to communicate more effectively in personal relationships, taking on the role of helper with friends or family members can be detrimental for several reasons. First, it is difficult to be objective when listening to the problems of friends or family members. A lack of objectivity could have a negative impact on a helping session because the helper's own needs could interfere with assisting the client to act in her or his best interests. Second, the role of helper is powerful and could disturb the power dynamics in the relationship. For example, Alfonso began to rely on his friend to be his helper while he was going through a divorce. In time, Alfonso became dependent on this friend for assistance when problems emerged at work or with his children. His relationship with his friend-turned-helper was harmed because their interactions were always focused on Alfonso's problems.

Perhaps the most blatant example of harmful dual relationships involves a helper having a sexual relationship with a client. Sexual involvement with clients (and former clients) has been shown to have negative outcomes (Pope, 1994). Thus, many professions have developed explicit rules prohibiting sexual intimacies between helpers and clients. In addition, providing counseling to someone with whom one has been sexually involved in the past can be destructive to the client. Helpers typically cannot be objective and provide quality services to clients with whom they have been intimately involved. (For discussion about sexual attraction, see chap. 13.)

DEVELOPING APPROPRIATE BOUNDARIES

Helpers need to think about boundaries, or the ground rules and limits of the helping relationship. Boundaries can be about the structure of helping (e.g., length, fees, policies about touching and violence, confidentiality) or about the interpersonal nature of the interaction (no sexual intimacies, friendships, or business relationships with clients outside of helping). Considerable research has been conducted on the practices of experienced therapists regarding boundaries (see Borys & Pope, 1989; Conte, Plutchik, Picard, & Karasu, 1989; Epstein, Simon, & Kay, 1992; Holroyd & Brodsky, 1977).

Initially, helpers need to clarify the rules about confidentiality, the length of helping, and any fees involved. Helpers typically choose to avoid involvement in social activities with clients outside of sessions because such activities may make it difficult for helpers to be objective and for clients to feel comfortable disclosing in the therapy setting. I encourage beginning helpers to provide the phone number at a work setting so clients can reach them for emergencies, but I suggest they not give a home phone number. The reason to not give out home phone numbers is that some clients take advantage of beginning helpers, who have difficulty setting limits about not talking on the phone at any hour for any reason. I vividly recall one of my first clients in a practicum during graduate school. She called for several nights at midnight because I had not clarified that calling was not appropriate. When I finally told the client that she could not keep calling every night, she felt hurt and abandoned, and the therapeutic relationship was damaged. It would have been better if I had discussed this limit with her initially to clarify the rules and expectations.

Developing appropriate boundaries is often quite difficult. It is probably better for beginning helpers to start out being overly cautious and then relax their boundaries as they gain experience. Consultation with supervisors can be helpful when in doubt about which boundaries are appropriate and how to set them. Furthermore, exploring one's own countertransference issues (i.e., personal reactions to clients) is important when thinking about establishing boundaries in general. It is even more important for helpers to examine their own issues when they want to violate or adjust boundaries with a particular client, as these urges to violate boundaries often reflect countertransference issues.

BE AWARE OF YOUR VALUES

Empirical literature has shown that helpers' values influence clients (e.g., Beutler & Bergin, 1991), so helpers need to be aware of this influence of values and beliefs in their interactions with clients. For example, a helper who believes that all women should work outside the home in high-status, nontraditional occupations may inadvertently discourage a client from selecting a traditional career that seems to be a good fit for her interests and that would enable her to focus on her family. Beginning helpers, like advanced clinicians, should work to understand their biases. Thus, I encourage helpers to increase their awareness of their values and to ascertain the influence of these values on the helping process.

The influence of values in helping can be subtle. Helpers can influence the direction of sessions and clients' selection of actions through nonverbal behavior of which they are unaware, such as smiling or nodding their heads at particular moments. Beginning helpers sometimes struggle with inadvertently encouraging clients to talk about situations that are comfortable for or interesting to the helper. For example, a helper might use nonverbal behaviors to indicate great interest when the client is talking about her romantic relationship but seem somewhat less interested when the discussion moves to roommate concerns.

ETHICAL BEHAVIOR RELATED TO CULTURE

Ethical behavior mandates that helpers be mindful of differences among individuals and use basic helping skills that reflect an understanding of the people with whom they are working (see also American Psychological Association, 2003). Beginning helpers should not assume that helping skills transfer across cultures and individuals. One example is the assumption that maintaining eye contact is a sign of openness, interest, and willingness to participate in the session. In some cultures (e.g., Asian cultures), however, a lack of eye contact signifies respect for an authority figure and thus should not be interpreted according to American societal norms in helping sessions.

At times, helpers who are working with clients from a different culture either neglect or attach too much significance to the culture of their clients when providing interventions. It is important for helpers to realize that helping in the traditional manner may (or may not) be sufficient for these clients. For example, heterosexual helpers who are working with lesbian or gay clients should investigate the literature about working with these clients and be aware of the special challenges that may be present for these clients, while also understanding that lesbian and gay clients may share many similarities with heterosexual clients. For example, Shawn was depressed and felt hopeless when he sought help at the university counseling center. His helper assumed that because Shawn was a gay man, his depression ensued from the discrimination that gay men experience on campus. The helper told Shawn that he understood how painful it must be to be a gay man on a predominantly heterosexual college campus. Shawn was stunned and angry at the helper: He had sought assistance because his sister had recently been killed in a car accident and he was having trouble grieving the loss, not because of problems related to his sexual orientation. Thus, it seems critical to be aware of the client's culture as influencing the client deeply but never to assume that the client's cultural background and related experiences are the primary motivators for seeking assistance.

Furthermore, a helper who is working with a client from a different culture should not assume that the client's goals are to assimilate (or not assimilate) into the majority culture. For example, Bridget immigrated to the United States from another country and asked for assistance in selecting a career. She explained to her helper that her parents wanted her to go to medical school, but she was doing poorly in her science courses. The helper incorrectly assumed that Bridget did not want to pursue a medical career and directed her to select a different occupation on the basis of her interests, values, and abilities (because making career decisions in terms of individual needs and abilities is a cultural value for many people living in the United States). However, if the helper had listened carefully to Bridget, he would have discovered that she was feeling devastated about her inability to meet her parents' expectations and dreams in part because of her cultural background, which valued familial harmony and parental approval.

Demonstrating interest in clients' cultures is important, but helpers should not expect clients to educate them about culture. For example, an African American client who worked in a battered women's shelter expressed frustration not only with being a member of a group of people who have less power in American society but also with being asked to train and educate European American helpers about her culture.

Helpers can educate themselves about culture through talking with people from different cultures, trying foods from different places, and watching movies. Above all, though, perhaps the best idea is to read relevant materials. Several excellent texts provide further information about multicultural counseling and counseling with specific groups (D. R. Atkinson & Hackett, 1998; D. R. Atkinson, Morten, & Sue, 1998; Helms, 1990; Helms & Cook, 1999; McGoldrick, 1998; McGoldrick, Giordano, & Pearce, 1996; Muran, 2007; Pedersen, 1997; Pedersen, Draguns, Lonner, & Trimble, 2002; Ponterotto, Casas, Suzuki, & Alexander, 1995; D. W. Sue & Sue, 1999). It is important always, however, to remember that much of what one learns about other cultures through reading involves stereotypes. Although these stereotypes are perhaps accurate in general terms, they may not apply to individuals within a given culture. Thus, it is important to learn the stereotypes about cultures but also to listen to the individual client for how the culture has influenced him or her.

All of us need to engage in serious self-examination to discover our cultural values and beliefs as well as our prejudices and biases. Being aware of our cultural beliefs (e.g., valuing independence, autonomy, religion, and family) is important so that we can recognize what we value; but it is also important so that we do not automatically assume these values are right for everyone else. Understanding our prejudices and biases is important so that we do not harm clients who are culturally different from us.

All of us have been raised with prejudices and biases that can surface when we are least aware of them. Sometimes we are so used to these feelings that we do not even question their validity. Refer back to Exercise 2 about hot buttons in Lab 1 in chapter 1. If you had different reactions to different clients (e.g., to working with a male vs. female client), step back and try to understand these reactions.

It is also important to think about what biases clients might have toward you as a helper. For example, an African American client might automatically not trust a White helper. On the other hand, the African American client might be very used to being in a White environment and not have an issue with having a White helper. Furthermore, it is important to take the whole person into consideration rather than just one aspect, such as race. An African American person with a middle-class background will likely share many of the values of a White middle-class helper.

In addition, ethical behavior goes beyond having an awareness of individual and cultural differences to embracing a commitment to eliminate bias and discrimination in one's work. This commitment may involve actively examining our biases, confronting colleagues who act in a discriminatory manner, advocating for those with less power, and working for social change. For example, some helpers facilitate growth or empowerment groups for clients who have been marginalized in society. Another helper used her experience as a counselor, teacher, and researcher to write a book about empowering clients through the process of counseling (McWhirter, 1994).

BEING A CULTURALLY COMPETENT HELPER

D. W. Sue and Sue (1999) asserted that becoming a culturally skilled helper is an active, ongoing process that never reaches an end point. It is something helpers aspire to, and work toward, rather than accepting complacency. The following are characteristics of culturally sensitive helpers (Arredondo et al., 1996; Skovholt & Rivers, 2003; D. W. Sue & Sue, 1999):

- They strive to understand their culture and how it influences their work with clients.
- They strive to understand how their beliefs about helping (e.g., style, theoretical orientation, definition of helping) are influenced by their culture.
- They honestly confront their biases, prejudices, and discriminatory behaviors and work to keep them out of the helping process.
- They have a wide range of helping skills and use them flexibly to fit the needs of clients from different cultures.
- They are knowledgeable about the cultures of their clients.
- They understand the extent to which discrimination and oppression influence clients' lives and contribute to their problems.
- They acknowledge and address cultural differences between themselves and their clients while still communicating willingness to help.
- They seek supervision or refer when necessary.

ACT IN A VIRTUOUS MANNER

Professionals concerned with ethical behaviors have begun to move from a focus on behaving in an ethical manner (i.e., following the guidelines delineated in an ethical code) to behaving in a virtuous manner. Virtues are not as concerned with laws and rules as much as with striving to be a person of positive moral character (Meara et al., 1996). Part of this change results from the reality that ethical codes, in and of themselves, cannot provide exact specifications for behaviors. Helpers need to internalize the six basic ethical principles discussed earlier in this chapter (autonomy, beneficence, nonmaleficence, justice, fidelity, and veracity), practice a comprehensive ethical decision-making model, and monitor themselves and their behaviors to ensure respectful interactions with clients.

For example, a helper had a very successful helping session with a client at the university counseling center. She used her basic helping skills to provide a safe and open environment. The client shared much personal information in the session and struggled with concerns of importance in his life. The following weekend, the helper ran into the client at a party. She was confused about how to deal with this situation because her training had not addressed guidelines for meeting clients in social situations. However, the helper was a sensitive and respectful woman, so she waited for the client to speak to her first and returned his brief greeting as they passed. Her response was consistent with virtuous behavior. It is important to recognize that it is not possible to provide helpers with answers to every ethical situation they might encounter; instead, helpers need to behave with clients in a caring and respectful manner that is consistent with acting in a virtuous manner (which is most likely also ethical).

TAKE CARE OF YOURSELF TO ENSURE THAT YOU CAN CARE FOR OTHERS

One final often-ignored dimension of ethical behavior involves helpers taking care of themselves. Helping can be an exhausting enterprise that requires helpers to give much of themselves to others. The fastest road to burnout involves taking care of others without paying attention to relaxation and caring for one's own needs. It behooves helpers to monitor their health and energy to ensure that they can provide quality services to others. Helpers might evaluate regularly the presence of added stressors, poor health, and exhaustion. Helpers can try to achieve balance by integrating rewarding work, supportive relationships, regular exercise, and healthy eating habits into their lives. Helpers can also seek counseling when they need support or assistance with pressing concerns.

Working Through an Ethical Dilemma

Although beginning helpers may not encounter many ethical dilemmas, learning how to work through these situations can be helpful so that helpers can be prepared when ethical dilemmas arise. Ethical dilemmas occur when there are competing ethical guidelines (Kitchener, 1984). At times, the actions that helpers could take to uphold one ethical principle would violate another ethical principle. Kitchener described inherent contradictions that exist in ethical codes (e.g., individual autonomy vs. making decisions for clients; confidentiality vs. protecting others). For example, ethical codes often ensure a client's right to privacy and confidentiality. They also endorse the importance of working to minimize harm to others. These important standards can, at times, conflict with one another. For instance, one helper worked with an adolescent client who was threatening to kill herself but did not want the helper to discuss this with her parents. The adolescent felt her parents would not take her seriously and might punish her for disclosing these thoughts to her helper. The helper was faced with an ethical dilemma that was not easily resolved by examining the profession's ethical code. In this case, the helper talked with the adolescent about the importance of disclosing this information to her parents to ensure her safety. Then, in the presence of the client and with the client's permission, the helper discussed the client's concerns with her parents.

Helpers can follow the A-B-C-D-E strategy for ethical decision making (Sileo & Kopala, 1993) when they are confronted with an ethical dilemma. To illustrate its application, let us consider a situation in which a client discloses to a helper that she was raped by an acquaintance the previous night. The helper in this case is a beginning helper who feels outraged by the crime and wants to call the police immediately. The client, however, is concerned about her relationship with her boyfriend and definitely does not want the rape to be reported. The helper realizes that this is not a situation in which he is legally required to break confidentiality and report the rape, but instead is an ethical dilemma between reporting a crime against the client's wishes and maintaining confidentiality. The helper uses the A-B-C-D-E strategy for ethical decision making to work toward resolving how to proceed in this challenging situation.

A: ASSESSMENT

The helper identifies the situation; the client's status and resources; and the helper's values, feelings, and reactions to the situation. In this case, the helper notes that the client is a well-adjusted, bright, and competent young woman who is finishing her 4th year in college, majoring in business administration. She reports having a good relationship with her boyfriend. Two close friends have promised to support her through her recovery from the rape, and she has indicated an interest in attending a rape survivors' group. The helper, however, feels strongly that the rapist should be punished for what he did to the client. When he reflects more on the issue, however, the helper acknowledges that the strength of his emotions may result from his feeling helpless when he discovered that his younger sister had been raped.

B: BENEFIT

The helper evaluates what is most likely to benefit the client, the helping relationship, and the client's significant others. In this case, the helper believes that disclosure of the rape to the police and subsequent prosecution of the rapist could benefit the client, her boyfriend, and possible future victims. However, he also acknowledges that the client believes that she would be helped most by discussing the rape with her helper, her best friends, and a rape survivors' support group. As with many ethical dilemmas, different benefits are present for several possible solutions.

C: CONSEQUENCES AND CONSULTATION

Moving on to the ethical, legal, emotional, and therapeutic consequences that could result from possible actions, the helper consults with a supervisor who provides assistance in identifying and working through salient issues. In this case, the supervisor helps the helper identify that his disclosure of the rape to the police would undermine the trust he had worked to develop with the client. Moreover, the helper would be violating the client's confidentiality and right to privacy. His reporting of the rape might reinforce feelings of powerlessness that the client felt after being raped.

D: DUTY

The helper next considers to whom a duty exists. In this case, the helper's primary duty or responsibility is to the client rather than to her boyfriend or other women that the rapist might harm. His job as a helper is to do no harm to his client and to provide services that enhance her growth and potential. The helper is beginning to realize how important it is to abide by the client's wish for nondisclosure, despite his own desire to prosecute the rapist.

Sometimes, the helper may have a duty to protect someone other than the client (i.e., an identifiable person whom the client is threatening to harm). In situations in which a child is being abused, helpers are mandated by law to report the abuse or to assist the client in reporting the abuse. Furthermore, in cases in which the client threatens to harm self or others, the helper must ensure the safety of the individuals identified to be at risk for harm. For example, if this client told her helper that she planned to murder the rapist and had enlisted the assistance of an assassin to carry out the plan, the helper would have a responsibility to prevent harm to the rapist.

E: EDUCATION

The helper reviews his education to determine what he has learned about appropriate actions to take in dealing with similar ethical dilemmas. The helper refers to his notes from his courses, consults current Web sites (see Exhibit 3.1), and determines that in this situation, the best strategy is to maintain the client's confidence and assist in her recovery from the rape. The helper also decides to go for therapy to address his residual feelings about his sister's rape.

Concluding Comments

Ethical dilemmas can be aptly described by the two Chinese symbols representing *crisis:* danger and opportunity. Ethical dilemmas can be dangerous in that the welfare of the client may be compromised, but they also present an opportunity for helpers to reflect on what they have learned and what they value and then to act in a manner consistent with professional and (one hopes) personal values. Ethical dilemmas provide a unique challenge for helpers to confront and resolve important questions and to ensure, to the best of their abilities, that their clients' needs are being served. In my experience when ethical issues arise in classes (and they have a few times), it provides a great opportunity to think through important pedagogical issues and make sure that the best possible educational services are being delivered.

What Do You Think?

■ How do you feel about professional groups imposing ethical restrictions on helpers?

■ What do you think the consequences should be if someone violates the ethical standards?

■ What is your opinion about cultural considerations in ethics? Discuss how your response may be influenced by your cultural background.

■ Discuss the possible positive and negative consequences of discussing confidentiality and informed consent and how they influence the therapeutic relationship.

■ What are some ways, other than those covered in the chapter, that helpers could inadvertently cause clients harm?

■ Do you agree that taking care of oneself as a helper helps to prevent problems in the helping role?

i LAB 3. Ethical Awareness

A downloadable PDF of this Lab is available in the student resources area of the Helping Skills, *3rd ed. Web site: http://www.apa.org/books/resources/Hill3.*

Goal: For helpers to become knowledgeable about how to resolve ethical issues that might emerge during their helping sessions.

Instructions: Gather into four small groups. Identify the ethical issues in each situation and then apply each step of the A-B-C-D-E strategy for resolving ethical dilemmas to the case. Afterward, get together as a large group and present your conclusions.

Case 1: A beginning helper (Jack) wants to practice his helping skills and notices someone in his residence hall (Sam) who seems to have a lot of problems and few friends. What issues should Jack consider if he wants to act in accordance with the ethical guidelines described in this chapter?

Case 2: A beginning helper is interested in working with clients who have eating disorders because she went through counseling for the issue. Recently, she has been under a lot of stress and her eating has become erratic and uncontrollable. She is assigned a client who has an eating disorder. What should be the helper's response if she were acting in accordance with the ethical guidelines described in this chapter?

Case 3: A beginning helper has been working with a client for three sessions. The client is a single, attractive male who has many qualities that the helper (also a single male) admires in a romantic partner. During the third and final session, the client indicates an interest in talking more over drinks. The helper is attracted to the client yet uncertain about what to do, given that the helping relationship is ending and that it may or may not have risen to the level of "real" counseling. What should be the helper's response if he were acting in accordance with the ethical guidelines described in this chapter?

Personal Reflections

- What issues arose for you personally in trying to apply the A-B-C-D-E strategy to these cases?
- What would you do to prevent yourself from making ethical "mistakes" if you were a practicing therapist?
- How do the ethical principles and standards mesh with your personal morality?

EXPLORATION STAGE ‖

Overview of the Exploration Stage | 4

When one pours out one's heart, one feels lighter.

—Yiddish proverb

Yusef was feeling miserable, lonely, and worthless
after his recent move to the United States. He
desperately wanted to have a close friend with
whom he could talk about his deepest feelings. His
parents were concerned about him and suggested
that he talk with a helper. During his first session
with the helper, Yusef indicated that he felt like he
was going to "burst from loneliness." Since moving
to this country, he had not talked to anyone other
than his parents. He was hesitant to tell them how
badly he felt because he worried that they would
get too concerned and he felt they could not really
do anything to help him. The helper listened
carefully and reflected Yusef's feelings of isolation,
sadness, and rejection. Yusef began to cry and was
able to talk about how he felt different from the
other kids because he was from another culture.
The helper let him talk and express all his feelings.
She accepted him and listened nonjudgmentally,
interested in understanding his experiences. At the
end of the session, Yusef told the helper that he felt
much better and had renewed energy to make
friends. Talking to a caring, understanding person
helped lift Yusef's burden and made him feel better.

This overview chapter presents the theoretical background
for the exploration stage and describes the major goals of
this stage. Chapters 5 through 7 of this volume describe the
major skills used to reach the goals of the exploration stage.

Chapter 8 presents clinical issues new helpers face in implementing this stage.

Theoretical Background: Rogers's Client-Centered Theory

Much of what takes place in the exploration stage is influenced by Carl Rogers's theory of personality development and psychological change (see Rogers, 1942, 1951, 1957, 1959, 1967; Rogers & Dymond, 1954). Rogers had a profound influence on the field of psychology with his optimistic and hopeful assertion that all people have the potential for healthy and creative growth. His client-centered orientation was rooted in phenomenology, which places a strong emphasis on the experiences, feelings, values, and inner life of the client. Rogers believed that perceptions of reality vary from person to person, that subjective experience guides behavior, and that people are guided by their internal experience rather than by external reality. Similarly, he believed that the only way to understand individuals is to enter their private world and understand their internal frame of reference. In other words, to understand another person, one needs to suspend judgment and try to see things as the person sees them.

According to Rogers (1942, 1951, 1967), the only basic motivational force is the tendency toward self-actualization, which propels people to become what they are meant to become. He believed that each person has an innate "blueprint," or set of potentialities, that can be developed. Rogers likened the forces toward self-actualization in people to the natural order. He noted that plants and animals grow without any conscious effort, provided that the conditions for growth are optimal. Similarly, he believed that people have an inherent ability to fulfill their potential. Furthermore, Rogers believed that people are resilient and can bounce back from adversity given this innate growth potential.

THEORY OF PERSONALITY DEVELOPMENT

According to Rogers (1942, 1951, 1967), infants evaluate each experience in terms of how it makes them feel; Rogers called this the *organismic valuing process* (OVP). Rogers believed that because behavior is governed by the OVP, infants can perceive experiences as they actually occur without distorting them. With the OVP, no experiences are more or less worthy; they just are. In other words, every event is interesting and open for investigation without prior prejudice. Infants thus evaluate experiences as to whether they enhance or maintain the organism.

For example, if an experience (e.g., being hugged) enhances the organism, the infant feels good and is satisfied and might smile or laugh. However, if experiences do not enhance the organism (e.g., being cold or having a dirty diaper), the infant does not feel good, is not satisfied, and so might cry. Infants evaluate events by how they actually feel, not by how someone else tells them they should feel. The OVP, then, is an internal guide that everyone has at birth, and it leads the person toward self-actualization (see Figure 4.1). People freely seek those experiences that enhance them when they trust this internal guide. Rogers believed that because infants have positive strivings toward self-actualization and a natural curiosity about life, they can trust these inner feelings.

In addition to having the OVP, children also have a need for unconditional positive regard. In other words, they need acceptance, respect, warmth, and love without *conditions of worth* (COW); that is, they need to be loved just because they are themselves and not because they do anything. When children feel prized, accepted, and understood by others (usually parents), they begin to experience self-love and self-acceptance and develop a healthy sense of self with little or no conflict. A prized child is able to attend to his or her OVP and make good choices on the basis of inner experiencing.

Unfortunately, because parents themselves are not perfect, they place COW on their children, demanding that children fulfill certain requirements to be loved. For example, parents may give messages such as "I will not love you unless you are a 'good girl,' " "I will not love you unless you keep your room clean," or "You must be intelligent to receive my love." Because parents communicate (through words or actions) that children are lovable and acceptable only when they behave in accordance

FIGURE 4.1

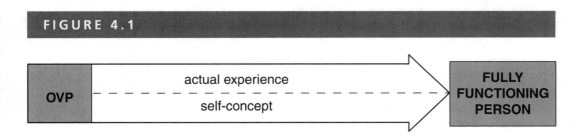

The self-actualizing tendency. Psychologist Carl Rogers's hypothesized path between the organismic valuing process (OVP) and the "fully functioning person." All people, Rogers believed, have a "self-actualizing tendency," a drive to encounter actual experience according to one's own self-concept. When there is such congruence, self-concepts are valued in terms of basic, genuine feelings and self-regard; experiences are evaluated according to the OVP—that is, according to the basic needs and desires of the organism.

with imposed standards, children come to believe that they must be and act in certain ways to earn their parents' love.

Given the need for love, the COW, rather than the OVP, come to guide a child's organization of her or his experiences (see Figure 4.2). In other words, children sacrifice their OVP to receive love from their parents (e.g., children give up being spontaneous and playful to sit "properly" and be "good" to please their parents). When a child introjects (i.e., internalizes) his or her parents' COW, these conditions become a part of the child's self-concept. The more COW there are, the more distorted the person becomes from his or her own experiencing.

COW lead children to feel conflict between their self-concept and their inner experience. For example, a mother may communicate to a young girl that it is not acceptable for her to hate her brother. The girl may feel that to be loved, she must be a good girl, and so she may disown the hate as not being part of herself. Hence, rather than learning that she may feel hate but cannot hurt her brother, she learns that her feelings are not acceptable. Another example is parents who punish or ridicule a boy for crying when he is hurt or needs help with a difficult task. The boy might repress his feelings of pain and dependency and become extremely independent to maintain his parents' approval. These two examples illustrate how externally imposed values can sub-

FIGURE 4.2

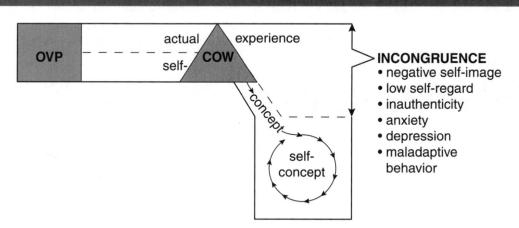

Conditions of worth and incongruence. The self-actualizing tendency can be derailed when the self-concept is altered by conditions of worth (COW), which supplant a person's basic, positive self-regard with others' conditional evaluations of worth. The incongruence between actual experience and self-concept, according to Rogers, typically results in inauthentic expressions of feelings, low self-regard, defensiveness, anxiety, and depression.

stitute for the OVP. When feelings of hate or dependency get aroused, these children cannot identify or repress these feelings and, thus, are not in touch with their inner experiencing.

Children experience positive self-regard only when their self-experiences are consistent with feedback that they get from others (e.g., if a girl feels talented in playing the violin and others tell her that she is talented). Feelings of self-worth become dependent on the COW that are learned in interaction with significant others. A child with too many COW would not be open to experience, accepting of feelings, capable of living in the present, free to make choices, trusting, capable of feeling both aggression and affection, and capable of creativity. He or she would have a conflicted sense of self.

Obviously, children must become socialized to live in their families and society. Children cannot act on all their innate desires or get all of their needs met immediately because the world is not a perfect place and also because other people may have needs that conflict with theirs. Parents, for example, cannot always immediately meet the infant's needs because they have other demands on their time. In addition, parents cannot allow a child to hurt a sibling or another child. The manner, however, in which parents socialize their children is crucial. For example, a parent can empathize with a young girl but still place limits on her (e.g., "I know you are angry at your brother, but you cannot hurt him"). The girl may feel frustrated but does not learn to deny her feelings. Instead, she learns to experience her feelings but channel them in a more socially acceptable direction. In contrast, when parents humiliate a child (e.g., "Real men don't cry," "Shut up, or I'll give you something to cry about") or deny that the child has feelings (e.g., "You don't hate your teacher," "You don't feel hurt"), the child becomes confused about her or his feelings. The child may feel sad or feel hatred, but the parents say he or she does not have these feelings. What should the child trust—the inner experience or what parents tell him or her to feel? If the child does not pay attention to his or her parents, she or he risks losing parental approval and love. If she or he does not pay attention to inner feelings and instead tries to please others and the COW, the child loses her or his sense of self. One can easily see how children come not to trust their inner experiences. Children must survive, so they often choose parents' attention and "love" over inner experiencing.

When COW are pervasive and the OVP is disabled, the sense of self is weakened to the point at which a person is unable to experience or recognize feelings as belonging to the self. For example, a woman might not even be aware of feeling angry and hurt when being verbally and physically abused by her husband because she thinks she deserves the abuse. When people cannot allow themselves to have their feelings, they often feel a sense of emptiness, phoniness, or lack of genuineness.

This lack of genuineness about one's feelings leads to a split or incongruence between the real and ideal self and is the source of anxiety, depression, and defensiveness in relationships.

DEFENSES

Rogers (1957) suggested that when there is an incongruence between experience and sense of self, the person feels threatened. For example, a person who acts pleasant and happy but is actually feeling grumpy and depressed is in danger of losing touch with his inner self. If he were to perceive his depression accurately, his self would be threatened because he has built an image of himself as always happy. When a person feels such a threat, she or he typically responds with anxiety, a signal that the self is in danger. Feeling this anxiety, the person invokes defenses to reduce the incongruity between experience and sense of self, thereby reducing anxiety.

One major defense is perceptual distortion, which involves altering or misinterpreting one's experience to make it compatible with one's self-concept. By distorting experiences, clients avoid having to deal with unpleasant feelings and issues and can maintain their perceptions of themselves. For example, a man may perceive himself as being of average weight even though he is quite overweight and no longer fits into chairs. He might tell himself he does not eat any more than other people. As another example, a person with a sense of worthlessness who is promoted at work might misinterpret the reason for the promotion to be congruent with her negative sense of self. She might say that the only reason she got the promotion was that "the boss had to do it" or "no one else wanted the job."

A second defense is denial, which involves ignoring or denouncing reality. In this situation, people refuse to acknowledge their experiences because they are inconsistent with the images they have of themselves. By denying their experiences, clients avoid anxiety. For example, a woman who is treated unfairly at work might ignore her anger at her boss because she has internalized her parents' belief that anger is bad and that she will not be loved if she expresses anger. Rather than allow herself to experience her anger, she may say she is not trying hard enough or she is not smart enough for the job.

Defenses block incongruent experiences from full awareness and minimize threats to one's sense of self and thus allow the self to function and cope. A certain level of defenses is necessary for coping, but excessive use of defenses can take a toll on the self in at least three ways. First, the subjective reality (what one allows oneself to experience) can become incongruent with the external reality (the world as it is). At some point, the person may no longer be able to distort or deny the experience, which could lead to overwhelming feelings of threat and anxiety and disintegration of the self. For example, a child might struggle to maintain the illusion that things are fine between his parents despite their nightly battles. However, when his mother leaves without warning, the boy may not be able to handle the loss and may stop attending school and talking to others. In another example, a person might partition off parts of self that are unacceptable and exclude them from awareness (e.g., deny to oneself that sexual abuse occurred). Second, a person might develop a rigidity of perception in areas where she or he has had to defend against perceiving reality. For example, a woman might have such a strong need to believe in the curative effects of a quack medicine for cancer that she does not listen to any disconfirming evidence, resulting in her not seeking proven strategies for treating her cancer. Third, the real self can become incongruent with the ideal self, suggesting a discrepancy between who one is and who one wishes to be. A woman might be average in intelligence but feel a need to be smart (particularly if she has internalized parental COW that she should be extremely intelligent). If the real–ideal discrepancy is large, the person may feel dissatisfied and become maladjusted (e.g., depressed, anxious).

REINTEGRATION

According to Rogers (1957), to overcome disintegration, rigidity, or discrepancies between real and ideal selves, a person must become aware of the distorted or denied experience. In other words, a person must allow the experience to occur and accurately perceive the event. The woman described above must acknowledge to herself that she has average intelligence and accept and value herself rather than distort or deny her feelings. Rogers theorized that for reintegration to occur, the person must (a) reduce the COW and (b) increase positive self-regard through obtaining unconditional positive regard from others. COW lose their significance and ability to direct behavior when others accept the person as he or she is. In effect, individuals return to the OVP and begin to trust the inner self, thus becoming more open to experience and feelings (see Figure 4.3).

A person can reintegrate without unconditional positive regard from another person if there is minimal threat to the self and the incongruity between self and experience is minor, but this is difficult. Typically, individuals respond to years of having COW imposed on them by becoming increasingly defensive. Once developed, defenses are difficult to let go because the person anticipates being vulnerable and hurt again. In effect, defenses are adaptive to help children cope, but fear and habit make them difficult to shed when they are no longer needed.

A helping relationship, then, is often crucial for assisting individuals in overcoming their defenses and returning to trusting their OVP.

FIGURE 4.3

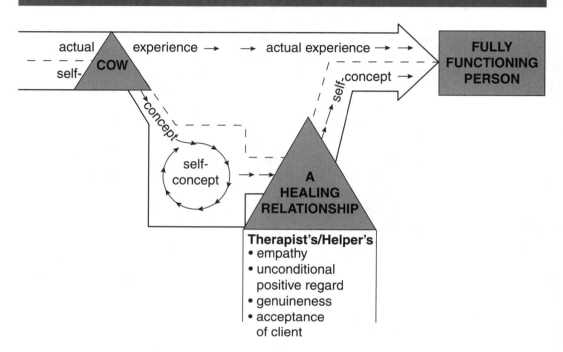

A healing relationship. Only through a healing relationship that offers empathy, unconditional positive regard, genuineness, and acceptance—typically from a therapist/helper—can the self-concept be restored to congruence with actual experience, according to Rogers (1957). The self-concept returns to evaluations of actual experience based on the OVP, thereby facilitating self-actualization and the drive to become a "fully functioning person"—one who can realize the self's maximum potentiality for independence, creativity, authentic expressions of feelings, and love. COW = conditions of worth.

A helping relationship allows the individual's self-actualizing tendency to overcome the restrictions that were internalized in the COW. In a helping relationship, the helper attempts to enter the client's subjective world and understand the client's internal frame of reference. The helper also tries to provide an experience in which the client is accepted and cared for without COW. This helping relationship does not necessarily need to be from a professional helper, and in fact, people often seek healing relationships from supportive people in their environment (e.g., friends, relatives, rabbi, minister, priest).

Rogers (1951) believed that the helping relationship, in and of itself, produces growth in the client: "I launch myself into the therapeutic relationship having a hypothesis, or a faith, that my liking, my confidence, and my understanding of the other person's inner world, will lead to a significant process of becoming" (p. 267). Rogerian helpers believe that most clients benefit greatly from being listened to, understood, and accepted. The power of this kind of relationship can be highly therapeutic and constructive. In the Rogerian approach to helping, the helper enters the therapeutic relationship with the facilitative attitudes of congruence (genuineness), unconditional positive regard, and empathy.

Rogers (1957) postulated six conditions that he considered to be necessary and sufficient for change to occur.

1. *The client and helper must be in psychological contact.* A therapeutic relationship or emotional connection between the helper and client is essential.
2. *The client must be in a state of incongruence.* There must be a discrepancy between self and experience that leads the client to feel vulnerable or anxious. If a client feels no anxiety, she or he is unlikely to be motivated enough to engage in the helping process.
3. *The helper must be congruent (genuine) or integrated in the relationship.* The helper must be open to her or his own experiences and be genuinely available to the client. The helper cannot be phony in the helping relationship.
4. *The helper must feel unconditional positive regard for the client.* The helper values all feelings (although not necessarily all behaviors) and places no judgment on the feelings. Essentially, a helper is trying to understand a client's feelings and experience but is not trying to judge whether the person "should" or "should not" have the feelings or whether the feelings are "right" or "wrong."
5. *The helper must experience empathy for the client.* The helper tries to immerse herself or himself in the client's feeling world and understand the client's inner experiences. The understanding comes out of the helper's experiencing of the client's feelings, using the helper's inner processes as a referent. The helper not only experiences the client's feelings but also has his or her own reactions to the client's feelings; the helper is thus able to go beyond words to understanding the client's implicit feelings (Meador & Rogers, 1973). The helper tries to feel as if she or he were the client and temporarily living in the client's life, without ever losing the awareness that they are separate individuals. The helper tries to sense and uncover feelings of which the client is unaware because they are too threatening. Rogers emphasized that empathy is not passive but requires thinking, sensitivity, and understanding. He described *empathy* as follows:

   It means entering the private perceptual world of the other and becoming thoroughly at home in it. It involves being sensitive, moment by moment, to the changing felt meanings which flow in this other person, to the fear or rage or tenderness or confusion or whatever that he or she is experiencing. It means temporarily living in the other's life, moving about in it delicately without asking judgments. (Rogers, 1980, p. 142)

Empathy can be distinguished from sympathy, in which the helper feels pity for the client and often acts from a position of power rather than as an equal. Empathy also differs from emotional contagion, in which a helper feels the same feelings as the client (e.g., becomes just as depressed as the client) and cannot maintain objectivity. Empathy involves a deep understanding of the client's feelings. Bohart, Elliott, Greenberg, and Watson, (2002) indicated that empathy is effective because it creates a positive relationship, provides a corrective emotional experience, promotes exploration, and supports the client's active self-healing efforts.

Another construct that is similar to empathy is compassion, which means to resonate with the client's suffering (see Vivino, Thompson, Hill, & Ladany, in press). Probably Rogers considered compassion as a part of empathy, but it is helpful for therapists to cultivate compassion in addition to empathy because it allows them to feel deeply for what their clients are going through.

6. *The client must experience the helper's congruence, unconditional positive regard, and empathy.* If the client does not experience the facilitative conditions, for all practical purposes they do not exist for the client, and the sessions are not likely to be helpful.

Rogers (1951) stated that a facilitative attitude (being genuine, unconditionally positive in regard, and empathic) on the part of helpers is what is most beneficial for helpers. He indicated that skills were important, but that the facilitative attitude served as the basis for the skills. Skills without a facilitative attitude might not only not be helpful but might be harmful.

In summary, Rogers speculated that if helpers can accept clients, clients can come to accept themselves. When clients accept themselves, they can allow themselves to experience their real feelings and accept that the feelings come from themselves. Hence, the OVP is unblocked, and the person becomes open to his or her experiences. The client can begin to experience love, lust, hatred, jealousy, joy, competitiveness, anger, pride, and other feelings; accept the feelings; and come to accept self. It is important to remember that acceptance of feelings is distinct from decisions about what to do about the feelings. Allowing oneself to have the feelings provides more of a basis for making decisions about what to do because the actions are then based on inner feelings rather than on "shoulds."

CURRENT STATUS OF CLIENT-CENTERED THEORY

Meta-analyses have shown that client-centered therapy and human-istic therapy are indeed effective and that they are as effective as other approaches to psychotherapy (Elliott, Greenberg, & Lietaer, 2004). In addition, some reviews of the empirical literature have confirmed the importance of the facilitative conditions, particularly of empathy, in lead-ing to positive outcome of therapy (Bohart et al., 2002; Farber & Lane, 2002; Klein, Kolden, Michels, & Chisholm-Stockard, 2002). It appears that empathy is important to allow clients to feel safe and supported, to help clients have a positive relationship experience, to promote explo-ration, and to support clients' active self-healing efforts.

Recent research, however, has focused more on the working alliance, or the relationship between the therapist and the client, rather than just the therapist-offered facilitative conditions (e.g., Horvath & Bedi, 2002). Thus, contemporary researchers consider the interaction between ther-apist and client to be more important than just looking at what the ther-apist offers.

In their reformulation of Rogers's theory, Bohart and Tallman (1999) stressed that clients are self-healing but can get off track. They suggested that when helpers provide appropriate conditions, clients are once again able to be self-healing. Similar to Rogers's argument that an empathic attitude is more important than the use of specific skills, Bohart and Tallman argued that specific techniques are not as important as using whatever techniques work to help the client get back to self-healing.

THE RELATIONSHIP OF ROGERS'S THEORY TO THE HELPING SKILLS MODEL

Rogers's theory forms the foundation for the exploration stage and informs the insight and action stages. I agree with Rogers that helpers should maintain an empathic client-centered stance of trying to under-stand the client's experience as completely as possible with as little judg-ment and as few prior assumptions as possible. Empathy and a therapeutic relationship can be very effective in helping clients begin to accept themselves and trust their experiences.

In contrast to Rogers's assertion that a facilitative attitude is more important than the specific skills, I believe a facilitative attitude and skills are inseparable (Hill, 2005b, 2007). Skills are used to express a facilita-tive attitude, and a facilitative attitude is needed to express the skills.

For some people, being understood and encouraged to express their feelings is enough to get them back to a self-healing mode so they can function again and make needed changes. Others need more assistance in learning how to deal with feelings and experiences, many of which may be new to them. Furthermore, some people need to be assisted in moving toward insight and action. In addition to maintaining the facilitative conditions, then, helpers need to be able to facilitate insight and action. Additional theories (psychoanalytic, cognitive, behavioral) are needed to assist some clients in moving beyond exploration of thoughts and feelings; these are described in later chapters.

Furthermore, I do not completely agree with Rogers that people are inherently good and striving for self-actualization. There seems to be minimal evidence for these postulates. My assumption is that people are neither good nor bad at birth but rather develop depending on temperament, genetics, the environment, parenting, and early experiences (see chap. 2, this volume). More is known now about genetic and biological contributions to human functioning than was known when Rogers was proposing his theory. Despite these differences in beliefs about human nature and biological contributions, though, I agree with Rogers about the importance of the facilitative conditions for establishing the therapeutic relationship and helping clients explore concerns and achieve self-acceptance.

Goals for the Exploration Stage

The goals for the exploration stage are establishing rapport and a trusting relationship; attending, listening, and observing; helping clients explore thoughts; facilitating the expression of emotion; and learning about clients. The sections that follow define these goals in more detail.

ESTABLISHING RAPPORT AND DEVELOPING A THERAPEUTIC RELATIONSHIP

Helpers establish rapport (i.e., an atmosphere of understanding and respect) with their clients so that clients feel safe to explore. Rapport sets the stage for development of the therapeutic relationship, which is very important in helping. Clients are most likely to reveal themselves when they believe they have a caring, therapeutic relationship with their helpers. Clients generally need to feel safe, supported, respected, cared for, valued, prized, accepted as individuals, listened to, and heard in their interactions with helpers. In everyday relationships, people often do not fully listen to others, so it is a gift to clients for helpers to listen attentively to them without rushing to say something next (e.g., telling a competing story, as friends often do).

During the exploration stage, helpers try to understand their clients from the clients' frame of reference. They attempt to "walk a mile in the clients' shoes" and view the world through their clients' eyes. Helpers try to understand clients' thoughts and feelings without imposing their thoughts or values on clients. They attempt not to judge clients and figure out whether they are "right" or "blameworthy," but instead try to understand how clients came to be the way they are and how it feels to be who they are. Helpers try to align or attune themselves (i.e., try to feel what it is like to be the client) so they can understand each client's feelings.

If helpers can assist them in becoming aware of their inner experiencing, clients can begin to trust and then to heal themselves. Rogers (1957) hypothesized that clients typically need to feel accepted and prized by others before they can begin to accept and value themselves. To do this, helpers need to accept clients as they are as much as possible and provide them with the facilitative conditions of empathy, unconditional positive regard, and genuineness. As mentioned earlier, *empathy* refers to understanding another person and feeling as if you are the other person (i.e., trying to put yourself in her or his place even though you are not that person and can never understand the person completely). *Unconditional positive regard* refers to accepting and appreciating another person without judgment. *Genuineness* (or what has also been termed *congruence*) refers to helpers' being open to their own experiences and genuinely available to clients rather than being phony or inauthentic. A large part of establishing a relationship is having an attitude of acceptance, empathy, and respect. Helpers need to listen and understand clients without judging them. In addition, having knowledge of helping skills, feeling competent in being able to use the skills, and the appropriate use of skills places helpers in the framework whereby they are more likely to have a therapeutic attitude.

Helpers should not think they can simply establish a relationship at one point in time and ignore it thereafter. They need to be aware of maintaining the relationship throughout the helping process. At any time throughout the process, the relationship can, and often does, rupture and need repair (see Hill, Nutt-Williams, Heaton, Thompson, & Rhodes, 1996; Rhodes, Hill, Thompson, & Elliott, 1994; Safran, Muran, Samstag, & Stevens, 2002).

Beginning helpers often worry about the possibility of not liking a client or not being able to establish rapport with a client. For example, many beginning helpers think they could never work with rapists or child abusers because they would be repulsed and horrified. However, the goal of being a helper is not to make friends with clients. Helpers do not need to "like" clients in the same way they like or choose to spend time with close friends. Rather, helpers have a responsibility to understand and assist clients and to feel compassion for the human beings underneath the exterior presentations. Often if a helper can get insight into how the client got to where he or she is, the helper can begin to have compassion for the client.

For example, the greatest challenge for one helper was working with women in prison. The crimes committed by the women made it difficult for her to empathize and respect them. However, after getting to know the women and their life circumstances, she became aware that these women had feelings similar to hers. Even though helpers may not have experienced the same life events as their clients, they have surely experienced many of the same emotions; thus, helpers can empathize with clients' feelings, even if they disagree with their behaviors.

ATTENDING, LISTENING, AND OBSERVING

The major way that we as helpers establish rapport and build a therapeutic relationship is through attending, listening, and observing. We orient ourselves nonverbally toward clients so that we are receptive to listening to whatever they say. We listen intently to what they say rather than assuming we know anything about them. We observe carefully to see how they are feeling and reacting to everything that happens in the session.

HELPING CLIENTS EXPLORE THOUGHTS

Clients need a chance to talk about their problems. It often helps to talk out loud about what is going on inside. All too often, people just continue with their ordinary routines without exploring their problems in any depth. As Frank and Frank (1991) noted, "How can I know what I think until I have heard what I have to say?" (p. 200). Having a forum to express their thoughts allows clients to hear and think about the content of what they are saying. Clients need to realize what they are thinking and have a chance to express these thoughts out loud.

Furthermore, by realizing what one is thinking, one has a better chance to hear the inconsistencies and logical fallacies. Talking about one's thoughts provides the client the opportunity to think about whether she or he really believes what is being said, especially when the client knows someone else is hearing it. In addition, the process of talking to a helper about a problem is useful because it allows the client to think about it, take it out and examine it, put thoughts into words, and get another person's reactions.

ENCOURAGING EXPRESSION AND EXPERIENCING OF FEELINGS

Emotions are a key element in the helping process because they represent fundamental experiencing and are connected integrally to cognitions and behavior. In fact, mental health could be defined as allowing oneself to have a whole range of feelings and expressing these feelings in an appropriate manner.

One major goal of the exploration stage is for helpers to assist clients in experiencing feelings about their presenting problems. Many clients learned as children to suppress their feelings. They had to distort or deny their actual feelings to survive and gain approval from parents or other significant persons, so many clients are not aware of their feelings. For example, if clients cannot allow themselves to feel hurt, they limit their range of emotions and might feel hollow or empty inside. Some clients feel that their "inner cores" are rotten. Clients might not know who they are and might rely on other people to tell them how they feel. In significant relationships, they might ignore their feelings and feel distant without knowing why. Hence, being able to feel their true feelings and put words onto the feelings can be liberating for clients.

Sometimes the content of what the client says is not as important as the feelings about the topic, particularly if there is a discrepancy between content and feelings. Helpers need to listen to the "music" (i.e., the underlying message) in addition to listening to the words. They need to try to hear both the content and what the client feels.

In addition, clients need to focus on what they are feeling immediately in the present moment. Experiencing immediate feelings often is not comfortable, so clients may want to run away and avoid their feelings. Through support and encouragement by helpers, clients often are able to tolerate the anxiety and discomfort of exploring their immediate feelings. For example, Joel spent much of the session telling the helper about events that occurred during the week. When the helper gently encouraged him to explore his feelings in the present regarding these past events (e.g., "How do you feel right now about the event?"), Joel talked about his feelings and the session became more intense and productive than it previously was.

Helpers sometimes need to be assertive and ask about feelings that clients are not discussing. For example, clients might need to be invited to talk about difficult feelings such as shame or being depressed or suicidal. In friendships, people often do not probe beyond what their friends choose to reveal because they feel that would be overstepping implicit boundaries. In helping relationships, by contrast, helpers encourage clients to explore painful feelings that are hard to express. However, helpers need to respect the rights of clients not to go any deeper than they choose. Helpers walk a fine line between inviting clients to disclose feelings and not forcing them into unwanted disclosure.

Another reason for encouraging clients to talk about feelings is that emotional arousal seems to be necessary for change to occur (Frank & Frank, 1991). Without emotional arousal, clients typically are not involved in the helping process and are not motivated to change. Many times, people deny or defend against their feelings because they do not want to deal with the overwhelming or painful nature of their feelings. In contrast, when people have strong emotional arousal (e.g., fury, despair), they are most aware of feelings and more likely to be open to changing. Because emotional arousal is important in terms of setting the stage for change to occur, helpers need to assist clients in becoming aware of and experiencing their emotions.

LEARNING ABOUT CLIENTS

The exploration stage provides an important opportunity for helpers to learn about their clients. When a client first comes to a session, the helper has no way of knowing how to help that particular person. Helpers cannot assume that they know anything about particular clients or their problems, even (or perhaps especially) if helpers have similar problems. Encouraging an individual client to explore often requires a substantial amount of time because most people and problems are quite complex. In addition, because our goal is to help clients come to their own conclusions and decisions, helpers need to listen carefully to what clients say and how they feel before constructing an action plan to help them solve their problems.

In learning about clients, helpers must follow the lead of the individual client. Helpers can be prepared in general by knowing theories of therapy and by practicing the helping skills, but they must learn more specifically about how to help each client from that client. A parallel example is having a baby. Expectant parents can read lots of books about babies and generally be prepared for having a child, but they really learn parenting skills from attending to the needs of their own unique infant. Similarly, each client is different because of culture, family, and experiences; helpers cannot make assumptions about who the client is or what she or he needs.

Furthermore, on the basis of observing and learning about the client, the helper starts to conceptualize the client and the client's problems during the exploration stage. This conceptualization enables the helper to implement the insight and action stages. Knowing something about the origin of and factors maintaining the problem can aid helpers in deciding whether clients can profit from insight and action.

Exploration Stage Skills

In the next few chapters, I focus on three sets of skills that helpers can use to attain the above goals. The goals of establishing rapport and building the therapeutic relationship and learning about the client are meta-goals—they happen as a result of the more specific goals. So in the next chapters, we focus on the goals of attending, listening, and observing; exploring thoughts; and exploring feelings.

Within each goal, helpers can use several skills somewhat interchangeably. To attend, listen, and observe, helpers use eye contact, facial expression, head nods, body posture, body movements, space, grammatical style, silence, no or minimal interruptions, no or minimal touch, encouragers, and approval-reassurance. To facilitate exploration of thoughts, helpers use restatements or open questions about thoughts. To facilitate exploration of feelings, helpers use reflections of feeling, disclosures of feeling, or open question about feeling. It may be that what is important is not so much which skill within the set is used as that the skills are used for the right goal and are implemented in a helpful manner (i.e., with good attending skills and empathy). See Exhibit 4.1 for a list of goals and skills used to facilitate these goals.

Concluding Comments

The exploration stage is important because it facilitates the development of the helping relationship, gives clients a chance to explore concerns and immerse themselves in their immediate experiencing, and provides helpers with an opportunity to learn about clients' presenting issues and to assess clients' appropriateness for what helpers can offer. For Rogerians, the exploration stage is all that is needed for helping. Rogerians

EXHIBIT 4.1

Skills for Facilitating the Goals of the Exploration Stage

Goal	Skill
Attending, listening, observing	Eye contact
	Facial expression
	Head nods
	Body posture
	Body movements
	Space
	Grammatical style
	Silence
	No interruptions
	No touch (or minimal touch)
	Minimal encourager
	Approval-reassurance
To explore thoughts	Restatement
	Open question about thoughts
To explore feelings	Reflection of feelings
	Disclosure of feelings
	Open question about feelings

believe that the facilitative attitudes of empathy, unconditional positive regard, and genuineness allow clients to begin to accept themselves, which releases the inner experiencing and unblocks the potential for self-actualization. Indeed, some clients need only a listening ear to get them back to their own self-healing processes. Hence, helpers generally should spend a lot of time in the exploration stage because it can be helpful by itself. However, because many clients cannot make progress with exploration alone, insight and action are often necessary to help them change. In this case, exploration sets the stage for everything else that follows.

Exploration skills are used throughout all three stages. Thus, even when helpers move to insight and action, the most frequently used skills are the exploration skills because these skills help clients continue to feel safe and encourage deeper exploration.

An important caveat throughout the exploration stage (and the rest of the helping process) is that there are no absolute "right" interventions to use. Although there are general guidelines, it is not possible to provide a cookbook to tell helpers exactly what to do in different circumstances with different clients. Individual clients require different things at different times from helpers. It is up to helpers to determine which interventions are productive and which are not useful by paying attention to the individual client's reactions and responses (refer back to chap. 2 for a review of the moment-by-moment process).

What Do You Think?

- Rogers has been charged with being too optimistic about human nature and as reflecting American culture in the mid-20th century (as compared with the pessimistic view of Europeans such as Freud). Debate whether Rogers's view is too simplistic and optimistic.
- Take each of Rogers's six conditions and debate its merits.
- Do you think that it is the therapist's facilitative conditions or the relationship between the helper and client that is most crucial?
- How well do the tasks of the exploration stage fit your personal style?
- Discuss whether establishing a relationship is more a matter of attitudes or implementing helping skills.
- Describe the challenges you would face in developing a relationship with someone you believe has done awful and despicable things (e.g., rape, murder).
- Do you believe that it is necessary for clients to "tell their stories"?

Attending, Listening, and Observing Skills 5

The one who listens is the one who understands.

—African (Jabo) proverb

The students in one class prearranged to manipulate
their professor's behavior through nonverbal
responding. Whenever the professor moved to the
right, they looked up, paid rapt attention, and smiled
encouragingly. Whenever the professor moved to the
left, they looked down, rustled their papers, coughed,
and whispered. The professor soon had moved so
far to the right, he fell off the stage! This example
illustrates the power of attending skills.

The skills covered in this chapter are rarely ones that show up
on transcripts of helping sessions because they are mostly
nonverbal. They are what has been called the "back channel"
of communication, similar to the oil that greases the mechanism to make a machine run smoothly or the glue that
holds things together. Helpers need to attend to clients,
listen to them, and observe them carefully for the process
of helping to move forward. These skills help clients feel
safe and comfortable, which allows them to explore their
thoughts and feelings. Helpers do not usually think consciously about and are not aware of these skills, but they can
have a big impact on clients.

Attending, Listening, and Observing

Attending refers to helpers orienting themselves physically toward clients. The goal of attending is for helpers to communicate to clients that they are paying attention to them and to facilitate clients in talking openly about their thoughts and feelings. In effect, attending lays the foundation for the implementation of all the other helping interventions. Clients feel they are valued and worthy of being listened to when helpers attend to them. Attending can encourage clients to verbalize ideas and feelings because they feel helpers want to hear what they have to say. Furthermore, attending behaviors can reinforce clients' active involvement in sessions.

Attending is communicated mostly through nonverbal behaviors, which help convey both what helpers are trying to express and what they do not intend to express (or might be trying to hide). For example, although a helper might try hard to be empathic and look concerned, he or she might feel bored and irritated with the client, which might be expressed through foot tapping or stifled yawns.

Attending orients helpers toward clients, but listening goes beyond just physically attending to clients. *Listening* refers to capturing and understanding the messages that clients communicate (Egan, 1994). Listening involves trying to hear and understand what clients are saying. Reik (1948) talked about listening with a third ear, or trying to hear what the client really means, not just what she or he says overtly. In effect, the helper puts the verbal and nonverbal messages together and hears what the client is thinking and feeling at a deep level.

Attending behaviors set the stage for allowing helpers to listen, but attending does not necessarily ensure listening. Helpers could attend physically but not be listening (e.g., they could be thinking about dinner that night and not hear what clients are saying). Listening provides the raw material from which helpers develop their verbal and nonverbal interventions, but listening should not be confused with the ability to deliver these interventions. Helpers could listen without being helpful, but it would be very difficult to be helpful without listening. Thus, from watching sessions, one could not actually tell if helpers were listening; however, one could infer they were listening if they were able to produce statements that reflected what they heard.

Observing involves paying attention to what is going on overtly with clients in terms of nonverbal behaviors. Whereas listening focuses more on the words and nuances of what the client is saying, observing focuses on trying to pick up on the behavioral cues of the client. Observing is particularly important for noting times when clients have negative reactions, feel ambivalence, have difficulty expressing emotions, or are distracted or uninvolved.

Clearly, there is a lot of overlap among the attending, listening, and observation skills, which is why they are presented together in this chapter. As a helper, you will want to do all of these to form the foundation for your relationship with clients. Before I describe nonverbal behaviors, let's think about cultural issues in attending, given that such issues can have a profound impact on the helping process.

Cultural Issues in Attending and Listening

Each culture develops rules for nonverbal communication (Harper, Wiens, & Matarazzo, 1978). An example of such a cultural rule is the pattern of greeting that might take no more than one third of a second. This pattern involves looking at the other person, smiling, lifting the eyebrows, and nodding the head. These behaviors seem to act as a releaser in that they elicit the same response from another person. Rules for nonverbal behaviors are typically outside of conscious awareness. Most people probably could not articulate the nonverbal rules in their own culture because they learn these rules as young children through social interactions and example rather than by explicit verbal instruction.

Nonverbal behaviors that are appropriate in one culture might not be appropriate in another. A whole industry has developed to teach diplomats and travelers about nonverbal rules of other cultures. For example, in Asia, it is important for people not to praise themselves and instead to appear humble (Maki & Kitano, 2002). Therefore, an American who boasts might not be well received in Asian countries.

If you are involved in interpersonal interactions in which your rules for nonverbal behaviors are not followed by the other person, you might feel intense discomfort. You might not be able to understand or articulate why you feel uncomfortable, but you probably know that something does not feel right. For example, if someone stares at you, you might feel uncomfortable because it is inappropriate in your culture to stare for a long time. If someone stands too close and grabs your arm when you are talking, you might feel an urge to move away because the person has violated your personal space.

Helpers need to adapt their style to fit clients' nonverbal styles rather than expect clients to adapt to them. Helpers can take their cues from clients as to what makes them feel comfortable. For example, if a client acts nervous and initiates too much eye contact, the helper might look away and observe whether the client responds differently. In addition, helpers might ask clients for feedback about what feels comfortable or uncomfortable for them.

Nonverbal Behaviors

Helpers typically communicate much of their attending and listening through nonverbal behaviors, and helpers observe what clients may be experiencing through noting their nonverbal behaviors. Indeed, some researchers (e.g., Archer & Akert, 1977; Haase & Tepper, 1972) have suggested that nonverbal behaviors play a more important role in the communication of emotions than verbal behaviors. These researchers suggested that people communicate true emotions more through nonverbal than verbal expressions, and that nonverbal behaviors are more reliable indicators of true emotion when there is a discrepancy between verbal and nonverbal behaviors. In my opinion, there is not enough empirical evidence to indicate the relative importance of verbal and nonverbal behaviors; however, enough evidence exists to suggest that helpers should pay attention to what they and their clients communicate nonverbally as well as verbally.

So let us examine the different kinds of nonverbal behaviors. *Kinesics* refers to the relationship of bodily movements (arm and leg movements, head nods) to communication. Bodily movements can be categorized into several types, each of which has a different function (Ekman & Friesen, 1969). *Emblems* are substitutes for words (e.g., a wave is a universal greeting). *Illustrators* accompany speech (e.g., measuring the size of a fish with the hands). *Regulators* (e.g., head nods, postural shifts) monitor the conversation flow. *Adaptors* are habitual acts that are often outside awareness and have no communicative purpose (e.g., head scratching, licking one's lips, playing with a pen).

Helpers can use emblems, illustrators, and regulators to accompany verbal messages, but they should avoid using adaptors. Adaptors detract from the helper's effectiveness by turning the focus away from the client to the helper. Too many adaptors or an inappropriate use of emblems, illustrators, or regulators is often a sign of "nonverbal leakage" (i.e., the person does not want to communicate or is trying to hide, but the feeling leaks out through nonverbal channels).

In the next few sections, I take up a number of nonverbal behaviors that might be important for the helping process. These behaviors both can enable the helper to attend to the client and are important things for the helper to be aware of in listening to and observing the client. Obviously, these nonverbal behaviors all operate together, and sometimes one nonverbal behavior can compensate for another, but here I break them apart to describe how each one operates.

EYE CONTACT

Eye contact is a key nonverbal behavior. Looking and gaze aversion are typically used to initiate, maintain, or avoid communication. With a gaze, one can communicate intimacy, interest, submission, or dominance (Kleinke, 1986). Eyes are used to monitor speech, provide feedback, signal understanding, and regulate turn taking (Harper et al., 1978). One could say we meet people with our eyes or that "the eyes are the windows into the soul." In contrast, gaze avoidance or breaking eye contact often signals anxiety, discomfort, or a desire not to communicate with the other person. In general, a person who violates the rules of eye contact will have a hard time communicating with others.

In typical noncounseling interactions, people make eye contact with each other (i.e., mutual gaze) in 28% to 70% of their interactions (Kendon, 1967), although usually for no more than 1 second at a time. Dyads typically negotiate when and how much to look at each other, although this is not a conscious negotiation and takes places at a nonverbal level. Too little eye contact can make one feel the listener is uninterested in the conversation and is avoiding getting involved. By contrast, too much eye contact can make the other person feel uncomfortable, intruded on, dominated, controlled, and even devoured. Likewise, staring can feel rude, insulting, and threatening.

Norms for eye contact differ among cultures. In White middle-class North America, people tend to maintain eye contact while listening but look away when speaking, checking back from time to time to get feedback; in African American culture, people typically look at others while speaking but look away when listening (LaFrance & Mayo, 1976; Sommers-Flanagan & Sommers-Flanagan, 1999). In some Native American groups, sustained eye contact is considered offensive and a sign of disrespect, especially if by a younger to an older person (Brammer & MacDonald, 1996). Several cultural groups (some Native American, Inuit, or Aboriginal Australian groups) avoid eye contact, especially when talking about serious topics (Ivey, 1994). And, as noted in chapter 3 (this volume), a lack of eye contact signifies respect for an authority figure in some cultures.

In sum, helpers ideally use moderate amounts of nonintrusive eye contact. They use enough so that clients feel attended to, but they should not stare or look intently without an occasional break in gaze. And, helpers should be aware of cultural norms regarding eye contact.

FACIAL EXPRESSION

Darwin (1872) speculated that before prehistoric people had language, they communicated threats, greetings, and submission through facial expressions. He believed that this shared heritage explains why all humans express basic emotions through similar facial expressions. He wrote,

> [T]he movements of expression in the face and body, whatever their origin may have been, are in themselves of much importance for our welfare. They serve as the first means of communication between the mother and her infant; she smiles approval, and thus encourages her child on the right path, or frowns disapproval. The movements of expression give vividness and energy to our spoken words. They reveal the thoughts and intentions of others more truly than do words, which may be falsified. . . . These results follow partly from the intimate relation which exists between almost all the emotions and their outward manifestations. (p. 366)

The face is perhaps the body part most involved in nonverbal communication because people communicate so much emotion and information through facial expressions (Ekman, 1993). People pay a lot of attention to facial expressions because they give clues about the meaning of the verbal message. In Shakespeare's (1623/1980) *Macbeth,* Lady Macbeth says to her husband, "your face, my thane, is a book whereon men may read strange matters" (Act 1, Scene 5, p. 17).

The following are some common facial expressions and possible meanings (remember that these are only possible meanings), according to Nirenberg and Calero (1971):

- A frown might indicate displeasure or confusion.
- A raised eyebrow may suggest envy or disbelief.
- An eye wink might indicate intimacy or a private matter.
- Tightened jaw muscles may reflect antagonism.
- Eyes squinted might reflect antagonism.
- Upward rolling of the eyes may imply disbelief or exasperation.
- Both eyebrows raised may denote doubt or questioning.

Ekman and Friesen (1984) showed photographs of facial expressions to people around the world and found that several facial expressions had the same meaning across cultures. People around the world cry when distressed, shake their heads when defiant, and smile when happy. Even blind children who have never seen a face use the same facial expressions to express emotions as sighted people (Eibl-Eibesfeldt, 1971). In addition, fear and anger are expressed mostly with the eyes and happiness mostly with the mouth (Kestenbaum, 1992).

Although people in different cultures share a universal facial language, they differ in the manner and depth of expression of their emotions. For example, while emotional displays are often intense and prolonged in Western cultures, Asians display emotions of sympathy, respect, and shame but rarely display self-aggrandizing or negative emotions that might disrupt communal feelings (Markus & Kitayama, 1991; Matsumoto, Kudoh, Sherer, & Wallbott, 1988).

An important facial feature used in helping is smiling. Although smiling makes a person look friendly and can encourage exploration, I caution helpers against smiling too much during helping sessions because smiling can be perceived as ingratiating or inappropriate when clients are talking about serious concerns. Helpers who smile excessively could be seen as not genuine, as mocking the depth of clients' problems, or as uninvolved.

Helpers need to be aware what they are communicating through their facial expressions. Expressing active interest and concern is important, and matching facial expression to what the client is saying is crucial. In other words, helpers may smile or laugh when clients say something funny, and they may cry when clients say something very sad, as these imply a human connection.

HEAD NODS

The appropriate use of head nods, especially at the end of sentences, can make clients feel helpers are listening and following what they are saying. Indeed, verbal messages are sometimes unnecessary because helpers communicate through head nods that they are "with" clients and that clients should continue talking.

As with other nonverbal behaviors, there is an optimal level of head nods. Too few head nods can make clients feel anxious because they might think that helpers are not paying attention; too many can be distracting. For example, one helper nodded her head constantly to show support, but her nodding distracted the client who thought the helper looked like a bobblehead or a puppet on a string.

BODY POSTURE

An often-recommended body posture is for helpers to lean toward clients and maintain an open body posture with the arms and legs uncrossed (e.g., Egan, 1994). This leaning, open body posture often effectively conveys that the helper is paying attention, although helpers can appear rigid if they stay in this position too long. Also, if the open, leaning position is uncomfortable, it can be hard for helpers to attend to clients.

One body posture some students (especially men) use is slouching back in their chairs with legs spread wide apart. This posture, although comfortable, can seem like a sexual advance, so helpers need to be aware what they convey with their body posture.

BODILY MOVEMENTS

Bodily movements provide information one often cannot obtain from either verbal content or facial expression. As Freud (1905/1953a) eloquently stated, "He that has eyes to see and ears to hear may convince himself that no mortal can keep a secret. If his lips are silent, he chatters with his fingertips, betrayal oozes out of him at every pore" (p. 94). Van den Stock, Righart, and de Gelder (2007) found that body expressions were particularly important in addition to those of the face and voice in helping responders recognize emotions. Similarly, Beattie and Shovelton (2005) suggested that spontaneous hand gestures enabled people to get their messages across more clearly.

Ekman and Friesen (1969) noted that leg and foot movements are the most likely sources of nonverbal leakage because they are less subject to conscious awareness and voluntary inhibition. The hands and face are the next best sources of clues for nonverbal leakage. Hence, if a helper finds him- or herself repeatedly tapping his or her foot, the helper might think about what he or she is feeling.

Gestures often communicate meaning, especially when they are used in conjunction with verbal activity. According to McGough (1975), the following are some possible meanings (again, remember that these are just possible meanings):

- Steepling of fingers might suggest that a person feels confident, smug, or proud.
- Touching or rubbing the nose tends to be a negative reaction.
- Hand to mouth often occurs when a person has blurted out something that should not have been said.
- Finger wagging or pointing implies lecturing or laying blame.
- Tugging at the collar suggests that the person feels cornered.
- Pinching the bridge of the nose implies that the person is deep in thought.
- Locked arms or crossed legs can be a defensive or critical position.
- Clenched fists is sometimes a defensive or hostile gesture.
- Hand over the eyes can be a gesture of avoidance.
- Sitting back in chair with hands behind the head may communicate confidence or superiority.

SPACE

The term *proxemics* refers to how people use space in interactions. E. T. Hall (1968) described four distance zones for middle-class Americans: intimate (0–18 inches), personal (1.5–4 feet), social (4–12 feet), and public (12 feet or more). If rules for prescribed distances are not followed, people can feel uncomfortable, although they are not usually aware of what is making them uneasy. Hall noted that once these patterns for space are learned, they are maintained largely outside of conscious awareness. Typically, the personal to social distance is considered appropriate for seating arrangements in helping relationships, although individuals vary in the amount of distance that feels comfortable for them. Some helpers place chairs close together, whereas others, when they have control over the arrangements, place the chairs far apart. Some helpers place a number of chairs in their offices and allow clients to choose where they sit; where the client sits then provides information that the helper can later use in speculating about the client's needs (e.g., to be close or to be distant).

Space is used in very different ways in different cultures (E. T. Hall, 1963). American and British people generally prefer to be relatively distant from other people and rarely touch. In contrast, Hispanic and Middle Eastern people generally prefer less distance. For example, Arabs and Israelis often stand close, touch, talk loudly, and stare intently. In their review of the literature in work environments, Ayoko and Hartel (2003) found consistent evidence that space violations triggered conflict for people from different cultural backgrounds. In addition, Norman (1982) noted that space is a specialized elaboration of culture. He claimed that space reflects status, power, and expressions of personality. For example, a client would probably react very differently to a helper sitting behind a desk than to a helper sitting without a barrier in between, given that desks can communicate power.

Helpers need to take cultural considerations into account rather than just reacting unconsciously to someone who uses different proxemic patterns. In addition, helpers need to be aware of differences within cultures. For example, a helper should not assume all Latino/Latina clients want to be hugged at the beginning and end of each session just because Latino people often hug when greeting and leaving. Differences exist within cultures, and acculturation to the dominant culture may influence clients' comfort with physical closeness.

TONE OF VOICE

Consider how you feel when someone speaks slowly, with a soft, gentle, inviting voice as opposed to when a person speaks quickly, in a loud, brash, demanding voice. You are probably more likely to disclose to the first person than to the second. Similarly, in helping, clients are more likely to explore when the helper speaks softly and gently than loudly and commandingly.

In addition, helpers need to match the client's pace of speech, within some limits. Helpers might use a slower pace of speech with clients who speak slowly. In contrast, helpers might speak somewhat faster with clients who talk rapidly. If a client is manic and is speaking too rapidly, however, the helper might use a slower pace to encourage the client to slow down.

GRAMMATICAL STYLE

Another way helpers communicate attending is through matching the client's language and grammatical style. Language must be appropriate to the cultural experience and educational level of the client, so the helper can form a bond with the client. If a client says, "I ain't never gonna make it with chicks," it would probably be better for the helper to say something like, "You're concerned about finding a girlfriend," rather than "Your inferiority complex prevents you from establishing relationships with appropriate love objects." The latter statement sounds too discrepant from the client's statement. The helper must sound natural and helpful rather than stilted or condescending.

Helpers should not compromise their integrity by using a language style that feels uncomfortable to them, but they can modify their style to be more similar to that of their client. Each of us has a comfortable range of behaviors, and helpers need to find the place within that range to meet each client. After all, the goal of helpers is to facilitate client change rather than to add additional barriers to change.

SILENCE

A silence is a pause during which neither helper nor client is speaking. The silence can occur after a client's statement, within a client's statement, or after a simple acceptance of the helper's statement. For example, after the client says something like, "I just feel so confused and angry and don't know what to say," the helper might pause to allow the client time to reflect on the feelings and see if the client has anything new to add. If the client pauses in the middle of saying something and is obviously still processing the feelings, the helper might be silent to let the client think without interruption. If the client responds minimally to something the helper said, the helper might be silent to see if the client can think of something else to say. It is important to note that to say nothing is not necessarily to do nothing. Helpers can be attentive and supportive, and they can listen without saying anything. In fact, sometimes the most useful thing a helper can do is to say nothing.

I often recommend the use of brief silences for beginning helpers because it gives them a chance to listen to clients without having to formulate an immediate response. Thus, when clients pause, the helper then starts pondering what to say to reflect all that they have heard (while of course still attending to the client). Often, beginning helpers are surprised to discover that clients keep talking, indicating that they just need permission to talk.

Silence can be used to convey empathy, warmth, and respect and to give clients time and space to talk (Hill, Thompson, & Ladany, 2003; Ladany, Hill, Thompson, & O'Brien, 2004). Silence can also allow clients time to reflect or think through what they want to say without interruption. Some clients pause for a long time because they process things slowly and thoroughly or because they are in the middle of thinking through something and need time to get in touch with their thoughts and feelings. At such times, silence is respectful because it provides space for clients to think without feeling pressured to say anything. Warm, empathic silences give clients time to express their feelings. By allowing clients the space, helpers can encourage clients to express feelings from which they might otherwise run away. Silence can indicate to clients that helpers are patient and unrushed and have plenty of time to listen to whatever comes out. During these empathic silences, helpers can sit attentively focused on being with the client while the client is deeply immersed in thoughts and feelings. Hence, I suggest that helpers avoid interruptions and give clients several seconds after speaking to see whether they have anything else to say. Likewise, some empirical evidence suggests that clients talk more when therapists delay speaking (Matarazzo, Phillips, Wiens, & Saslow, 1965).

In contrast to the use of silence to provide empathy and warmth, silence can also be used to challenge (Hill, Thompson, & Ladany, 2003; Ladany et al., 2004). In this use of silence, helpers challenge clients to take responsibility for what they want to say. Rather than rushing in and taking care of the client, helpers wait and encourage the client to say something. Silence is used by psychoanalytic therapists during long-term therapy to encourage free association (i.e., saying whatever comes to mind; see Basch, 1980). During free association, silence can be used to raise the client's anxiety because the client does not receive feedback about what the helper wants or feels. Like a stimulus deprivation experiment, silence sometimes increases discomfort and forces clients to rely on their inner resources and to examine their thoughts, or as one therapist said, "to let clients stew in their juices." Although challenging silences may be helpful in long-term therapy when there is a good working alliance, it can be potentially damaging to use silence for these reasons if the client does not trust the helper or understand the purpose of the silence. Silence can be frightening for clients who feel isolated and out of touch with the helper or who do not know how to express themselves. Helpers have to assess what is going on for clients during the silence and determine whether it is better to continue the silence or break it.

Silence also is often inadvertently used for negative or inappropriate reasons (Hill, Thompson, & Ladany, 2003; Ladany et al., 2004). Some helpers are silent because they are anxious, angry, bored, or distracted. Many beginning helpers are uncomfortable with silence. They do not know what to do and are often concerned about how clients might perceive them. To relax, helpers can breathe deeply, relax, and think about the client and what might be going on inside the client. In other words, helpers should try to establish an empathic connection with clients during silence rather than focusing on themselves. If silences go on for a long time (i.e., more than a minute) or a client is obviously uncomfortable, helpers should consider breaking the silence and asking the client how she or he is feeling.

As with other skills, the acceptability of silence varies by culture. D. W. Sue and Sue (1999) noted that in Japanese and Chinese cultures, silence can indicate a desire by the person to continue talking after making a point. In contrast, European Americans are less comfortable with silence and often rush to fill the space.

Here is an example of how silence might be used therapeutically (note that here and throughout the book the helper's speech is italicized when it illustrates the specific intervention):

Client: My dog Sam just died. I'm really upset because I've had that dog since I was very little. I grew up with the dog.

Helper: (Silence of about 1 minute) *How are you feeling?*

Client: I was just thinking about how I got the dog. I begged my parents forever to get me a dog. I said I would take care of it. Of course I didn't much at first, but I did later. Sam was kind of like Red Rover in the comics— he waited for me at the bus stop, and we had great adventures together. I could tell Sam everything.

Helper: (Silence of 30 seconds)

Client: Sam helped me get through my parents' divorce. I felt like I could rely on him then like no one else. It's like losing my best friend—we went through so much stuff together. I felt so terrible when I left for college and couldn't take him with me. He looked so sad, and I didn't even say goodbye to him.

Minimal Verbal Behaviors

There are two minimal verbal behaviors that helpers can use to facilitate client exploration. These are minimal encouragement and approval-reassurance.

MINIMAL ENCOURAGERS

Helpers encourage clients to keep talking through nonlanguage sounds, nonwords, and simple words such as "um-hmm," "yeah," and "wow." Helpers use minimal encouragers to acknowledge what the client has said, communicate attentiveness, provide noninvasive support, monitor the flow of conversation, and encourage clients to keep talking. Minimal encouragers are often used in conjunction with and serve the same purpose as head nods.

Helpers sometimes use too few or too many minimal encouragers. Too few can feel distancing, whereas too many can be distracting and annoying to the client. I suggest helpers use minimal encouragers and acknowledgments, mostly at the end of client sentences or speaking turns (i.e., everything a client says between two helper interventions), to encourage clients to keep talking (assuming they are actively involved in exploration). A minimal encourager here suggests to the client that you are giving up your speaking turn and would like him or her to continue speaking. Interrupting a client to provide minimal encouragers, however, can be distracting, so helpers should pay attention to the appropriate timing of this intervention.

APPROVAL-REASSURANCE

Approval-reassurance is a helpful skill that can be used occasionally (and I stress occasionally) to provide emotional support and reassurance, indicate helpers empathize with or understand clients, or suggest that clients' feelings are normal and to be expected. The key is to use approval-reassurance to foster exploration and to make clients feel safe enough to keep talking at a deep level about their concerns. For many clients, approval-reassurance that their problems are normal and that they are not alone in their feelings can be empowering and help clients go further in exploring their concerns. The following are some examples of approval-reassurance:

- "That's really hard to handle."
- "That's a devastating situation."
- "How awful!"
- "Wow! That's an awesome opportunity!"
- "Good try!"
- "It was really terrific that you were able to express your feelings to him!"
- "I've felt that too."
- "Yeah, I know what you're going through."
- "I've been there too."

Approval-reassurance can also be used to provide reinforcement, indicating that the helper values something the client has said or done and wants to encourage the client to continue the effort to change. Some clients need support or acknowledgment that they have done something well. In addition, approval, reassurance, and reinforcement can help some clients persist in exploring because they know someone is listening and sympathetic; this is especially important if clients are exploring difficult or painful topics.

When using approval-reassurance, it is important that the helper stay close to where the client is and know the client well enough to know what behavior is being approved. For example, a client who has been working on being assertive came into her session and told her helper that she finally told her boss that she wanted more control over her schedule. The helper said, "Wow, that is great that you were able to stand up for yourself." The client burst into tears and said that she was fired from her job. It perhaps would have been more helpful for the helper to, instead of giving approval-reassurance, to say something like, "And how did that go for you?"

Helpers, of course, must be cautious not to minimize clients' feelings or cut short exploration. In addition, approval-reassurance is inappropriate if used to alleviate anxiety or distress, to minimize feelings, or to deny feelings (e.g., "Don't worry about it," "Everyone feels that way"). When used in this manner, approval-reassurance is typically counterproductive to our work as helpers because it stops rather than facilitates clients' exploring and accepting feelings. Such statements can make clients feel they have no right to their feelings. Helpers sometimes use these interventions as misguided attempts to reassure others that everything is okay. Unfortunately, problems typically do not go away because they are minimized or denied. Most of us have heard the old sayings, "Give it time" or "Time cures all." It is not "time" that makes feelings go away; in fact, feelings often fester when they are bottled up or denied. Rather, it is awareness, acceptance, and expression of feelings that aid in resolution of painful affect. To reiterate, our goal as helpers is to help clients identify, intensify, and express feelings rather than minimize or deny them.

Although helpful in some situations, approval-reassurance can sound false if used excessively, prematurely, or insincerely. If such interventions are used to promote helper biases (e.g., "I think you're right to feel guilty about getting an abortion"), they can also be problematic because they stop client exploration or make clients feel compelled to agree or comply.

In general, then, if done judiciously and sparingly, approval-reassurance can encourage clients and facilitate exploration of thoughts, feelings, and experiences. Approval-reassurance should not be used, however, to diminish feelings, deny experiences, stop exploration, or provide a moral judgment. When helpers find themselves using approval-reassurance in a counterproductive way, they may want to think about what is going on in their own lives.

Here is an example of a positive use of approval-reassurance (in italics):

> *Client:* I just learned that my sister needs to have a kidney transplant. She's been sick a lot lately and hasn't been getting better.
>
> *Helper:* *That's too bad.*

Client: Yeah, I feel terrible for her. She's only 21 and has always been active, so this is a real shock for her. I feel guilty that she got this horrible disease while I'm healthy and able to function.

Helper: *It's pretty natural to feel some guilt.*

Client: Really? I'm glad to hear that. I have been trying to do more for her. I'm thinking of organizing a campaign to find a donor and raise money for her treatment. Because she has an unusual blood type, it will be difficult to find the right person, and it's going to cost a lot of money.

Helper: *That's terrific that you would do that for her.*

Client: I feel like it's the least I can do. It does interestingly bring up a lot of issues for me about obligation versus doing things because I want to. (Client continues exploring her thoughts.)

Nonverbal Behaviors to Avoid

As mentioned earlier, helpers should pay attention to what they communicate nonverbally to clients. Some nonverbal behaviors to avoid include interrupting, note-taking, and touching.

INTERRUPTIONS

One particularly distracting behavior is interruptions. When the client is exploring productively (i.e., talking about innermost thoughts and feelings), the helper does not need to interrupt. Often the helper simply has to attend and listen and stay out of the client's way, so that the client has the opportunity to keep talking. Matarazzo et al. (1965) stressed that helpers should not interrupt and should delay talking for several seconds after the end of client statements. This pause (noninterruption) allows clients to continue thinking and talking without undue pressure from helpers. Matarazzo et al. found inexperienced helpers used far more interruptions than did experienced helpers. If, however, the client is stuck, cannot think of what to say, or is rambling or talking nonstop but not exploring productively, the helper may need to interrupt to help the client get back on track through the use of exploration skills (see chaps. 6, 7, and 18, this volume).

NOTE-TAKING

Another potentially distracting behavior is note-taking, which tends to reduce the ability of helpers to attend to clients. While the helper is taking notes, the client is often unengaged and passively waiting for the helper to finish writing, which reduces the intensity of the immediate experience. Clients may also be suspicious about what helpers are writing and curious about why they record some things and not others. For helpers who want to take notes to remember what occurred during sessions, a less intrusive method would be to tape sessions and later listen to the tapes to recall specific details of the session. An exception is when the helper is conducting a more formal intake session and needs to take notes (see chap. 18); even then I recommend that the note-taking be kept to a minimum and that the helper make sure to maintain eye contact with the client.

TOUCH

Touching is a natural inclination when helpers want to indicate support to their clients and in fact can make clients feel understood and involved in a human relationship (Hunter & Struve, 1998). Montagu (1971) noted that touch is a natural physical need and that some people hunger for touch because they do not receive enough physical contact. Unfortunately, touch can sometimes have negative effects. Clients can feel that their space has been invaded. If the touch is unwanted, or if clients have a history of unwanted touch, touch can be frightening and make clients feel unsafe.

Highlen and Hill (1984) reported that the few studies conducted on touching in therapy were inconclusive. Some studies have shown positive effects of touching, whereas others have found no effects. A survey of practicing therapists indicated that about 90% never or rarely touched clients during sessions (Stenzel & Rupert, 2004). The only type of touch that was used much at all was a handshake, typically before or after a session. Some therapists, however, were reluctant to even shake hands due to concern that any touch could be misinterpreted as sexual or exploitative and result in harm or litigation. Furthermore, therapists indicated that they were more likely to accept a hug or handshake than to initiate such behaviors.

Given the potential benefits and misunderstandings harm related to touch, it clearly requires clinical judgment to know when to use touch. Therefore, other than a possible handshake at the beginning or end of the session if it seems culturally appropriate, it is probably better for beginning helpers to refrain from touching. General guidelines for touch for more advanced helpers, as suggested by Kertay and Reviere (1998) and E. W. L. Smith (1998), are to

(a) seek consent from the client prior to touch,
(b) explain the use of touch to the client, and
(c) discuss the experience with the client afterward.

Relax and Be Natural but Professional

Within the bounds of looking professional, each helper needs to determine which attending behaviors feel comfortable and natural to use. For example, sitting in an uncomfortable but technically correct counselor posture will probably communicate discomfort to the client.

It is important not to just appear relaxed but to actually be relaxed. Many beginning trainees try so hard to maintain an attending stance that they come across as artificial or posed. They perform all the "right" behaviors but end up being too attentive, which makes clients feel they are being examined too closely. One of the most difficult tasks facing helpers is to relax and be themselves. However, when helpers integrate attending and listening behaviors into their way of being, clients often respond by exploring their concerns.

When you are not able to relax, you can try to learn more about what is going on inside you. For example, if you feel your muscles tensing or note you are withdrawing physically from clients, you might reflect about what is going on for you at that moment. Awareness is the key to handling situations. Once you know how you feel, you can make informed decisions about how to act rather than having the reactions "leak out." Paying attention to bodily reactions provides an incredible amount of information about clients. If you feel bored, anxious, attracted, or repulsed by a client, chances are other people feel this way toward the client. See chapter 12 on immediacy for ideas about how to use these reactions therapeutically during the insight stage.

One way to maintain a professional stance is through clothing. I often suggest that beginning helpers dress one notch better than their clients. If clients in your agency typically wear casual clothes like jeans and T-shirts, then you might wear nice slacks and a shirt. It is particularly important to avoid seductive clothing.

One problem that helpers often have is being distracted by internal thoughts and feelings. For example, helpers often engage in negative self-talk (e.g., "I'm not doing this right," "I'm not sure the client likes me," "I wonder if I'm giving too much eye contact"). If they are distracted by what they are thinking, helpers will have a hard time focusing on clients and listening attentively. So once you catch yourself being distracted, you might try refocusing and thinking about what is going on with the client. After the session, you might think about your own issues.

Another difficulty is that some helpers are not sensitive to cultural differences in nonverbal behaviors. When someone from another culture does something nonverbally that is different from their custom (e.g., using eye contact differently), some helpers judge these clients according to their own cultural standards. So become aware of this tendency and try not to judge using your own standards.

An effective way to obtain feedback about attending behaviors is for helpers to record themselves in a helping situation (with the client's permission) and later carefully observe their nonverbal behaviors and the client's reactions. Helpers can also experiment with nonverbal behaviors with friends or classmates. When friends are talking about something important, helpers might use attending behaviors appropriately and observe the friend's reaction. Helpers then might use attending behaviors inappropriately (or not at all) and see if friends react differently. Helpers can later tell their friends what they were doing and solicit feedback about reactions to different nonverbal behaviors.

Listening and Observation Skills

Listening and observing involve paying attention to both the verbal and nonverbal messages of the client and trying to determine what the person is thinking and feeling.

VERBAL MESSAGES

Clients communicate with helpers in a variety of ways, the most obvious being the words they use to express thoughts, feelings, and experiences. Helpers can listen carefully to the words. Helpers get into a listening stance by using attending skills, minimal encouragers (e.g., "um-hmm"), and freeing their minds from distractions. Helpers can imagine themselves in the client's position. Thus, helpers listen by seeking to understand what a client is experiencing from the client's perspective rather than from the helper's viewpoint. For example, an adolescent client, Kathleen, complained she felt devastated and worthless because she had not been asked to the prom. From the perspective of the helper, a 35-year-old married woman, not being asked to the prom was not a catastrophic event. However, by listening to Kathleen with a third ear, the helper could imagine that Kathleen felt awful.

A key to listening is for helpers to pay attention to clients without formulating the next response. All too often, people are half listening to what someone is saying because they are thinking about what to say next. It is better to listen and say nothing (especially if the client is exploring productively) than to rush in and say something that interrupts the client's exploration.

In addition, clients who have different verbal styles than their helpers can cause confusion for their helpers. Helpers who are introverted might assume that talkative clients are comfortable, when they could be talking too much out of anxiety. It is important for helpers not to project their feelings and personal style onto their clients.

NONVERBAL MESSAGES

Not only is it important that helpers listen to clients' words, but they also can learn a lot by "listening" to clients' nonverbal behaviors. Clients who are nervous often use a lot of adaptors, are very quiet, stutter, or cannot speak coherently. Clients who are defensive or closed often cross their arms and legs, almost as a barricade to the helper. Clients who are ashamed might look down as they speak. Clients who are scared might speak softly, look away, or have a closed posture. In contrast, clients who are comfortable and feel safe with their helpers often lean forward and talk with animation and feeling in their voices.

As noted earlier, helpers should not interpret nonverbal behaviors as having fixed standard "meanings." Fidgeting can reveal anxiety, but it can also reveal boredom; folded arms can convey either irritation or relaxation. For example, if a client sits with arms and legs crossed, he or she is not necessarily withholding or defending. It could mean he or she is cold or just habitually sits with arms and legs crossed. Helpers cannot "read" another's body language as having universal meaning but can use observations as hints or clues about what a client might be feeling. If a client is sitting with arms and legs crossed and has scooted the chair back, the helper might hypothesize that the client needs distance from the helper. The helper needs to investigate this hypothesis further, however, by talking about it with the client (using skills covered in this book). Thus, helpers can use nonverbal data to form hypotheses and then gather more data to determine the accuracy of these hypotheses.

It also appears that some emotions are hard to read. Results from two studies (A. P. Atkinson, Dittrick, Gemmell, & Young, 2004; Van den Stock et al., 2007) suggest that fear and anger are harder to recognize than happiness and sadness. In addition, fear and anger are difficult to distinguish. These results indicate that it is important that helpers not make assumptions about what clients are feeling.

Helpers also need to be aware of possible misinterpretations when someone from another culture uses nonverbal behaviors differently than they do. For example, if a European American helper greets an African American client who does not make eye contact, the helper should not assume the client suffers from guilt or low self-esteem, but should pay close attention to whether this nonverbal behavior has a different meaning in the client's culture.

Helpers are often confused when clients have different nonverbal styles from theirs. For example, a helper who does not like to make a lot of eye contact might assume that a client who makes eye contact feels comfortable and in control of the situation. However, too much eye contact can be as much a defense or indication of anxiety as too little eye contact; both styles make it difficult for people to get close to others.

A key to listening is to pay attention to context. Rather than becoming fixated on the meaning of specific nonverbal behaviors, helpers need to pay attention to everything about the client: the verbal and nonverbal behaviors, the setting, the culture, and the presenting problem. For example, Archie appeared angry and hostile to the helper, but his behavior made sense when he revealed that he had just been stopped and frisked by a police officer for no apparent reason other than that he was an African American man in a White neighborhood.

When Rosenthal, Hall, DiMatteo, Rogers, and Archer (1979) showed clips of emotionally expressive faces and bodies, they found that some people were better at detecting emotion than others, and that women were generally better at detecting emotion than men. J. B. Miller (1976) used social learning theory to explain why women might be better at detecting emotion than men:

> Subordinates (women), then, know much more about the dominants than vice versa. They have to. They become highly attuned to the dominants, able to predict their reactions of pleasure and displeasure. Here, I think, is where the long story of "feminine intuition" and "feminine wiles" begins. It seems clear that these "mysterious" gifts are in fact skills, developed through long practice, in reading many small signals, both verbal and nonverbal. (p. 10)

It is interesting to note that although some people are better than others at picking up nonverbal cues, some evidence showed that counselors were no better than noncounselors at nonverbal acuity (Sweeney & Cottle, 1976).

Helpers who are aware that they are not as natively sensitive to nonverbal cues can try harder to pay attention to these behaviors. A few studies have suggested that trainees can be taught to increase their sensitivity to nonverbal communication (e.g., Delaney & Heimann, 1966; Grace, Kivlighan, & Kunce, 1995). It seems that self-awareness and practice can help people become more sensitive to nonverbal cues.

EXAMPLE OF INAPPROPRIATE ATTENDING AND LISTENING

Helper: (leaning back, arms folded, and looking at the ceiling) So, how come you came today anyway?

Client:	(very softly) Well, I'm not sure. I just haven't been feeling very good about myself lately. But I don't know if you can help me.
Helper:	(shifts forward in seat and looks intently at client) Well, so what is happening?
Client:	(long pause) I just don't know how to . . .
Helper:	(interrupts) Just tell me what the problem really is.
Client:	(long pause) I guess I really don't have anything to talk about. Sorry I wasted your time.

EXAMPLE OF APPROPRIATE ATTENDING AND LISTENING

Helper:	Hi. My name is Debbie. We have a few minutes to talk today so that I can practice my helping skills. What would you like to talk about?
Client:	(very softly) Well, I'm not sure. I just haven't been feeling very good lately about myself. But I don't know if you can help me.
Helper:	(matches the client's soft voice) Yeah, you sound kind of scared. Tell me a little bit more about what's been going on lately.
Client:	I've been kind of down. I haven't been able to sleep or eat much. I'm behind on everything, and I don't have the energy to do any schoolwork.
Helper:	(pauses, softly) It sounds like you feel overwhelmed.
Client:	(sighs) Yes, that's exactly how I feel. It just seems like there's a lot of pressure in my first year of college.
Helper:	Um-hmm (head nod)
Client:	(continues talking)

Concluding Comments

Attending behaviors set the stage for helpers to listen and to let clients know they are being heard. Helpers also need to listen carefully to clients' verbal and nonverbal behaviors to hear what clients are saying and to pick up clues about underlying thoughts and feelings. In addition, attending and listening provide the foundation for all the other skills taught in this book, so helpers should be particularly attentive to learning these skills. Finally, observing nonverbal behaviors provides clues for how clients might be feeling, so it is important to pay attention to them.

What Do You Think?

- Do you think that attending is different than listening?
- What are some rules for nonverbal behavior in your culture?
- How do you think rules are established for nonverbal behaviors? Can these rules be changed?
- What do you think about the role of culture in attending and listening?
- What are your thoughts about manipulating your nonverbal behaviors to achieve desired goals with clients?
- Reflect about how much of communication is nonverbal versus verbal.
- How do you feel about using silence? How was silence used in your home?
- How might touching help or hinder the helping process? How was touching used in your family?

i LAB 4. Attending and Listening

A downloadable PDF of this Lab is available in the student resources area of Helping Skills, *3rd ed. Web site: www.apa.org/books/resources/Hill3.*

Please note that the first few labs might feel somewhat artificial because each helping skill is first practiced separately. In real helping sessions, you will not use just one skill at a time The best way to master the helping skills is to focus on each one intensely and separately before trying to integrate them.

In addition, some students feel overwhelmed with these lab exercises because they worry that they will not remember everything they are "supposed" to do. You probably will not remember everything. It takes a lot of practice before you can begin to use everything you have learned. Try to relax and do your best—you do not have to be perfect. Just get in there and try the exercises and see what happens. These exercises are designed to give you the opportunity to practice the skills in a relatively safe place.

Exercise 1: Attending

Goals

1. To allow helpers a chance to communicate empathy just through attending behaviors.
2. To enable helpers to become accustomed to being in the helper role.

Helper's and Client's Tasks During the Helping Exchange

1. Students pair up and take turns being helper and client.
2. The helper uses appropriate attending behaviors with the client, who talks about an easy topic (see Exhibit 1.1 in chap. 1). The helper should communicate empathy *but not say anything verbally.*
3. Continue for 3 minutes. Switch roles.

Exercise 2: Listening

Goals

1. To enable helpers to become accustomed to the helper role.
2. To allow helpers an opportunity to try different attending behaviors to see which feel most comfortable and congruent.
3. To provide feedback to helpers about their attending behaviors.
4. To allow helpers an opportunity to observe and learn about the meanings of clients' nonverbal behaviors.
5. To give helpers an opportunity to practice listening skills without interpreting, making judgments about what clients say, or thinking of what they want to say.

Helper's and Client's Tasks During the Helping Exchange

1. Students should be arranged in groups of three, alternating roles so each person participates at least once in each role (helper, client, and observer).
2. The helper can relax, use appropriate attending skills, introduce him- or herself, and ask what the client would like to talk about.
3. The client should talk *briefly* for one or two sentences about an easy topic.
4. The helper should first pause to think and then repeat verbatim (except for changing "I" to "you") what the client said. Repeating verbatim probably will feel awkward to many helpers, but it enables helpers to listen carefully and make sure they hear what clients are saying. Be sure to focus on this task and not talk about life in general.
5. Continue for 8 to 10 client speaking turns. Although it is difficult (especially the first time), stay in the helper and client roles.

Observer's Task During the Helping Exchange

1. Take notes on your observations of the helper's ability to repeat exactly what the client said. Note one positive and one negative attending behavior.
2. Encourage the helper and client to stay on task.

After the Helping Exchange

1. The helper first discusses which attending behaviors felt comfortable and how it felt to repeat what the client said.
2. The client can give feedback about the helper's attending and listening skills.
3. The observer can give positive and then negative feedback to the helper.

Personal Reflections

▪ What was it like for you to be silent in the first exercise?
▪ What was your experience in the roles of helper, client, and observer?
▪ Which attending behaviors did you find most helpful as a helper and as a client?
▪ How did you feel about repeating everything verbatim?
▪ What multicultural issues (e.g., gender, race, ethnicity, age) arose in your dyads?

Skills for Exploring Thoughts 6

The world is made of stories, not atoms.

—Muriel Rukeyser

After Jason's parents were killed in a random drive-by shooting, he needed a chance to talk with someone who would not judge him. His helper listened supportively, showed appropriate and encouraging attending behaviors, rephrased the content of what Jason was saying (e.g., "You're still trying to understand what happened," "You can't make sense of their deaths," "You want to hurt their murderer"), and asked open questions to help Jason clarify his thoughts. Jason left feeling better about having someone listen and being able to express what he was thinking.

Rationale for Exploring Thoughts

When clients come into a helping situation, we as helpers need to hear what their problems are so that we can figure out how to help them. Because the problems we work with are related to clients' thoughts and feelings, we need to hear about those. In this chapter I focus on thoughts, and I focus on feelings in chapter 7. Obviously, thoughts and feelings cannot really be separated, but I have separated them into two chapters to provide maximum attention to each.

As helpers, we want to hear from clients about what they think about their problems. We want to hear about the problem and help clients to explore thoughts about the problem. By talking about the problem, clients often hear themselves fully for the first time, and then they can begin to understand their reactions.

I am not just referring here to the client telling stories and entertaining us. The purpose of helping is not for the helper to be entertained but for the client to think deeply about his or her concerns. And I am not referring to just obsessing about problems and endlessly listing complaints. A recent study found that adolescent girls tend to coruminate (Rose, Carlson, & Waller, 2007) or endlessly obsess and worry about issues and bring each other down. Ruminating obviously does not help. Rather, helpers want to hear about what troubles clients about these issues. Helpers want clients to slow the process down and think about their situation, to have a chance to talk about the different pieces of the problem in a supportive, nonjudgmental setting. By explaining things to someone else, clients often hear themselves in a new way.

When I talked about this issue in class recently, a student asked me how we can tell whether a client is truly exploring versus ruminating or telling a story to entertain us. Good question! If a client is telling a story (at least if she or he is a good storyteller), there is a polished quality to it—there is a clear beginning, a build up to a climax, and then a conclusion. If the client is ruminating, there is also a steady tone, often boring and said in a monotone. In contrast, when a client is truly going inward and exploring thoughts, there are often pauses to check things out, and the voice tone often varies as if the person is discovering new things as he or she talks. It is usually very engaging to listen to people when they are searching inward for what they are thinking.

The primary skill this chapter focuses on for helping clients explore thoughts is restatements because they help clients feel heard, encourage them to continue talking, and help to focus on the most important aspects of their problems. Open questions for thoughts are also helpful but are used somewhat less often. Closed questions are only occasionally helpful but might be used in rare circumstances.

Restatements

Restatements are a repeating or paraphrasing of the content or meaning of what a client has said (see Exhibit 6.1). Restatements typically contain fewer but similar words as the client's, are more concrete and clear than the client's statement, can be phrased either tentatively (e.g., "So you seem to be saying that maybe you were a little bit late?") or more

EXHIBIT 6.1

Overview of Restatement

Definition	A *restatement* is a repeating or rephrasing of the content or meaning of the client's statement(s) that typically contains fewer but similar words and is more concrete and clear than the client's statement. Restatements can be phrased either tentatively or as a direct statement. Restatements can paraphrase either the immediately preceding material or material from earlier in session or treatment (i.e., summaries).
Examples	"You want to be an effective helper." "Your parents are breaking up." "To summarize, you seem clearer on what you would like to do about attending the wedding."
Typical helper intentions	To clarify, to focus, to support, to encourage catharsis (see Web Form D)
Possible client reactions	Supported, understood, clear, negative thoughts or behaviors, stuck, lacking direction (see Web Form G)
Desired client behavior	Cognitive–behavioral exploration (see Web Form H)
Helpful hints	Focus on the content of what the client is trying to communicate Pick the most important part of the client's statement to paraphrase—the "cutting edge," the part that is most salient, for which the client has the most energy Keep restatements short and simple Pause before restating to see if the client has finished talking Give restatements slowly and supportively Focus on the client rather than on other people Vary the manner in which you deliver restatements

directly (e.g., "You were late"), and refer to things the client just said or to things the client said earlier in the session or treatment.

Summaries, a kind of restatement, tie together several ideas or pick out the highlights and general themes of the content expressed by the client. Summaries do not go beyond what the client has said or delve into the reasons for feelings or behaviors but consolidate what has been said. For example, the helper might say to an adolescent, "So here's what I think we've learned so far. You get angry at your parents for being too intrusive. They barge in your room without knocking and give you no privacy. You don't feel that they listen to you."

WHY USE RESTATEMENTS?

The use of restatement goes back to Rogers (1942), who believed that helpers need to be mirrors or sounding boards, enabling clients to hear what they are saying without judgment. Thinking about one's problems alone is often difficult because one can get blocked or stuck, may not have enough time or energy to examine problems thoroughly, may rationalize behaviors, or may give up and quit trying. Having another person who listens and serves as a mirror of the content offers clients a golden opportunity to hear themselves think.

Given that clients often feel confused, conflicted, or overwhelmed by their problems, receiving accurate restatements allows them to hear how their concerns sound to others. It is important that clients hear back what they have said, so they can evaluate what they are thinking, add things they have forgotten, think about whether they actually believe what they have said, and think about things at a deeper level. Because statements often sound different when repeated by someone else, restatements allow clients to ponder what they really think. Restatements also can enable clients to clarify matters, explore certain aspects of the problem more thoroughly, and think about aspects they had not considered before. Just taking the time to think through a problem carefully with the benefit of an interested listener can lead to new understanding. In fact, with healthy clients who are trying to understand major problems or make decisions, helpers might never need to go beyond this type of intervention because these clients only need an opportunity to hear what they are thinking.

An additional reason for helpers to use restatements is that helpers are required to put their listening into words and play an active role in the helping process. Rather than assuming they have understood what clients have said, helpers use restatements to check out the accuracy of what they have heard. Having to listen to clients and summarize their words in fewer and more concise terms requires that helpers attend carefully and determine the key components of what clients have revealed. Saying "I understand how you feel" or asking questions can be easy but is often empty; restating what the client has said is much harder and requires that helpers not only listen but also struggle to understand enough of what clients have said so they can restate the essence of their messages. Although at first it may seem that restatements are a passive mode of responding, helpers actually are engaged actively in trying to capture the essence of clients' experiences and paraphrase it back for clients to hear.

Restatements seem most appropriate to use when clients are talking cognitively about their problems (i.e., are trying to explain a situation or thought). Clients who are cognitively oriented rather than affectively oriented often like restatements. Such cognitively oriented clients like to analyze their thoughts about problems and might be threatened if asked to focus too much on feelings, especially early in a helping relationship. Restatements also seem to be appropriate when affectively oriented clients are talking about issues that are too affect laden because the feelings might be overwhelming and need to be contained.

As with restatements, helpers also use summaries to reassure clients that they have been listening and to check the accuracy of what they have been hearing. Summaries can be particularly useful when clients have finished talking about a particular issue or at the end of sessions, as a way of helping clients reach a sense of closure regarding what has been explored. Summaries also can be helpful at the beginning of subsequent sessions to recap past sessions and provide a focus for the upcoming session.

HOW TO RESTATE

The goal of restatements is to enable clients to focus and to talk in more depth about an issue, as well as to assist clients in figuring out issues rather than just restating what the client already knows. Hence, helpers try to capture the "cutting edge" of what clients have revealed—what clients are most uncertain about, what is still unexplored, or what is not completely understood. A student used a metaphor of Wayne Gretzky, a star hockey player, saying that it is important in hockey to go to where the puck is going, not where it has been. Helpers, then, should pick out the most salient message or the issue clients are working on to facilitate further exploration on this issue.

Clues for determining what is most important to restate can be gathered by attending to what the client focuses on most, what the client seems to have the most involvement in talking about, what the client seems to have questions or conflicts about, and what is left unresolved. Attention to nonverbal messages (e.g., vocal quality might indicate that the client is deeply engaged in what he or she is talking about) can also assist helpers in determining the salient content of the client's message.

Helpers sometimes worry that selecting the most important part of the client's statement requires a judgment call and removes them from a client-centered approach to helping. I would argue that restatement allows helpers to stay within a client-centered approach because they are trying to use their empathic skills to figure out the most important aspect for the client. Helpers have to listen to clients at a deep level to hear what clients are most concerned about. The attitude of being client-centered is important for helpers when formulating restatements.

Rather than paraphrasing everything clients say, helpers try to capture the essence of what they have said, although formulating a restatement can be difficult when the client has talked for a long time. Beginning trainees often think they need to capture everything the client has said, but capturing everything not only would be impossible but would probably be counterproductive. The focus would shift from the client to the helper because the repeating would take too much time. The momentum would be lost in the session. The client would be put in a position of trying to remember everything he or she said to determine whether the helper repeated everything accurately. In contrast, an effective restatement keeps the focus on the client and is almost unnoticeable in subtly guiding and encouraging the client to keep talking. Focusing on one piece of an issue at a time is important to allow clients the opportunity to delve deeply into a concern. Helpers can return later to other important aspects of the problem after one part is explored thoroughly.

Restatements are generally shorter and more concise than clients' statements, focusing on the most important material rather than repeating everything verbatim. For example, if the client has been talking at some length about the many things that have been getting in the way of studying, the helper might give a restatement such as, "So you have not been able to study lately" or "Studying has been difficult for you lately," because these statements focus the client on what is important to explore at a deeper level.

The emphasis of restatements should be on the client's thoughts rather than on other people's thoughts. This focus enables the client to focus inwardly rather than blaming others or worrying about what others think. For example, a client was discussing her decision to move to the West Coast. During the session, she continuously focused on her colleagues' and friends' reactions to her decision. The helper worked to focus the restatements on the client ("You would like to move") rather than on her friends and colleagues ("Your friends don't want you to move").

The emphasis is on helping clients explore more deeply without having an agenda for what content should emerge. Helpers should not be judgmental and should not assume they know or understand what clients are experiencing. Helpers should not be invested in solving problems or disclosing their own problems; rather, they should be focused on hearing the client's story and facilitating exploration.

To reduce the tendency to become repetitive, helpers can vary the format of restatements. There are several ways to introduce restatements, for example:

"I hear you saying . . ."
"It sounds as though . . ."
"I wonder whether . . ."
"You're saying that . . ."
"So . . ."

Alternatively, helpers can just repeat and slightly draw out a key word clients have said, such as *divorce, music,* or *headache.* If the key word is presented in a questioning or inviting tone, it encourages the client to tell the helper more about the topic. For example, if a client has been talking about her daughter having just been tested and found to have an incredibly high IQ score, and the helper wants the client to explore more about IQs, she might simply say, "IQ . . . ?," thereby inviting the client to tell her more about what IQ means to her.

Although it is helpful when restatements are relatively close to what the client has said, it is not necessary (or often even possible) for the restatements to be perfectly accurate. For example, if a client presents a confused and jumbled statement of her concerns and the helper provides restatements that do not encapsulate the content accurately, the client can clarify what she means so both of them understand the situation better. Restatements thus allow clients a chance to clarify helpers' mistaken impressions.

EXAMPLE OF RESTATEMENT

The following shows a helper using restatements (in italics) in a session:

Client: I have to go on a pilgrimage to Mecca. I don't really want to go because it's the middle of my last semester in college and I'm worried that my grades will suffer if I leave for 2 weeks, but I don't have much choice. According to my religion, I have to go.

Helper: *You have to go.*

Client: Yeah, for my religion, we all have to do a pilgrimage before we get married. It's just expected. My father has to go with me because a man has to be on the pilgrimage, but I don't have a very good relationship with him, and he's not well, so I don't know if he can withstand the rigors of the trip. The last time he went with my brother, it was pretty disastrous.

Helper: *You said you don't have a very good relationship with your father.*

Client: Right. He wasn't around much when I was growing up. He was always too busy. And now to spend 2 weeks with him is a lot. I don't even know what we could talk about. I feel like I don't know him. I get anxious just thinking about spending a lot of time with him. But on the other hand, I wish I knew him better, so maybe this is an opportunity to get to know him.

Helper: *Really know him.*

Client: Yeah, really know him. I've always wanted to have a good relationship with him. People say that we're a lot alike. And he could teach me a lot about my religion and culture, things I don't know much about, given that I came to the United States when I was very young.

Helper: *So you could learn something from your father.*

Client: Oh yeah, I think I could learn a lot from him. He is a wise person. I just hope I can be myself with him.

I've always felt like such a little kid, and I would rather feel like an adult with him the way I can with my mother.

Helper: *Feel like an adult.*

Client: Yeah, I want to feel like myself when I am around him. I want to be able to behave like I do with other people. I want to get to know him as a person instead of feeling afraid of him. (Client continues to explore.)

DIFFICULTIES HELPERS EXPERIENCE IN RESTATING

Many helpers initially feel awkward and stilted using restatements because people do not typically paraphrase what another person has said in regular social communication. Many beginning helpers worry that clients will feel annoyed and say something like "I just said that." In fact, the reaction of clients is usually quite different when they are given a good restatement—they feel heard. Once students learn how to use restatements, they can be very useful not only in helping relationships but also with friends and family to demonstrate that one is really listening.

Another difficulty beginning helpers face is sounding like parrots if they continually use the same format to introduce restatements (e.g., "I hear you saying . . .") or if they repeat clients' messages verbatim. Clients often get annoyed with parroting and become distracted from focusing on their concerns. In a related vein, some helpers are so afraid of making a mistake when choosing key aspects of clients' messages that they repeat everything, taking the focus off the client and halting the flow of the interchange. Not surprisingly, clients quickly become bored and annoyed with such restatements, saying things like, "That's what I just said." Moreover, clients might feel stuck and aimless when restatements are mere repetitions of what they have said. By choosing the key components, focusing on the "cutting edge" of clients' concerns, varying the format, and keeping the restatements short, helpers can deal with these problems. It is also important to focus on being empathic rather than restating robotically. Some helpers get so caught up in capturing the content accurately that they forget the most important thing is to show the client that they are struggling to understand.

Some helpers feel frustrated when they use restatements because they feel they are not "doing" anything or giving the client specific answers. Restatements are used to help clients explore and tell their stories rather than come to insight or action, so helpers rarely feel brilliant when using them. In fact, clients often are not able to remember restatements because the focus is on them rather than on the helper.

EXHIBIT 6.2

Overview of Open Questions About Thoughts

Definition	*Open questions about thoughts* ask clients to clarify or explore thoughts. Helpers do not request specific information and do not purposely limit the nature of the client response to a "yes," "no," or one- or two-word answer, even though clients may respond that way. Open questions can be phrased as queries ("How do you think about that?") or as probes ("Tell me how you feel about that"), as long as the intent is to help the client clarify or explore.
Examples	"What were you thinking when you said that?" "Tell me more about your thoughts about that."
Typical helper intentions	To focus, to clarify, to encourage catharsis, to identify maladaptive cognitions (see Web Form D)
Possible client reactions	Clear (see Web Form G)
Desired client behaviors	Recounting, cognitive–behavioral exploration (see Web Form H)
Helpful hints	Make sure your questions are open instead of closed Vary the format of the open question Avoid multiple questions Avoid "why" questions Focus on the client rather than on others Focus on one part of the issue rather than trying to cover everything Have an intention for every question Observe client reactions to your questions

Open Questions About Thoughts

Open questions about thoughts help clients clarify and explore their thoughts. When using these leads, helpers do not want a specific answer from clients but instead want clients to explore whatever comes to mind. In other words, helpers do not purposely limit the nature of clients' responses to a "yes," "no," or one- or two-word answer, even though clients may respond that way (see Exhibit 6.2).

WHY USE OPEN QUESTIONS TO GET AT THOUGHTS?

Many researchers have found that open questions are used frequently in therapy and are generally perceived as being moderately helpful for the therapy process (Barkham & Shapiro, 1986; Elliott, 1985; Elliott, Barker, Caskey, & Pistrang, 1982; Fitzpatrick, Stalikas, & Iwakabe, 2001; Hill, Helms, Tichenor, et al., 1988; Martin, Martin, & Slemon, 1989). These studies suggest that open questions can be a useful intervention for encouraging clients to talk longer and more deeply about their concerns.

Open questions serve several purposes. They can be particularly useful when clients are rambling, repeating the same thoughts but not really exploring deeply. They can also be used to help clients clarify their thoughts when they are confused, lead clients to think about new things, help clients unravel conflicting thoughts, or provide structure for clients who are not very verbal or articulate. Clients often get stuck describing their problems and need open questions to help them think about different aspects of the problem. Open questions can also be used to clarify or focus and are particularly helpful when clients are starting the session, rambling, being vague or unclear, or stuck. As with restatements, open questions demonstrate that the helper is listening and interested in the client. They show the helper is tracking what the client says and is interested enough to encourage the client to keep talking.

In addition, if a client cannot think of what to talk about, open questions are a good way for helpers to provide direction. For example, if Justin has been talking about receiving a bad grade and has explored his feelings and then the dialogue stops, the helper might ask Justin what a bad grade means for the future. Other possible open questions might be to ask Justin to compare how this situation relates to past experiences with grades or how this grade affects his relationship with his parents. These open questions could help Justin talk more completely about other important aspects of the problem. I like comparing problems to a ball of yarn; with each probe helpers encourage clients to take out a bit of the yarn and talk about it. When one piece is explored thoroughly, helpers gently guide clients to talk about another piece of the problem.

Probes for thoughts can be considered as a subcategory of open questions about thoughts. With a probe, the helper makes a statement (e.g., "Tell me more about that") rather than asking a question, but the intent and consequence is the same. I recently heard a person say that the three kindest words you could hear are "Tell me more." Indicating curiosity and interest through judicious use of open questions for thoughts can truly be a gift.

In addition, open questions about examples are helpful when clients are talking generally and vaguely about problems. Asking for specific examples can give helpers a clearer picture of what the client is talking about (e.g., "Tell me about a specific time when you felt distant from your father").

HOW TO ASK OPEN QUESTIONS ABOUT THOUGHTS

There are several ways that open questions can be asked. For example:

- "Tell me about the last time you thought x."
- "Tell me more about x."
- "What's that like for you to think x?"

- "What do you think about that?"
- "What do you mean by that?"
- "What does x mean?"
- "Can you give me an example of that?"
- "What comes to mind when you think about x?"

Helpers should maintain the appropriate attending behaviors because the manner of presenting open questions is important. The tone of voice should be kept low and soft to convey concern and intimacy, the rate of speech should be slow, and the open question should be phrased tentatively to avoid sounding as though helpers are interrogating clients. Helpers should be supportive, nonjudgmental, and encouraging no matter what clients say because there are no right or wrong topics to explore and no right or wrong answers to questions.

Open questions should be short and simple. Clients may have difficulty following lengthy questions. Helpers should also avoid asking several questions at once because this can be confusing for clients. Multiple questions ("What did you do next, and what were you thinking, and what did you mean by that?") can have a dampening effect on the interaction if clients do not know which question to respond to first or feel bombarded. Clients might ignore important questions because they cannot respond to all of them.

Another guideline is that open questions about thoughts are most effective when helpers focus on one part of the problem at a time. Clients cannot talk about everything at once and may have difficulty choosing a single topic, so it can be helpful for helpers to pick the most important or salient issue to focus on and return to others later. Typically, the best issue to focus on is the one for which clients have the most energy or affect, or for what is at the "cutting edge" of a client's awareness. For example, if Juan is talking about several different topics, the helper might ask Juan a question about the topic that seems most unresolved or pressing.

In addition, helpers should keep the focus of the open question on the client ("How did you feel about your mother's behavior?") rather than turning the attention to other people ("What did your mother do in that situation?"). Keeping the focus on the client helps him or her explore what is going on inside rather than deflecting to other people. For example, if Jean often argues with her mother, the helper can ask about Jean's thoughts ("What are your thoughts when your mother starts yelling at you?") rather than asking Jean about her mother's thoughts ("What do you think your mother would say about this?"). Although it could be helpful to understand more about the mother, she is not in the room, and the helper is likely to get a one-sided view of her. The person the helper is most likely to help is the client, so it is typically better to focus on the client.

It is also important to keep the client focused on current thoughts rather than telling stories about past thoughts (e.g., "What do you think now about your procrastination?"). However, it is important to ask the client about previous experiences or memories related to the current problem (e.g., "What are your memories of other fights with your mother?") because such memories might have great relevance to how the client views the current situation. Helpers should avoid interrupting to ask open questions if the client is exploring productively (i.e., exploring at a deep level). It is better to allow the client to keep talking and only ask questions when the client is stuck or needs guidance about what to explore further.

One particular kind of open question I like to ask is, "Tell me your memories about that." This open question is particularly helpful when a client is describing a troubling current situation that you suspect might be influenced by past experiences. Thus, when Selina was talking about the effects of her father and stepmother breaking up, I asked about her memories of her mother and father's divorce. Selina was able to talk about painful memories that obviously were still affecting her and influencing how she was dealing with the current situation.

Helpers should also avoid "why" questions (e.g., "Why did you blow up at your boyfriend the other night?" "Why are you not able to study?") in the exploration stage because they are difficult to answer and can make the client defensive. As Nisbett and Wilson (1977) indicated, people rarely know why they do things. If they knew why they act as they do, they probably would not be talking to helpers. When someone asks why you did something, you might feel she or he is judging you and deriding you for not being able to handle the situation more effectively. Instead of "why" questions, helpers could use "what" or "how" questions (e.g., instead of "Why didn't you study for your exam?" the helper could ask "What was going on that kept you from studying?" "What was going through your mind when you were trying to study?" or "What is going on that makes it difficult for you to study?").

Finally, helpers should be aware of cultural differences in clients' responses to questions. D. W. Sue and Sue (1999) noted that people from some cultures may be uncomfortable when they are questioned or asked to initiate the dialogue (e.g., "What would you like to talk about today?") because it may be disrespectful. In such cases, helpers may have to be more direct, either in educating the client about the helping process or in suggesting topics to discuss. Helpers cannot assume, however, that clients from other cultures will not like open questions, but if they observe that clients seem uncomfortable with open questions, they can instead try other skills.

EXAMPLE OF OPEN QUESTIONS ABOUT THOUGHTS

The following shows a helper using open questions about thoughts (in italics) in a session:

> *Client:* My younger sisters are fighting a lot with each other. They really get nasty and have been hurting each other. My youngest sister was caught stealing from a store recently. My parents aren't doing anything about it, and my sisters are just going wild. I wish there was more I could do to help them. If I were still at home, they would listen to me. I think they don't have anyone to turn to. My parents are divorcing, so they're just not available to my sisters.
>
> *Helper:* *Tell me more about what it's like for you not to be there.*
>
> *Client:* On one hand, I'm delighted to be away from the mess. On the other hand, I feel guilty, like I survived the Titanic crash and came out alive but they're sinking.
>
> *Helper:* *What is it like when you are with your family?*
>
> *Client:* My parents are still living together, but they fight all the time. Things are pretty scary around the house because my parents get pretty violent with each other. I have to look out for my sisters. I am really more their parent than either of my parents are. I got to be pretty strong by having to fend for myself so much.
>
> *Helper:* *Can you give me a specific example of a time when you had to look after your sisters?*
>
> *Client:* Oh, yeah, just last night when I called home. My younger sister said that mom has started to throw dishes around and dad left the house in a huff and they haven't talked. No one even asks them about their schoolwork any more and they are running around wild. I don't know what to do for them from here. (Client continues exploring.)

DIFFICULTIES HELPERS EXPERIENCE IN DELIVERING OPEN QUESTIONS ABOUT THOUGHTS

A common problem is that helpers tend to ask the same type of open questions repeatedly, most often "What do you think about that?" Many clients become annoyed when they continually hear the same type of question and have a hard time responding.

Similarly, some beginning helpers use only open questions rather than interspersing open questions with restatements. Helpers tend to use open questions excessively when anxious because this skill is relatively easy and already exists in most helpers' repertoires. Unfortunately, the interaction can become one-sided if helpers use too many open questions. In this situation, helpers are not demonstrating that they are listening to what the clients are saying or struggling to understand the clients. The tone of the session can become stilted rather than being a mutual struggle to explore and understand the client's concerns.

DISTINGUISHING OPEN AND CLOSED QUESTIONS

Closed questions request a one- or two-word answer ("yes," "no," or a confirmation) and are used to gather information or data. Closed questions can ask for specific information, for example, "What was your test grade?" "How old were you when your parents were divorced?" or "Did you call the counseling center?"

Closed questions have a limited role in the helping process. The primary reason for using closed questions is to obtain specific information from clients, perhaps because the client has been vague and the helper needs more information to understand the situation. The most direct way to get this specific information is through closed questions. For example, when a client is vague about his or her family situation and the helper is struggling to understand the family dynamics, the helper might ask, "Are you the oldest child?" or "Where are you in the birth order?" In such situations, asking for needed information is better than making assumptions or being confused. The key is that the information is important for the therapeutic process.

Helpers can also use closed questions occasionally to ask for clarification, because they did not hear what the client said, or because they want to determine if clients understood or agreed with what they said. For example:

- "What did you say?"
- "Am I right?"
- "Is that what happened?"
- "Does that sound right to you?"
- "Did I understand you correctly?"

Another situation in which closed questions are important is during a crisis situation. If there is a crisis (e.g., the potential for suicide, homicide, violence, or abuse of any kind or decompensation into serious mental illness), the process changes from helping to crisis management. In these situations, helpers need to ask clients directly about what is happening so they can make appropriate referrals (see also chap. 18). If such a situation occurs while you are in training, immediately seek out supervisors who can help you figure out how to handle the situation.

Closed questions are appropriate for certain types of interview situations, such as a medical doctor gathering information to make a diagnosis, interrogations by lawyers during courtroom trials, or job interviews. In these situations, the roles between the interviewer and interviewee are often distinct. The interviewer asks the question to get the desired information; the respondent answers the questions. The control of the interview usually stays with the interviewer, who directs the interaction by asking questions.

An example of an interview situation in which closed questions are useful is in academic advising. When a student comes to me in my role as an academic advisor asking about her or his chances of being accepted into graduate school, my goal is to gather enough information about the student's credentials (e.g., grade point average, Graduate Records Exam [GRE] scores, research and clinical experience, career goals) to make an assessment. The best and most efficient way of gathering such information quickly is typically through closed questions (e.g., "What are your grade point average and GRE score?" "What research experiences have you had?" "Where do you hope to be employed after graduate school?"). I try to ask the closed questions in a supportive, empathic, nonjudgmental fashion, without attempting to determine what students should do with their lives or pass judgment on their effectiveness as human beings. Once I have the information, I can assess how likely it is that the student will be admitted to graduate school. If I think the student needs help in exploring values, feelings, options, and talents, I typically refer the student to the campus counseling center because these tasks are not part of my role as an academic adviser.

Although closed questions can be helpful in interview situations, they have limited applicability in helping settings because they typically do not help clients explore. Helpers slip into an interviewer role and quickly become responsible for directing the interaction. They become interviewers rather than helpers. Once trapped in the interviewer role and having to think about the next question, helpers often have difficulty changing the course of the session and encouraging exploration. In these situations, clients can become dependent on helpers for the next question. Rather than exploring problems deeply, clients often respond passively and wait for the next question.

Given the theoretical premise that helpers are trying to facilitate clients in their self-healing efforts rather than acting as experts who diagnose and "treat" clients, they do not typically need much specific information. Specific information does not help facilitate exploration of values, feelings, options, and talents. Before asking questions, helpers should thus think about what they are going to do with the information once it is provided. Helpers can ask themselves, "Whose need am I fulfilling with the information I gain from closed questions?" If the information will be used to facilitate the process of exploring for the client, helpers should ask the question. If the information is desired for voyeurism, curiosity, to fill the silence, or to make a diagnosis and fix the problem, helpers should probably not ask the closed question during the exploration stage.

When helpers use closed questions, they follow the same guidelines for implementation as were proposed for open questions. In other words, helpers should use an empathic and inviting manner to encourage the client to explore rather than just answer the simple question. Furthermore, helpers should refrain from asking multiple closed questions. As with too many open questions asked at once, clients can feel bombarded and have a hard time knowing which questions to answer first. Helpers should also avoid closed questions (questions that have a specific desired answer, e.g., "yes," "no," or specific information) that limit exploration. More important, helpers need to notice what happens when they use closed questions. Helpers should determine for themselves whether control of the interaction shifts back to them when they use too many closed questions. Do closed questions make you feel like a grand inquisitor? Helpers can also ask clients for their reactions to closed questions to determine the effects of these interventions.

Most beginners use too many closed questions because this skill is a familiar way of interacting outside of the helping situation. In social interactions, people often ask a lot of closed questions to get the details of exactly what happened. The goal in these interactions is to get the facts of the story rather than to help another person express or explore feelings, as it is in helping.

Helpers sometimes use closed questions inappropriately to satisfy their curiosity. They might ask for information out of voyeurism rather than to help the clients explore. For example, Martha was working on her feelings of jealousy of and competitiveness with her older sister. Martha came into the session and announced that her sister had a date with a "hot" movie star. The helper exclaimed, "Wow, how did she meet him?" or "What was he like?" Although extreme, this example illustrates how helpers can get carried away with asking for specific information to satisfy their own curiosity rather than to help clients explore. It also illustrates how the focus can easily shift away from the client to others.

A particularly egregious type of closed question occurs when the helper is condescending or tries to coerce the client into responding a particular way (e.g., "You really don't want to keep drinking, do you?"). Such questions take the focus away from the client and make the helper seem like an expert who knows how the client should behave.

I would not go so far as to say that helpers should never use closed questions, given that they can occasionally be helpful. I do, however, encourage beginning helpers to reduce the number of closed questions they use and instead use more open questions and restatements. When helpers do need to use closed questions to gather specific necessary information (sometimes history is important for gaining awareness of context), they can follow up with the other exploration skills to help clients get back to exploration.

Students often ask how to distinguish closed and open questions. I suggest that you see whether the question can be made to be more open. If it can be made more open, it is probably a closed question. For example, the closed question "Did you get an A?" can be changed to "How do you feel about how you did on the test?" The latter question is much more open. One important thing about open questions is that they allow the client to explore what is important to them. For example, Mary was wondering where her client Sam was in the family birth order. She almost asked him this as a closed question but decided to practice making it open. She said, "Tell me more about your siblings," which led to Sam exploring in detail the many conflicts and tensions in the family and how he felt everyone babied him because he was the youngest. Mary got far more information than she probably would have with a closed question.

A Comparison of Skills for Exploring Thoughts

Restatements help clients hear what they have been saying and enable them to correct mistakes and expand further. With restatements, clients often feel that helpers are listening to them and understand them. In contrast, open questions about thoughts directly ask the client to explore more, so they give guidance about what the helper wants the client to do at that moment and therefore can be helpful when the client is not sure what to do or needs a little direction. I recommend using mostly restatements, with occasional open questions.

What Do You Think?

- Debate the efficacy of restatements compared with responses that are more typically used in friendships, such as advice and self-disclosure.
- Compare and contrast restatements and open questions about thoughts.

- In his early theorizing, Rogers (1942) promoted restatement at the most important skill, whereas later he focused more on other skills. What do you think about restatements?
- How do you respond when people use restatements or open questions in conversation with you?
- What cultural considerations can you think of in using restatements or open questions?
- Do you agree that helpers should not ask "why" questions in the exploration stage?
- Debate the merits of focusing on thoughts versus feelings?

i PRACTICE EXERCISES

A downloadable PDF of this chapter's Practice Exercises is available in the student resources area of the Helping Skills, *3rd ed. Web site: http://www.apa.org/books/resources/Hill3.*

Pretend that a client makes the following statements to you. Read each of these statements, and then write both a restatement and a probe for thoughts. Compare your responses with the possible helper responses provided at the end of this practice exercise. The helper responses that are given are not the "right" or "best," but they are provided to give you some idea of the different possibilities of ways to respond.

Statements

1. Client: "I have a lot of work to do for my classes. But I don't know when I'm going to do it because I have to work 20 hours a week at my job. When I come home from classes and working, I just don't have any energy to do schoolwork. I feel like I need a chance to just 'veg' out and watch TV."

   Helper restatement: _____

   Helper open question about thoughts: _____

2. Client: "After I graduate, I am going to take a cross-country trip. At first I was just going to go by myself, but then my roommates heard about it, and both of them said they wanted to go. I rearranged my schedule to accommodate them, and now one of them says he isn't going."

   Helper restatement: _____

   Helper open question about thoughts: _____

3. Client: "My mother is going through a divorce. She talks to me every night about it, which seems a little odd since I'm only 9 years old. She says she has no one else to talk to. The guy she married after my father left her is a real jerk. He beat her up and is an alcoholic."

   Helper restatement: _____

   Helper open question about thoughts: _____

Possible Helper Responses

1. "You don't have much energy right now for your schoolwork."
   "When you get home from work, you don't really want to do schoolwork."

"Tell me more about that."

"What thoughts go through your head when you 'veg' out?"

2. "You've made a lot of adjustments in your plans for your friends."

"You just learned that your friend will not accompany you on your trip."

"Tell me more about your relationship with this friend."

"What are you hoping for from this trip?"

3. "You're thinking a lot about your mother lately."

"Lots of responsibility."

"What is it like for you to hear your mother talk about this divorce?"

"Give me an example of what your mother said last night?"

---

i LAB 5. Exploring Thoughts

A downloadable PDF of this Lab is available in the student resources area of the Helping Skills, *3rd ed. Web site: http://www.apa.org/books/resources/hill3.*

Goals:
1. To give helpers an opportunity to attend and listen to clients.
2. To encourage helpers to focus on the most important part of the client's statements.
3. To practice using restatements and open questions to help the client explore thoughts.

Exercise 1: One-Word Restatements

The helper repeats the single most important word or phrase the client has said. For example, if the client says, "I am having a terrible dilemma. I just found out my best friend's boyfriend cheated on her. I don't know whether I should tell her, because she would be so hurt," the helper might say, "dilemma" or "best friend." Continue for 8 to 10 client-speaking turns.

Exercise 2: Practice Formulating Restatements

1. In a large group, the group leader verbally gives an example of a client statement (keep it simple, brief, and not very emotional). Each student writes a restatement and then reads his or her restatements out loud. Continue with examples until the leader is certain that students understand and can deliver restatements.
2. Still in a large group, the leader asks one student to be the client and talk about something easy—something about which he or she does not have many feeling (suggested topics: cars, politics, weather, technology, hobbies, extracurricular activities). After the "client" talks for a while, the students all write down a restatement. Once everyone is done writing, the leader asks them in turn to deliver their restatement to the client. The client should respond as he or she would if talking to this person.

Exercise 3: Practice Formulating Open Questions for Thoughts

Do the same as for Exercise 2 but with open questions for thoughts.

Exercise 4: Practice Integrating Skills in Role-Play

Students should be arranged in groups of three, with lab leaders monitoring the groups. Within groups, choose one person to be the helper, one to be the client, and one to be the observer.

Helper's and Client's Tasks During the Helping Exchange

1. The helper introduces him- or herself (see Lab 1 for possible format).
2. The client talks briefly on a topic about which he or she does not have a lot of strong feelings/emotions.
3. The helper listens attentively during the client statement without thinking of what she or he is going to say next. After the client statement, the helper pauses, takes a deep breath, thinks of what to say, and then either restates what the client said (using fewer words and focusing on the most essential part of the statement) or asks open questions about thoughts. For this exercise, the helper focuses on content rather than feelings. Remember to use appropriate attending behaviors throughout the exercise.
4. Continue for 5 to 10 turns.

Observer's Task During the Helping Exchange

Take notes about the helper's attending behaviors. Write down each helper statement in sequence and note whether it is a restatement, an open question, or other.

After the Helping Exchange

1. The helper talks about how it felt to do restatements and ask open questions.
2. The client says how it felt to receive restatements and open questions. The client also gives feedback to the helper about what was most and least helpful.
3. The observer gives feedback to the helper about the use of restatements, open questions, and attending skills. Give positive feedback first and then only one piece of negative feedback (go back and read about feedback in chap. 1).

Switch Roles

Keep doing role-plays as described above until everyone has had a chance to be the helper, client, and observer at least once.

Large Group Go-Round

Going around the circle one at a time, each person should say first what he or she did well. In a second go-round, each person can say what he or she is going to continue to work on and how he or she might do that.

Personal Reflections

- How did you handle any anxiety you might have experienced giving restatements and open questions about thoughts?
- In the past, students have had difficulty formulating short concise restatements, focusing on content instead of feelings, figuring out what to focus on in the client's statements, talking too much, and keeping the focus on the client. Which of these experiences did you have? How might you handle such challenges?
- What did you learn about yourself in trying to be a helper?
- What difficulties did you have combining skills?

Skills for Exploring Feelings 7

It seems to me that clients who have moved significantly in therapy live more intimately with their feelings of pain, but also more vividly with their feelings of ecstasy; that anger is more clearly felt, but so also is love; that fear is an experience they know more deeply, but so is courage.

—Carl Rogers

Tyler, an aspiring actor, had been in an automobile accident that left him with a disability and made it unlikely he would ever be able to act again. Throughout the session, his helper used a number of reflections (e.g., "You feel angry because you can no longer do what you love to do," "I wonder if you feel afraid that people will laugh at you," "It sounds like you feel anxious about going out in public") to help Tyler talk about his many feelings so he could identify and accept what was going on inside him. The helper also asked some open questions (e.g., "How do you really feel about that?") that helped Tyler stop and think about what he was really feeling and then try to express his feelings. Once he was able to express his feelings, Tyler felt relieved.

Rationale for Exploring Feelings

Clients typically seek helping because they are distressed. Therefore, it makes sense to help them explore their feelings of distress. As Rogers noted (see chap. 4), emotions are a key part of our experience. They tell us how we are reacting to the world. Often we ignore, deny, distort, or repress feelings because we have been told they are unacceptable (e.g., being told "big boys don't cry"). Hence, we grow apart from our inner experiencing and cannot accept ourselves. We need to return to and allow ourselves to feel our emotions because only then can we decide what to do about them.

Feelings are at least as important as content or thoughts in client communication. Clients seem to be most able to solve their problems when they get in touch with their feelings (see also Elliott, Watson, Goldman, & Greenberg, 2004). Experiencing feelings allows clients to evaluate events in terms of their inner experiencing.

Clients' expression of emotions enables helpers to know and understand them. People respond differently to events, so helpers need to know how experiences are interpreted by individual clients. For example, when Varda came to a helper's office because her father died, the helper initially assumed that Varda felt sad, depressed, and lonely because that is how the helper felt when her father died. But in fact, Varda felt angry because she had been having intrusive memories of childhood sexual abuse since her father died. It was safe for Varda to remember the abuse only when her father was no longer able to hurt her. In addition, Varda felt relief that her father died because she no longer had to deal with him. This example illustrates the importance of listening carefully and not imposing assumptions on clients.

If clients accept their emotions, they can become open to new feelings and experiences. Feelings are not static but change once they are experienced. When a person experiences a feeling fully and completely, new feelings often emerge. For example, once Varda experienced her anger, she became aware of other feelings such as sadness, which then led eventually to feelings of acceptance and peace.

In contrast, unaccepted feelings are likely to "leak" out, sometimes in destructive ways. For example, Robert became subtly rude or hostile to a friend who was accepted into a prestigious law school after Robert learned that his own application had been rejected. All of us know people who do not directly say they are angry but indirectly communicate subtle, nasty messages that make it difficult to respond to them. Other people get stuck because they cannot accept their feelings. Similar to the obstruction that occurs when a river gets dammed up, these people get blocked if they do not allow themselves to have and express their feelings.

Feelings are rarely simple or straightforward; therefore, it is important to note that clients might have several conflicting feelings about a topic. For example, Diana might feel excited about taking a new job and pleased that she was selected over other candidates. However, she might also feel anxious about what is required of her, afraid of working too closely with the boss (who reminds her of her father), insecure about how others may view her, and worried about whether she can make enough money to pay the rent. It is important for helpers to encourage clients to experience and express as many feelings as possible without worrying about whether the feelings are rational, ambiguous, or contradictory.

Anger, sadness, fear, shame, pain, and hurt seem to be the most important emotions involved in therapeutic change (Greenberg, 2002). These negative emotions are often bottled up and not expressed or experienced because of shame and fear of disapproval. Many people cannot allow themselves to even think about such feelings. Hence, clients require a supportive environment to feel safe enough to express these feelings openly.

In addition, it is important to note that sometimes emotions exist in layers (Greenberg, 2002; Teyber, 2006). For example, after anger is expressed and experienced, sadness and shame often emerge. Inversely, after sadness is expressed and experienced, anger and guilt often emerge. Similarly, gestalt therapists believe every feeling has two sides. If clients talk only about fear, helpers might wonder about wishes; if clients talk only about love, helpers might wonder about hate. By fostering deeper thought about the feelings, helpers enable clients to admit the multitude of feelings they might not otherwise have been able to acknowledge.

Clients who can experience, accept, and own their feelings can then decide how to behave. Clients do not have to act on the feelings, but they can make more informed decisions about what to do when feelings are out in the open. In fact, being aware of one's feelings makes one less likely to act on them unintentionally.

There are lots of ways to help clients explore feelings, and it is probably best to vary the approach so that helpers do not start to sound robotic. My favorite skill is reflection of feelings because, when used appropriately, it conveys empathy, that the helper is listening to the client, and that the helper is struggling to understand the client. Disclosures of feelings and open questions about feelings are also helpful skills for identifying and intensifying feelings.

Reflection of Feelings

A *reflection of feelings* is a helper statement that explicitly labels the client's feelings (see Exhibit 7.1). The feelings may have been stated by the client (in either the same or similar words), or the helper may be able to infer the feelings from the client's nonverbal behavior or from the content of the client's message. The reflection may be phrased either tentatively (e.g., "I wonder if you're feeling angry?") or more directly (e.g., "It

EXHIBIT 7.1

Overview of Reflection of Feelings

Definition	A *reflection of feelings* is a repeating or rephrasing of the client's statements, including an explicit identification of feelings. The feelings may have been stated by the client (in exactly the same or similar words), or the helper may infer feelings from the client's nonverbal behavior, the context, or the content of the client's message. The reflection may be phrased either tentatively or as a statement.
Examples	"You feel angry at your husband for not being home."
	"You seem pleased that you told your boss you didn't want to work late."
Typical intentions	To identify and intensify feelings, to encourage catharsis, to clarify, to instill hope, to encourage self-control (see Web Form D)
Possible client reactions	Feelings, negative thoughts or behaviors, clear, responsibility, unstuck, scared, worse, misunderstood (see Web Form G)
Desired client behavior	Affective exploration (see Web Form H)
Helpful hints	Listen for the underlying feelings
	Capture the most salient feeling to reflect to the client
	Reflect only one feeling at a time
	State the feeling tentatively, with empathy, and without judgment
	Try to match the intensity of the feeling
	Reflect what the client is feeling presently
	Keep the reflection short and simple
	Focus on the client's feelings rather than on the feelings of other people
	Vary the format of reflections
	Vary the feeling words you use

sounds to me like you're feeling angry"). The emphasis can be just on the feeling (e.g., "You feel upset") or on both the feeling and the reason for the feeling (e.g., "You feel upset because your teacher did not notice all the work you have done").

Helpers use reflections to help clients identify, clarify, and experience feelings on a deeper level. Reflections encourage clients to become immersed in their inner experiences. Rather than just stating a feeling, however, helpers need to stress the importance of helping clients experience feelings in the immediate moment (i.e., an experience is more important than an explanation). For example, a couple might recount an incident in which they became angry with one another. The helper would encourage them to express their current feelings and talk to each other about how they are feeling about the incident now. Another intention is to encourage emotional catharsis with reflections. Cathartic relief occurs when feelings begin to flow rather than being stuck or bottled up and when clients accept their feelings.

BENEFITS OF REFLECTIONS OF FEELINGS

Reflections of feelings are ideal interventions for enabling clients to enter into their internal experiences, especially if delivered with concern and empathy for clients' reluctance to experience the painful feelings. Clients often need such assistance to recognize and accept their feelings and themselves.

Clients often have difficulty identifying and accepting feelings on their own, perhaps because they do not know how they feel, are ambivalent or negative about the feelings, or have been punished for having had such feelings in the past. Furthermore, it can be difficult to articulate feelings because they are often sensations rather than fully understood awarenesses. People often do not have words to symbolize feelings, so working together with helpers to struggle to label feelings helps clients identify the feelings.

Hearing reflections also enables clients to rethink and reexamine what they really feel. If a helper uses the term *disgusted,* this forces the client to think about whether *disgusted* fits his or her experience. This searching can lead to deeper exploration of the feelings in an attempt to clarify the feeling. It is often difficult for clients to verbalize their deepest, most private thoughts and feelings. In a safe and supportive relationship they can begin to explore the feelings, which are often complex and contradictory. They can feel a combination of love, hatred, and guilt toward the same person in the same situation. Being allowed to admit these ambivalent feelings to another person without rejection can enable clients to accept feelings as their own.

Reflections also validate feelings. Laing and Esterson (1970) suggested that people stop feeling "crazy" when their subjective experience is validated. It is easy to feel that one is the only person who has ever felt a certain way, so hearing helpers calmly label feelings can help clients see that such feelings are acceptable and that helpers accept clients as they are.

Reflections of feelings can also be used to model the expression of feelings, which could be useful for clients who are out of touch with their emotions. Many people experience an emotion but do not have a label for the feeling. For example, saying "I wonder if you feel frustrated with your sister" suggests that frustration is a feeling a person might have in this situation. By labeling feelings, helpers also imply that they are not afraid of feelings, that feelings are familiar, and that clients are acceptable regardless of their feelings. By suggesting a feeling, reflections might circumvent clients' defenses or possible embarrassment about having the feelings. Helpers thus indicate through reflections that the feelings are normal and that they accept the person who has the feelings.

Coming up with reflections requires that the helper work at least as hard as the client is working. Reflections demonstrate that the helper is actively engaged in trying to understand the client. It also forces the helper to communicate his or her understanding of the client's feelings so the helper can investigate the accuracy of his or her perceptions. The helper could say, "I understand exactly how you feel," but this statement does not demonstrate to the client the content of the understanding. Reflections provide an opportunity for helpers to show their understanding. Beginning helpers quickly discover that accurately perceiving and communicating how another person feels is difficult. Although we can never truly understand another person, as helpers, we can struggle to get past our own perceptions and try to immerse ourselves in the client's experiences and empathize with the client.

Finally, reflections can help to build the relationship because helpers are working hard to understand their clients. If clients feel the helpers' empathy and understanding and are able to talk with them openly and explore their feelings, the therapeutic relationship is likely to build.

Reflections of feelings are thus ideal interventions for encouraging client expression of feelings because helpers give examples of what clients might be experiencing. Clients can then begin to recognize and accept feelings, and helpers accept clients' feelings as natural and normal. In addition, clients can give helpers feedback about what they did or did not understand if helpers clearly articulate what they think clients are feeling.

HOW REFLECTION OF FEELINGS RELATES TO EMPATHY

Some authors have equated reflection of feeling with empathy (e.g., Carkhuff, 1969; Egan, 1994). I disagree with this stance because it is too narrow to define *empathy* as just reflection of feeling (see also Duan & Hill, 1996). I agree with Rogers (1957) that empathy is an attitude or way of being in tune with the experience of another person. If delivered appropriately, however, a reflection of feelings could be a manifestation of empathy. A technically correct reflection of feelings, on the other hand, could be unempathic if it is delivered at the wrong time or in an inappropriate manner. For example, if a helper says, "you feel humiliated" in an all-knowing, firm voice, the client may feel put down or misunderstood. The client may feel that the helper understands her better than she understands herself, which could make her mistrust her own feelings and submit to the helper as the authority.

There are times when it is more empathic to use a helping skill other than a reflection (e.g., a challenge). A helper responding to a client who feels stuck in an abusive relationship might challenge the client's decision to stay in the abusive situation. This response might be very empathic given the dangerous situation in the home and the helper's valuing of the client as a person deserving of a healthy relationship.

HOW TO REFLECT FEELINGS

Clients need to feel safe enough in the therapeutic relationship to risk delving into their feelings. They must feel that they will not be disparaged, embarrassed, or shamed but rather accepted, valued, and respected when they reveal themselves. Hence, reflections must be done gently and with empathy.

When learning to do reflections, a helpful format is to say:

- "You feel ____"

or

- "You feel ____ because ____"

In other words, helpers can say just the feeling word to highlight the feeling (e.g., "Angry" or "You feel angry"). Or, they can say both the feeling and the reason for the feeling (e.g., "You feel frustrated because you didn't get your way") to provide supporting data for why the client has the feeling.

Once helpers grasp how to do reflections, they can vary the format so clients do not become annoyed with repetitiveness. If the helper says, "It sounds like you're feeling . . ." 20 times in a row, it is not surprising that the client would notice, which would take away from the client's exploration. The following are some alternative formats:

- "I wonder if you're feeling ____"
- "Perhaps you're feeling ____"
- "You sound (or seem) ____"
- "Could you be ____?"
- "From your nonverbals, I would guess you're feeling ____"
- "It sounds like you feel ____"
- "Perhaps you feel ____"
- "So you're feeling ____"
- "And that made you feel ____"
- "I hear you saying you feel ____"
- "My hunch is that you feel ____"
- "You're ____"
- "Upset" (or whatever feeling word is most appropriate)

Using a metaphor instead of a feeling word can also be helpful. For example, the helper might say, "It's like you're in a fog" or "It sounds like you felt like you were run over by a truck."

Helpers should pick the most salient feeling rather than reflect all of the feelings in a single reflection. Selecting the most salient feeling requires a judgment call, so helpers need to be attentive to clients' verbal and nonverbal behavior. To detect the most powerful immediate feelings, helpers can pay attention to where the most energy is in what the client is saying or how the client is reacting nonverbally.

Not only is the specific feeling important, but helpers also need to try to match the intensity of the feeling (Skovholt & Rivers, 2003). For example, the intensity of anger could range from a mild "irritated" to a stronger "mad" to an even stronger "enraged." Similarly, the intensity of happiness could range from "okay" to "happy" to "ecstatic." Helpers can also vary the intensity of a feeling word by using modifiers, such as "somewhat" or "very" (e.g., "somewhat upset" vs. "very upset").

It is also sometimes useful for helpers to state the feelings tentatively (e.g., "Perhaps you're feeling upset?") to encourage clarification. Stating feelings too definitely (e.g., "You obviously are angry at your mother") can preclude exploration because clients might feel that there is no reason to struggle to identify the inner feeling. Hence, it is best to adopt a quizzical tone, such as "I wonder if you might be feeling ___?"

In addition, given that the goal of helpers is to allow clients to immerse themselves in their feelings so they can come to accept these feelings, helpers should focus on what the client is feeling in the present moment about the situation because these are the feelings that are very alive. By focusing on feeling present in the moment, helpers guide clients to experience their immediate feelings rather than telling stories about past feelings (e.g., "You sound irritated right now as you talk about your mother" rather than "It sounds like you were upset with your mother when that happened"). Remember that a person can have feelings in the present about something that happened in the past (e.g., "You still feel angry as you think about what he said").

I also suggest that helpers allow clients time to absorb and think about the reflections that are presented rather than rushing quickly to the next feeling. If the client starts crying or getting upset, the helper can encourage him or her to experience and express these feelings rather than trying to "take away" the feelings or make the client feel better. Pause, go slowly, and do not interrupt when the client is experiencing feelings; at the same time, be there with the client and reflect her or his feelings.

Helpers need to remember that feelings are multifaceted and change over time. New feelings emerge as old feelings are experienced and expressed. Understanding and reflecting feelings at one point in time are just the beginning of entering into an experiential process; helpers need to constantly look for new feelings that emerge during the exploration process.

Because the goal is to reflect feelings and keep the focus on the client, helpers need to be aware of staying in the background and facilitating exploration. Helpers can reach this goal by maintaining a supportive and listening stance. Good reflections should almost not be noticed by clients because these interventions help clients continue exploring and paying more attention to themselves than to the helper.

IDENTIFYING FEELING WORDS

Many beginning helpers have difficulty coming up with a range of words to describe the emotions expressed in a given situation. Exhibit 7.2 is a checklist of emotion words developed from several sources (Greenberg, 2002; Hill, Siegelman, Gronsky, Sturniolo, & Fretz, 1981; student feedback; lists collected from various unknown sources). Feel free to highlight favorite words and also to add words to the list to personalize it. (The Emotion Words Checklist is available as a downloadable PDF in the book's Web area, at http://www.apa.org/books/resources/Hill3.)

Note that this list includes both positive and negative emotions. Negative emotions outnumber positive emotions by about two to one (Izard, 1977), especially in a helping situation; however, helpers need to remember to focus on positive as well as negative emotions so clients feel encouraged about changes they are making.

SOURCES OF REFLECTIONS

Clues about what a client is feeling can be found in four sources: (a) the client's portrayal of his or her feelings, (b) the client's verbal content, (c) the client's nonverbal behavior, and (d) the helper's projection of his or her own feelings onto the client. Helpers need to be aware that the last three sources only provide clues and may not necessarily accurately reflect a client's feelings.

Client's Expression of Feeling

Sometimes clients are aware of their feelings and express them openly. For example, a client might say, "I was really upset with my teacher. I was so mad that she wouldn't even listen when I told her my feelings." The helper might use another word (e.g., "furious") to describe the feelings so the client can experience feelings at a deeper level and explore other aspects of the feelings. The client has signaled her or his readiness to talk about feelings, so the helper can help the client move into deeper exploration. I recommend using synonyms rather than repeating the exact feeling word the client has used. In this way, the client can find the best label for the feelings and also experience the different parts of the feelings.

EXHIBIT 7.2

Emotion Words Checklist

Calm–relaxed

at ease	at peace	calm	comforted	comfortable
complacent	composed	contented	easygoing	mellow
peaceful	quiet	relaxed	relieved	safe
satisfied	serene	soothed	tranquil	warm

Joyful–excited

amused	animated	blissful	captivated	cheerful
delighted	eager	elated	ecstatic	enchanted
energized	enthusiastic	euphoric	exhilarated	excited
fantastic	glad	gleeful	happy	high
hopeful	joyful	jubilant	lighthearted	loved
lucky	marvelous	optimistic	overjoyed	pleased
positive	superb	thrilled		

Vigorous–active

active	adventurous	alert	alive	ambitious
animated	bubbly	busy	daring	energetic
free	invigorated	lively	motivated	reckless
refreshed	renewed	revitalized	spirited	vibrant
vigorous	vivacious	wild		

Proud–competent

accomplished	admired	attractive	beautiful	bold
brave	capable	competent	confident	courageous
deserving	effective	efficient	empowered	fearless
forceful	gifted	handsome	heroic	important
independent	influential	intelligent	invincible	looked up to
lovely	mighty	pleased	powerful	prosperous
proud	purposeful	respected	responsible	satisfied
self-reliant	steady	strong	successful	sure
talented	triumphant	victorious	wise	worthy

Loved–loving

accepted	affectionate	attached to	cared for	desire for
devoted to	encouraged	fond of	included	love/loved
needed	protected	safe	secure	supported
trust/trusted	understood	wanted		

Concerned–caring

accepting	caring	charitable	comforting	compassionate
concerned	considerate	cooperative	empathic	forgiving
generous	gentle	giving	helpful	interested
kind	loving	nice	pity	protective of
receptive	responsive	responsible for	sensitive	sorry for
sympathetic	tender	understanding	unselfish	warm
worried about				

Luck–deserving

appreciative	deserving	entitled	fortunate	grateful
justified	lucky	thankful	warranted	

EXHIBIT 7.2 *(Continued)*

Emotion Words Checklist

Inspired

enlightened	enriched	impressed	inspired	transported
uplifted				

Completed–finished

completed	done	finished	fulfilled

Surprised–shocked

amazed	astonished	astounded	awestruck	flabbergasted
immobilized	numb	paralyzed	shocked	shaken
speechless	startled	stunned	surprised	taken aback

Anxious–afraid

afraid	agitated	alarmed	anxious	apprehensive
at a loss	defenseless	desperate	dread	edgy
fearful	fidgety	frantic	frightened	horrified
hysterical	ill at ease	impatient	insecure	jumpy
jittery	out of control	overwhelmed	panicky	petrified
nervous	on edge	restless	scared	stressed
tense	tentative	terrified	threatened	uncomfortable
uneasy	vulnerable	worried		

Bothered–upset

annoyed	bothered	burdened	distressed	disturbed
perturbed	troubled	rattled	restless	shaken
shook	upset	uptight	unbalanced	worried

Angry–hostile

aggravated	agitated	angry	bitter	defiant
displeased	dissatisfied	enraged	exasperated	frustrated
furious	hateful	heartless	hostile	incensed
indignant	infuriated	irate	irked	irritated
mad	miffed	nasty	outraged	pissed off
provoked	rebellious	resentful	resistant	ruthless
spiteful	unforgiving	vehement	vengeful	vindictive
violent	vicious			

Contempt–disgust

better than	contemptuous	disgusted	indignant	look down
nauseated	repelled	repulsed by	revulsion	righteous
scornful	sickened	superior	turned off	

Sad–depressed

blue	distraught	down	defeated	dejected
demoralized	depressed	despondent	discouraged	down
gloomy	glum	grief	heartsick	low
melancholy	miserable	morose	mournful	numb
pessimistic	resigned	sad	somber	sorrowful
tearful	unhappy			

Shame–guilt

apologetic	ashamed at	fault	bad	belittled
blameworthy	culpable	degraded	disgraced	embarrassed
				(continued)

EXHIBIT 7.2 (*Continued*)

Emotion Words Checklist

exposed	foolish	guilty	humbled	humiliated
mortified	naughty	put down	mocked	regretful
remorseful	ridiculous	rotten	scorned	shamed
sorry	stupid			

Inadequate–weak–helpless

cowardly	deficient	feeble	fragile	helpless
hopeless	impaired	inadequate	incapable	incompetent
ineffective	inefficient	inept	inferior	insecure
insignificant	overwhelmed	pathetic	powerless	rejected
small	stupid	unable	unacceptable	unfit
unimportant	unqualified	unworthy	useless	vulnerable
weak	worthless			

Intimidated–controlled

bossed	bullied	controlled	dominated	intimidated
intruded on	obligated	overpowered	picked on	pressured
pushed around	put upon			

Lonely–unloved–excluded

abandoned	alienated	alone	apart	cut off
discounted	distant	empty	homesick	ignored
isolated	left out	lonely	lonesome	neglected
overlooked	rejected	uncared for	unimportant	unloved
unpopular	unwanted	unwelcome		

Hurt–cheated–criticized–blame

abused	accused	belittled	betrayed	blamed
cheated	criticized	crushed	degraded	deprived
devastated	disappointed	disliked	forsaken	hurt
judged	injured	let down	mistreated	misunderstood
overlooked	pained	put down	rejected	victimized
wounded				

Burdensome–tolerated–obligated

burdensome	endured	indebted	in the way	obligated
put up with	tolerated			

Manipulated–exploited

abused	exploited	imposed upon	manipulated	managed
maneuvered	overworked	placated	pressured	used

Tired–apathetic

apathetic	bored	disinterest	drained	exhausted
fatigued	indifferent	lukewarm	resigned	run down
sleepy	sluggish	tired	unconcerned	unimpressed
uninterested	unmoved	weary		

Confused–bewildered

baffled	bewildered	conflicted	confused	disorganized
doubtful	flustered	hesitant	lost	mixed up
mystified	perplexed	puzzled	stuck	torn
uncertain	undecided	unsure		

EXHIBIT 7.2 *(Continued)*

Emotion Words Checklist

		Reluctant		
cautious	guarded	hesitant	inhibited	reluctant
shy	timid	wary		
		Compelled–determined		
compelled	determined	driven	haunted	obsessed
obstinate	stubborn	tormented		
		Jealous–mistrustful		
envious	jealous	mistrustful	paranoid	suspicious

Client's Verbal Content

Another source of clues about feelings is verbal content. Although the client may not be mentioning feelings directly, it may be possible to infer the feelings from the client's words. For example, clients often respond to a major loss with feelings of sadness, respond to success with feelings of pleasure, and respond to anger directed at them with fear. Hence, helpers can make preliminary hypotheses about what clients might feel. For example, an adolescent client might mention that she received her report card and had improved her grades in almost every subject. The helper might say, "You must feel proud of yourself for raising your grades." Helpers need to be cautious, tentative, and ready to revise their reflections, however, on the basis of feedback from the client. Helpers cannot know everything about clients and will need to amend their reflections as they gather more information and as the feelings emerge and change in sessions.

Nonverbal Behaviors

How the client appears nonverbally is a third source of clues for feelings. For example, if the client is smiling and looks pleased, the helper might say, "I wonder if you feel happy about that." Helpers also need to look at all the nonverbal behaviors, especially discrepancies between different nonverbal behaviors, for clues. Thus, for example, the client may have a composed facial expression but have excessive arm and leg movements (see chap. 5, this volume). When a client is kicking his or her foot, a helper might wonder out loud if the client is nervous or angry. The meaning of nonverbal behaviors is not always the same (see chap. 5, this volume), however, so helpers must use nonverbal behaviors as clues to possible feelings rather than assuming that nonverbal behaviors have fixed meanings.

Projection of Helper's Feelings

A final source for detecting client feelings is ourselves: How would I feel if I were in that situation? For example, if a client is talking about an argument with a roommate over cleaning their apartment, helpers can recall how they have felt in arguments with roommates, siblings, or friends. Helpers are not judging how the client "should" feel but are attempting to understand the client's feelings by placing themselves in a similar situation. Helpers can use these projections as long as they remember that the projections are possibilities rather than accurate representations of the client's reality. The helper's feelings might not apply to someone else. However, the helper can hypothesize about the client's feelings using her or his own projections and then search for supporting evidence in the client's verbal content and nonverbal behaviors.

ACCURACY OF REFLECTION OF FEELINGS

The feeling word provided by the helper does not have to be perfectly accurate to be helpful, although it does need to be "in the ballpark." As long as the feeling word is relatively close to what the client is feeling, it can enable the client to clarify the feeling. For example, if a client has been talking about feeling scared and the helper uses the word *tense*, the client can clarify and say the feeling is more like *terror*. Clarifying the feelings gives the helper a clearer understanding of the client and allows the client to clarify what he or she is experiencing internally. One could argue that reflections that are too accurate could halt client exploration because there would be no reason for the client to try to clarify or explore the feelings. On the other hand, feeling words that are "out of the ballpark" can be damaging. If a helper uses the word *happy* after the client has said *tense*, the client might feel that the helper is not listening or does not understand, and the client might quit exploring.

Helpers are rarely accurate with every reflection. More often, they struggle in each reflection to understand the client more completely. Clients often appreciate the helper's struggle to understand as much as the specific reflection. Understanding another person's feelings is something helpers strive for but remain humbly aware of how difficult it is to achieve. Hence, helpers should not be as concerned with assessing the accuracy of a particular reflection as with trying to understand clients and communicating to clients that they are struggling to understand.

WHEN TO USE REFLECTIONS OF FEELINGS

Reflecting feelings can have positive benefits by helping clients explore the affective component of the problems, experience relief from tension, come to accept their feelings, and feel proud that they had the courage to express and face their feelings. According to Greenberg (2002), a good time to focus on emotions is when

- there is a therapeutic bond between a helper and a client,
- the helper and client agree on the task of working on emotions,
- a client is avoiding feelings (e.g., the client obviously has a feeling but is interrupting it or is avoiding emotion by intellectualizing, deflecting, or distracting),
- a client behaves maladaptively because of a lack of awareness of feelings (e.g., becomes passive when abused, depressed when angry, overly inhibited from feeling happy or sad and so lacking vigor), or
- a client needs to reprocess traumatic experiences (although not usually immediately after the event).

WHEN NOT TO USE REFLECTIONS OF FEELINGS

Reflection of feelings can be problematic if clients reveal more feelings than they can tolerate at the time. If their defenses are overwhelmed, clients can deteriorate under prolonged emotional catharsis. They may not be ready for the feelings and may not feel supported enough to risk deep exploration. It is probably better not to focus on emotions in the following situations (Brammer & MacDonald, 1996; Greenberg, 2002):

- The therapeutic relationship is not strong (e.g., the client does not feel safe or does not trust the helper, the helper does not have enough information about the client).
- The client feels overwhelmed by emotions due to severe emotional disorder, delusional thinking, or extreme anger.
- The client is going through severe emotional crises, and discussing feelings would add more pressure than he or she could handle.
- The client has a history of aggression, falling apart, substance abuse, self-harm, not being able to regulate emotions, or lack of coping skills.
- The client shows strong resistance to expressing feelings.
- There is not enough time to work through the feelings.
- The helper is not experienced in dealing with emotionally distraught clients.

During crises or when the client is feeling emotionally overwhelmed or distraught, it is perhaps most appropriate to help clients regulate their emotions rather than pressing them to go deeper into feelings (Greenberg, 2002). Emotion regulation techniques such as relaxation training (e.g., suggest that the client take a deep breath) are discussed in chapter 16 of this volume.

An additional concern is that clients might accept the helper's reflection as accurate, not because it necessarily is but because the helper is in a position of authority. Clients might feel their helpers know more about them than they actually do. Helpers thus need to observe whether clients comply too readily with what helpers say rather than experiencing their own feelings. As tempting as it might be, acting as an omniscient authority with regard to clients' feelings often leads to dependency, misunderstandings, or a difficult realization of the helper's limitations.

Helpers should also be aware of cultural considerations in using reflections, given that cultures differ in beliefs about how emotion should be expressed. In the United States, people are generally encouraged to be open about their feelings and experiences. One only needs to turn on radio and television talk shows to see how people share their innermost experiences freely. People from non-American cultures, however, are often more reserved about admitting and expressing feelings, especially with nonfamily members (Pedersen, Draguns, Lonner, & Trimble, 2002). There are also gender differences in the expression of emotion, in that men may have a harder time expressing feelings than women. Men are not typically socialized to be sensitive to feelings and often feel threatened if asked to say what they are feeling (Cournoyer & Mahalik, 1995; Good et al., 1995; O'Neil, 1981).

My intent in presenting these cautions is not to discourage helpers or make them fearful about dealing with client feelings but to increase helpers' awareness about potential hazards of reflecting feelings. In general, reflection of feelings is appropriate and beneficial but can occasionally lead to clients feeling overwhelmed by uncontrollable feelings, so helpers need to be aware and responsive to client reactions.

EXAMPLE OF REFLECTION OF FEELING

The following shows a helper using reflection of feelings (in italics) in a session:

Client: I had to miss classes last week because I got a call right before class that my father had been in a serious car accident. He was on the beltway and a truck driver fell asleep at the wheel and swerved right into him, causing a six-car pile-up. It was really awful.

Helper: *You sound very upset.*

Client: I am. All the way to the hospital, I kept worrying about whether he was okay. The worst thing is that he already had several bad things happen to him recently—his third wife left him, he lost money in the stock market, and his dog died. He just doesn't seem to have anything left.

Helper:	*You're concerned because of all the bad things that have happened lately.*
Client:	Yeah, he doesn't have much will to live, and I don't know what to do for him. I try to be there, but he doesn't really seem to care.
Helper:	*It hurts that he doesn't notice you.*
Client:	Yeah, I have always tried to please my father. I always felt like I couldn't do enough to make him happy. I think he preferred my brother. My brother was a better athlete and liked to work in the shop with him. My father just never valued what I did. I don't know if he liked me very much.
Helper:	*Wow, that's really painful. I wonder if you're angry too?*
Client:	Yeah, I am. What's wrong with me that my father wouldn't like me? I think I'm a pretty nice guy. (Client continues to explore the situation.)

DIFFICULTIES HELPERS EXPERIENCE IN DELIVERING REFLECTION OF FEELINGS

Beginning helpers are often nervous about dealing with clients' expressions of intense negative feelings, such as sadness or anger. They get anxious when clients cry because they feel uncomfortable with crying, uncertain about how to handle emotions, and unsure about ever really understanding another person. Feelings of guilt might also emerge when clients cry, because helpers might think their interventions upset the clients or caused the pain. Furthermore, helpers might be afraid that if they encourage clients to express their feelings, the clients will get stuck in the feelings and not be able to emerge from them. Helpers might also have difficulty accepting intense feelings both in themselves and in their clients. It is important to stress, however, that feelings are natural and clients need to express their feelings so they can begin to accept them. When helpers accept clients' feelings, it conveys to the clients that their feelings are okay. Helpers are encouraged to learn to accept and cope with their anxieties so they can enable clients to express and accept their feelings. Many helpers find that taking a deep breath and focusing on the client and the client's feelings rather than focusing on themselves helps them allow clients to express and accept their feelings (Williams, Judge, Hill, & Hoffman, 1997).

At times, beginning helpers have difficulty capturing the most salient feeling to reflect back to the client. They might hear several feelings and be confused about which is most important to reflect first. Helpers should pay attention to the feeling that seems to elicit the most intensity or depth of feelings. They can always come back later and reflect other feelings when they become more salient. There is plenty of time in the exploration stage to cover any feelings in depth, so it is better to focus on each feeling individually and thoroughly. Practice helps tremendously. Helpers can practice by guessing the most salient emotions displayed in movies, reflecting strong feelings of friends when they are talking about problems, and role-playing in practice exercises.

Some helpers also have difficulty separating their own feelings from the client's feelings. They assume clients must have the same feelings they do. Other helpers overidentify with a client and feel the client's emotion so strongly (i.e., feel sympathy or emotional contagion) that they cannot be objective and helpful. Helpers need to become aware of their own feelings so that they can differentiate what is coming from clients and what is coming from themselves. As mentioned before, personal therapy and supervision can be invaluable in this task.

Finally, helpers sometimes state the client's feelings too definitely (e.g., "You obviously feel angry") rather than tentatively (e.g., "I wonder if you feel angry"). If clients are passive and have difficulty disagreeing with their helpers, direct statements of feelings by helpers can be problematic because clients are not thinking for themselves or examining their experiences. A tentative statement about feelings can be more respectful and encourages clients to verify, dismiss, or modify the feeling words.

Disclosure of Feelings

Disclosure of feelings is when the helper suggests a feeling that he or she had in a similar situation (see Exhibit 7.3). This disclosure can be real ("When I was in that situation, I felt stressed"), hypothetical ("If I were in your situation, I might feel stressed"), or how the helper feels hearing the client talk (e.g., "Hearing you talk about that makes me feel stressed").

Disclosures of feelings can be used to model for clients what they might be feeling (e.g., "When I was applying for my first job, I felt terrified about what I would say in the interview"). After hearing a disclosure of feelings, clients might recognize that they had similar (or very different) feelings. In other words, disclosures of feelings can stimulate clients to recognize and express their feelings. In effect, the disclosure of feelings is similar in intention and consequences to reflection of feelings. Disclosure of feelings can be helpful for clients who are afraid to experience their feelings, especially feelings of shame and embarrassment.

An additional goal of disclosure of feelings is to help clients feel more normal because they learn other people have similar feelings. Many of us think we are the only ones who ever feel lousy, inadequate, phony, or depressed. Hearing that others have felt the same way can be a tremendous relief. In fact, Yalom (1995) posited that universality (i.e., a sense that others feel the same way) is a curative agent in therapy.

EXHIBIT 7.3

Overview of Disclosure of Feelings

Definition	A *disclosure of feelings* is statement about a feeling that the helper had in a similar situation as the client.
Examples	"When I was breaking up with my boyfriend, I felt sad." "If I were in your situation, I might feel angry."
Typical intentions	To identify and intensify feelings, to encourage catharsis, to clarify, to instill hope, to encourage self-control (see Web Form D)
Possible client reactions	Feelings, negative thoughts or behaviors, clear, responsibility, unstuck, scared, worse, misunderstood (see Web Form G)
Desired client behavior	Affective exploration (see Web Form H)
Helpful hints	Listen for the underlying feelings Choose feelings that you think the client is experiencing Disclose only one feeling at a time Disclose feelings that are not too "hot" at the moment for you (this is about the client, not about you) State the feeling tentatively, with empathy, without judgment Keep the disclosure short and simple Turn the focus back to the client immediately (e.g., I wonder if you feel that way?")

Disclosures of feelings can be a good way for helpers not to impose feelings on clients. Rather than saying "You feel ___," the helper says "I felt ___ in the past, and I wonder if you might feel that way?" Helpers are being respectful by owning that they are the ones who have the feelings. They acknowledge their projections and then ask how clients feel. After disclosures of feelings, helpers should turn the focus back to the client. For example, the helper might say, "I wonder how you feel?"

It is important that beginning helpers not use disclosures of feelings for their own needs. Beginning helpers often want to disclose feelings because they want to shift attention to their own problems or show clients how knowledgeable they are about certain issues. Helpers have to be thoughtful about their intentions for disclosing feelings and must be careful to turn the focus back on the client after disclosing feelings. In summary, disclosures can sometimes be helpful to inform clients and help them recognize their feelings, but helpers need to be careful that the attention does not shift from the client to them.

EXAMPLE OF SELF-DISCLOSURE OF FEELINGS

The following shows a helper using self-disclosure of feelings (in italics) in a session:

Client: How did you learn to be a therapist?

Helper: I am just in the process of learning to be a helper. It will be many years and lots of training before I

Client: am qualified to consider myself a therapist. Perhaps you're curious about my credentials?

Client: I just wonder if you're going to be able to help me.

Helper: I can understand that fear. *I was very nervous about going to see a therapist the first time too.*

Client: I am a bit nervous. This is the first time I've talked to anyone about my problems. I feel like I'm weak if I talk to anyone. My father always used to say that only crazy people go to therapists.

Helper: *That would make me angry.*

Client: It did make me angry. My father is hardly one to talk given his problems. I really want to have an opportunity to talk more about my feelings about my family—they are pretty messed up, and I guess I am too.

The helper might shift at this point to using other helping skills (e.g., reflections and restatements) to help the client explore more about her feelings about her family.

Open Questions About Feelings

If the helper wants clients to express feelings, the most reliably efficient skill is probably probe for feelings (see also Goates-Jones, Hill, Stahl, & Doschek, in press; Hill & Gormally, 1977) because this skill specifically tells the client what it is the helper wants him or her to do. With a probe for feeling, the helper asks something like, "I wonder how you're feeling about that?" Thus, the helper indicates directly to clients how they should respond (see Exhibit 7.4).

The material presented in chapter 6 for open questions about thoughts also applies to open questions about feelings (recall that probes for feelings would be under this category). I would highlight the need to vary open questions about feelings, so that helpers are not saying only, "How do you feel about that?" Instead, helpers might say, "What was that like for you?" or "Tell me about that experience."

EXAMPLE OF OPEN QUESTIONS ABOUT FEELINGS

The following shows a helper using open questions about feelings (in italics) in a session:

Client: I think I want to go to the local community college when I graduate from high school because my par-

---

EXHIBIT 7.4

Overview of Open Questions About Feelings

Definition	*Open questions about feelings* ask clients to clarify or explore feelings. Helpers do not request specific information and do not purposely limit the nature of the client response to a "yes," "no," or one- or two-word answer, even though clients may respond that way. Open questions can be phrased as queries ("How do you think about that?") or as probes ("Tell me how you feel about that"), as long as the intent is to help the client clarify or explore.
Examples	"What are you feeling right now?" "Tell me more about your feelings."
Typical helper intentions	To focus, to clarify, to encourage catharsis, to identify maladaptive feelings (see Web Form D)
Possible client reactions	Clear, feelings (see Web Form G)
Desired client behaviors	Recounting, affective exploration (see Web Form H)
Helpful hints	Convey empathy with your question Make sure your questions are open instead of closed Vary the format of the open question Avoid multiple questions Avoid "why" questions Focus on the client rather than on others Focus on one part of the issue rather than trying to cover everything Have an intention for every question Observe client reactions to your questions

---

ents don't have enough money to send me anywhere else.

Helper: *What are you feeling right now?*

Client: Well, I feel a little disappointed because I had always assumed that I would go to a big university. I've gotten good grades, and it just doesn't seem fair that I cannot go wherever I want.

Helper: *You sound angry.*

Client: I probably am. My parents told me I could go wherever I wanted, but then they got divorced last year and nothing has been the same.

Helper: *I know that when my parents got divorced, I felt totally abandoned. I wonder if you feel like that?*

Client: I do. They are both into their own stuff now. They are both dating other people and acting like silly teenagers. I feel older than them. But because they got divorced, we no longer have enough money for me to go to the university.

Helper: *I wonder if you feel betrayed.*

Client: That's exactly the right word. I do feel betrayed. They always promised me I could go to the university. I was always the smartest kid and they praised me a lot for that. But now, they don't even know I exist. It just feels like the bottom has fallen out. (Continues)

A Comparison of Skills for Exploring Feelings

Reflections of feelings help clients get into their feelings, come to accept these feelings, and then move to new feelings. With reflections, clients often feel that helpers are listening to them and understand them. Sometimes, it can be helpful to soften the reflection by using a disclosure of feelings, especially if the helper turns it back to the client (e.g., "Does that fit for you?").

Of course, using only reflections or disclosures of feelings could get to be too much. There are times, for example when clients do not get into their feelings, that they need a more direct open question about feelings to help them. In this situation, an open question about feelings is a good way to encourage clients to talk about their feelings. If clients have difficulty identifying their feelings, though, they might feel anxious and unsure when helpers ask, "How are you feeling about that?" Such questions can confuse or concern clients because they are not sure what helpers want to hear or how they "should" feel. Sometimes asking how they feel stimulates defenses and makes clients shut down. Clients can also feel annoyed that helpers are not really listening to what they are saying or trying to empathize with their feelings.

It can also be helpful to follow up reflections with open questions about feelings. For example, the helper might say, "You sound sad," give the client a chance to respond, and then say, "Can you tell me more about the feeling of being sad?" Or, the helper might comment, "It's really hard to be in touch with all that sadness."

What Do You Think?

■ Compare and contrast the effects of using reflections of feeling, self-disclosures of feelings, and open questions about feelings. in terms of their ability to help clients explore.

- Compare and contrast focusing on feelings versus thoughts for exploration.
- How does your culture influence how you feel about experiencing and expressing your feelings and talking about other people's feelings?
- How do you choose which feeling to reflect if a client has a lot of different feelings?
- How can you tell whether clients agree with your reflections because they are accurate, because you are in the "power position," or because they want to please you?
- How much should you mirror feelings that the client is aware of versus encourage the client to experience feelings of which he or she might not be aware?
- Some therapists do not like to ever disclose anything. What would be their reasoning? Do you agree?

i PRACTICE EXERCISES

A downloadable PDF of this chapter's Practice Exercises is available in the student resources area of the Helping Skills, *3rd ed. Web site:http://www.apa.org/books/resources/Hill3.*

For each of the following client statements, write a reflection of feelings, a self-disclosure of feelings, or a probe for feelings. Compare your responses with the possible helper responses provided at the end this practice exercise.

Statements

1. Client: "I'm really having difficulty with my schoolwork right now. I have a hard time concentrating because there are so many other things going on. My mother is in the hospital, and I wish I could be there to be with her because she may die soon. When I'm thinking about her, it's hard to get into my work. But I know that what would upset her most is if I got bad grades and didn't finish school."

   Helper reflection of feelings: _____

   Helper disclosure of feelings: _____

   Helper open question about feelings: _____

2. Client: "When I'm trying to sleep, I keep hearing my parents arguing. I try to hide my head under the pillow, but I still hear them."

   Helper reflection of feelings: _____

   Helper disclosure of feelings: _____

   Helper open question about feelings: _____

3. Client: "My roommate is really nice. I really like her. She is so much like the sister I wish I had when I was younger. It's really nice to have somebody to do things with. I was so lonely on campus last year, but having her as a roommate makes me feel like I belong. She's from a really poor family and she hardly has any money. Fortunately, my parents send me a lot of money, so I'm glad I can share some with her."

Helper reflection of feelings: _____

Helper disclosure of feelings: _____

Helper open question about feelings: _____

4. Client: "I just got into the worst fight ever with my mother. She was saying awful things to me, like I would never succeed in school because I'm lazy. I got so angry at her, I was shaking. I just don't know what to say to her when she does that. Why can't she be supportive like my friends' mothers?"

Helper reflection of feelings: _____

Helper disclosure of feelings: _____

Helper open question about feelings: _____

Possible Helper Responses

1. "You're really worried about your mother."
   "When my little sister was sick and then died, I felt incredibly vulnerable. I wonder if you feel that way?"
   "I wonder how you feel about your mother's illness?"

2. "You're upset that your parents are arguing so much."
   "If I were you, I might feel angry at them. How does it make you feel?"
   "How do you feel about your parents?"

3. "You feel relieved that you finally feel like you belong."
   "I remember feeling embarrassed when I had more money than my friends."
   "How do you feel about sharing your resources with her?"

4. "I can see how mad you are at your mother."
   "I feel angry at your mother just hearing you talk."
   "I wonder what you feel inside when you compare your mother to your friends' mothers?"

i LAB 6. Skills for Exploring Feelings

A downloadable PDF of this Lab is available in the student resources area of the Helping Skills, *3rd ed. Web site: http://www.apa.org/books/resources/Hill3.*

Goal: For helpers to learn to help clients explore their feelings. The focus is on learning how and when to use reflections of feelings, disclosures of feelings, and open questions about feelings. An additional goal is for students to hear how others phrase the skills.

Exercise 1: Awareness of Own Feelings

In a large group the leader asks each student to say feeling words to reflect about how she or he is currently feeling. Students should practice using feeling words that they would not typically use so they can broaden their feeling word vocabulary. See Exhibit 7.2, Emotion Words Checklist, for ideas, but remember to add words to personalize the list.

Exercise 2: Formulating Reflections

1. In a large group, the leader role-plays a brief emotionally laden example of a client problem. Each student writes down a reflection of feeling. The leader asks the group members to take turns delivering their reflections. The leader continues with examples until students grasp the concept of reflections.
2. Still in a large group, the leader asks one student to play a client and talk about something easy that he or she has some feelings about (suggested topics: academic issues, career, pets, problems at work, roommate issues, problems with health, romantic relationships). After the "client" talks for awhile, the students all write down a reflection of feelings. Once everyone is done writing, the leader asks each one in turn to deliver their reflection of feelings to the client. The client should respond as he or she would if talking to this person.

Exercise 3: Formulating Disclosures of Feelings

This exercise is the same as Exercise 2, except that it focuses on disclosures of feelings.

Exercise 4: Open Questions about Feelings

This exercise is the same as Exercise 2, except that it focuses on open questions about feelings.

Exercise 5: Exploring Feelings

Divide into groups of three students. Everyone takes turns with each role (helper, client, and observer).

Helper's and Client's Tasks During the Helping Exchange

1. The client talks briefly about a topic for which he or she has strong (but not overwhelming) feelings.
2. After the client finishes speaking, the helper gives a reflection of feelings, a disclosure of feelings, or an open question about feelings. Helpers should take their time, pause, and then consider how the client is feeling, what nonverbal behaviors reveal about feelings, and how they would feel if they were the client. Keep the intervention short and simple.
3. Continue for 5 to 10 turns. Vary which skill you use.

Observer's Task During the Helping Exchange

Take notes about the helper's attending behaviors and manner of delivery of the skills. Write down each exact intervention to provide a record for later discussion. Note the client's reactions to the interventions.

After the Helping Exchange

1. The helper should talk about how it felt to try to help the client explore feelings.
2. The client should talk about how it felt to be the recipient of the interventions. Discuss specific interventions that were more and less helpful.
3. The observer should give lots of positive feedback to the helper about her or his attending behaviors and interventions, and then give one idea for what she or he could do differently.

Switch Roles

Keep doing role-plays as just described until everyone has had a chance to be the helper, client, and observer at least once.

Large Group Go-Round

Going around the circle one at a time, each person should say first what he or she did well. In a second go-round, each person can say what he or she is going to continue to work on and how he or she might do that.

Personal Reflections

- What did you learn about yourself when delivering reflections?
- What would you do if a client started to cry?
- In the past, some students have had a hard time selecting the most important feeling; some have become overwhelmed by lengthy client descriptions and could not differentiate "the forest" (feelings) from "the trees" (all the words); some were worried about hurting the client if they gave a "bad" reflection; some had difficulty figuring out the feelings if the client did not explicitly state feelings; and some had trouble when clients were very articulate about their feelings because they did not want to repeat the client's feeling words. What was your experience?
- Are there particular feelings (e.g., anger, guilt) that you have difficulty using with clients because of your own discomfort or problems?
- In the past, many students have reported that their confidence dropped dramatically after beginning to learn helping skills but then increased with practice. What pattern do you see emerging with regard to your confidence as a helper?

Integrating the Skills of the Exploration Stage | 8

It is a luxury to be understood.

—*Ralph Waldo Emerson*

Dmitry, a new helper, was in his first session with a client, Joe. He asked several closed questions, and Joe answered them briefly and then sat waiting for more questions. Dmitry panicked because he did not know what to do next. He felt himself sweating and wanted to run out of the room. Instead, he paused, took a deep breath, and thought about what he had learned about helping. His teacher's words echoed in his head: "Try to feel what the client is feeling." So he said, "I wonder if you're scared right now?" and was amazed when the client started talking about feeling depressed because he was doing poorly in his courses. Joe went on to talk about how his father was very critical and shamed him when he did not meet his unrealistic standards. Dmitry quickly became so engaged in listening to Joe that he forgot his own anxiety.

The goals of the exploration stage are to establish rapport and help clients explore thoughts and feelings. In addition, helpers are laying the foundation during the exploration stage to move to insight and action. It is important foremost to be empathic and to accept clients unconditionally so they can begin to accept themselves. By keeping an awareness of the goals in this stage, helpers can be more grounded in trying to facilitate the process. Otherwise, it is easy for helpers to get lost and let clients talk aimlessly or in circles.

This chapter covers issues that arise for helpers during the exploration stage. First, I cover the goals and skills of the exploration stage, then talk about the difficulties that helpers typically face in the exploration stage, and then present several possible strategies for coping with the difficulties. Finally, I present an example of the exploration stage.

Choosing Goals to Facilitate Exploration

In trying to decide what to do during the exploration stage, the helper has to first ponder what his or her goals are for helping the client. In general, the helper wants to put the client at ease, help the client feel safe, create an atmosphere in which the client can talk, listen attentively to the client, and observe the client. This set of goals is accomplished through the nonverbal and minimal verbal attending, listening, and observation skills discussed in chapter 5.

The helper also wants to help the client explore the content of the problem, to tell the story about what is troubling him or her. For clients to be able to talk, it helps to have someone listening attentively and struggling with them to help them figure out what they are trying to say and what they mean. So when the helper wants to facilitate the client in talking, using restatements and open questions about thoughts can be very helpful.

Arousal of emotions is also important. The client needs to focus not only on the story but also on the feelings attached to the story, to experience and express what is going on internally. Experiencing the emotions within the context of an accepting relationship allows the client to accept the emotions and thus come to trust his or her inner experiencing. To facilitate this emotional experiencing, the helper often uses reflections of feelings, disclosures of feelings, and open questions about feelings.

But of course, these goals are often overlapping. Helpers want to support clients and to help them talk about both thoughts and feelings. So how do helpers decide which skills to use at any given moment in the session? There are no fixed rules, but I can share with you some ideas based on my clinical experience.

Choosing Skills to Match the Goals

To help clients explore deeply, helpers typically rely on reflection of feelings (my absolute favorite skill). Reflections demonstrate that the helper is listening and struggling to understand the clients' experience and are particularly helpful when clients need encouragement to keep talking, when clients need to experience their feelings (whether or not they are actively expressing the feelings), or when helpers want to show support or understanding. Reflection of feelings is also a useful way to identify possible feelings for clients who are out of touch with their feelings. Helpers can disclose about their own feelings as a softer, more tentative way of proposing feelings that clients might have. Most clients respond to reflections of feelings or disclosure of feelings by talking about their feelings. However, some clients do not, perhaps because reflections do not request that clients talk about their feelings. For these clients, helpers can alternate reflecting feelings with asking open questions about the feelings. This way, helpers not only suggest possible feelings but also encourage clients to identify and express their own feelings. This method helps clients become comfortable expressing their feelings.

If helpers want to focus the discussion or clarify what clients are talking about, they might use restatements (e.g., "so you flunked your exam" or a repetition of the key word *exam*). When clients are confusing, rambling, or just need to talk, restatements can serve as mirrors that reflect back to clients what they are saying. Restatements help clients clarify and think more deeply about what they are saying.

Throughout the session, a helper can use open questions to maintain the session's flow (e.g., "How are you feeling about that?" "Tell me more about that"). If clients seem stuck or are repeating the same material over and over, helpers can use open questions to ask about other aspects of problems the client has not addressed. Using a variety of open questions helps clients explore the complexity of situations and think about things they might not have considered.

Helpers can follow clients' responses to open questions with a reflection of feelings or restatement to show they understand what clients have said and to encourage them to say more. Open questions request that clients respond in a particular way. In contrast, reflections of feelings are a gentler way of suggesting feelings without seeming as demanding. Restatements and reflections shift the responsibility for initiating dialogue back to clients and show that helpers are listening to clients. Alternating among open questions, restatements, and reflections can keep helpers from getting stuck in an interviewer mode and can make the session seem less contrived and more interesting.

Occasionally, helpers ask closed questions to gather specific, important information from clients (e.g., "Is your mother alive?" "When did you graduate from high school?"). Helpers need to remember to use closed questions to benefit clients rather than to satisfy their own curiosity. Before using closed questions, then, helpers need to be clear about what they are going to do with the information and whose needs are being met (the helpers' or the clients'). Generally, however, I recommend that helpers try to rephrase closed questions into open questions, restatements, or reflections of feelings.

Beginning helpers may have problems in the exploration stage if they are not able to facilitate deep exploration in their clients. Their clients seem to go around in circles, repeating themselves over and over rather than going deeper into their problems. Generally, circling occurs when helpers use too many closed questions or use restatements or reflections that are focused on someone other than the client, are too general or vague, or do not ask about other aspects of problems. Beginning helpers sometimes worry about being too intrusive, so they often skim the surface of issues rather than helping clients explore deeply with the skills suggested in this book. They might forget to attend and listen, or they might forget to be empathic and caring. It is not enough just to use the right skills; helpers must use them in an empathic manner to fit what clients need at the time.

Helpers should pay attention to clients' reactions to their interventions. If the client is exploring and going deeper into problems, that is great. The helper is obviously on the right track. However, if the client becomes very quiet, passive, or does not explore, the helper should assess what is not working. Perhaps the helper is not attending or listening, is asking too many closed questions, is focusing on someone other than the client, or is giving inaccurate restatements and reflections. The client might be bored, confused, or overwhelmed with negative feelings and retreat from further exploration. By assessing the problem, a helper can change what she or he is doing and try different skills. It is crucial that the helper pay close attention to the client's reactions in order to select appropriate interventions.

When the client is productively exploring, the helper fades into the background as much as possible. The client is obviously able to work and needs the helper just to be there supporting the work. Jung (1984) phrased this well in talking about dream interpretation: "The greatest wisdom [a dream analyst] can have is to disappear and let the dreamer think [the dream analyst] is doing nothing" (p. 458). Our job as helpers is to have clients so immersed in exploration that they do not notice our skills—the interventions should facilitate, rather than intrude on, the process. This might involve the helper giving a minimal number of head nods, being silent, and working to be empathic and to communicate empathy.

Finally, it is important not only to observe the client to see how she or he is reacting to the process but also to ask the client about their reactions (remember that clients often hide negative reactions; see chap. 2, this volume). By checking in with the client frequently, the helper can modify the process to make it more suitable for the client.

A SAMPLE PROCESS

In this section, I describe several steps that helpers can use in their first session. These steps include getting started, facilitating explanation, deciding when the client has explored enough, dealing with difficult client situations, and developing own style.

Getting Started

Before the session, it is ideal for the helper to take some time to "center," to get in touch with current feelings and take some time to relax enough (use deep breathing), put aside (bracket) other issues and concerns, and focus on being present in the moment with the client. At the beginning of the session, the helper can take a deep breath and assume a helping posture that is comfortable yet professional. The helper then introduces himself or herself to the client, explains what will happen in the session, and describes confidentiality. Then the helper turns the floor over to the client by asking the client what she or he would like to talk about today. The helper listens attentively and allows the client to do the talking.

Facilitating Exploration

If the client seems focused mostly on content, the helper might start by giving restatements when the client pauses, to demonstrate that the helper understands and to encourage further clarification and exploration. If the client has difficulty continuing, the helper might ask open questions to encourage exploration of other aspects of the problem. After establishing some rapport, the helper might introduce some reflections of feelings to gently help the client think about feelings, and then follow these reflections up with open questions asking the client about feelings.

If the client is clearly in touch with feelings and able to experience and express them, the helper might start with reflections of feelings and open questions about feelings to help the client go deeper into the feelings. The helper will probably occasionally intersperse these feeling-oriented interventions with restatements and open questions about feelings to help the client explore other aspects of the problem.

Deciding When Client Has Explored Enough

Clients have explored enough when helpers can answer the following questions:

- What is the client's problem?
- What is motivating the client to seek help now?
- How does the client think and feel about the problem?

When helpers sense that clients have explored the situation thoroughly, they might use a restatement to summarize, to see whether the client has anything else to add, to provide closure, and to set the stage for insight. For example, a helper might say, "You've been talking a lot today about your feelings about your roommate. You seem concerned that the two of you are not as close as you have been in the past. You are not sure what you can do to fix the relationship. How does this summary fit for you?" Alternatively, helpers might ask clients to summarize (e.g., "Could you sum up what you learned so far?") to get a sense of how much clients have absorbed. Ideally, summaries are a joint effort, with helpers and clients trying together to explicate what has been learned. Sometimes, of course, summarizing is not necessary because clients naturally move directly to insight.

Dealing With Difficult Client Situations

I can hear trainees asking, "But what do I do when the client won't talk, or when the client is too talkative, or when the client is suicidal, or when I'm attracted to the client?" and so on. For now, I'll ask you to hold off on the questions and focus of your skills. Once you begin to master your skills, then it is time to turn to focus on difficult client situations—these are covered in chapter 18.

Developing Own Style

There is no "right" way to implement this (or any other) stage in this helping model. Each helper has to modify this approach to fit his or her personal style, and then be able to modify that style to fit the needs to individual clients (all of whom have different needs and reactions). I suggest that you try out the skills and see how they work for you. Practice a lot. Get feedback from clients and observers. Become a personal scientist—see what works and what does not work. Trust your experience.

Helper Self-Awareness

Helpers can use their inner experiences as tools for understanding what is happening in the helping process. By being aware of their reactions, helpers can make better decisions about how to intervene and are less likely to act out their reactions in helping situations (Williams, Hurley, O'Brien, & DeGregorio, 2003). Moreover, helpers' reactions can provide valuable clues about how other people react to clients. For example, if the helper feels bored when a client talks in a monotone voice, chances are that other people in the client's life also feel bored when the client talks that way. Hence, helpers have some firsthand information about how the client comes across to other people, which is important data for the insight stage.

It is important that helpers learn about themselves so personal issues do not intrude on sessions with clients. An ideal place to examine these issues is in supervision (i.e., consultation with a trained professional). With the help of an experienced supervisor, helpers can begin to identify which feelings come from personal issues, which are stimulated by clients, and which are due to a combination of personal issues and client behavior.

Cultural Considerations

There are a number of cultural considerations to consider when implementing the exploration stage. First, the humanistic theory behind the exploration stage is in tune with a Western philosophy, which encourages open examination of thoughts and feelings and emphasizes self-healing and self-actualization. Other cultures, particularly Eastern cultures, value collectivism more than a strong emphasis on self (Pedersen, Draguns, Lonner, & Trimble, 2002; D. W. Sue & Sue, 1999). Clients from non-Western cultures may be less amenable to exploration than to action, so the exploration stage may need to be shorter than with a Western client (note that some Western clients are also uncomfortable exploring feelings). Helpers must be mindful of not imposing their own values about open communication on people from other cultures. I caution, however, that some exploration is necessary to get a firm foundation of understanding before rushing to action. Furthermore, helpers must be careful not to stereotype clients from other cultures or assume all people from a given culture have similar values. Remember that there is more variation within a given culture than between cultures (D. R. Atkinson, Morten, & Sue, 1998; Pedersen, 1997).

A general guideline is that it is important to explore cultural differences when these seem salient to the client. The helper can mention cultural differences in the first session and ask about these (e.g., "I am aware that we are from different cultural backgrounds. I wonder how that is for you?"). The helper can also be attentive to client discomfort throughout the helping process and ask the client whether this discomfort is due to cultural differences (e.g., "I notice you seem uncomfortable when I probe for feelings. I wonder if opening up to a stranger is frowned on in your family or culture?"). In addition, it can also be helpful to ask about cultural values related to the helping process (e.g., "What is the reaction in your family and culture to people seeking help from counselors or helpers?"). Finally, helpers can ask clients to talk about their culture, so that they can learn more about the experience for each client uniquely (e.g., "Tell me about what it is like for you to be a Korean student who just arrived in the United States").

Difficulties Implementing the Exploration Stage

Here are some difficulties that beginning helpers have talked about when they are first learning to implement the exploration stage. If you are aware of these obstacles ahead of time, you will be more likely to cope when difficulties inevitably arise.

INADEQUATE ATTENDING AND LISTENING

Several factors might interfere with helpers' ability to attend and listen adequately to their clients. Many helpers get distracted from listening because they are thinking about what to say next or are distracted about something unrelated to the session (e.g., what's for dinner tonight). Helpers sometimes judge the merits of what clients are saying rather than listening and understanding them. One type of judgment that is hard to avoid is evaluating clients using one's own cultural standards. For example, a European American, middle-class, female helper might have difficulty listening to and understanding an upper-class African American man or a very poor Asian woman. Sympathy can be another impediment to listening because helpers sometimes become so involved with and feel so badly for clients that they cannot maintain objectivity; they try to "rescue" clients instead of attending to feelings.

ASKING TOO MANY CLOSED QUESTIONS

Beginning helpers often ask too many closed questions because they feel they need to gather all the details of a problem. Many helpers think the helping process is similar to a medical model in which they should collect a lot of information to diagnose the problem and provide a solution for the client. However, in this stage the helper's task is to aid clients in coming to their own solutions, so there is little need to know all the details. Instead, such skills as facilitating exploration of thoughts and feelings are important for helping clients explore.

Some helpers ask too many questions simply because they do not have anything better to say. These helpers do not necessarily want to hear the answers to their questions; they just want to fill time or satisfy their curiosity. When asking questions, it is important to clarify for whom the question is being asked (i.e., to assist the client or to fulfill the helper's need).

TALKING TOO MUCH

Some helpers talk too much in helping sessions. They might talk because they are anxious, want to impress clients, or like to talk in general. However, if helpers are talking, clients cannot talk and, hence, cannot explore their concerns. Research has found that clients generally talk about 60% to 70% of the time (Hill, 1978; Hill, Carter, & O'Farrell, 1983). In contrast, in nonhelping situations, both people in an interaction ideally talk about 50% of the time; therefore, it can be difficult for beginning helpers to adjust to listening more than talking.

NOT ALLOWING SILENCE

One of the most daunting tasks for beginning helpers is to cope with silence. Trainees often rush to fill voids in sessions out of fear that clients are bored, anxious, critical, or stuck. Rushing to fill voids can result in superficial and unhelpful comments. Helpers should try to understand their fears about silence in sessions, asking themselves what concerns they have (e.g., not appearing competent, not helping the client). Once they figure out these concerns, they can work on these fears outside of sessions, rather than rushing to fill silences in sessions.

URGE TO DISCLOSE

One of the biggest problems beginning helpers have is the urge to disclose too much. Because client issues are often similar to their own issues, beginning helpers want to share their experiences with their clients. It seems natural to disclose and tell one's stories, as one would with friends. Helpers also may want help for themselves and may be distracted by their own problems while listening to clients. It can be difficult to listen to someone else's issues when one is going through the same thing. For example, beginning helpers in their early 20s often have difficulty listening to students their own age talk about identity issues, relationship difficulties, problems with parents, and plans for the future because these are issues for the helpers. Beginning helpers who are older might have difficulty listening to problems about parenting and aging. Adopting the professional identity of a helper who listens but does not disclose much is a major and challenging shift in perspective for beginning helpers. However, because inappropriate self-disclosure can be detrimental and can hinder the therapeutic relationship, helpers need to learn to restrain themselves.

GIVING TOO MUCH (OR PREMATURE) ADVICE

Beginning helpers often rush into giving advice. They feel pressured to provide answers, fix problems, rescue clients, or have perfect solutions. Many clients and beginning helpers are under the misguided notion that helpers have a responsibility to provide solutions to problems. Giving clients answers or solutions is often detrimental because clients have not come to the solutions on their own and, therefore, cannot own them. Furthermore, when given answers, clients do not learn how to solve future problems without depending on other people. Clients most often need a sounding board or someone to listen to them think through their problem or help them figure out how to solve their problems, rather than someone just telling them what to do. It is critical to realize that the need to provide answers often originates in the helper's insecurity and desire to help, which are normal feelings at the start of learning helping skills.

It is important, however, to recognize that some clients *do* want answers from helpers and do not want to explore. It is sometimes appropriate to move more quickly to the action stage with such clients. Sometimes such clients will be more eager to explore after they have made some specific changes in their lives; other clients, however, just want changes without deep exploration and understanding. Helpers can educate clients about the benefits of coming to their own solutions after a thorough exploration of their problems, feelings, and situation, but helpers should be careful not to be judgmental about clients who do not want to explore.

BEING "BUDDIES"

Sometimes beginning helpers err by acting like "buddies" with clients instead of being helpers. The role of helper necessitates providing a connected yet clearly defined relationship to maintain objectivity and offer maximum assistance. Being a buddy can be limiting because helpers might choose interventions to make clients like them rather than to help clients change. For example, Sam, a beginning helper, began every session by talking with his client, Tom, about recent sporting events. Tom responded enthusiastically to talking about sports but was reluctant to discuss more personal issues. Sam avoided changing the topic because he wanted to maintain a friendly connection with Tom. Unfortunately, because of his desire to be buddies, Sam was not able to help Tom explore his personal issues.

DISCOURAGING INTENSE EXPRESSION OF AFFECT

Beginning helpers sometimes feel awkward when clients express intense affect, such as despair, intense sadness, or strong anger (especially if the anger is directed toward the helper). Sometimes helpers are uncomfortable with negative feelings because they do not allow themselves to feel their own negative feelings. They may deny or defend against their internal "demons." For these helpers, hearing clients' negative feelings can be very stressful. Sometimes helpers feel a need to make clients feel better immediately because they do not want their clients to suffer. They mistakenly think that if clients do not talk about their feelings, the feelings go away. They might be afraid to have clients get into the negative feelings because they feel inadequate to help. Guilty feelings might emerge for helpers if their interventions result in clients crying. These helpers err on the side of keeping things "light" or minimizing feelings so they do not have to face "tough" situations in which they feel helpless. Recently, an attractive adolescent client told her helper she felt totally fat and ugly. She expressed disgust with her body and astonishment that anyone would want to be around her. A helper who is uncomfortable with intense negative feelings might give the socially sanctioned response of reassuring this client that she is attractive and suggesting that her feelings are not accurate. Ironically, this response would negate the client's feelings and could make the client feel worse because she would feel misunderstood.

Now might be a good time to ask yourself how you feel about overt expressions of affect. What do you instinctively want to do when someone begins to sob uncontrollably? Most of us feel an urge to get the person to stop crying and to feel better. How do you react when someone is acting hostile and angry toward you? Many of us get defensive or react with hostility. Helpers need to be aware of their tendencies to respond in these types of situations so they can practice other, more therapeutic ways, to respond. The exploration skills can be particularly valuable tools for helping clients stay with their intense emotions.

DISSOCIATING AND PANICKING

Sometimes beginning helpers become so anxious about their performance that they feel they are outside their bodies observing themselves in the helping role, instead of being fully present and interactive in the helping session. At the worst, these helpers become completely frozen and cannot say anything. These experiences can frighten helpers, who then panic and tell themselves they can never be good helpers. In fact, anxiety is often more of a problem than lack of skills, but fortunately I have seen many students overcome their anxiety and become gifted helpers.

FEELING DISCOURAGED ABOUT ABILITY TO BE A HELPER

At about this point in the course, some students say they feel like they are getting worse at being able to be a helper rather than getting better. They are so focused on each skill and on watching everything they do that it is hard to perform at all. An analogy can be drawn to learning to ski. When you first learn to ski, you are conscious of every little thing you do. Like beginning skiers, beginning helpers focus on each thing they do in the helping encounter. In learning helping skills, helpers practice the individual skills (and often unlearn habits that were not facilitative to helping) and then put all the skills together. Although difficult initially, it often begins to feel easier when you put them all together. Students often feel better after practicing for a few more weeks, although some students come to realize that they do not want to be helpers.

Coping Strategies for Managing Difficulties

To overcome a lack of skills, helpers can practice helping skills taught in this book. The skills can be compared to tools in a toolbox; helpers learn about the different tools available for different tasks. Some tools work better than others for some helpers and some clients. It is important that helpers have many tools (e.g., helping skills and methods for managing anxiety) in their toolboxes so they have a lot of options to help clients and to manage their own anxiety in sessions.

Several ideas are offered in this section for helpers to manage anxiety (see also Management Strategies Scale in Web Form J), based on findings of research with beginning helpers (Williams, Judge, Hill, & Hoffman, 1997). Helpers can use the first few strategies before they do sessions to prepare themselves, and they can use the last few in sessions to deal with anxiety. I hope all helpers find some strategies they can use.

OBSERVING MODELS

Watching skilled helpers in helping sessions is an excellent way to observe skills being used appropriately. The skills come alive when one sees them demonstrated by experts. Although reading about theories and skills is important, imagining how they come across is hard unless models are available. Bandura (1969) showed the effectiveness of watching a model as one step in the learning process. I recommend watching many different helpers to illustrate that there are many ways and styles of helping (especially see this book's accompanying DVD, *Helping Skills in Practice: A Three-Stage Model*).

IMAGERY

Through sports psychology, we know that when athletes have the requisite skills, practice through imagery can be a beneficial addition to actual practice (Suinn, 1988). Helpers can imagine themselves using appropriate attending behaviors and helping skills in different situations. For example, a beginning helper who feels uncomfortable with silence might close her eyes and visualize herself in a session with a quiet client. She might imagine herself sitting comfortably with the client and allowing the silence to occur. She might also visualize breaking the silence after a period of time by asking how the client is feeling.

ROLE-PLAY

Before sessions with clients, helpers can role-play using specific helping skills. Helpers can also role-play the mechanics of sessions, such as starting and stopping the session, responding to silence, and dealing with anger directed toward the helper. By using role-plays with supportive partners (e.g., classmates), helpers are more likely to learn the skills at a comfortable pace.

PRACTICE THE SKILLS

Perhaps the best method for managing anxiety is practice. The more helpers practice and pay attention to what they do well and how they can improve, the better and more comfortable they are likely to become in helping sessions. Throughout the book, I provide exercises for helpers to practice the helping skills. I encourage helpers to participate in many practice sessions with sympathetic and helpful volunteer clients.

DEEP BREATHING

One way helpers can manage anxiety during sessions is to breathe deeply from the diaphragm instead of taking short breaths from high in the chest. To determine whether you breathe from the diaphragm, put your hand over your stomach. When you breathe, you should feel your hand move in and out. Deep breathing serves several functions. First, it allows one to relax. When the diaphragm is relaxed, it is harder to be anxious physiologically. Second, taking a deep breath gives helpers a moment to think about what they want to say. Helpers can take time to focus their energy instead of being distracted by thinking about what to say in the next intervention. Third, deep breathing gives clients a chance to think and consider whether they have anything else to say.

FOCUS ON THE CLIENT

All too often, beginning helpers are so concerned with their own behavior that they cannot listen attentively to clients. By shifting focus to be more concerned with the client than with themselves, helpers can listen more attentively (Williams et al., 1997). The goal is to facilitate clients in exploring feelings, not for helpers to show off how much they understand clients. By focusing on the client and attempting to immerse oneself in the client's world, many beginning helpers are able to lessen their anxiety.

POSITIVE SELF-TALK

We all talk to ourselves as we do things. We say things like "I can do this" or "I think I am going to panic." Some people have called this the "inner game" because it occurs beneath the surface. Positive self-talk has a positive influence on performance in helping sessions, whereas negative self-talk has a negative influence on performance (see Nutt-Williams & Hill, 1996), so helpers need to be attentive to what they are saying to themselves. Helpers can practice using positive self-talk before sessions so they have positive sentences ready to use to coach themselves. Alternatively, helpers can write down positive self-statements (e.g., "I know the skills," "I am competent") on index cards and glance at them before or during practice sessions.

Example of the Exploration Stage

The following is a sample of an interchange in which the helper facilitates client exploration through an integration of the exploration skills. This example is not meant to be perfect but rather a realistic example of what might occur with a beginning helper. After each helper response, I label the skills used and give an explanation of what the helper was trying to accomplish. As you go through the example, cover the helper's responses and formulate your response first. You can then see how similar the helper's response is to yours and determine which is most effective and which you would be most comfortable trying.

> *Helper:* Hi! My name is Sandra. We have 30 minutes today to explore whatever you would like to talk about. (The helper intends to set limits by providing information about what the client can expect from the session.)
>
> *Client:* Okay.

Helper: So, where would you like to begin? (The helper uses an open question to focus.)

Client: I'm feeling anxious about a paper I have to write. I always end up waiting until the last minute to begin, and then I panic because I don't have enough time to write it. I know I do this, but I can't seem to stop myself.

Helper: You're really upset with yourself. (The helper gives a reflection to help the client experience feelings.)

Client: Yeah, I'm worried that I'm going to ruin my chances of getting into graduate school because I'm not doing as well in my courses as I should be.

Helper: You feel scared because your current behaviors might limit your future goals. (The helper gives another reflection because she wants to stay with the feelings and help the client explore further.)

Client: Exactly, I really think I could succeed in graduate school, and I know I need a graduate degree to do what will make me happy. I'm so worried that I'll stay in this rut and ruin everything I've worked for.

Helper: Tell me about the last time you had a paper to write. Take me through what went on inside your head. (The helper wants information about what goes on and wants to get the client to talk more concretely about the problem, so uses open questions about thoughts.)

Client: Well, actually, I have a paper due tomorrow, and I haven't started it yet. I've gathered all the material I need, and I've taken notes on the books, but I haven't written anything. And I've been up late several nights already this week, so I'm short on sleep.

Helper: I can hear the panic in your voice. (The helper reflects nonverbal behavior to help the client recognize feelings.)

Client: Yeah, I'm scared that I won't be able to pull it off this time. Usually I can just pull an all-nighter and get it done, but it seems too big this time. The paper's supposed to be 20 pages.

Helper: What are your plans for this evening? (The helper wants the client to get more specific about the situation to provide a clearer picture and again focuses by using an open question about action.)

Client: Well, I just want to go home and sleep. I just don't want to do it.

Helper: Is anything else going on in your life that makes it difficult for you to work on the paper right now? (The helper notes that the client seems stuck and thinks that perhaps the situation is more complicated than the client has expressed. Hence, the helper uses an open question to ask about other issues.)

Client: It's funny you should ask about that. I just had a big fight with my boyfriend, and I feel very upset. He wants to get married and have kids right away, but I really want to go to graduate school. But if I go to graduate school, I will have to move away, at least for a while.

Helper: So you feel conflicted between being with your boyfriend and going on to school. (The helper feels pleased that the client has opened up about other parts of the situation. Because the helper wants to get the client to talk about her feelings about this conflict, the helper uses a reflection that focuses on both parts of the problem.)

Client: That's really true. It just feels like everything has to go his way. Just because he's already finished his school and is working, he wants me to be done too.

Helper: I wonder if you're somewhat confused. (The helper's intent is to identify feelings through reflection, but the helper has inappropriately projected her confusion onto the client because she is in a similar situation.)

Client: No, not really. As I think about it, I feel angry. I shouldn't have to give up my career for his. My mother did that, and she is very unhappy. She never even learned how to drive. She did everything for her kids, and now that we have all left home, she's depressed and lonesome. I think I want to have a career, but I don't know. I don't know if it's fair, and I don't want to risk losing my relationship with my boyfriend.

Helper: (in a softer voice) It sounds like you are really torn up inside. (The helper realizes that the last intervention was inaccurate and shifts focus back to the client's feelings by using a reflection.)

Client: (cries softly) Maybe I can't write the paper because I'm so confused about this fight with my boyfriend and what's going on with my mother.

Helper: (The helper is silent for 30 seconds to give the client a chance to experience her feelings of sadness.)

Client: (cries and then blows her nose)

Helper: (softly) I'm sure this is very difficult for you to talk about. (The helper wants to support the client and gives an approval-reassurance.)

Client: Yeah, it sure is. What do you think I should do?

Helper: Well, I think you should go talk to your instructor and see if you can get out of writing the paper tomorrow. Then I think you need to talk to your boyfriend and try to work things out. Perhaps you should encourage your mom to get counseling. (The helper inappropriately gets caught up in the client's request for help and gives direct guidance about what client should do.)

Client: Oh. (silence) Well, I don't know. (The client stops exploring and becomes passive.)

Helper: Sorry, I got carried away with too much advice. How do you feel about a career? (The helper realizes the client has stopped exploring and so apologizes briefly. She then tries to go back to the exploration by using open question to return to the last major issue they were discussing before the client got stuck.)

Client: (Client continues to explore.)

What Do You Think?

- How would you have handled the situation as the helper in the extended example?
- How do you explain the client's being able to gain insight (i.e., "Maybe I can't write the paper because of my fight with my boyfriend and what's going on with my mother") in the example when the helper did not provide interpretations?
- Discuss whether you think helpers need to go on to the insight stage or whether the exploration stage is necessary and sufficient for clients' change.
- Is it possible for clients to explore too much?
- Check the obstacles you are likely to face in your development as a helper:

  ____ inadequate attending and listening

  ____ asking too many closed questions

  ____ talking too much

  ____ giving too much or premature advice

  ____ being "buddies"

  ____ not allowing silence

_____ inappropriately self-disclosing

_____ discouraging intense expression of affect

_____ dissociating and panicking

_____ feeling inadequate

■ Identify strategies you might use to cope with obstacles as a helper:

_____ observing models

_____ imagery

_____ role-playing

_____ practice

_____ deep breathing

_____ focusing on the client

_____ positive self-talk

i LAB 7. Integration of Exploration Skills

A downloadable PDF of this Lab is available in the student resources area of the Helping Skills, *3rd ed. Web site: http://www.apa.org/books/resources/Hill3.*

You are ready to integrate the skills you have learned so far. In this lab, you will meet with a client and use these skills to facilitate client exploration.

Goal: For helpers to have an oppurtunity to integrate the skills of the exploration stage.

Execsice 1. Helping Exchange

Helper's and Client's Tasks During the Helping Exchange

1. Each helper pairs up with a volunteer client selected from outside the class.
2. Helpers bring the necessary forms with them to the session: Session Review Form (Web Form A), Helper Intentions List (Web Form D), Client Reactions System (Web Form G), Session Process and Outcome Measures (Web Form I), and Self-Awareness and Management Strategies Survey (Web Form J). Supervisors bring the Supervisor Rating Form (Web Form B).
3. Helpers bring an audio- or videotape recorder (tested ahead of time to ensure it works) and a tape. They turn on the recorder at the beginning of the session.
4. Helpers introduce themselves, inform clients about confidentiality, and indicate whether sessions will be recorded and observed.
5. Each helper conducts a 20-minute session with a client who talks about any easy topic (see Exhibit 1.1). The helper should be as helpful as possible, using all the exploration skills. Watch for the client's reactions to each of your interventions and modify subsequent interventions when appropriate.
6. Watch the time carefully. About 2 minutes before the end of the session, let the client know that time is almost up. At the end, let the client know when time is up by saying something like, "We need to stop now. Thank you for helping me practice my helping skills."

Supervisor's Tasks During the Session

Supervisors use the Supervisor Rating Form to record observations and evaluations.

Postsession

1. Both helper and client complete the Session Process and Outcome Measures (Web Form I). Each helper also completes the Self-Awareness and Management Strategies Survey (Survey Form J).
2. After the session, each helper reviews the tape with the client (review of a 20-minute session takes about 40 to 60 minutes). Helpers stop the tape after each intervention (except minimal acknowledgments such as "um-hmm" and "yeah"). Helpers write down the key words on the Session Review Form (Web Form A) so the exact spot on the tape can be located later for transcription.
3. Helpers rate the helpfulness of the intervention and record the numbers of up to three intentions (responding according to how they felt *during* the session). Use the whole range of the Helpfulness Scale and as many categories as possible on the Helper Intentions List. Do not complete these ratings collaboratively with clients.
4. Clients rate the helpfulness of each intervention and record the numbers of up to three reactions (responding according to how they felt *during* the session). Clients should use the whole range of the Helpfulness Scale and as many categories as possible on the reactions system (helpers learn more from honest feedback than from "nice" statements that are not genuine). Do not collaborate with helpers to complete the ratings.
5. Helpers and clients record the most helpful and least helpful event in the session.
6. Supervisors give feedback to helpers based on the Supervisor Rating Form (Web Form B).

Lab Report

1. Helpers should type a transcript of their 20-minute session (see the sample in Web Form C). Skip minimal utterances such as "okay," "you know," "er," and "uh."
2. Divide the helper speech into response units (essentially grammatical sentences), using the directions provided in Web Form F.
3. Using the Helping Skills System (see Web Form E), determine which skill was used for each response unit (grammatical sentence) in your transcript.
4. Indicate on the transcript which different words you would use for each intervention if you could do it again. Use the Helping Skills System (Web Form E) to indicate which skill fits for each response unit of what you would say differently.
5. Erase the tape. Make sure no identifying information is on the transcript.
6. Compare the skills used in this session with the skills in the initial session (Lab 2).
7. Compare the helper and client scores on the Session Process and Outcome Measures and the Self-Awareness and Management Strategies Scales with those of other students (go to references cited in Web Forms I and J).

Execsice 2: Watching the Exploration Stage in the DVD

The leader plays the exploration stage portion of the DVD that accompanies this book, *Helping Skills in Practice: A Three-Stage Model*. After all participants have viewed this portion of the DVD, the leader facilitates a discussion about what was helpful and not helpful, and about conceptualizing the client.

INSIGHT STAGE

Overview of the Insight Stage 9

Daring as it is to investigate the unknown, even more so
is it to question the known.

—*Kaspar*

Juan had been to a behavioral helper who taught him
relaxation, assertiveness skills, and time management
skills. He was now more organized, relaxed, and better
able to carry on a conversation, but he still felt empty
inside. He could not understand why he felt life had no
meaning. He went to a helper who believed in insight,
and they began exploring his feelings about himself
and his childhood. Through the new helper's gentle
questioning, challenges, interpretations, and
disclosures of insight, he came to the understanding
that perhaps his anxiety and loneliness had roots in the
fact that his mother died when he was 2 months old
and his father sent him to live with his grandparents.
Although his grandparents were very loving, he had
always felt that he was interfering with their retirement
plans and that he was out of place. He realized that in
social situations, he always placed himself on the
outside so others would not have the chance to reject
him. He lived his life as a defense against being
abandoned again. He also came to realize that by
removing himself from social situations, he had no
opportunity to have close, satisfying relationships. In
sessions, he found himself constantly worrying that
the helper was bored and would rather be with other
clients. Through the helper's talking about their
immediate relationship, Juan came to understand that
his feelings were a transference onto the helper of his
feelings about his parents abandoning him. Once he
understood more about himself and could see that the

helper indeed cared about him, Juan began to rethink the idea that he was not lovable. He was able to reframe his perceptions of his grandparents to see that they did love him and had chosen to raise him. Juan felt better because he now had some explanations for his feelings and behaviors.

During the exploration stage, helpers work to establish a therapeutic relationship with clients, help clients explore thoughts about the many facets of their problems, and help clients experience feelings related to their problems at a deep level. For some clients, this supportive, nonjudgmental listening is all that is needed to help them make important changes in their lives. The helper's acceptance enables these clients to experience their feelings and accept what is going on inside them. They become unblocked, able to think about how they want to be and what they want to do about their problems. Their actualization potential is released, and they become creative and active self-healers and problem solvers. They no longer "need" outside intervention, although they might enjoy sharing their thoughts and feelings with a good helper and benefit from deeper examination of their concerns.

Unfortunately, not all clients can progress on their own after exploring their thoughts and feelings. Some clients have a hard time understanding the origins and consequences of their feelings and behaviors. Other clients get stuck and need someone to help them get past obstacles and defenses they learned in childhood that protect them against internal pain and external harm. It is difficult to give up protective defenses because there is no assurance that the world is a safe place. When painful events occur, clients often compartmentalize experiences in their minds so that they do not have to think about them, making it difficult to integrate these experiences into their lives. Some clients have done things a certain way for so long that they never question their actions or think about the reasons for what they do. Other clients are eager to learn more about themselves and their motivations but need an objective perspective to help them move beyond their blind spots. For these situations, it is important for helpers to be able to use insight skills.

The insight stage builds on the foundation of the exploration stage. Going beyond exploration to insight and understanding requires a deep sense of empathy and belief in clients. In this stage, helpers see beyond defenses and inappropriate behaviors to the client's inner self, accept who clients are, and help clients come to understand themselves more deeply.

What Is Insight?

When clients come to insights, they see things from a new perspective, are able to make connections between things, or have an understanding of why things happen as they do (Elliott et al., 1994). For some, gaining insight is like a light bulb going off, a sudden feeling of "aha!" For example, Yinyin might suddenly realize her strong reactions to her boyfriend when he said he would not go to a party stem from her rarely having gotten her way as a child. Her anger may be due to perceived past injustices and a belief that her boyfriend is doing the same thing to her that her parents did. For others, however, insight does not occur suddenly. Rogers (1942) noted that "insight comes gradually, bit by bit, as the individual develops sufficient psychological strength to endure new perspectives" (p. 177). For example, Robert might slowly, and only after several challenges and interpretations, come to realize that his indecision over his career choice might be due to unhappiness with his wife. Hill et al. (2007) talked about this range of insights as gold nuggets versus gold dust—sometimes clients are lucky and hit a gold nugget of insight, but more often there is a smattering of gold dust as they work hard to gain insight over time.

INTELLECTUAL VERSUS EMOTIONAL INSIGHT

Insight usually must be emotional as well as intellectual to lead to action (Reid & Finesinger, 1952; Singer, 1970). In other words, the insight must be deeply felt as well as cognitively understood. Intellectual insight provides an objective explanation for a problem (e.g., "I am anxious because of my Oedipal conflict"); it has a barren, sterile quality that keeps clients stuck in understandings that lead nowhere (Gelso & Fretz, 2001). Many of us know people who can give a comprehensive history of their psychological problems and the sources of their difficulties but who cannot express their feelings fully. Emotional insight, on the other hand, connects affect to intellect and creates a sense of personal involvement and responsibility (Gelso & Fretz, 2001). For example, when Jason suddenly realizes his conflict with his wife for having her own interests is really due to the hurt he felt because his father did not spend much time with him, he can feel that hurt deep inside himself. He may feel the relief of a burden lifted from him. This emotional and intellectual insight might help Jason decide that it is okay for his wife to have separate activities from him. Jason might start thinking that he needs to develop his own interests and might begin to question why he allows his whole identity to be based on his wife. The deep insight Jason achieved would not have been possible if he had been given an interpretation that sounded right "on paper" but was not something he could acknowledge as his own or feel at a deep level.

The attainment of emotional insight is thought to result in behavior change (Ferenczi & Rank, 1925/1956). For example, a client who understands only intellectually that she screams at her boyfriend because she is angry with her father does not achieve the same kind of growth and change that both intellectual insight and emotional insight engender. If this client were to experience the feelings associated with this intellectual understanding (e.g., how badly she feels about transferring negative feelings toward her mostly innocent boyfriend, and how deeply frustrated she is that her father continues to have a negative influence on her life), she might develop the motivation to change her behavior toward her boyfriend (which then might help her gain more insight about the problem). Emotional insight is typically easier for clients to attain when they are fully and actively involved in the helping process. They need to be personally involved and eager about trying to understand themselves. It is usually better for helpers to work with clients to help them achieve insight rather than telling them what to think.

WHY IS INSIGHT NECESSARY?

According to Frank and Frank (1991), the need to make sense of events is as fundamental to human beings as the need for food or water. They suggested that people evaluate internal and external stimuli in view of their assumptions about what is dangerous, safe, important, good, bad, and so on. These assumptions become organized into sets of highly structured, complex, and interacting values, expectations, and images of self that are closely related to emotional states and feelings. These psychological structures shape, and in turn are shaped by, a person's perceptions and behaviors. They viewed insight as a reworking of the past that leads to the discovery of new facts, as well as a recognition of new relationships between previously known facts and a reevaluation of their significance.

Similarly, Freud (1923/1963) believed psychological problems are developmental and resolution can only be reached by obtaining insight into the problems. Symptoms generally make sense in the context of past and present life experiences. For example, Jenna's fear of public speaking made sense in the light of her reluctance to achieve and possibly outdo her passive and depressed mother. Her insight that she had been limiting herself to placate her mother led her to understand why she made the choices she did throughout her life. This understanding gave her a sense that she could make different choices in the future.

Frankl (1959) emphasized the importance of having a life philosophy to transcend suffering and find meaning in existence. He argued that our greatest human need is to find a core of meaning and a purpose in life. Frankl's experience in a German concentration camp bears out his theory: Although he could not change his life situation, he was able to change the meaning he attached to this experience. By drawing on the strengths of his Jewish tradition, he was able to survive and help others survive. Similarly, Wampold (2001) suggested that people need an explanation, sometimes any explanation, to make sense out of their lives.

Clients' interpretations of events determine subsequent behaviors and feelings, as well as their willingness to work on certain topics in a helping setting. For example, John, an 18-year-old client, is reluctant to learn to drive. If he believes his reluctance to drive is due to fears about having a major accident, John might say fear is the main problem. If John believes the fear is due to a reluctance to grow up and become independent, he might feel more of a need to work on separation issues. Helpers need to learn how clients currently construe events (both consciously and unconsciously) so they can help them develop more adaptive constructs.

It is usually best to attain insight before moving on to action. If clients did whatever helpers told them to do, with no understanding of or explanation for why these actions were important, they would not have a framework to guide their behavior when new problems develop. Clients would be dependent on others to tell them what to do as each new problem arose. In contrast, if clients learn how to think about their problems, they are more likely in the future to explore their problems, achieve understanding, and decide what they would like to do differently on their own. In effect, helpers are teaching clients a problem-solving approach.

In the example of the reluctant driver, if John comes to understand that his reluctance is due to anxiety and guilt about leaving his sick mother, he can make an informed decision that fits his values about what he wants to do about his mother. Hence, insight is especially important in the helping process.

Theoretical Background: Psychoanalytic Theory

Psychoanalytic theory began with Sigmund Freud and has evolved through many subsequent theorists (notably Adler, Jung, and Sullivan). Over the century that psychoanalytic theory has existed, many changes have been made in the theory (Mitchell, 1993), with current emphasis given to the relationship between therapist and client (e.g., Safran & Muran, 2000; Strupp & Binder, 1984; Wachtel, 2008). In this section, the focus is on a few important aspects of psychoanalytic theory that are currently salient and applicable to the helping skills model.

I have often found that students are quite disdainful of Freud when they first take helping skills classes. Many have learned in their undergraduate psychology classes that Freud is outdated and irrelevant. Yet, as students progress through graduate school and particularly as they become master therapists, they often have increasing awareness of the beauty and relevance of Freudian theory as a way of explaining the depths of human nature. They rarely swallow the theory whole but do become intrigued with this theory and especially with modern versions of it. So I encourage you to have an open mind about psychoanalytic theory.

Psychoanalysis presents a complex, rich description of the development of personality and treatment. In this section, I touch on only a few of the ideas. I encourage interested readers to explore other sources to learn more about other psychoanalytic theories (e.g., Basch, 1980; Gelso & Hayes, 1998; Greenson, 1967; Kohut, 1971, 1977, 1984; Mahler, 1968; McWilliams, 2004; Mitchell, 1993; Patton & Meara, 1992).

FREUDIAN THEORY OF PERSONALITY

In his attempt to understand personality development, Freud postulated a number of models that have become so well known that they have become household terms. Although quite controversial, these models help us think more deeply about human nature. They need not be taken literally but rather as metaphors for thinking about development. And of course, as we gather more knowledge, these models constantly evolve.

Freud (1940/1949) suggested that all children go through several psychosexual stages of development. In the first stage, energy is focused on oral (eating) satisfaction. As the child has to learn to control urination and defecation, energy shifts to the anal region. Then, Freud suggested that a latent period occurs, in which the child is more free for other pursuits. As the child develops, energy shifts to the genital regions. Here, Freud postulated that children begin to become attracted to parents of the opposite sex. The resolution of this conflict (the Oedipal conflict for boys; the Electra complex for girls) leads children to give up the opposite-sex parent as a sex object and identify and ally with the parent of the same sex. As children go through each stage, they can become stuck if they are either deprived (e.g., given too little to eat) or overindulged (e.g., given too much to eat). If people have difficulty they may regress back to a stage in which they felt gratified (e.g., regress to overeating).

Looking back over 100 years from a different culture, it is clear that Freud's developmental sequence was heavily culturally bound and is not so readily relevant for the present day. But rather than dismissing it out of hand, it is useful to recognize that indeed there are psychological developmental sequences that are important. Indeed, many theorists since Freud have built on these theories and offered different stage models (e.g., Erikson, Kohlberg, Mahler). Perhaps one of Freud's greatest contributions here was the notion that we can be either overindulged or underindulged at each of several developmental stages and that these early experiences clearly influence us in later life. Also, having raised both a boy and a girl, I can tell you that there is something to the notion of boys and girls reacting differently to mothers and fathers.

Furthermore, Freud postulated that at birth, infants are totally governed by the *id,* or primitive urges that seek immediate gratification. As the child develops, the *ego* forms to help the child delay gratification and negotiate with the outside world. As the child develops further and internalizes society's morals and values through resolution of the Oedipal/Electra conflict, she or he develops a *superego* (which involves both morals and ideals). Throughout life, people struggle with conflicts between primitive impulses, the moderating ego, and societal restrictions and ideals. For example, Maria continually struggled with her weight. On the one hand, she wanted to eat whatever and whenever she wanted (influence of id), but on the other hand she relentlessly scolded herself for her lack of control (harsh superego), and compromised by allowing herself a small dessert every night if she had exercised during the day (the ego at work). Once again, the id, ego, and superego are metaphors that help us understand psychological principles rather than being actual physiological structures that could be found in the brain or body. They help us tell the story of how and why people struggle to cope with life.

A related Freudian concept is consciousness. Freud divided awareness into the unconscious, preconscious, and conscious. He postulated that the largest percentage of mental activity is unconscious, or not available to immediate awareness. A small amount of energy is in the preconscious, suggesting that one can access these thoughts and experiences if a great deal of attention is paid to them. An even smaller amount of awareness is conscious, or currently in our awareness at any given time. Freud proposed that most people act out of unconscious motivations and are unaware why they act the way they do. To illustrate the power of the unconscious, think about a recent time you did something that seemed out of character for you (e.g., became suddenly angry, acted differently from your values)—these feelings and behaviors may have been motivated by unconscious feelings.

Yet another important Freudian construct relates to defenses. Not everything goes smoothly in the development of personality. Children do not always receive everything they need to develop psychologically. One way people cope with adversity is by developing defense mechanisms. Freud (1933) and more recent psychoanalysts have theorized that defense mechanisms are unconscious methods for dealing with anxiety through denial or distortion of reality. Everyone has defense mechanisms because everyone has to cope with anxiety inherent in living. Defense mechanisms can be healthy if used appropriately and in moderation, but repeated and frequent use of defense mechanisms can be problematic. Some examples of defense mechanisms include the following:

- Repression (not allowing painful material into one's conscious thought)
- Intellectualization (avoiding painful feelings by focusing on ideas)
- Denial (actively rejecting painful affect)
- Regression (engaging in behaviors from an earlier stage of development at times when one is anxious)
- Displacement (shifting uncomfortable feelings toward someone who is less powerful and less threatening than the individual from whom the feelings originated)
- Identification (emulating characteristics in others)
- Projection (perceiving that others have the characteristics that are unconsciously disliked in one's self)
- Undoing (behaving in a ritualistic manner to take away or make amends for unacceptable behaviors)
- Reaction formation (acting in a manner that is opposite to what one is feeling)
- Sublimation (changing unacceptable impulses into socially appropriate actions)
- Rationalization (making excuses for an anxiety-producing thought or behavior)

For example, Antonio has marital problems because he projects onto his wife that she is dominating like his mother. He is unable to see that her questions are motivated by concern rather than by a desire to control. He is afraid of telling his wife about his anger at her for being dominating, and so he displaces his feelings by kicking the dog. If asked about his anger, he denies it and regresses to acting like a whiny 7-year-old who expects to be punished. These defense mechanisms protect Antonio from the anxiety that comes from being aware of how he felt toward his mother when he was a child and from learning how to deal with his feelings more appropriately to the current situation with his wife.

ATTACHMENT THEORY

Another important analytic construct is attachment, which has been the focus of much recent theorizing and research (e.g., Bowlby, 1969, 1988; Cassidy, & Shaver, 2008; Meyer & Pilkonis, 2002). Bowlby developed attachment theory to explain the behavioral and emotional responses that keep young children in close proximity to caregivers. In optimal attachment, caregivers provide for the infant a comfortable presence that reduces anxiety and promotes a feeling of security. From this secure base, infants are able to explore their environment. Through an observational study of young children, Ainsworth, Blehar, Waters, and Wall (1978) found three patterns of attachment: secure, anxious–ambivalent, and anxious–avoidant. Infants who were securely attached explored freely in their mother's presence, showed some anxiety upon separation, and were easily comforted when reunited. Infants with an anxious–ambivalent pattern were excessively anxious and angry, and they tended to cling to their mothers to an extent that interfered with their exploration. They were also distressed during separation and were difficult to comfort on reunion with mothers. Anxious–avoidant infants showed minimal interest in their mothers and displayed minimal affect throughout the observation. These observations have been replicated with other children, and the results have been extended to adulthood, suggesting that attachment patterns in childhood carry over to relationships in adulthood (Ainsworth, 1989). Bowlby's theory has been used extensively to explain the difficulties clients have in forming relationships with other people, including therapists (e.g., Mallinckrodt, Gantt, & Coble, 1995).

TREATMENT FROM A PSYCHOANALYTIC PERSPECTIVE

Freud (1923/1963) believed that deep examination and insight into troubling issues could assist in the resolution of problems. As a foundation for treatment, the helper listens patiently, empathically, uncritically, and receptively to the client (Arlow, 1995).

To facilitate insight, the helper encourages the client to free associate—to say whatever thoughts come to mind without censure as a means to make the unconscious conscious, which is a primary focus of psychoanalytic treatment. When appropriate, the helper offers interpretations that are just beyond the client's current understanding to encourage the client to think more deeply about the issues (Speisman, 1959). The focus of interpretations is typically about the origins of behaviors and the influence of early childhood experiences on current behaviors. Psychoanalysts talk about the importance of doing an "archeological dig" to determine the early reasons for current behaviors.

The goal of psychoanalytic treatment is to make the unconscious conscious, or stated another way, to replace the id with the ego. Although the majority of the mind is unconscious, according to Freud, one can strive to make oneself as aware as possible of these primitive influences. Because of the difficulty of dealing with unconscious material, Freud proposed analyzing dreams, fantasies, or slips of the tongue, where the ego does not have as strong a control. Psychoanalytic helpers also assist clients in developing an awareness of frequently used defense mechanisms and in gaining more control over the use of these unconscious strategies to reduce anxiety.

Freud believed that manifestations of unresolved problems from early in childhood are repeated throughout the client's life. Often, the repetition is uncovered through analysis of the way the client relates to the therapist. For example, a client whose mother was cold and unable to fulfill the client's attachment needs as an infant may demonstrate neediness in her relationship with the therapist. The client might call the therapist at home, ask for extra sessions, and try to get the therapist to extend the time limits of each session. The client might also project onto her therapist that the therapist is cold and unable to meet her needs. Placing on the therapist characteristics that belong to other people with whom one has unresolved issues is termed *transference* (Freud, 1920/1943). Freud indicated that the analysis and interpretation of transference can be a powerful therapeutic tool to facilitate understanding of the client's relationships with others (see also Gelso & Carter, 1985, 1994). Recent research, however, suggests caution in using transference interpretations, especially with clients who have a lot of difficulty with interpersonal relationships (Crits-Christoph & Gibbons, 2002).

The helper's unresolved issues can also influence the process and outcome of helping. This process has been called *countertransference* (see also Gelso & Hayes, 1998, 2007) and is defined as the helper's reactions to the client that originate in the unresolved issues of the helper. In the previous example, the therapist may have had unresolved needs to take care of others (perhaps related to having an alcoholic mother who relied on the helper to care for younger siblings) and so might respond to the client's neediness by allowing the client to call her at home, stop by the office at any time, and delay payment until the client earns more money. If unrecognized, countertransference behaviors can influence therapy negatively. However, awareness of countertransference feelings can actually facilitate the process. For example, if Jeff becomes aware that he has a hard time empathizing with a passive older female client because the client reminds him of his mother, Jeff can talk with his own therapist about his issues with his mother and talk with his supervisor about how to understand the client. Thus, Jeff can come to understand the client separate from his own difficulties with his mother.

Since Freud, one major change in psychoanalytic theory has been the recognition that the therapist is not a blank screen but rather plays a key role in the therapeutic relationship. Theorists now refer to this as *two-person psychology*, to emphasize the fact that the therapist and client are both contributors to the relationship based on their own issues (see review in Hill & Knox, 2009). From this perspective, it is not possible to talk about client transference and therapist countertransference as separate issues.

Building on this idea, psychoanalytic and interpersonal helpers emphasize working on the therapeutic relationship as a central change mechanism within therapy. By talking openly about what is going on between the helper and client, it is possible to work through problems in the relationship, clarify distortions in the transference and counter-transference, model healthy interpersonal functioning, and encourage clients to interact differently with others outside of therapy.

HOW PSYCHOANALYTIC THEORIES RELATE TO THE THREE-STAGE MODEL

The emphasis in psychoanalytic theories on the importance of early relationships, defenses, insight, and dealing with the therapeutic relationship is consistent with my thinking about the insight stage. More specifically, the emphasis on the importance of early childhood experiences is in concert with my thinking about the importance of early experiences, particularly with significant others. Similarly, the emphasis on defenses is important in helping clients cope with establishing moderate levels of defenses that protect them yet allow them to interact with others. I also believe strongly that insight is helpful in enabling clients to make lasting changes and to solve new problems as they arise. Furthermore, to me, psychotherapy would indeed be dull and lack depth if we just focused on exploration or behavior change instead of asking deeper questions about meaning. Finally, dealing with problems as they occur in the therapeutic relationship is crucial because it provides clients with corrective relational experiences and teaches skills to handle relationships outside of therapy more effectively.

I emphasize that the helper's role in the insight stage involves coaching the client to gain insight rather than the helper being the one who provides the insight. Often, clients are capable of coming up with their own insights when helpers provide the appropriate atmosphere and ask thoughtful questions. In fact, clients often feel better about insights they have attained on their own rather than interpretations that are foisted on them. Some clients, however, want more input from helpers, and such input can be helpful if offered in a collaborative, tentative, empathic manner.

A departure I make with psychoanalytic theory is with regard to helping clients move to the action stage. Helpers using psychoanalytic theories do not usually focus on helping clients make specific behavior changes (Crits-Christoph, Barber, & Kurcias, 1991). In contrast, I contend that the action stage can be very useful, especially when it follows the insight stage (although some clients want or need action before insight). Similarly, helpers using the three-stage model tend to be more active agents in helping, and the length of treatment tends to be shorter than in classic psychoanalytic therapy. Despite some differences in theoretical assertions, however, I stress that psychoanalytic techniques are helpful for guiding clients toward increased insight and self-understanding (which set the foundation for action).

Developing Hypotheses About Client Dynamics

To make decisions about how to intervene in the insight stage, helpers need to have some idea about what is going on at a deeper level for the client. Helpers need to start thinking about client dynamics. To do so, they rely in part on their perceptions and intuitions of the client dynamics. They use themselves as barometers of what is going on in the relationship. Helpers have to allow themselves to have inner reactions and then think about how the client contributes to these reactions. Helpers can ask themselves the following questions to begin to assess client dynamics:

- Are there discrepancies or contradictions in feelings, actions, or thoughts expressed by the client?
- What might be causing the client to behave this way at this time?
- What contributes to keeping this client from changing at this time?
- What are the client defenses, resistances, and transferences operating in this situation?
- How am I feeling in the therapeutic relationship, and could others react similarly to this client?

Teaching students about conceptualization skills can be built into training programs. After role-plays, the instructor can ask students to begin to think about client dynamics. For example, in one training session, Kunal (a student in class who was the volunteer client) talked about not having been accepted into graduate school and feeling unsure about what he wanted to do—did he really want to go to graduate school or did he want to do something else with his life? After one student acted as the helper going through the exploration stage, I stopped the interaction, asked Kunal to sit quietly and observe but not respond, and initiated a discussion about emerging conceptualizations of this client. We wondered, respectfully of course, whether Kunal had problems with commitment in other areas, and we speculated about family pressures with regard to attending graduate school. These speculations were helpful in identifying issues for further probing in the insight stage. Not that all the speculations were right, but they did provide ideas about where to go, always recalling the need to be flexible and revise ideas based on emerging information. Similarly, it could be helpful for helpers to talk with supervisors about conceptualizations as a way to stimulate one's thinking.

On the basis of their conceptualizations, helpers can develop clearer intentions. Thus, by hypothesizing about the client's problem, the reason the client is talking about the problem at this particular time, and what the helper can do to help, the helper is able to better determine what to do next in the session. Conceptualization thus enables helpers to have a focus and intentions for interventions instead of just wandering aimlessly without a clear focus in sessions.

Goals and Skills of the Insight Stage

In the insight stage, I focus on three main goals: facilitating awareness, facilitating insight, and working with the therapeutic relationship. These goals all work synergistically to help clients move to new depths of self-understanding. A number of skills are used to implement each of these goals. See Exhibit 9.1 for a list of the goals and the skills to facilitate those goals.

EXHIBIT 9.1

List of Skills to Facilitate Goals of the Insight Stage

Goal	Skill
Foster awareness	Challenge
Facilitate insight	Probe for insight
	Interpretation
	Disclose insight
Work on the therapeutic relationship	Immediacy

FACILITATING AWARENESS

It is important that clients become aware of their thoughts and behaviors. People have lived with themselves for so long and developed defenses to protect themselves from interpersonal injuries, so they are often unaware of thoughts and behaviors that are not adaptive. They need to hear how others honestly react to them so they can begin the self-examination process. For example, a client may be unaware that he comes across in a hostile manner, which makes others avoid him. Awareness involves becoming more conscious about one's thoughts, feelings, behaviors, and impact on others. Thus, awareness is often a precondition for insight. To facilitate awareness, helpers primarily challenge thoughts and discrepancies.

FACILITATING INSIGHT

Once a person becomes aware of some feeling, thought, or behavior, he or she often wants to understand more about it. One of the hallmarks of our existence as human beings is the desire for an explanation for our thoughts, feelings, and behaviors. An explanation, right or wrong, helps most people feel more in control of their world and is a potent ingredient in therapeutic change (Hanna & Ritchie, 1995). In the insight stage, helpers search for clues regarding what motivates clients, what causes them pain and happiness, and what hinders them from achieving their potential (remembering to be empathic and compassionate). Here, helpers use probe for insight, interpretations, and disclosures of insight.

WORKING WITH THE THERAPEUTIC RELATIONSHIP

Another specific goal of the insight stage is for clients to gain awareness and insight into their interpersonal interactions. Because clients are often unaware how they come across to others, one goal of helping is to provide clients with feedback about how they come across in the helping relationship. The assumption is that they act toward others in similar ways as they do toward the helper, so looking closely at the therapy relationships provides a microcosm of clients' interpersonal relationships. Of course, clients do not behave exactly the same with everybody as they do with helpers (especially given that helpers have different personal styles and countertransference issues), but observations of the therapy relationship provide an opportunity to work on one immediate relationship. Helpers can then work with clients in the action stage to generalize learning to other relationships. To work on the therapeutic relationship, helpers use immediacy (again with empathy, compassion, and tentativeness).

Concluding Thoughts

In comparison with the exploration stage, in the insight stage helpers rely somewhat more on their own perspectives and reactions to help clients understand where they are getting stuck and what might be motivating them. Thus, helpers move away somewhat from the receptive stance of facilitating client exploration during the exploration stage and not presenting their own thoughts and conceptualizations (although they are thinking about them) to a slightly more active (but still empathic) stance of trying to help clients understand issues that prevent them from functioning fully.

I emphasize that helpers do not have "the" insight or right perspective and should not force clients to accept their perspectives. Rather, helpers primarily encourage clients to discover new things about themselves and occasionally and tentatively offer their own perspectives to help clients come to new awarenesses and insights.

There remains a sense of working together, with helpers aiding clients in discovering things about themselves. The goal is for clients to have a sense of discovery of the new understandings. Even when helpers suggest insights, clients need to try them and discover if they fit rather than accepting them blindly. Understanding what is going on inside oneself is an "aha" experience that is invaluable, but it must be discovered and experienced by the client to be truly beneficial. Helpers have to be careful when using their own perspective to make sure they are motivated by the best interests of the clients rather than by their own needs. When helpers are motivated by their own needs (i.e., countertransference), their interventions tend to be less helpful. Helpers need to be aware of their countertransference reactions so they do not inappropriately act on them in sessions.

Helpers also have to be prepared for clients not agreeing with their challenges or interpretations. Sometimes these skills are used prematurely or are inaccurate or inappropriate, some are done insensitively, and sometimes clients become defensive and anxious. Helpers need to pay attention to these reactions to see how they can intervene differently with the client.

The skills unique to the insight stage are much harder to learn and use than the skills in the exploration stage. I do not expect students to master the insight skills quickly in their initial exposure to the model. In fact, it takes most students many years and much practice to learn the insight skills and apply them in the appropriate situations in a helping setting. But it is important for beginning helpers to be aware of the insight skills, even though they will probably initially be appropriately hesitant to use these skills.

The exploration skills (attending and listening, restatement, reflection of feelings, and silence) are also frequently used in the insight stage. Once the helper has presented a challenge, interpretation, disclosure of insight, or immediacy, the client is at a new level, and the helper has to facilitate the client in exploring thoughts and feelings.

What Do You Think?

- What is the role of insight in your life? Describe several situations in which you naturally sought out (or avoided) insight.
- Describe your thoughts about whether insight is necessary before action.
- Describe your thoughts about how much interpretive input the helper should provide and how it should be done.
- Compare and contrast psychoanalytic theory with Rogers's client-centered theory. Which theory makes most sense to you personally in terms of the personality development and therapy?
- Which defense mechanisms do you use most often in your life?

Skills for Fostering Awareness 10

And the trouble is, if you don't risk anything, you risk
even more.

—*Erica Jong*

Ethan says he wants to go to graduate school, but then
he doesn't study and so ends up with bad grades. The
helper gently challenges Ethan by saying, "Hmmm, on
the one hand you say that you want to go to graduate
school, but on the other hand you don't seem to want
to study. What do you suppose is going on?" This
challenge was presented in a gentle, nonthreatening
manner and followed by an open question to
encourage Ethan to become curious about himself. It
raised Ethan's awareness about his behaviors and
encouraged him to think more about his commitment
to attending graduate school. Ethan realized he was
not ready for graduate school and began pondering
why he might be sabotaging himself.

This chapter focuses primarily on challenges as a skill for fostering awareness. In addition, a few other skills that can be
useful to foster awareness are covered briefly.

Challenges

Challenges point out maladaptive beliefs and thoughts, discrepancies, or contradictions of which the client is unaware
or unwilling to change (see Exhibit 10.1). When a helper uses

EXHIBIT 10.1

Overview of Challenge

Definition	A *challenge* points out maladaptive thoughts, discrepancies, or contradictions of which the client is unaware, unwilling, or unable to change.
Example	"You're feeling sad that your husband died, but I wonder if you're also angry at him for leaving you."
Typical helper intentions	To challenge, to identify maladaptive behaviors, to identify maladaptive cognitions, to identify and intensify feelings, to deal with resistance, to promote insight (see Web Form D)
Possible client reactions	Challenged, unstuck, negative thoughts and feelings, clear, feelings, responsibility, new perspective, scared, worse, stuck, confused, misunderstood (see Web Form G)
Desired client behaviors	Cognitive–behavioral exploration, affective exploration, insight (see Web Form H)
Helpful hints	Observe the client to develop challenges (look for inconsistencies, maladaptive thoughts)
	Challenges should be done carefully, gently, respectfully, tentatively, thoughtfully, and with empathy
	The helper's tone should be one of puzzlement and curiosity, trying to help the client figure out a puzzle
	Work collaboratively with clients to raise awareness
	Do not make judgments when you challenge
	Be humble—remember how difficult it is to be aware
	Present the challenge as soon as possible about the behavior occurs
	Ask for client reactions

challenges, he or she is inviting clients to become aware of their maladaptive issues, thoughts, feelings, and behaviors. Maladaptive beliefs and thoughts are important because these influence feelings and behaviors. If clients can become aware of their maladaptive beliefs and thoughts, they can decide whether to change them.

Discrepancies and contradictions are important because they are often signs of unresolved issues, ambivalence (mixed feelings), or suppressed (or repressed) feelings. Often these discrepancies come up because clients have not been able to deal effectively with feelings as they arise. With challenges of discrepancies, helpers juxtapose two things to make the client aware of the contradiction between them, thus paving the way to understanding the cause of the discrepancy. Helpers can focus on several types of discrepancies:

- Between two verbal statements (e.g., "You say there's no problem, but then you say you're annoyed with him.")
- Between words and actions (e.g., "You say you want to get good grades, but you spend most of your time partying and sleeping.")

- Between two behaviors (e.g., "You're smiling, but your teeth are clenched.")
- Between two feelings (e.g., "You feel angry at your sister, but you also feel pleased that now everyone will see what kind of person she really is.")
- Between values and behaviors (e.g., "You say you believe in respecting others' choices, but then you try to convince them that they are wrong about abortion.")
- Between one's perception of self and experience (e.g., "You say no one likes you, but earlier you described an instance where someone invited you to have lunch.")
- Between one's ideal and real self (e.g., "You say you want to achieve, but you also say you can't.")
- Between the helper's and the client's opinions (e.g., "You say you are not working hard, but I think you are doing a great job.")

The term *challenge* is used in this book instead of the more typical term *confrontation* because challenge conveys less of a confrontational or aggressive manner. However, I use the two terms somewhat interchangeably in the discussion.

RATIONALE FOR USING CHALLENGES

Challenges are used to help clients recognize feelings, motives, and desires of which they are not aware. If clients are angry at others but unable to admit it, they might make a lot of sarcastic comments and inadvertently wound others. In other words, their anger "leaks" out. Furthermore, clients might be invested in not being aware of their inappropriate behaviors. They may blame other people rather than take responsibility for their actions. For example, a middle-aged person might continue to blame his parents for all of his problems rather than take responsibility for them, because taking responsibility would mean he would have to give up his rage at his parents and change his unhealthy behaviors. Challenges are often needed to nudge clients out of denial, help them see their problems in a different light, and encourage them to take appropriate responsibility for their problems.

Challenges can also help clients become aware of ambivalent feelings. Most of us have ambivalent feelings but cannot allow ourselves to feel both sides of issues because of beliefs about how we "ought" to be (e.g., "Nice girls don't get angry"). Challenges can be used to unearth thoughts and feelings so that clients begin to experience and take responsibility for their thoughts and feelings.

Challenges also enable clients to admit to having different or deeper feelings than they were previously able to acknowledge. For example, Angela said over and over that everything was going well until the helper challenged her about her poor grades. This challenge encouraged Angela to think about what might be going on at a deeper level and made her realize that she was trying too hard to ignore problems. Another example involves Gianni, who indicated that his relationship with his wife was great. The helper pointed out that Gianni's wife was never home and they had not had sex for 3 years. This challenge invited Gianni to examine closely what was happening in his relationship with his wife.

Even though the goal of challenges is to raise awareness, sometimes challenges help clients gain insight. Although helpers are not interpreting or providing reasons when they challenge, sometimes simply hearing a challenge leads clients to insight. For example, a helper may challenge a client by telling him that he says he wants help, but he does not disclose anything about his situation. This challenge might lead the client to realize that he is reluctant to reveal anything because he is afraid of being rejected.

These interventions can also be used to help clients become aware of their defenses (see chaps. 4 and 9 for more discussion of defenses). Defenses exist for a reason—they help us cope. All of us need some defenses to survive in the world. However, most of us have defenses that are not very adaptive. Sometimes we develop defenses to protect ourselves from unreliable, punitive, or abusive parents or others, and we rigidly use these defenses later in life even when they are no longer needed. Although everyone needs defenses sometimes, the helper's goal is to help clients become aware of their defenses and make choices about when and how much to use them. For example, a helper might challenge a client by saying, "You say that you keep up a wall to protect yourself against everyone, but I wonder if you really need to keep it so high with everyone. Maybe there are some people you can trust." By providing a safe place to examine defenses, helpers can work with clients to distinguish situations in which defenses are needed to protect the client and when it is safe to let go of unnecessary defenses.

Our goal as helpers is not to break down or remove all of the defenses but to give clients the option of choosing when and how often to use defenses. We need to help clients look carefully at their reasons for maintaining defenses and determine whether the defenses are still needed. For example, in the face of a hostile attacker, a defense of withdrawal might be appropriate, whereas withdrawal might be counterproductive in an intimate relationship.

In addition, it is important to note that not all challenges of discrepancies relate to pointing out negative aspects that the client is not ready to face. Some relate to positive things that clients are not ready to admit to themselves. For example, Marita constantly put herself down in front of other people, making disparaging remarks about what a "klutz" she was or how anyone else could do things better. Her helper challenged her gently that in fact she was quite competent at expressing her feelings and interacting with him. She was surprised and then started crying, later saying that no one had ever said anything positive to her before.

THEORETICAL PERSPECTIVES ON CHALLENGES

Several theorists have talked about the benefits of challenges. They have used the more traditional term of confrontation, however, so I use this term for this section.

Carkhuff and Berenson (1967), humanistic theorists, stated that the purpose of pointing out discrepancies is to help reduce ambiguities and incongruities in the client's experiencing and communication. They suggested that confrontations encourage clients to accept themselves and become fully functioning. Confronting clients with the discrepant facets of their behaviors challenges them to understand themselves more fully. As Carkhuff (1969) noted, "At the point of confrontation the client is pressed to consider the possibility of changing and, in order to do so, utilizing resources that he [or she] has not yet employed" (p. 93). "The challenge in a sense creates a crisis in the client's life. The crisis poses the client with the choice between continuing in his [or her] present mode of functioning or making a commitment to attempt to achieve a higher-level, more fulfilling way of life" (p. 92).

Another perspective about confrontation comes from Greenson (1967), a psychoanalyst. Greenson defined confrontation as a demonstration to the client of his or her resistance: "all the forces within the patient that oppose the procedures and processes of psychoanalytic work" (p. 35). He suggested that confrontations should be delivered before interpretations because defenses first need to be confronted and brought into awareness before they can be understood. For example, he noted that before he could interpret why a client was avoiding a certain subject, he would first have to get the client to face that she or he was avoiding something. Thus, the confrontation points out that the client is resisting; the questions of how and what the client is resisting are then addressed through clarification and interpretation.

EMPIRICAL EVIDENCE ABOUT CHALLENGES/CONFRONTATIONS

A number of studies show that challenges or confrontations are used infrequently, accounting for about 1% to 5% of all therapist statements (Barkham & Shapiro, 1986; Hill, Helms, Tichenor, et al., 1988). Furthermore, Hill, Helms, Tichenor, et al. found that clients and therapists rated confrontations as moderately helpful but that clients had negative reactions to confrontations (i.e., felt scared, worse, stuck, confused, or misunderstood; lacked direction). They also found that clients did not explore their feelings after hearing confrontations and that therapists viewed sessions in which they did a lot of confrontations as not very smooth or satisfactory. Other studies indicate that confrontations are powerful, arousing interventions that can lead to defensiveness and resistance (W. R. Miller, Benefield, & Tonigan, 1993; Olson & Claiborn, 1990; Salerno, Farber, McCullough, Winston, & Trujillo, 1992). These studies suggest that challenges can be helpful in pointing out contradictions but need to done carefully and empathically so clients can hear and use them.

HOW TO DO CHALLENGES

A major task for helpers is presenting challenges in such a way that clients can hear them and feel supported rather than attacked. Quite unlike the exploration skills that convey acceptance, challenges can imply criticism. With challenges, helpers indicate that some aspect of a client's life is incongruent or problematic and imply that a client should change to feel, think, or act differently, and so the helper needs to be careful about how the challenge is phrased and presented. Challenges should be done carefully, gently, respectfully, tentatively, thoughtfully, and with empathy.

One might think of the client as building a wall around him- or herself. Rather than attacking the wall directly with major weapons or armaments, the helper might do better to point out the wall. When the client is aware of the wall, the helper and client together can try to understand the purpose for the wall and decide whether the wall is needed. Rather than battering down the wall, the helper might encourage the client to build a door in the wall and learn when to open and close that door.

The helper's manner should be one of puzzlement rather than hostility, of trying to help the client figure out a puzzle and make sense of discrepant pieces. One can simply point out the discrepancy in a nonthreatening manner and ask the client to clarify. Similarly, Lauver and Harvey (1997) suggested using "collegial confrontations," which point out the helper's confusion about what he or she perceives as discrepant; they recommended against trying to persuade the client to come around to the helper's viewpoint. In essence, helpers empathically point out discrepancies and then follow these challenges with reflections of feelings and open questions about how it felt to be challenged.

Furthermore, it is important that helpers not make judgments when they challenge. A challenge should not be a criticism but an encouragement to examine oneself more deeply. The goal is to work collaboratively with clients in raising awareness. If helpers are judgmental, clients may feel shamed and embarrassed and hence be more resistant to recognizing problems. Helpers need to remember that all of us have discrepancies and irrationalities and that we are not "better than" our clients. We need to be humble and empathize with how difficult it is to understand ourselves and make necessary changes. It is usually easier to see someone else's inconsistencies than it is to see our own.

When learning to challenge discrepancies, I recommend that helpers use the following formats to make sure they include both parts of the intervention:

On the one hand _____, but on the other hand _____.
You say _____, but you also say _____.
You say _____, but nonverbally you seem _____.
I'm hearing _____, but I'm also hearing _____.

Sometimes the first part of the discrepancy is implied, and the helper states only the "but" clause. For example, the client might say that there are no problems, and the helper might respond, "But you said he was angry at you" (implying "You just said there were no problems, but . . ."). Or the helper might challenge by simply saying, "really?" "oh yeah?" or "hmmm?" which questions the client in a gentle challenging manner and encourages the client to think about what he or she is thinking.

Challenges should be used as soon as possible after an example of the client's inconsistency. If a helper waits too long, the client might not remember what the helper is talking about. For instance, if the helper says, "Last session when you spoke about your mother, you smiled in a strange way," the client is not likely to remember the incident. Thus, helpers should act fairly quickly (if they have enough data), while the behaviors and feelings are still recent (e.g., "Just then you smiled in a strange way. I wonder what's going on?").

Helpers also need to think about whether challenges are appropriate for the particular client. Direct, blunt challenges are not likely to be as effective with Asian, Latino/Latina, and Native American clients (Ivey, 1994) because they are not culturally appropriate. Ivey presented the example of a Chinese counselor's first efforts to counsel in China after training in the United States. He confronted an older Chinese man using the standard format for challenges: "On the one hand you do X, but on the other hand you do Y; how do you put these two together?" The older man politely said his farewell and never came back. The counselor had forgotten that when Chinese people see the need to express disagreement, they generally take great care not to hurt the other person's feelings or cause the other person to "lose face." His direct confrontive technique was considered ill-mannered and insensitive, especially because it came from a younger person. Ivey suggested that it is not impossible to confront a Chinese person but that helpers need to be sensitive and gentle. It might be better to present the challenge in a more tentative manner and to perhaps precede it by saying something positive. On the other hand, direct (but still empathic and respectful) confrontation may be especially appropriate with some male European American or African American clients who find the soft and gentle approach meaningless and who may even denigrate the helper for using it. Ivey (1994) stressed the need for flexibility and responsiveness to each person.

Furthermore, the need for challenges varies on the basis of where the client is in the change process. Clients who are at precontemplation and contemplation stages of change (see chap. 2, this volume, for details) are more likely to need challenges to jolt them out of their complacency and encourage them to change (Prochaska, DiClemente, & Norcross, 1992). Clients in the later stages of the helping process (e.g., action, termination, and maintenance) are less likely to require challenges to get them past defenses and barriers to changing.

Because challenges can have such a strong impact on clients, helpers need to observe clients' reactions carefully by listening attentively and observing the client's nonverbal behavior (recall the research cited in chap. 2 that clients often hide negative reactions). Thus, helpers should not expect that they necessarily know when clients feel badly after a challenge. Clients could withdraw, and helpers would not know that they were upset. Hence, helpers often have to ask clients how they reacted to challenges and probe beneath the surface to understand the complete reaction (e.g., "You just got quiet. What are you thinking?"). In addition, helpers need to remember to reflect feelings to encourage clients to talk about their reactions to challenges (e.g., "You seem upset").

From observing the client's reactions, a helper can make more informed decisions about how to proceed:

- If the client responds to challenges with denial, the helper needs to rethink how he or she is presenting the challenges, whether the client is ready to hear the challenge, or whether a challenge was a good intervention.
- If the client says that she or he has no reaction to the challenge, the helper might evaluate whether she or he presented the challenges effectively, whether the challenge was accurate, or whether the client was defensive.
- If the client responds with partial examination or acceptance and recognition but no change, the helper can continue to confront gently to help the client move further. The helper also can reflect how scary it is to change and help the client to explore fears.
- If the client responds with new awareness and acceptance, the helper can summarize and then perhaps move on to interpretation.

Helpers should not be surprised when clients react strongly to challenges. Instead, they should help clients express and work through their emotions. This is the exciting and potentially potent, albeit scary for both clients and helpers, stuff of helping.

A final issue is the timing of challenges. If you think your challenge was accurate but your client denies or dismisses it, you may need to back off until the client can handle the challenge or until you have more evidence for your observations. For example, you may experience a client as being extremely hostile and pushy with you although he perceives himself as being friendly and accommodating. Your first challenge, "You say you're easygoing, but you sound like you act somewhat aggressively with your friends," might be negated by the client ("Nah, they all love me"). You might want to obtain more examples from the client about how he behaves with friends, or you may want to ask the client to observe his own behavior or ask his friends for feedback. Despite his reaction, you can trust your impression that this client was aggressive with you (although of course you need to search yourself for countertransference issues related to aggression). In time, you might present another challenge with more specific behavioral evidence. For example: "You say you are never hostile, but you sounded like you were hostile in your interaction with your friend yesterday. From what you said, you completely disagreed with everything your friend said and refused to talk about it. I wonder what your experience was?"

AN EXAMPLE OF CHALLENGES

The following shows a helper using challenges (in italics) in a session:

Client: My husband wants his parents to come and live with us. His father has Alzheimer's, and his mother takes care of his father, but she can't drive and is not feeling too well herself. They are both old and need more help around the house.

Helper: How do you feel about them moving in with you?

Client: Well, I think they need to do something. The situation is not improving, and they are getting old. My husband really wants to take care of them. He feels some obligation since he's the oldest child.

Helper: (gently) *I hear that your husband wants to take care of them, but I am not hearing how you feel about it.*

Client: I have been brought up to believe that family takes care of family when they need help. I didn't take care of my parents, so I feel like we should do what we can to help them if they want it. They may not even want to move in. They might rather do something else.

Helper: *I'm struck by how hard it is for you to talk about your feelings.*

Client: That's interesting. You're really right. I feel like I don't have a right to my feelings. I feel like it's something I "should" do. I don't have any choice, so I'm trying not to have any feelings. If I'm really honest with myself, I'm terrified of what it will be like if they move in. His mother can be very critical.

Helper: You sound upset.

Client: Yeah, but it makes me feel guilty. I just don't know what to do. I guess I've always had a hard time standing up to his parents. Actually, I have a hard time standing up to most people, so this is just another example. I think it stems from my childhood. (Client continues to talk.)

Other Techniques for Fostering Awareness

There are a number of other techniques that can be used to facilitate awareness, including cognitive therapy, two-chair technique, humor, nonverbal referents, and owning responsibility. To avoid overwhelming the beginning helper, I mention each of these briefly but encourage you to seek further training if you want to become competent in using them.

COGNITIVE THERAPY

Cognitive theorists suggest that irrational thinking keeps people from coping effectively and makes them unhappy. Two major theorists have been Ellis and Beck.

Ellis (1962, 1995) suggested that people say irrational things to themselves, such as "I must be loved by everyone," "I must be completely competent and perfect to be worthwhile," "It is awful if things are not the way I want them to be," "There should be someone stronger than me who will take care of me," and "There is a perfect solution to human problems, and it is terrible if I don't find it."

The main goal of cognitive restructuring is to help clients recognize their faulty thinking and change it. To enable clients to recognize their maladaptive thoughts, helpers such as Ellis (1962, 1995) use persuasion and challenges. They attack the irrational thoughts; for example: "What are you telling yourself now?" "You are telling yourself that it would be awful if you did not succeed at being a physicist, but what would be the worst thing that would happen?" "What would be so horrible about that?" "You say you can't stand it, but is that true, would you fall apart?" "It might not be pleasant, but would it actually be catastrophic?" It is important, however, that helpers attack the beliefs, not the person.

Ellis's approach is didactic, in that he teaches clients an ABC model, where A is the activating event, B is the irrational beliefs, and C is the consequent negative emotional reactions or behaviors. Whereas clients make the assumption that events (A) cause emotions (C), Ellis believes that it is the irrational beliefs (B) that lead to negative emotions (C). For example, if Sam gets a C on an exam (A), he might think that the failure makes him feel bad (C); in fact, it is what he tells himself about getting a C (e.g., "I'm a failure as a person; I should be perfect"). Hence, if we replace the irrational beliefs (B) with more rational cognitions (D), clients have more positive emotions (E). In this example, Sam might be taught a more rational thought such as, "It's too bad that I got a C on the exam but that doesn't make me a bad person. It just means that I have to study harder next time, instead of going out drinking the night before." Ellis would also give clients homework to test the validity of irrational beliefs. He might suggest that Sam study more before the next exam to see if that improves his grade. He would also encourage Sam to record his irrational thoughts and combat them with more rational thoughts.

Beck and his colleagues (Beck, 1976; Beck & Emery, 1985; Beck & Freeman, 1990; Beck, Rush, Shaw, & Emery, 1979; Beck & Weishaar, 1995) developed a cognitive theory that is slightly different from Ellis's theory. They postulated that automatic thoughts and dysfunctional interpretations are the major source of problems for clients, and that clients misconstrue events on the basis of faulty logic and beliefs in the cognitive triad of the self, world, and future. Hence, clients often view themselves as defective, inadequate, or unlovable; the world as unmanageable, uncontrollable, or overwhelming; and the future as bleak and hopeless.

Beck's gentle therapeutic approach is quite different from Ellis's direct confrontational style. He recommended that helpers work collaboratively with clients as scientists to uncover faulty logic and examine its impact. Helpers ask a series of questions to help clients arrive at logical conclusions ("What happens when you say X to yourself?"). Helpers also actively point out cognitive themes and underlying assumptions that work against clients. Beck suggested that people often draw conclusions without having adequate evidence (e.g., a person might conclude that he is unlovable just because he has no one with whom to eat lunch one day). People also take details out of context (e.g., focus on one negative comment about a presentation in class and ignore several positive ones), develop general rules out of a few instances (e.g., because she made a mistake one time, a person generalizes that she cannot handle any responsibility), and make something more or less important than it is (e.g., perceive a person not saying "hello" as meaning that he is angry; minimizing the importance of failing a course). In addition, people attribute blame to themselves without any evidence (e.g., a secretary believing that a company's going out of business is due to her not coming into work one day) and engage in rigid, either-or thinking (e.g., a man may think that women are either goddesses or whores). For those who want to learn more about cognitive therapy, I recommend the widely used self-help book by Burns (1999).

TWO-CHAIR TECHNIQUE

A two-chair technique can be particularly useful for identifying unrecognized feelings or when there is a polarity of feelings (e.g., love–hate) or a denial of feelings. This technique comes from process-experiential therapy (see Greenberg, Rice, & Elliott, 1993) and helps clients become aware of and resolve conflicting feelings. Sometimes doing and acting out feeling is easier and has more impact than talking about feeling. Similarly, Fromm-Reichmann (1950) said that clients need an experience, not an explanation.

The two-chair technique could be used when there is a marker of a major conflict expressed with two opposing sides. The helper asks the client to put one side of a conflict in one chair and speak from that side. Once the client has expressed feelings, she or he is asked to move to another chair and talk from that side with full expression of feelings. Usually what happens is that one side (the topdog) engages in a lot of criticism, and the other side (the underdog) whines and acts helpless. By having both sides speak fully and express the feelings as well as listen and let the other side talk, the client comes to allow both sides to emerge and exist equally and thus integrate them. The videos of Leslie Greenberg and Marvin Goldfried produced by the American Psychological Association provide good examples of the two-chair technique.

HUMOR

Sometimes challenges can be softened by using humor, as long as the client feels that the helper is laughing *with* rather than laughing *at* him or her. Helping clients laugh at themselves can help them think about their problems in a different way. An example from Falk and Hill's (1992) study of the effects of therapist humor involved a case in which the client had just described how her daughter, an honor student at a prestigious college, had belittled her A average at a community college. The therapist said, "It's not quite so often that I've run into a daughter's being so overtly competitive with her mother. Not that competition between mothers and daughters isn't a hallmark of our society for heaven's sake, but it's usually masked or disguised or, you know, somewhat less overt." The client responded to this statement with laughter and it helped relieve some of the tension that she was feeling.

In another example from the Falk and Hill study, a helper and client were dealing with issues related to control and perfectionism in the client's life, particularly with regard to eating and schoolwork. The client excitedly described her weekend in which she contacted several friends, coordinated their activities, and eagerly took on the role of the designated driver. She exclaimed, "I had so much fun." The helper commented, "And so much control." They both laughed, and the client began to talk about how her need for control pervaded many aspects of her life.

If clients can start laughing, they can sometimes begin to see things in a different light. Of course, as with other types of challenges, helpers need to have established a relationship with clients and use the humor to raise awareness rather than to make fun of the client.

NONVERBAL REFERENTS

In chapter 7, nonverbal behaviors were presented as sources for reflections of feelings. In this chapter, based on Gestalt therapy, this idea can be carried a little further such that nonverbal referents can serve as stimuli for challenges. Clients are encouraged to be aware of what their bodies might be saying to them. The helper might direct the client who is tapping his foot to "be your foot. What are you saying right now?" And the helper might even ask the client to exaggerate the feeling to help him or her begin to identify the feeling. By asking the client to be the body part, helpers enable clients to get out of rationalization and into their experiencing—the client has to look inward to see whether there is something going on (e.g., "What am I feeling?"). Recall from chapter 5 that nonverbal behaviors often reflect leaks of emotions, so we can use these to raise awareness. Of course this intervention needs to be done cautiously and for the benefit of the client. It is often easy for helpers to use this type of intervention to show-off (e.g., "Aha, I caught you").

OWNING RESPONSIBILITY

Many people in conversation use "you" and "everyone" instead of saying "I" (e.g., "Everyone gets upset at their parents" rather than "I am upset at my parents"). In other words, they make it seem that everyone feels or acts a certain way rather than taking responsibility for their own thoughts and feelings. Simply asking the client to say "I" and make the statement for himself or herself can raise the client's awareness and encourage him or her to take responsibility and differentiate from other people.

Other phrases that indicate a lack of taking responsibility can also be challenged. For instance, the client can be asked to change "can't" to "won't" (e.g., "I can't ask for a raise" to "I won't ask for a raise") and "shouldn't" to "I choose to" (e.g., "I shouldn't play computer games" to "I choose to play computer games"). Once they change their language, clients can be asked to talk about how it feels with the different phrases.

Difficulties Helpers Experience
Using Challenges

Challenge is a difficult intervention for many beginning helpers. One set of difficulties relates to helpers not doing enough challenges. Many beginning helpers use too few challenges because they are afraid of being intrusive, forcing clients to examine their "dirty laundry," offending clients, sounding accusatory or blaming, destroying the therapeutic relationship, causing clients to feel unsupported, or afraid that clients will not like them. Furthermore, confronting people is not considered polite in some cultures, so helpers from such cultures may feel reluctant to use challenges. However, if clients are being contradictory or confusing or are stuck, it is difficult for them to clarify their thinking without outside feedback. In fact, if done appropriately, challenges can be a gift that lets the client know the helper is willing to say unpleasant things that others may not say (e.g., "You say you want to have friends, but you criticize everything anyone does").

Another set of difficulties involves using challenges inappropriately. Some helpers who feel afraid of negative feelings might use challenges to deny or minimize negative feelings. For example, if a client talks about suicidal feelings, a helper might use a challenge that indicates that the client has a lot to live for and should not be thinking about suicide. A statement that a client has a lot to live for might sound like the helper is pointing out strengths, but in this situation the helper is minimizing the negative feelings and falsely reassuring the client so he or she does not have to deal with the suicidal feelings.

A third set of difficulties involves using too many challenges or using challenges too harshly. Some helpers become too invested in having clients recognize their discrepancies. They might argue with clients to convince them of their observations. Or they become like detectives who present the evidence and want to force clients to admit their problems and confess that they are not being consistent. These helpers are like lawyers cross-examining witnesses in the courtroom; they seem eager to "catch" clients in their discrepancies. Some helpers use challenge, often unconsciously, as an opportunity to get back at clients they do not like or who upset them in some way. Needless to say, such challenges can make clients feel unsupported and confronted.

Finally, helpers often have trouble knowing how to respond when clients disagree and challenge the helper in return. For example, the helper might say it seems like the client is coming across hostilely or seductively, and the client might deny it and say it is the helper's problem. Some helpers do not know whether to keep trying to get clients to see the evidence or whether to give up and try again later after they have more data to support the challenge. Helpers may even begin to distrust their perceptions when clients challenge them. At times, helpers might misperceive the situation because of their own issues or insufficient data. At other times, however, clients might be defensive, unwilling to examine themselves, or have a hard time acknowledging their behaviors. Having supervisors listen to tapes of sessions and provide feedback is useful for helpers to determine whether they were distorting because of their own needs, whether the challenge was accurate but presented in a nontherapeutic manner, or whether the client was not ready. Showing a videotape of the session to the client can also provide a powerful self-confrontation if the client is not aware of his or her behavior.

What Do You Think?

- Do you think that there is a benefit to awareness, or should helpers just focus on behavior change?
- Are challenges of discrepancies necessary and helpful?
- Compare and contrast the different skills for facilitating awareness (e.g., challenges of discrepancies, two-chair technique, humor).
- How can helpers maintain an attitude of curiosity and compassion for clients with their challenges rather than attacking them and getting invested in confronting clients?
- What types of helpers might be likely to use challenges inappropriately?
- Discuss cultural differences in using and reacting to the different ways of facilitating awareness.

i PRACTICE EXERCISES

A downloadable PDF of this chapter's Practice Exercises is available in the student resources area of the Helping Skills, *3rd ed. Web site: http://www.apa.org/books/resources/Hill3.*

Read each of the following client statements and write a challenge you might use if you were a helper with the client.

Statements

1. Client: "My family is really important to me. They mean more to me than anyone else in the world. I think about them a lot. I go home about once a year, and I call them every month or so when I'm running out of money."

   Helper challenge: _____

   _____

2. Client: "I really want to go to graduate school, but I have lots of things going on right now, and I just want time for myself to travel and play. I don't think I want to study as much as I know I would have to in graduate school, but I do want to be able to get a good job as a psychologist so that I can do therapy with kids."

   Helper challenge: _____

   _____

3. Client: "My parents are very religious. They tell me I have to go to church every Sunday as long as I'm living at home. I know I have to do it to please them, but I feel so confused about the whole topic. I don't know what I believe, and nothing makes sense. I feel like I'm going through the motions. I feel guilty even talking about this though, because they would be so upset that I don't agree with everything they say."

Helper challenge: _____

_____

4. Client: "The guy I was going with said that he wants us just to be friends. He asked me to go to California with him on a big trip, but just as friends. I don't know if I should go. I still like him a lot. Maybe if I went, he would start liking me again. I don't know what I did that made him quit liking me."

Helper challenge: _____

_____

Possible Helper Responses

1. "You say your family is important to you, but you don't call them."
   "You told me your family is important to you, but you seem to talk to them only when you want money."

2. "You want the things that come from having a graduate degree, but you aren't so sure you want to do what it takes to get the degree."
   "You say you want to get a graduate degree, but your voice doesn't sound very enthusiastic as you talk."

3. "You want to please your parents, but you also really want to figure out for yourself what you believe."
   "You feel guilty that you might believe something that your parents don't, but perhaps you also feel angry that they don't allow you to have your own feelings."

4. "You want to go, but you're not sure if you should."
   "You are really upset that this guy doesn't want to be romantically involved anymore, but you think you can get him to change his mind."

---

i LAB 8. Challenge of Discrepancy

A downloadable PDF of this Lab is available in the student resources area of the Helping Skills, *3rd ed. Web site: http://www.apa.org/books/resources/Hill3.*

Goals: For helpers to continue practicing exploration skills (reflection, restatement, and open questions) and then to challenge once they have established a supportive relationship with a client and identified discrepancies. In groups of four to six, one person will be the client and another person will be the initial helper. The rest should be ready to take over as helper or give backup to the helper. Everyone will take turns being the client. Each group should have a designated lab leader (other than the helper) to organize and coordinate the session.

Helper's and Client's Tasks During the Helping Exchange

1. The client talks about something that he or she feels conflicted or confused about (e.g., future career choices, lifestyle issues). The client should plan on being at least moderately disclosing, although clients always have the right not to disclose when they are uncomfortable doing so.
2. The initial helper starts by using exploration skills to help the client explore. If one helper gets stuck, another helper can take over to facilitate a thorough exploration.
3. After several minutes of exploration, the group leader stops the helper and asks each person in the group to try a reflection of feelings. (Quite often students have forgotten to do reflections of feeling, and this is an excellent opportunity to affirm the importance of this intervention.) The client should respond to each person.
4. The group leader then asks each person (except the client) to write down a challenge. Helpers can ask themselves whether they hear any "sour notes," discrepancies, or defenses. Once all helpers have written challenges, they take turns delivering their challenges to the client, who responds briefly to each challenge.

Processing the Helping Exchange

After everyone has had a turn and the client has responded, the client can talk about which challenges were most helpful and why. Clients should be as open and honest as possible so helpers can learn what they did well and what they did not do so well.

Switch Roles

Keep doing role-plays as described above until everyone has had a chance to be the client, initial helper, and other helpers.

Personal Reflections

- What issues did using challenges raise for you?
- What are your strengths and weaknesses in terms of using challenges?
- How can you deliver challenges that clients can hear and absorb without being too aggressive or too passive?
- Describe what your intentions were for challenging and whether your clients reacted as you hoped.
- What role did your culture play in your giving or receiving challenges?

Skills for Facilitating Insight 11

Men go abroad to wonder at the heights of mountains, at the huge waves of the sea, at the long courses of the rivers, at the vast compass of the ocean, at the circular motions of the stars; and they pass by themselves without wondering.

—*St. Augustine*

Jim told his helper that he was feeling depressed and aimless. He felt that nothing made sense and that he had no purpose in life. He also talked extensively about how his parents were anxious about him taking risks since his older brother had died in a motorcycle accident. On the basis of this and other information the helper had learned about Jim through several sessions, the helper said, "I wonder whether your lack of purpose in life is because you are still grieving the loss of your brother and you haven't been able to make your own decisions and figure out who you are as a person." This interpretation helped Jim make sense of his depression and aimlessness. After talking further with the helper and trying to understand what was going on inside, Jim was able to see his life in a new perspective and to think about how he wanted to be.

Helpers ideally begin the interpretive process with an attitude of empathic curiosity. They wonder what it is that makes clients act a certain way. And they invite clients to think more deeply about what causes and maintains their problems. Furthermore, they help clients develop their own insights because discovered insights are typically better than those that are imposed. The skills that helpers use to facilitate insight are open questions for insight, interpretations, and disclosures of insight.

Open Questions for Insight

Clients often come up with ideas and insights on their own if granted the space and support to do so. They often just need therapists to give them permission to be curious and to join them in the process of trying to figure out what is going on. Open questions for insight, which are questions that invite clients to think about deeper meanings for their thoughts, feelings, or behaviors, can be used for this purpose (see Exhibit 11.1). These questions gently guide the client to explore and become curious about possible explanations. These open questions might be phrased in the following ways:

- "What are your thoughts about what is going on there?"
- "What do you make of your feelings about the ending of the relationship?"
- "What connection do you make between your feelings and the event?"

EXHIBIT 11.1

Overview of Open Questions for Insight

Definition	*Open questions for insight* invite clients to think about deeper meanings for their thoughts, feelings, or behaviors.
Examples	"What is your understanding about your lack of interest in sex?"
	"What do you think might be going on when you compulsively want to eat?"
Typical helper intentions	To promote insight (see Web Form D)
Possible client reactions	Clear, feelings (see Web Form G)
Desired client behaviors	Recounting, affective exploration (see Web Form H)
Helpful hints	Convey empathy and curiosity with your question.
	Make sure your questions are open instead of closed.
	Avoid multiple questions.
	Focus on the client rather than on others.
	Observe client reactions to your questions.

Open questions for insight are similar to those used for thoughts and feelings (see chaps. 6 and 7). The only difference is that the focus is on asking the client to think about insight rather than thoughts or feelings. Refer back to the earlier chapters for more detail on how to use open questions.

As discussed with open questions for exploration, open questions for insight should be done gently and with an air of curiosity. The helper is collaboratively inquiring and helping the client to think about insight. Helpers should be careful not to ask too many questions at one time, should make sure to give clients time to respond, and should vary questions with other skills so that they do not sound repetitive.

A way to develop open questions is to think about aspects of the narrative that do not quite fit. For example, in one session when a client was talking about her inexplicable and sudden bursts of anger at her boyfriend, the helper asked, "What is it about your boyfriend that allows you to blow up at him?" and "What might be some reasons that he doesn't deserve your respect?" These questions came directly from what the client was talking about and helped the client gain insight into her anger.

Although I advised against asking "why" questions in the exploration stage, they are more appropriate in the insight stage if done well. Because the aim of the insight stage is to achieve insight, it can be really useful to ask clients about their understanding, as long as helpers are careful not to sound blaming, accusatory, or demanding. Again, the goal is for the helper and the client to work together to construct meanings, so helpers need to be respectful, gentle, and genuinely eager to help the client attain insight when asking "why" questions. So rather than saying, "Why do you do that?" (especially in an accusatory tone), the helper might empathically say, "I wonder if you could think about why you do that?" The helper's goal, of course, is to stimulate curiosity rather than defensiveness.

Interpretations

Interpretations are interventions that go beyond what a client has overtly stated or recognized and present a new meaning, reason, or explanation for behaviors, thoughts, or feelings so clients can see problems in a new way (see Exhibit 11.2). Interpretations can work in the following ways:

- Make connections between seemingly isolated statements or events (e.g., "Could your anger at your husband right now be connected to your grief over your mother's death?")
- Point out themes or patterns in a client's behaviors, thoughts, or feelings (e.g., "It seems that you get fired from every job after

EXHIBIT 11.2

Overview of Interpretation

Definition	An *interpretation* is a statement that goes beyond what the client has overtly stated or recognized and gives a new meaning, reason, or explanation for behaviors, thoughts, or feelings so the client can see problems in a new way.
Examples	"Maybe you don't want to clean your room or do your work because you're angry with your mother."
	"Ever since your friend committed suicide, you have been on edge and having a hard time coping. I wonder if you feel responsible for her death?"
	"I wonder if I remind you of your father. You said he acts like he knows everything."
	"Perhaps you're trying to get her to distrust you so you can get angry and leave. Otherwise it might be too hard to leave since she's alone."
Typical helper intentions	To promote insight, to identify and intensify feelings, to encourage self-control (see Web Form D)
Possible client reactions	Better self-understanding, new perspective, clear, relief, negative thoughts or feelings, responsibility, unstuck, scared, worse, stuck, lack of direction, confused, misunderstood (see Web Form G)
Desired client behaviors	Insight, cognitive–behavioral exploration, affective exploration (see Web Form H)
Helpful hints	Interpretations should be done carefully, gently, respectfully, thoughtfully, empathically, and infrequently.
	Make sure that client is ready for an interpretation.
	Carefully observe client reactions.
	Work collaboratively with clients to construct the interpretations.
	Keep the interpretation short.
	Give interpretations only infrequently.
	Follow up interpretations with open questions asking the client about his or her reactions.

about 6 months. I wonder if somehow your fear of success makes it difficult for you to keep a job longer.")

- Explicate defenses, resistance, or transference (e.g., "I wonder if you're expecting me to respond like your father does.")
- Offer a new framework to understand behaviors, thoughts, feelings, or problems (e.g., "You say you were spoiled as a child, but it seems to me that you often felt abandoned and anxious as a child and that leads you to cling to other people.")

WHY GIVE INTERPRETATIONS?

One reason for using interpretations is that the empirical literature shows them to be valuable, at least for some clients. A number of studies show that therapists used interpretations moderately often compared with other skills (ranging from 6% to 8% of all therapist statements; Barkham & Shapiro, 1986; Hill, Helms, Tichenor, et al., 1988). Furthermore, interpretations were rated as being very helpful, helped engage clients in therapeutic work, led to high levels of client experiencing, and led clients to free associate (Colby, 1961; Hill, Helms, Tichener, et al., 1988; Spence, Dahl, & Jones, 1993). However, research on transference interpretations (interpretations about the client's distortion of the therapist based on previous significant relationships) has found mixed effects; better results have been found when therapists craft the interpretations to the beliefs and needs of the client and use them only with more well-adjusted clients (see the review in Crits-Christoph & Gibbons, 2002).

Interpretations can provide clients with a conceptual framework that explains their problems and offers a rationale for overcoming their concerns. Frank and Frank (1991) noted that interpretations increase clients' sense of security, mastery, and self-efficacy by providing labels for experiences that seem confusing, haphazard, or inexplicable. Frank and Frank asserted that interpretations relieve distress in part by relabeling client emotions to make them more understandable. They noted that the inexplicable loses much of its power to terrify when it is put in words. For example, if a helper interprets that Pablo's vague uneasiness at work is anger at the boss, who is a stand-in for the client's father, Pablo's uneasiness loses its power. Pablo is no longer unrealistically angry at his boss and instead can work on his feelings toward his father.

From a psychoanalytic perspective (e.g., Bibring, 1954; Blanck, 1966; Freud, 1914/1953b; Fromm-Reichmann, 1950), interpretations are the "pure gold" of therapy—the central technique for producing self-knowledge and change in clients. Psychoanalytic therapists create interpretations from client material that has been repressed and is unconscious. They postulate that interpretations are effective because they stimulate insight, which can lead to more reality-oriented feelings and behavior. Interpretations are thought to work by replacing unconscious processes with conscious ones, thus enabling clients to resolve unconscious conflicts. Although the exact mechanism by which insight works is vague and needs further explication, it is clear that insight plays a central role in the therapeutic change process.

In psychoanalytic theory, the role of early childhood is important because it serves as the template for everything that comes afterward. Hence, early childhood experiences are often the focus of interpretive behavior, although the childhood events that are focused on varies for different theorists. For Freudians (Freud, 1940/1949), the crucial early childhood event is the Electra–Oedipal conflict, in which the child seeks to have a romantic alliance with the parent of the opposite gender and to eliminate the parent of the same gender; the child must resolve this conflict to progress to maturity. Erikson (1963) postulated that the important early childhood events are interpersonal relationships. For Mahler (1968), the important early childhood event involves the symbiosis with the primary caregivers in very early years and the subsequent movement toward separation and individuation. Bowlby (1969, 1988) believed that attachment to the caregiver is the crucial event in childhood.

Because psychoanalytic helpers believe that early childhood relationships form the foundation for all ensuing relationships, interpreting the transference (i.e., a distortion by the client of the helper based on early childhood relationships) is one of the most important types of interpretation. The assumption is that the client recreates the problematic early relationship patterns with the helper either as a way to confirm or reject that the helper will act in the same way as the early caregiver (Weiss, Sampson, & the Mount Zion Psychotherapy Research Group, 1986). The client might act as he or she did as a child (the passive victim) and expect the helper to play the complementary role (the dominant or oppressive dictator). Conversely, the client might take on the role that the parent played in the relationship (the dominant one) and expect the helper to act like the client did as a child (the passive victim). The helper's reaction to the client's behavior is crucial for confirming or disconfirming the client's expectations. For example, the helper might say to Amanda, "I wonder if you get so furious at me for seeing other clients because you always felt that your mother preferred your brother to you, and you don't like to have to share me with other clients."

Although psychoanalytic theory is the basis for our thinking about using interpretations, other theoretical orientations also use interpretations but postulate different mechanisms by which they work. From an information-processing perspective, Levy (1963) suggested that interpretations reveal discrepancies between the views of the therapist and client. In other words, an interpretation makes it clear that the helper has a different perspective than the client. The helper does not "buy" the client's view about the issue and postulates a different explanation. If there is a discrepancy in perspectives, the client has three choices: to change in the direction of the helper's viewpoint, to try to change the helper's mind, or to discredit the helper. If the client resolves the discrepancy in the direction of the helper's interpretation, the client is able to reconstrue how she or he views the issue. Research has shown that clients are more likely to change in the direction of the helper's interpretation if they view the helper as expert, attractive, and trustworthy (Strong & Claiborn, 1982).

An example may help to illustrate the information-processing perspective. Joe explained his depression as a chemical imbalance and thus sought helping as a way to get medication. His helper suggested instead that Joe's depression was due to unresolved feelings about his mother's suicide and subsequent abandonment by his father. Because Joe valued the helper's opinion, he struggled to understand what the helper was saying about his depression. Initially, he argued with the helper, but then came to agree that in fact he did have anger at both of his parents. By shifting his perspective, he was then able to engage in the helping process to work through his feelings about his parents.

Cognitive psychologists (e.g., Glass & Holyoak, 1986; Medin & Ross, 1992) also construe the effectiveness of interpretations in different terms than do psychoanalytic theorists. Cognitive theorists believe that all thoughts, feelings, sensations, memories, and actions are stored in *schemas* (defined as clusters of related thoughts, feelings, actions, and images). With interpretations, helpers attempt to change the way that schemas are structured. They bring back the memories and try to come to new understandings about them on the basis of more current and complete information. In effect, the schemas are changed and restructured. The client has a new way of thinking, which must be reinforced or else it erodes. Hence, repeated interpretations with expansions to different areas of the client's life may be necessary for the connections to be made and retained. In addition, action and behavior change may be necessary to consolidate the changes in thinking.

An example for schemas relates to Katerina, who came to realize that she was lacking in self-esteem because she felt neglected as a child. However, she needed further interpretive work to understand the influences of the childhood experiences on her current life and change her schemas. In addition, making changes in her behaviors (e.g., getting a new job and leaving an abusive relationship) helped her begin to think more highly of herself and led her to understand why she stayed in such a bad situation for so long. So interpretive work helped Katerina change her schemas, and then action helped to reinforce or consolidate the schematic changes (connections).

To conclude this section, I should note that there is not enough evidence to support any one of these theories over the others. In fact, interpretations could work for all three reasons: because the unconscious is made conscious and more under ego control, because discrepancies between perspectives propel clients to change in the direction of resolving the discrepancy, or because interpretations cause changes in schematic connections.

SOURCES OF DATA FOR DEVELOPING INTERPRETATIONS

There are several sources of data that helpers can use for developing interpretations: verbal content of clients' speech, past experiences, defenses, developmental stages and culture, existential concerns and culture, and unconscious activities.

Verbal Content of Clients' Speech

A rich source of data for developing interpretations is in the content of what clients talk about. Given that people often compartmentalize things, listening carefully to what they say can reveal connections between relevant things that they had not put together. For example, if a client says she is having a hard time performing on her job and then goes on to talk about the seemingly unrelated topic of anxiety over her parents' health, the helper might connect the two if it seems probable that they are related (e.g., "Perhaps you're having a hard time concentrating because of anxiety about your parents").

Past Experiences

Helpers can speculate about how a client's behaviors might be related to how the client has interacted in the past with significant others. When the client's responses to the helper seem distorted because of experiences with others in the past or present, helpers have material for making a transference interpretation. For example, Keisha responded with silence and tears every time her helper provided positive feedback. Silence and tears are not typical responses to positive feedback, so the helper made some guesses about what might be going on with Keisha. The helper knew about Keisha's history with her father and suggested that perhaps Keisha was afraid of what might follow positive feedback, given that her father often told her something good and then yelled at her for her mistakes. (More discussion of transference interpretations is available in several texts: Basch, 1980; Freud, 1923/1961; Gelso & Carter, 1985, 1994; Greenson, 1967; Malan, 1976a, 1976b; Stadter, 1996; Strupp & Binder, 1984.)

A related way of examining transference is to look at the client's typical style of interacting and conceptualize what the client is trying to accomplish in interactions. The core conflictual relationship theme method (Book, 1998; Luborsky & Crits-Christoph, 1990) describes how people engage in typical interpersonal patterns. They have wishes or needs (e.g., the client may wish to control others or to have the approval of others), expected responses from others (e.g., submission or approval), and the consequent response from the self (e.g., depressed or pleased). For example, Keisha might wish for affection and love but also to be in control. She might expect others to hurt and control her as her father did, and hence she might feel anxious and lack confidence. Interpretations can thus be formulated about the client's characteristic way of interacting with others to help the client understand these patterns and to able to break out of them.

Defenses

Helpers can also provide interpretations based on observations of a client's defenses, for example, "I wonder if your difficulty at work stems from your avoiding interactions with others, something you learned to do as a child to protect yourself from fears of abandonment." In the previous chapter on challenges, helpers were encouraged to point out defenses to raise the client's awareness of them. Now the helper can work with the client to understand the role the defenses play. People develop defenses early in life to help them cope with situations but then may fail to give up the defenses even though they are no longer needed. It is perhaps hardest to give up things that we believe protect us from harm, given that they protected us in the past. Through interpretive activity, helpers can help clients realize why they started using defenses and then make choices about the need to continue using them. For example, while Jon was talking about his lack of being able to find a romantic relationship, the helper found himself feeling very sleepy. After fighting off the sleepiness, the helper became curious and wondered to himself whether Jon was using a defense by speaking in a monotone to keep away his anxiety. Thus, the helper challenged Jon to bring this defense into awareness (e.g., "You know, I can't help but notice that when you start to talk about romantic relationships, you start talking in a monotone and it's difficult to listen to you. Have you noticed a change in your behavior?"). Jon was intrigued but could not think of what might be going on. After a pause to give Jon a chance to reflect, the helper gently speculated, "I wonder if talking about romantic relationships is hard for you because of your anger over your parents and how they handled their divorce?"

Developmental Stages

An additional source of material for interpretations is the client's life stage, within the context of his or her culture. Are clients on or off course for mastering the developmental tasks that are important for them in their cultural context (e.g., developing friendships, separating from parents, completing schooling, making decisions about life partners and children, developing a satisfying career, developing satisfying adult relationships, letting go of children and careers, adjusting to illnesses and dying)? Interpretations can be developed linking clients' current emotions and functioning to what they might be expected to be feeling or not feeling at this stage of life within their culture. For example, Ken, a 50-year-old White man, might feel depressed because he compares himself with other people his age who have accomplished more in their lives. He dropped out of high school to rebel against his parents, who were both physicians, and worked in construction his whole life; now he wonders if he made the right choices. As another example, as Melania turns 35 and is not involved in a serious romantic relationship, she is feeling anxious about whether she will ever be able to have children.

Remember not to impose your own cultural values on others. For example, in Asian cultures, it is common for children to live at home through college. And it is becoming more common for young adults in the United States to return home to live with parents after college because they cannot afford the rent on apartments. To impose one's own demand for independence might not be appropriate in such cases.

Existential and Spiritual Issues

Helpers can also help clients understand themselves in terms of existential concerns. Yalom (1980), a well-known existential therapist, provided an excellent description of what he considered to be four universal existential concerns:

- *Death anxiety.* The fact that everyone dies at some point means we have to come to terms with the reality that we are not immortal. Particularly at times when one is ill or has been in an accident or attacked or when a significant other is ill or has recently been hurt or died, people feel vulnerable and attuned to loss and death.
- *Freedom.* Freedom refers to the lack of external structure and the need to take responsibility for one's destiny.
- *Isolation.* This includes isolation both from others and from the world. Each of us enters and exits the world alone; therefore, we must come to terms with our isolation in contrast to our wish to be part of a larger whole, to be taken care of and protected.
- *Meaning of life.* We must all construct our own life meanings, given that there is no predetermined path.

Yalom (1980) noted the benefits of introducing a client with terminal cancer into a therapy group. Having a group member dealing with issues of death brings up the existential issues more saliently for the rest of the group members. But Yalom also noted that clients in individual work frequently give clues about existential concerns if helpers just pay attention. For example, clients complain about physical aches and pains, of aging, of not being able to do what they used to do, of not knowing what to do with their time, of wanting to leave a legacy, about the death of a pet, or of wondering about spirituality. All of these topics can be explored further to help people deal with existential crises. Interestingly, Yalom suggested that clients often feel more rather than less anxious after talking about existential issues because they realize they cannot control many things in life.

Note that culture plays a role in existential concerns, particularly in terms of religious beliefs. A person who believes in life after death will probably experience less death anxiety than will someone who does not believe in life after death. By listening carefully to what clients say and asking them about relevant cultural beliefs, helpers can often hear underlying existential concerns and then assist clients, via interpretation, to understand these critical issues.

Unconscious Sources

Interpretations can be developed through indications of unconscious activities, most typically observable through dreams, fantasies, and slips of the tongue. Psychoanalytic theorists have long postulated that important unconscious material can be detected by looking at these manifestations. For example, if a client accidentally uses a former boyfriend's name when talking about her current boyfriend, one could wonder aloud with her whether there was some significance to the slip. Or if a client has a dream about the helper, this presents the helper with an ideal opportunity to look at what the client might be thinking about the helper. Similarly, if the helper has a dream about a client, this presents a valuable learning opportunity for the helper to speculate about the client, although helpers rarely reveal such dreams to clients, especially if they involve the helper's own unresolved personal issues (see Spangler & Hill, in press). For more detail on how helpers can work with dreams, I refer readers to a companion text that also uses the three-stage model (Hill, 2004).

ACCURACY OF INTERPRETATIONS

For psychoanalytic theorists, the accuracy of the helper's interpretation is important. The client and helper are on an "archeological dig" to uncover what actually happened in the client's past and understand how these events affect the client's current behavior. Of course, psychoanalytic therapists emphasize that what they hear in therapy is the client's perceptions about the events rather than actual events; thus, accuracy can never be determined.

Reid and Finesinger (1952), however, suggested that insight must merely be believed or make sense to have a therapeutic effect. They thought that the psychological relevance of the interpretation to the client's problems is more important than the truth per se (i.e., does the interpretation help the client understand more about his or her problems?). Similarly, Frank and Frank (1991) noted that interpretations do not have to be correct, only plausible. As an example, they cited a study by Mendel (1964) in which four clients responded with a drop in anxiety when they were offered the same series of six "all-purpose" interpretations (e.g., "You seem to live your life as though you are apologizing all the time"). I would not suggest that helpers ignore the "truth" and just have a set of standard interpretations to give clients. Quite the opposite: I believe that helpers should try as much as possible to develop interpretations that fit all of the data clients present. Helpers should remain humble, however, about how difficult it is to know all the data and to determine whether an interpretation is accurate.

Basch (1980), a psychoanalytic therapist, indicated that whether clients agree or disagree with interpretations is not a good indication of accuracy. Rather, he suggested, the criterion for accuracy should be whether clients subsequently bring up material that indicates they have gained insight into the problem. For example, if a helper interprets that Lao's fear of intimacy is based on feeling rejected by his father, the helper could conclude that the interpretation was accurate if Lao brings in additional memories of his father being distant and rejecting. I would caution, however, that clients sometimes bring in (and even make up) memories to please their helpers.

Frank and Frank (1991) noted that the client is the ultimate judge of the truth of the interpretation. They suggested that the helper's power to present an interpretation that is accepted by the client as valid depends on several factors:

- Whether the interpretation makes sense out of all the material the client has offered.
- The manner in which the interpretation is offered: Interpretations must be presented in ways that catch and hold the client's attention, such as with vivid imagery and metaphor, because clients need to be in a state of emotional arousal to be able to make use of interpretations.
- The client's confidence in the helper.
- The beneficial consequences for the client's ability to function and for the client's sense of well-being.

In sum, as helpers we can never really determine the accuracy of interpretations because we cannot go back and determine what actually happened in the past. In addition, we know that events are not just facts but also involve people's recall of them. We know that people perceive events idiosyncratically and then distort memories of events over time (Glass & Holyoak, 1986; Loftus, 1988). Research shows that people can "remember" events that never happened (Brainerd & Reyna, 1998), so helpers need to be careful not to try to persuade clients to have certain memories (e.g., repressed memories about childhood sexual abuse).

Thus, I suggest that perceived helpfulness is a more important criterion for evaluating interpretations than is accuracy. The following criteria may be used for determining whether interpretations are helpful for clients:

- When an interpretation is helpful, the client typically feels a sense of "aha," of learning something that "clicks," and has a feeling that things make sense in a new way.
- Clients typically have a feeling of energy and excitement about their new discoveries, particularly when they feel they have discovered the insight themselves.

- Clients present additional important information that confirms the insight.
- Clients start thinking about what to do differently based on the insight.

In short, when interpretations are helpful, clients arrive at personally relevant insights and can use these insights to talk more deeply about problems (emotional insight) and move to action.

HOW TO INTERPRET

The major task is to engage in an interpretive process in such a way that the client and helper are working together to construct interpretations. As with challenges, interpretations should be done carefully, gently, respectfully, thoughtfully, empathically, and infrequently.

If you decide that a client is ready for interpretive work, an excellent idea is to begin by asking the client for her or his interpretation (e.g., "What do you make of your flunking out of school even though you are obviously very bright?" "How do you make sense of your reluctance to retire even though your wife keeps pressuring you to do so?"). Asking clients for their interpretations before providing them with the helper's thinking encourages clients to think about themselves, gets helpers out of the position of being the ones who provide all the interpretations, gives helpers more information from which to formulate interpretations, and allows helpers to assess clients' current level of insight.

If the client seems interested and engaged in the insight process, the helper might give a gentle, tentative interpretation to augment or extend the client's initial understanding. Helpers should view this initial interpretation as something like a working hypothesis of what might be going on for the client; this working hypothesis will be revised as the interpretive process ensues and more information is gathered. The purpose of the initial tentative interpretation is to help the client take the next step in the interpretive process and think about the reasons for his or her behavior.

Interpretations can be phrased as a direct statement (e.g., "You are worried about whether you should get married, so you are diverting your anxiety about getting married into trying to make the wedding perfect"); phrased more tentatively (e.g., "I wonder if your fear of failure could possibly be related to feeling that you are not sure you can please your mother"); or phrased as a question (e.g., "Could it be that you distrust men because of your bad relationship with your father?"). Although the last intervention is phrased as a question, it is clearly an interpretation because the content of the question assumes a relationship that the client had not articulated and provides an explanation for the behavior.

Psychoanalytic theorists suggest that it is important to provide interpretations that are not too far beyond what clients already have recognized (e.g., Speisman, 1959). If interpretations are too deep, clients cannot understand what the helper is talking about; interpretations that are slightly beyond the client's awareness make more sense to the client and give the client a manageable stimulus for thinking. In the first session with a client who procrastinates, for example, the helper might not want to interpret the cause of the procrastination back to early childhood events because the client may not be ready to hear such an interpretation. Instead, the helper might interpret just beyond what the client is aware of to gently encourage the client to go to slightly new levels of understanding (e.g., "Perhaps it's hard for you to study because you're afraid of succeeding"). Later, when the client is comfortable about thinking psychologically, the helper might push for deeper interpretations, such as the client's reluctance to supersede his or her parents.

Helpers can develop these gentle, tentative interpretations by paying attention to what the client is half saying, saying in a confused way, or saying implicitly. The client may have almost put it all together and may only need a little help to begin to integrate the pieces.

The phrasing of interpretations is crucial to their acceptance by clients. Phrasing the interpretation tentatively and without jargon makes it easier for clients to understand. For example, "I wonder if you might be afraid of what I say because I remind you of your mother, who was sometimes mean to you" is easier for a client to hear than "Your transference of your Oedipal rage onto me has caused you to distort my meaning." The latter interpretation is difficult for most clients to hear because it is stated too definitely and with too much jargon.

It is important for the interpretation process to be collaborative, with the helper and client working together to understand new reasons for the present situation. The helper and client work together to construct insights that the client can hear and assimilate. The process is a creative attempt to understand a puzzling phenomenon. Natterson (1993) stressed that when a helper who wants to exert power over a client offers a shocking interpretation of a dream, it usually has an antitherapeutic effect because it discourages the client from sharing dreams. Similarly, Reik (1935) emphasized the deep, collaborative nature of the therapeutic encounter. He suggested that insights that come to clients as a result of interpretations should come as a surprise to both the helper and the client, rather than because the helper forced a predetermined interpretation on the client. Basch (1980) likewise noted that interpretations that are too obvious, easy, simplistic, or superficial connections are usually trivial or wrong, whereas the important insights are those that come as a surprise to both client and helper.

After effective interpretations, a client may add new information or suggest alternative interpretations. This new exploration is wonderful and gives a clear indication that the client is responding well to the interpretative process. Helpers can respond by reflecting feelings or asking open questions to draw out the client's thoughts.

On the other hand, if a client rejects an interpretation (says "Yes, but . . ."), the helper needs to evaluate the situation. If the helper thinks the interpretation was right but the client was not yet ready to hear it, the helper can return to the interpretation at a later stage when she or he thinks the client is more able to tolerate insight (interpretations sometimes are painful to hear). If the helper is wrong (which is possible because helpers never have all the relevant information), the helper can use exploration skills to obtain more understanding of the client before attempting again to interpret. Alternatively, helpers can ask clients to provide an interpretation that fits for them.

Helpers also need to extend interpretations to a variety of situations to help clients reach greater understanding. For example, if the interpretation involves the client being unorganized and sloppy as a reaction to an overly neat and compulsive mother, the helper can extend this insight to how the client is messy in her apartment, unorganized in terms of her studying behavior, and late for appointments. By talking about all these different areas, the client is more likely to begin to understand herself. Extending the interpretation to a number of situations also generalizes the learning, making it more likely that the client will begin to incorporate changes in thinking.

After hearing more information, helpers might restate a reformulated interpretation. The new interpretation might lead the client to new material that confirms or denies the validity of the interpretation. Thus, rather than helpers having and delivering the "correct" interpretations to clients, the helper and client work together to create or construct interpretations. This collaborative process requires that helpers be invested in the interpretive process rather than in specific interpretations, so they can revise interpretations when clients offer new information, explanations, or ideas.

EXAMPLES OF INTERPRETATION

A wonderful example of the whole working-through process comes from Hill, Thompson, and Mahalik (1989) in their examination of a single case of successful brief psychotherapy. The middle-aged client was the middle of 16 children. Her mother had married at a very young age; when her husband (the client's father) died, the mother abandoned the children. The client was divorced with three children and was depressed, blaming herself for being "spoiled." At the end of the therapy, the therapist and client both indicated that the most important interpretation was that the client's current difficulties resulted from a difficult childhood and inadequate parenting. Interpretations occurred only in the last half of the 12-session therapy, were of moderate depth, seemed to be accurate, and were interspersed with approval-reassurance, questions, restatements, and reflections aimed at catharsis. The therapist repeated the interpretation many times and applied it to many situations, which she referred to in postsession interviews as "chipping away" at the client's defenses. The client not only accepted the interpretation but also slowly began to incorporate it into her thinking (i.e., she changed from seeing herself as spoiled to seeing herself as neglected). The interpretation enabled her to disclose painful secrets (e.g., her father's attempted suicide and subsequent hospitalization in a mental institution). Finally, the therapist began to pair the interpretation with a directive that the client was a good parent to her children and thus could parent herself. The interpretation helped the client come to a greater self-understanding and, together with the direct guidance about parenting herself, enabled her to change in some fundamental ways (e.g., become a better parent, obtain a job, and begin an intimate relationship).

Here is another example with dialogue (interpretations are in italics). Note that the helper explores the problem before interpreting.

Client: Lately, when I'm in church, I have been getting very anxious. I have been starting to panic when we have to hold hands to say a prayer. My palms get very sweaty, and I feel very embarrassed. I start worrying about it so much ahead of time that I cannot concentrate on the church service. I just don't understand why I should get so nervous. I wish I could understand it, though, because it is making my experience of going to church very unpleasant.

Helper: It sounds like you feel upset about it.

Client: I do. I feel foolish. I mean, who cares about my sweaty palms? I'm sure the other people are just interested in going to church and don't really care about me. I don't know the people very well though, because I just started going to this church when I moved here this fall.

Helper: Tell me a little bit about the role of the church in your life.

Client: I was hoping to have a community like we had in my hometown. I need something apart from the people I know at work. But it hasn't worked out. I haven't really met anyone there yet.

Helper: So you just moved here and have been hoping to make friends through the church.

Client: Church was always important in my family. I don't know how much I believe in the religion, but I do feel a need for the connection that you get in church.

Helper: So you want to make friends and find a community, but you also feel some ambivalence and you're not sure what you believe.

Client: Wow, that is really true. I do feel like I'm supposed to go to church, but I'm not sure I really want to. I feel like my parents expect me to go. But I don't quite know what I believe. I haven't taken the time to figure out what I believe separate from what my parents told me to believe.

Helper: *I wonder if worrying about your sweaty palms takes your mind off thinking about what you believe.*

Client: Yeah, that's a good point. I sure cannot listen to much of the sermon if I'm worried about the person next to me and what they will think of me.

Helper: *Perhaps going to this new church is difficult because it reminds you so much of your family and what you were supposed to do as a child.*

Client: You're right. I feel like I've been trying to establish myself as an independent person. I moved across country so I could be on my own and make my own decisions, but I miss my family and my community. I don't know how much I want to be here. I feel like I'm struggling with trying to figure out who I am and what I want out of life. (Client continues exploring.)

DIFFICULTIES IN USING INTERPRETATION

Some helpers are hesitant to interpret because it feels intrusive to "poke around in clients' heads." They fear that they will be wrong, give interpretations prematurely, upset or anger clients, or harm the therapeutic relationship. They err on the side of passivity and do not offer any of their own thoughts to the interpretive exchange.

Other helpers are too eager to give interpretations and err on the side of aggressiveness. The interpretation process brings out the worst in some helpers. They become invested in the intellectual challenge of figuring out clients and are eager to use their powers of insight. They lose sight of the need for empathy and a strong therapeutic relationship and charge into putting all the pieces of the puzzle together. I agree that people are infinitely intriguing, interesting, and fun to figure out, but helpers must temper such sentiments with a strong compassion for clients and a desire to help clients understand themselves.

I caution helpers in the use and potential abuse of interpretations because they can be powerful interventions. Helpers have the responsibility to use power appropriately. I also caution helpers that clients may agree with interpretations because they want to please, but they may actually disagree with the interpretations and can feel wounded by them. Helpers thus need to observe client reactions and ask clients about their reactions.

Helpers also need to be careful to encourage clients to become actively involved in collaborating on constructing interpretations. In addition, timing is important, because clients need to be able to hear the interpretations and can build on them in constructing their own understandings.

Another problem helpers have is giving too many interpretations in one session. Clients often need time to absorb and think about each interpretation, so helpers should gauge their pace on the basis of clients' reactions.

A final problem is that some helpers are not experienced enough with interpretation and feel unable to put all the pieces together to formulate interpretations. If you feel this way, you might practice trying to understand your own behavior, focus more on asking the clients to come up with their own interpretations, and have patience that more interpretive ability will come with practice. I also suggest further readings in psychoanalytic theory (e.g., Basch, 1980; Book, 1998; McWilliams, 2004; Strupp & Binder, 1984).

Disclosures of Insight

Olga was very emotional and upset when she revealed that her husband had left her for a younger woman. She felt abandoned and humiliated and did not want any of her friends to know that her husband had left. She talked in her helping session about feeling depressed, isolated, alone, and hopeless, and she said that she was too old to start over. The helper said, "You know, I got divorced several years ago, and I never thought I would recover. I came to realize that I had believed my worth was dependent on whether I had a man, rather than who I was. I wonder if that's true for you?" Olga was momentarily taken aback, and then said, "I never thought of it that way. I think you may be right. I was always taught that I needed to be married and so I never prepared for anything else." The helper's disclosure thus enabled Olga to have an "aha" experience and think about why she was so upset about her husband's leaving her. She did not really miss him; they had not been getting along well for many years. Instead, she missed the sense of security that being married gave her. Once she understood that about herself, she could begin to adjust to the divorce.

A disclosure of insight reveals an understanding the helper has learned about him- or herself and is used to facilitate the client's under-

EXHIBIT 11.3

Overview of Disclosure of Insight

Definition	*Disclosure of insight* refers to the helper's presentation of a personal experience (not in the immediate relationship) in which he or she gained some insight.
Examples	"In the past, I often did not want others to feel upset by my successes, so I would underplay anything I did well. I wonder if that happens for you?"
	"I indulge in some bad habits just like you. I know they're bad habits, but just like you, I don't want to change them. I discovered that I just don't like the feeling of anyone controlling me because my mother was very controlling. Does that fit for you?"
Typical helper intentions	To promote insight, to deal with resistance, to challenge, to relieve the therapist's needs[3] (see Web Form D)
Possible client reactions	Understood, supported, hopeful, relief, negative thoughts or behaviors, better self-understanding, clear, feelings, unstuck, new perspective, educated, new ways to behave, scared, worse, confused, misunderstood (see Web Form G)
Desired client behaviors	Insight, affective exploration, cognitive–behavioral exploration (see Web Form H)
Helpful hints	Make sure that your intentions are to help the client gain insight rather to get attention for your own problems.
	Choose things to reveal that seem similar to what the client is going through.
	Keep it short.
	Do not reveal things about yourself that have not been mostly resolved (i.e., about which you still feel quite troubled).
	Make sure to turn the focus back to the client after disclosing.

standing of his or her thoughts, feelings, behaviors, and issues (see Exhibit 11.3). Instead of using challenges or interpretations, helpers share insights that they have learned about themselves in the hope of encouraging clients to think about themselves at a deeper level. Note that the intention is not to further the helper's understanding of him- or herself but to facilitate client insight.

Some students confuse disclosures of insight with other types of disclosures. The key feature here is that the helper has a hint about an insight that might help the client and uses his or her experience to present the insight in a more tentative way than an interpretation.

WHY USE DISCLOSURE OF INSIGHT?

A major reason for using disclosures is that they have been found to be helpful. Research suggests that therapists use disclosures infrequently, but clients rated them as very helpful and indicated that disclosures led them to gain insight, feel more normal, reassured them, and led to deeper therapeutic relationships (Hill, Helms, Tichenor, et al., 1988; Hill & Knox, 2002).

Helpers disclose their experiences to help clients attain realizations of which they had not been aware. This type of disclosure is useful when clients are stuck or are having a hard time achieving deep levels of self-understanding on their own. For example, if a client is talking about everything being just fine after leaving her abusive husband, but the helper suspects that the client has a lot of underlying turmoil, the helper might say, "I remember feeling like I wasn't sure if I made the right decision after I left my partner. It was real scary for me because my parents never allowed me to make my own decisions so I didn't trust myself. I wonder if something like that is true for you?" The helper hopes the client will understand more about herself by hearing about the helper's experience.

Another reason for using disclosure is to enable clients to hear things in a less threatening way than might happen with therapist challenges or interpretations. Hearing a disclosure such as "I also feel like a child when I go to visit my parents because I lose my identity and don't know who I am" or "I also have a hard time going to movies by myself because I feel like nobody loves me" provides an opportunity for clients to think about whether they have similar reasons for their behaviors. Rather than asserting an interpretation that may offend the client, helpers disclose personal insights and ask whether these insights might fit for the client, thus possibly facilitating new and deeper insight. By using disclosure, the helper admits that the insight may be a projection and allows the client to see if it fits. As with tentative interpretations, helpers are hoping that clients will feel freer to look for underlying reasons after they have heard helpers disclosing their insights. Thus, disclosures can have a modeling effect.

In addition, disclosures can alter the power balance of the helping relationship and lead to greater participation by the client. Rather than helpers being the experts with the answers and clients relying on helpers to solve their problems, disclosures make clear that helpers are also people who grapple with important human concerns. In addition, in dyads in which cultures differ, disclosures can be used to bridge the gap and make clients feel that their helpers can understand them.

THEORETICAL PERSPECTIVES ON THERAPIST DISCLOSURE

Humanistic theorists (e.g., Bugenthal, 1965; Jourard, 1971; Robitschek & McCarthy, 1991; Rogers, 1957; Truax & Carkhuff, 1967) have long valued therapist disclosure because they think that helpers should be transparent, real, and genuine in the therapeutic relationship, and they believe that helper disclosure can have a positive effect on treatment. Humanists believe that a personal and transparent style of intervention benefits both the process and the outcome of therapy because it allows clients to see helpers as real people who also have problems. In addition, humanists believe that when helpers disclose, there is more of a balance of control in the relationship, in that clients are not the only ones who are vulnerable. Humanists also contend that disclosure enhances rapport because clients feel more friendly toward and trusting of helpers who disclose. It is interesting that humanists also think that disclosure can help to correct transference misconceptions as they occur because helpers are direct and honest with disclosures and, hence, challenge distortions as they arise. Additional benefits claimed by humanists for disclosures are that helpers are able to be more spontaneous and authentic and can model appropriate disclosure. Moreover, helpers' disclosures can facilitate client disclosure and work on the therapeutic relationship. In effect, humanists believe that helpers' disclosures encourage an atmosphere of honesty and understanding between helpers and clients that fosters stronger and more effective therapeutic relationships.

Similarly, cognitive–behavioral theorists believe that helper disclosure within sessions, when used with appropriate boundaries, can strengthen the therapeutic bond and facilitate client change (see Goldfried, Burckell, & Eubanks-Carter, 2003). Of particular interest for the insight stage, cognitive–behaviorists use disclosure to provide feedback on the client's interpersonal impact and model effective ways of interacting.

In contrast, traditional psychoanalytic theorists (e.g., Basescu, 1990; Greenson, 1967; Simon, 1988) view psychotherapy as focused on working through patients' projections and transferences. They believe helpers should be neutral or blank screens so that clients can project onto them their feelings and reactions toward significant others. For example, a client's childhood experiences might prompt the client to transfer onto the helper a fear that the helper is going to be punitive. An analytic helper might sit behind the client to enable the client to focus inwardly rather than watching the helper's face for cues about his or her reactions. If a helper is in fact being neutral, she or he can assist the client in seeing that the belief that the helper will be punitive is a projection. If helpers deviate from neutrality, it is difficult to distinguish client projections from realistic reactions to what the helper is actually doing. For example, if a helper is consistently late, it would be difficult to determine whether the client's anger was a distortion based on previous experiences or legitimate anger at the helper's tardiness. Readers should not confuse neutrality with a lack of empathy, however, because competent analytic helpers are appropriately warm and empathic. It is not too surprising, given this emphasis on neutrality, that psychoanalytic helpers typically do not disclose.

In fact, psychoanalysts propose an inverse relationship between the client's knowledge of the helper's personal life, thoughts, and feelings and the client's capacity to develop a transference to the helper (Freud, 1912/1959). They believe that helper revelations contaminate the transference process and deleteriously demystify the therapy, thereby reducing the helper's status (Andersen & Anderson, 1985). In addition, Cornett (1991) suggested that helper disclosure might represent unresolved countertransference difficulties on the part of the helper, which would seriously compromise the client's ability to profit from treatment. Furthermore, psychoanalysts argue that helper disclosure can expose helper weaknesses and vulnerabilities, thereby undermining client trust in the helper and adversely influencing outcome (Curtis, 1981, 1982). I should note, however, that some current psychoanalytic theorists advocate the use of disclosure (see Geller, 2003), especially related to the therapeutic relationship (see chap. 12).

As you can probably tell, I agree more with the humanistic thinkers than with the traditional psychoanalytic thinkers about the value of helper disclosures. I have seen the power of disclosures in helping settings. But it is important to heed the concerns the psychoanalytic thinkers have about disclosures and make sure that they are used for the benefit of clients rather than for the needs of helpers.

In sum, helpers can disclose beneficially for clients if they do it for the appropriate intentions (not for their own needs) at the right moment. If helpers disclose in a manner in which they maintain an objective stance (i.e., are not overinvested), focus on the client, and observe client reactions, disclosures can be helpful. In fact, sometimes disclosures can be more helpful than other insight skills because the helper is not "putting something on" the client but is respectfully offering different possibilities to help the client gain insight.

HOW TO DISCLOSE ABOUT INSIGHT

Helpers need to think honestly about their intentions prior to disclosing. If they had an experience that could help clients understand more about themselves, it might be useful to disclose it for all the reasons noted above. Disclosures should not be used, however, to discuss or solve the helper's problems (e.g., "You think you've got it bad, let me tell you how bad it was for me"). Harm can result if helpers disclose because they have unresolved problems or have a desire to get attention for themselves. In this case, the focus shifts from the client to the helper, perhaps resulting in the client taking care of the helper.

To develop appropriate disclosures, helpers can think about what contributed to their behaviors when they were in situations similar to those of their clients. By focusing on insights they gained about themselves, helpers use their experiences to help clients attain insight. If helpers decide that disclosures are appropriate for the client at a particular moment, they should keep the focus of the disclosure on the insight rather than on recounting details of the experience. For example, rather than talking about the details of how his father died, the helper might say, "When my father died, I didn't know what I was feeling so I relied on everyone to tell me what I should be feeling. In the process, I lost myself. I wonder if that's happening to you?"

When helpers disclose, it is best to choose something that has occurred in the past, has been resolved, has resulted in a new perspective, can be helpful to the client, and does not make the helper feel vulnerable. Helpers should be honest about their experiences and should not make up things just to have a disclosure. If they have not had a similar experience that led to a new understanding, they should use a different skill.

In addition, disclosures that are short and immediately turn the focus back to the client tend to be most effective. Helpers can follow disclosures with open questions about whether the insight fits for the client (e.g., "I wonder how that fits for you?" or "I wonder if anything like that happens for you?").

If a disclosure does not work (e.g., the client denies or disavows having similar experiences or feels uncomfortable knowing information about the helper), it is probably best to refrain from making further disclosures. Several things could have happened. The helper could be right, but the client might not be ready to gain insight. Or, the helper could be projecting insight onto the client. In addition, the client could become upset about learning anything personal about the helper because it alters the distance between them. In such instances, the helper can collect more evidence to determine whether the helper's projection, the client's lack of readiness, or the client's need for distance is at issue. If lack of readiness is the problem, the helper can try other skills (e.g., reflection of feelings or challenge). If projection is the problem, the helper can seek supervision or therapy. If the client prefers not to know anything about the helper, the helper can change strategies and limit disclosures. Of course, any extreme reaction should be investigated further to assist in understanding and gaining insight into the client's underlying issues.

A specific situation that requires a bit more attention is how to respond when a client asks the helper for a disclosure. For example, a client might ask where the helper went for vacation or whether the helper is married or has children. A general rule would be to briefly provide information (if it feels comfortable) but also to then be curious about what motivates the client's desire for this personal information. Helpers might ask clients about their thoughts, fantasies, or concerns about them to learn more about what motivated clients to ask for information. In addition to providing the personal information, helpers can thus use the situation as an opportunity to investigate why clients want the information. Processing these issues in a gentle and supportive manner can provide the client with insight and strengthen the relationship.

EXAMPLE OF DISCLOSURE OF INSIGHT

The following example shows a helper using disclosure of insight (in italics) in a session.

> *Client:* I've been thinking a lot about death lately. I'm not thinking of suicide but more about the inevitability of death. There are so many senseless murders lately—the news is full of them. But I cannot quite grasp the idea of death—it doesn't make sense to me. It doesn't seem fair to be killed in the prime of life.
>
> *Helper:* You sound scared about the idea of dying.
>
> *Client:* Oh yeah, I really am. I really don't know what happens after death. Of course, my parents' religion talks about heaven and hell, but I can't quite buy all that. But if I don't believe what their religion says, I don't quite know what happens at death. And what is the meaning of life? I mean why are we here, and why does everyone rush around? What difference does it all make? I'm sure this all sounds very confusing, but I've been thinking about it a lot lately.
>
> *Helper:* No, it makes a lot of sense. I think all of us need to grapple with the meaning of life and the fact that we are going to die. You know, though, let me make a guess about something. *When I have been most concerned about death and meaning in life is when I have been in moments of transition and trying to figure out what I want out of life.* I wonder if that's true for you now?
>
> *Client:* Hmmm. That's interesting. I am about to turn 30, and it feels like a big turning point for me. I'm in a job I don't really like, and I haven't found the relationship that I always hoped I would find at this point. (Client continues talking productively about his personal concerns.)

POTENTIAL DIFFICULTIES IN USING DISCLOSURES OF INSIGHT

One danger in using disclosure is that helpers might project their feelings and reactions onto clients. For example, if a client has been talking about getting bad grades and a helper states, "I feel panicked when I get bad grades because I am still afraid of my parents' anger," the helper might have projected his or her own insight onto the client. The client might confirm that this is a projection by responding, "No, I feel more like I deserved the bad grade because I didn't study." Helpers need to remember that they are separate from their clients, have different experiences, and their personal insights might not apply to their clients.

Another problem is that some helpers use disclosure to satisfy their urge to reveal themselves, rather than using it intentionally to help clients gain insight. Similarly, some helpers mistake the notion of being open as an opportunity to say whatever is on their minds. Greenberg, Rice, and Elliott (1993) called such impulsive helper openness "promiscuous" disclosure. These types of disclosure may cause clients to feel uncomfortable and lose respect for the helper. For example, a client sought help to address her concerns about divorce. Unfortunately, her helper talked more about her own experiences with divorce than the client did. The client terminated and found a different helper who used disclosures more judiciously. Greenberg et al. suggested that disclosures need to be done with disciplined spontaneity on the basis of the helpers' accurate self-awareness of inner experience shared in a facilitative manner at a therapeutically appropriate moment. In other words, helpers need to be aware of themselves and of their intentions and deliver disclosures when they are most likely to help clients.

Beginning helpers tend to use too many disclosures. As with medical students seeing themselves in all the syndromes described in their medical texts, beginning helpers connect with many of their clients' struggles. They have a hard time setting aside personal issues to focus on their clients' problems. It is indeed difficult to shift from the mutual sharing that ideally occurs in friendships to the reduced amount of sharing that occurs in helping relationships. Paying attention to how a client's problems differ from the helper's can facilitate the helper to differentiate him- or herself from the client and use disclosures more judiciously.

Finally, some beginning helpers worry about making their disclosures perfect. They believe that disclosures could have negative effects if not done exactly right. They also worry about sounding patronizing, as if they have figured out everything for themselves whereas clients are still learning. They worry that they would feel too vulnerable and would lose any credibility they have as helpers if they disclose issues they are currently involved in and do not understand completely. Other helpers are concerned that they might not have an appropriate disclosure because they have not faced a similar situation or have not gained any insight into the situation—perhaps they are really in the same boat as the client. I recommend that helpers use other interventions if they feel uncomfortable or vulnerable using disclosures. I would also note that practice under close supervision helps greatly in terms of teaching beginning helpers the bounds of appropriate disclosures.

Suggested Reading

My colleagues and I recently did case studies of three different sessions of dream work to trace how clients gain insight (Hill et al., 2007; Knox et al., 2008). In two cases, clients gained insight into their dreams; in one case, the client did not gain insight into her dream. It is interesting that we found that open questions for insight were the most helpful therapist intervention. Read the cases and see whether you agree with our analyses of what factors led to insight.

What Do You Think?

- What role do you think culture plays in the interpretative process?
- When do you think it would be appropriate or inappropriate to offer interpretations, disclosures of insight, and open questions for insight?
- Do you agree about the necessity for developing a collaborative process of constructing interpretations with clients? Why or why not?
- Debate both sides of the idea that interpretations are a necessary prerequisite for change to occur (i.e., argue for and against the idea that interpretations are the "pure gold" of helping).
- Discuss whether clients can be taught to be more introspective.
- Debate whether interpretations should only be given after challenges.
- Debate how to determine the accuracy of interpretations.
- What theoretical approach do you prefer as a basis for developing interpretations?
- Discuss the notion that disclosure reduces the power imbalance between helpers and clients. What are the advantages and disadvantages of having a power imbalance in a helping relationship?
- What types of helpers might feel most comfortable disclosing?
- Debate the importance of helper neutrality in the insight stage.

i PRACTICE EXERCISES

A downloadable PDF of this chapter's Practice Exercises is available in the student resources area of the Helping Skills, *3rd ed. Web site: http://www.apa.org/books/resources/Hill3.*

For each of the following examples, write an open question for insight, an interpretation, and a disclosure of insight.

Statements

1. *Client:* I'm not doing very well in school right now. I'm sure it's my study skills. I just don't seem to be able to concentrate—I keep gazing out the window instead of getting my work done. I try to make myself stay at my desk more and more, but I seem to be getting less done. I broke up with my boyfriend so I could have more time to study, but it just doesn't seem to be working.

    Helper open question for insight: _____

    Helper interpretation: _____

    Helper disclosure of insight: _____

2. *Client:* I'm about ready to graduate and I need to decide what I'm going to do next with my life. I'm getting a lot of pressure from my parents, but I can't quite figure out what I want to do. I keep having this recurrent dream where I flunk out of a math class. I can never seem to get to class, and when I do get there, I don't understand any of the work. I never get to the tests on time, and I know I'm going to flunk out. I don't know why I keep having this dream. Math has always been difficult for me, but I got an A in my last math class.

    Helper open question for insight: _____

    Helper interpretation: _____

    Helper disclosure of insight: _____

3. *Client:* I really love my boyfriend and I want to get married, I really do. But, you know, recently I have not wanted to see him much. Every time we're together, I find myself criticizing him. You know, he does stupid things sometimes that just irritate me. I can just imagine him drinking beer and belching in front of my father. You know, my parents still haven't met him. I don't know quite why, but I haven't wanted to take him home.

    Helper open question for insight: _____

    Helper interpretation: _____

    Helper disclosure of insight: _____

Possible Helper Responses

1. "What do you think is going on?"
    "Maybe a fear of commitment keeps you from committing yourself to your schoolwork or a relationship."
    "When I was in a similar situation, I found that my feelings about the breakup interfered with my schoolwork. I wonder if that's true for you."

2. "What do you suppose causes your anxiety about the future?"
    "I wonder if your anxiety about your future is related to a fear of failing."

"I found that I was afraid that I would disappoint my parents if I didn't succeed. I wonder if that might be going on for you?"

3. "What thoughts do you have about why you don't want to take your boyfriend to meet your parents?"

"Maybe your fear about taking your boyfriend to meet your parents is because you're unsure about your feelings for him."

"You know there was one point for me where I realized later that I chose my partner specifically because he was so different from my father. Could that be true for you?"

---

i LAB 9. Facilitating Client Insight

A downloadable PDF of this Lab is available in the student resources area of the Helping Skills, *3rd ed. Web site: http://www.apa.org/books/resources/Hill3.*

Goals: For helpers to practice using the exploration skills (reflection, restatement, and open questions) and then learn to engage the client in the interpretive process.

Exercise 1

In groups of four to six people, one person should be the client, one person should be the initial helper, and the rest can wait to take over as helper or give ideas to the helper. Each person should take a turn being the client. Each group should have a designated lab leader (other than the helper) to organize and coordinate the session.

Helper's and Client's Tasks During the Helping Exchange

1. The client talks about a problematic reaction to a specific situation that he or she would like to understand. In other words, the client should talk about an event to which he or she had a strong reaction but did not understand why the reaction seemed out of proportion to the situation. For example, perhaps the client was driving along and someone swore at him and he became instantly enraged. Or perhaps the client was sitting in a classroom discussion and suddenly, for no obvious reason, felt like crying. The client should plan on being at least moderately disclosing—although, of course, clients always have the right to say that they do not want to disclose further.
2. The initial helper uses exploration skills (open questions, restatement, and reflection of feelings) for several minutes to help the client explore the problem. If the initial helper gets stuck, switch helpers to ensure a thorough exploration of the problem.
3. After several minutes of exploration, each group member should give a reflection of feelings, with the client responding to each reflection.
4. Each group member should ask an open question for insight (e.g., "What do you make of X?" "You mentioned Y, how does that fit with Z?").
5. Stop and have the group talk about the client (ask client to sit quietly and listen but not interrupt). Help the group conceptualize what is going on with the client and what might be helpful.
6. The group leader asks everyone (except the client) to write down an interpretation. Helpers can ask themselves, "What do I hear the person saying underneath the words?" "What are the themes in what the client is saying?" "What might be the reason for the client's feeling?" "What things might be connected to this problem?"
7. Each group member delivers his or her interpretation and allows time for the client to respond.

8. Everyone writes down a disclosure of insight. Helpers ask themselves, "When I was in a similar situation, what contributed to what I was doing? What did I learn about myself and my motivations that might be helpful to this client?"
9. Each helper in turn delivers a disclosure and gives the client a chance to respond.

Processing the Helping Exchange

After everyone has a turn and the client has responded, the client can talk about which interventions were most helpful and why. Helpers can talk about which interventions felt most comfortable and effective.

Switch Roles

Do another practice session with a different client, initial helper, and other helpers.

Exercise 2

Students should pair up, with one person as the helper and one as the client.

Helper's and Client's Tasks During the Helping Exchange

1. The client talks about a common problematic experience (e.g., schoolwork, adjustment to college, problems with friends).
2. The helper uses exploration skills (open question, restatement, and reflection of feelings) for about 10 minutes, allowing the client to explore.
3. The helper spends about 10 minutes giving some insight skills (challenge, open question for insight, interpretation, disclosures of insight), following up the insight skills with restatements and reflections of feelings.

After the Helping Exchange

The client can talk about his or her reactions to the insight skills. The helper can talk about his or her intentions and perceptions of the client reactions. Switch roles.

Personal Reflections

■ How did you feel giving open questions for insight, interpretations, and disclosures of insight?
■ Were you able to phrase the insight interventions so the client could hear them? Describe any discrepancies between the reactions you expected from the client and the actual reactions that the client had.
■ What are your strengths and weaknesses in engaging the client in the interpretive process?
■ How did you feel about receiving insight interventions as a client? What factors about the delivery of these interventions influenced your feelings?
■ What role does culture play in your ability to give and receive interpretive interventions?

Immediacy | 12

There are, in fact, no more important communications
between one human being and another than those
expressed emotionally, and no information more vital for
constructing and reconstructing working models of the self
and other than information about how each feels towards
the other . . . it is the emotional communications between
a patient and his therapist that play the crucial part.

—*John Bowlby* (1988, pp. 156–157)

Evita constantly got angry at her helper, Angela, and
criticized her for everything she said. Angela began
to feel inadequate and angry at Evita and did not
look forward to sessions. Angela consulted with her
supervisor, who reassured Angela that she was using
the helping skills appropriately and suggested that
perhaps Evita's personal issues caused her to denigrate
Angela. The supervisor suggested that Angela use
immediacy in the next session to let Evita know how
she was feeling. So in the next session, when Evita
criticized her for not saying the right feeling word,
Angela said, "You know, right now I'm feeling badly
because it feels like I cannot do anything right. I feel
frustrated because I don't know how to help you.
I wonder how you feel about our relationship?"
Evita broke into tears and said that she seemed to
push everyone away. Angela was able to listen and
reflect that Evita felt criticized. Eventually they came
to realize that Evita pushed people away because she
feared rejection. Using immediacy allowed Angela to
help Evita understand more about how she acted
with others, and its use strengthened the therapeutic
relationship.

mmediacy occurs when helpers disclose how they are feeling about the client, about themselves in relation to the client, or about the therapeutic relationship. Kiesler (1988, 1996) stated that *metacommunication* (his term for immediacy) occurs when helpers disclose to clients their perceptions of and reactions to a client's actions. He distinguished metacommunication from other helper disclosures of personal factual or historical information about life experiences because metacommunication relates specifically to the helper's experience of the client. Kiesler indicated that metacommunication is one of the most powerful interventions in the helper's repertoire because the helper responds to the client in a different manner from that to which the client is accustomed. Rather than ignoring inappropriate or obnoxious behavior, as is often the case in social interactions, for example, the helper confronts the client directly and describes the impact of the client's behavior on him or her. Similarly, Ivey (1994) called immediacy being "in the moment" with the client. He pointed out that most clients talk in the past tense about events but might profit from talking in the present tense about what is going on in the helping relationship.

Egan (1994) suggested that immediacy can focus on the overall relationship (e.g., "It feels to me that we are getting along well now that we have worked through our initial discomfort"), a specific event in the session (e.g., "I was surprised when you said that you appreciated the sessions because I wasn't sure how you felt about our work"), or present-tense personal reactions to the client (e.g., "I am feeling hurt right now because you reject everything I say"). See the overview of immediacy in Exhibit 12.1. For the insight stage, the primary interest is in immediacy statements that help clients gain greater understanding of how they come across in the therapeutic relationship, in the hopes that they can use this information to change how they act in relationships outside of helping.

Immediacy can be thought of as a type of disclosure because helpers disclose personal feelings, reactions, or experiences about the client or relationship to help the client gain insight. Immediacy can also sometimes be a type of challenge because it can be used to confront clients about issues in the relationship (e.g., "I feel annoyed that you avoid my questions"). In addition, immediacy can sometimes be a type of information if it is used to point out patterns in a client's behavior in relation to the therapist (e.g., "Whenever I go on vacation, you cancel the first two sessions after I return. I wonder if we could talk about this pattern?"). However, immediacy differs from feedback about the client (a type of information covered in the action stage, see chap. 15) because both people in the relationship are involved in immediacy interventions, whereas in feedback about the client the focus is only on the client (e.g., "You did a really good job when you spoke up to your mother").

EXHIBIT 12.1

Overview of Immediacy

Definition	*Immediacy* refers to the helper disclosing immediate feelings about the client, her- or himself in relation to the client, or the therapeutic relationship.
Examples	"Right now I'm feeling very tense because you seem to be angry at me." "I feel nervous too, but I'm pleased that you're sharing some very deep and personal feelings with me."
Typical helper intentions	To promote insight, to deal with the relationship, to challenge, to identify maladaptive behaviors, to identify and intensify feelings, to relieve therapist's needs[a] (see Web Form D)
Possible client reactions	Relief, negative thoughts or feelings, better self-understanding, clear, feelings, responsibility, unstuck, new perspective, challenged, scared, worse, stuck, confused, misunderstood (see Web Form G)
Desired client behaviors	Affective exploration, cognitive exploration, insight (see Web Form H)
Helpful hints	Be aware of your own feelings about the relationship. Observe the client for possible feelings about the relationship. Cultivate a sense of curiosity and try to understand your and the client's reactions. Be gentle, tentative, and empathic. State your own feelings as well as noting what might be going on for the client. Be nondefensive and encourage an open discussion of the relationship. Turn to focus over to the client (e.g., "What do you think?" "What is your reaction?").

[a]This intention is typically not therapeutic.

Although immediacy overlaps with other skills, I highlight it as a separate skill in the insight stage because it can be particularly valuable for helping the client gain insight into the therapeutic relationship.

In this chapter, I focus on four specific subtypes of immediacy. In the first subtype, *inquiries about the relationship,* the helper invites the client to share feelings about the therapeutic relationship. These inquiries are thus probes into the client's reactions to the relationship and have also been called *process statements* because they address what is going on in the immediate moment. These inquiries often involve the helper checking in with the client about feelings. For example, the helper might ask,

- "I wonder what reactions you had to the session today?"
- "How did you feel just now when I praised you?"
- "What would you like from me right now?"

The second subtype of immediacy is the helper's *statement of his or her reactions to the client.* Thus, the helper shares his or her own feelings and reactions in the moment and generally follows these up with an inquiry about how the client feels. For example, the helper might say,

- "I've been feeling a little disconnected from you today. I wonder how you've been feeling?"
- "I feel so much closer to you today when you share your feelings so deeply. I feel so moved by what you have said. How has it been for you?"

Making the covert overt is the third subtype of immediacy. Often the client is saying something to the helper indirectly, and through this intervention the helper attempts to make the client's intention more open. In this subtype, anything that happens in the helping relationship is open for processing to see whether something is going on in the relationship. For example, the helper might say,

- "You are late again today. I wonder if anything is going on in terms of your feelings about being here?"
- "You keep looking at your watch. I wonder if you're eager to leave?"
- "You seemed angry when I said that. I wonder what's going on inside?"

A fourth subtype, which also might involve covert communications, is *drawing parallels with outside relationships.* Again, the helper wonders aloud whether the client has reactions to him or her that are similar to those the client has to others. For example,

- "You mentioned that no one seems to understand you. I wonder if you might be saying that I don't understand you?"
- "You are talking about withdrawing from your friends lately. I wonder if that's happening in here with me?"
- "You've said that you get very upset if anyone criticizes you, and just now you pulled back when I talked about your procrastination. I wonder if you're worried that I will criticize you?"

RATIONALE FOR USING IMMEDIACY

The helping relationship provides a microcosm of how clients relate in the real world. If a client is compliant with the helper, for example, he or she is often compliant with others in the outside world. If a client is arrogant and shows off to impress the helper, chances are that she or he does similar things with other people. Therefore, the client's general interpersonal style can be examined, at least in part, by an investigation of his or her relationship with the helper. Thus, rather than having to rely completely on clients' reports of how they act with other people, helpers have a firsthand experience of how clients behave in an interpersonal relationship. Of course, clients do not always act toward all other people as they act toward the helper—it may be that they only act that way to people in positions of authority or to people of that gender or some similar characteristic. But observing the behavior does provide firsthand evidence of how the client comes across in interpersonal interactions, at least occasionally.

Helpers know from their own reactions how others might react to clients. So awareness of these reactions provides helpers with information that they can use to help clients understand more about themselves. Helpers first experience personally the impact of a client's behavior, which Kiesler (1988) and Cashdan (1988) called becoming "hooked." They noted that helpers are pushed into a constricted, narrow range of responses by the client's maladaptive behaviors. Helpers initially respond negatively to clients' unconscious demands (e.g., dominant clients elicit submissive behavior from helpers; hostile clients elicit hostile behavior from helpers). Thus, helpers experience firsthand how clients interact with at least some other people. If helpers become aware of these reactions without critical judgment of the client, they can begin to understand how other people react to clients in interpersonal relationships.

Resolving problems between the helper and client can also provide clients with a model of how to resolve interpersonal problems in relationships. If done well, clients learn that it is possible to talk about feelings, resolve problems, and develop closer relationships as a result of the discussion. Greenberg, Rice, and Elliott (1993) suggested that encountering another real human being who both cares and is authentic helps clients grow. Being able to resolve interpersonal problems can be a powerful experience, teaching clients that it is possible, although not always easy, to deal openly with issues.

In addition to addressing problems in relationships in general, immediacy can also be used to discuss issues of importance to the helping relationship. For example, a helper might want to process feelings with a client about running into each other at a party, or a helper could discuss with a client what has and has not worked in the helping process so that adjustments can be made. Many issues present themselves in a helping relationship, so immediacy is a critical tool for working out inevitable interpersonal problems.

Another reason for using immediacy is to challenge clients to change maladaptive behaviors. When helpers are honest about their reactions, clients learn how they come across to other people and thus might change their problematic behaviors. Some examples of interpersonal behaviors that can cause problems for clients in helping relationships (and other relationships) include being so talkative that the helper cannot speak, acting overbearing and arrogant and assuming that they are better than the helper, being passive and not saying anything without being asked, droning on and on in a monotone voice without maintaining eye contact, disagreeing with everything the helper says, constantly bringing gifts to the helper, or trying too hard to be helpful.

In the world outside of helping, friends and acquaintances might not be honest with each other about how they feel about what is going on in their relationship because it is difficult, may hurt feelings, and takes time and effort. Because they do not receive feedback, however, clients often are not aware of how they come across to others. If oblivious to their own behaviors (which they often are because they are so used to them), clients cannot change, and there could be negative consequences (e.g., if a client is not aware that she speaks with a hostile tone, it could negatively affect her evaluations in the workplace). The helping relationship thus provides an opportunity for clients to become aware of how their behaviors affect another person and to make changes in a safe setting.

Immediacy can also be used to make covert communication more direct. In some cases, clients talk covertly about the helping relationship because they are not sure how helpers will react if they say something directly. For example, a client might say that no one can help him. Because the helper is trying to help him, it is not a huge leap to guess that at least part of the communication is directed toward the helper. In any communication, helpers can ask themselves what clients are trying to communicate to them about the therapy relationship, although whether they use immediacy should be tempered by the clinical situation and the client's needs at the time.

Helpers who gently provide immediacy may be giving their clients a special gift. In effect, immediacy communicates that helpers are willing to take the time to let clients know about the effect of their behaviors so they can have an opportunity to increase awareness and change inappropriate behaviors. But it is important to emphasize that helpers must use immediacy in a caring way with deep compassion and empathy. Immediacy can be a powerful intervention that raises the temperature in the room, so helpers must be aware that it is a risky intervention that has great power to heal but can also be damaging if presented poorly.

It is also important to comment about cultural differences in terms of dealing immediately with relationship difficulties. In cultures in which typical communication is indirect, it can be considered rude to directly communicate about the relationship. I do not know of any culture where talking openly about immediate relationships is embraced, but it is probably even more difficult in shame-based and private cultures. Helpers may still be able to use immediacy, but they may need to be very gentle and tentative in their manner of delivery and carefully observe client reactions.

HOW TO USE IMMEDIACY

Immediacy is a difficult and demanding skill. Helpers need to be aware of what is happening in themselves and in the therapeutic relationship and have enough self-confidence and self-understanding not to react defensively to a client's open expression of feelings. Because they do not always openly deal with immediate feelings in nonhelping situations, helpers often feel frightened about doing so in helping situations. It takes courage, as well as skill, to be immediate with clients. But most importantly, it takes compassion; rather than taking the client's behavior personally, helpers try to understand what is going on with clients that keeps them from relating effectively and then compassionately try to help them become aware of these behaviors so that they can change and have more satisfying relationships. Drawing liberally from other theorists who have written about immediacy (Carkhuff, 1969; Cashdan, 1988, Ivey, 1994; Kiesler, 1988, 1996; Safran & Muran, 2000; Teyber, 2006), I propose the following ideas to enable helpers to use immediacy in helping sessions.

When using immediacy, helpers talk directly to clients about their interactions. In other words, helpers and clients metacommunicate about their communication. Kiesler (1988) stressed that the success of the metacommunication depends on the extent to which the helper balances the challenge of the metacommunication with being supportive and protective of the client's self-esteem. Helpers need to present the immediacy as a gentle examination of the process. Helpers communicate that they are committed to working with clients to understand their actions and the effects of their behaviors on relationships with other people.

Helpers should take appropriate responsibility for their feelings when using immediacy by using "I" statements (e.g., "I feel uncomfortable that you keep praising me" or "I feel bad that I interrupted you") rather than "you" statements (e.g., "You shouldn't praise me" or "You talk too much"). Clients often have an easier time owning their responsibility (e.g., "I was probably talking too much") when helpers have candidly admitted their contribution to the interaction. Furthermore, it is only fair for helpers to admit responsibility (if justified) if they demand that clients acknowledge their part. When helpers acknowledge their role in relationship problems, an open exchange can occur about how both people feel. Problems can be resolved, the therapeutic relationship can be enhanced, and clients can be encouraged to become actively involved in problem solving. For example, at mid-semester, a helper discovered that her client, Maria, was in the same practicum class as the helper's partner. The helper repeatedly asked Maria to process this situation even though Maria indicated that she had worked through her feelings on her own at the beginning of the semester. The helper later apologized and indicated that she realized she had many feelings about the situation and had inadvertently projected them onto the client.

It is crucial that helpers not prescribe how clients should change, because "should" statements imply that the helper knows more about the client than the client does, which goes against the client-centered nature of this model. Instead, helpers simply point out how they react when clients act in a particular way. It is also important that helpers are aware that their feedback about clients is based on their perceptions and reactions and that others might react differently to the clients. Helpers might even suggest that clients gather feedback about how others react to the behaviors. An awareness of how they are perceived by others can enable clients to make choices about how to behave and decide whether they want to make changes.

After being immediate with clients, helpers ask clients about their reactions to the immediacy, so that the communication is two-sided. Hence, after the helper says something like, "I find myself having a hard time staying awake when you talk," the helper can ask the client, "How do you feel about what I said" or "You became awfully quiet when I said I had a hard time staying awake. What was going on inside you?" Thus, the helper tries to engage the client in a discussion of the interaction. Research shows that it is important for helpers to be open about exploring the interaction (Rhodes, Hill, Thompson, & Elliott, 1994; Safran, Muran, Samstag, & Stevens, 2002).

Of course some clients will be happy to lay all the blame on the helper and turn the tables to talk about the helper's problems. If this happens, the helper can use that as an immediacy intervention (e.g., "You know, I'm feeling a little attacked. I wonder if we both can look at our parts in this interaction?").

Because helpers have indicated that it is permissible to process the relationship, they need to be aware that clients may give them feedback about what they do not like about the helper's behaviors. After all, helping is a two-way interaction, and helpers may be doing things that are not optimal for clients. Some of this information may be accurate and valuable—clients are often wonderful sources of feedback because they are the recipients of what helpers do and know how the interventions feel. However, helpers also must be aware that feedback is sometimes distorted (i.e., transference). For example, Yutta may say that the helper is mean, not because of what the helper has done but because of unresolved feelings she has about her critical mother that she projects onto the helper. Helpers have to determine what feedback is genuinely related to their behavior and what is related to transference issues. There is usually at least a grain of truth in most client feedback, however, so helpers should investigate both their own behaviors and the client's contribution.

EXAMPLE OF A HELPER USING IMMEDIACY

The following shows a helper using immediacy (in italics) in a session:

Client: I would really like to sleep with you. I think sex is very important and a natural way of relating to someone that you're close to. It's just a matter of time until you agree to sleep with me. I know you're attracted to me—I can see it in your eyes.

Helper: *It makes me uncomfortable when you talk about having sex with me. I wonder what your intentions are in talking with me about it?*

Client: Well, that's how men and women are supposed to relate. You say you're trying to help me. What I really need is for you to go to bed with me. That would give me some security that I am attractive.

Helper: So you have a hard time relating to me on a non-sexual basis.

Client: Yeah, I guess I do.

Helper: *I wonder if you have any ideas about what leads you to relate to me in a sexual way when it is not appropriate for what we are trying to do here?*

Client: That's interesting. My mother was always very seductive. I've always reacted to women on a sexual basis. Women are usually pretty eager to sleep with me.

Helper: *I wonder how it feels to talk about our relationship?*

Client: Well, I'm not used to it. I still can't see why you won't sleep with me.

Helper: *I can understand more now that when you get anxious about talking with me, you change the topic to talking about sex. Do you notice that?*

Client: Yeah, I guess I can see that. I am uncomfortable talking about my problems. I'm more of an action-type person and want to do something.

Helper: Are you willing to try to understand what's going on?

Client: Well, it makes me anxious, but I guess it's worth a try.

DIFFICULTIES HELPERS HAVE IN USING IMMEDIACY

Beginning helpers often have fears about intruding and making clients angry if they use immediacy, even if they do it empathically. Indeed, clients do sometimes become angry. For example, a helper gently suggested that Olivia was acting helpless when she expected the helper to take responsibility for her behavior and failures. Olivia became angry and adamantly denied that her behaviors were similar to those of victims. Several sessions later, however, Olivia acknowledged that the immediacy intervention was accurate and helped her become motivated to take more control of her life. If the helper had withheld the immediacy intervention for fear of hurting Olivia's feelings, Olivia would not have learned a valuable lesson about herself. Although it is sometimes painful to hear, such feedback can be motivational and subsequently life changing.

Another problem is that helpers often do not trust their feelings (e.g., "Maybe it is all my fault that I'm bored—if I were a better helper, I wouldn't feel bored"). They might feel unsure about their reactions and hesitant about communicating their feelings to clients appropriately and empathically. Some helpers simply avoid immediacy because it is frightening to talk directly and honestly about the immediate relationship. They are not used to such open communication in their relationships, and they feel vulnerable when sharing immediate feelings. They might feel anxious about dealing openly with interpersonal conflicts because their families had strong rules against addressing conflicts openly. In fact, most helpers have an easier time being empathic with clients who are sad or depressed but are less skilled when it comes to talking directly with clients about negative reactions and working through interpersonal problems. Once again, personal therapy can provide an opportunity for helpers to come to understand their own issues. Supervision can also provide a reality check for helpers because they can learn how someone else reacts to the client.

Finally, helpers sometimes inappropriately (and often unconsciously) use immediacy to deal with their own needs. For example, a helper who had recently been divorced was feeling particularly vulnerable and needed affirmation that he was attractive, so he encouraged his client to talk about her attraction to him. Usually, helpers are not aware that they are using immediacy to deal with their own needs. They might become aware that they are doing so, however, if their behaviors have negative consequences for their clients (e.g., a client quits after the helper gets angry at her for being too quiet). Hence, it is crucial that helpers are mindful of their needs so these needs do not intrude on the helping process.

It is often hard for beginning helpers to imagine using immediacy if they have only brief interactions with clients. They are right, because immediacy is often not appropriate in very brief interactions. However, it is still valuable for beginning helpers to practice this skill in role-plays and be aware of how it could be used in actual sessions with clients with whom they work for longer periods of time.

Suggested Reading

My colleagues and I have recently investigated therapist use of immediacy within two complete cases of brief psychotherapy (Hill, Sim, et al., 2008; Kasper, Hill, & Kivlighan, 2008). In these two cases, we found that therapist immediacy led to client immediacy, helped the dyads negotiate the rules of their relationship, helped the clients express immediate feelings, and enabled the clients to have corrective relational experiences. These two papers provide good examples of how therapists use immediacy in an actual setting.

What Do You Think?

- Discuss whether you think helpers can balance being direct with feedback and accepting clients for who they are.
- How might helpers respond when clients are angry at them?
- Discuss the idea that immediacy can be an enactment of a deep level of empathy.
- Discuss the advantages and disadvantages of using immediacy as compared with interpretations.

i PRACTICE EXERCISES

A downloadable PDF of this chapter's Practice Exercises is available in the student resources area of the Helping Skills, *3rd ed. Web site: http://www.apa.org/books/resources/Hill3.*

For each of the following examples, write an immediacy statement. Compare your responses with the possible helper responses provided at the end of this practice exercise.

Statements

1. *Client:* "You know, I thought about what you said last time, and I got really angry. I don't think you know what you're talking about when you suggest that I go to see my old boyfriend when I go into town to give a talk. He hasn't even tried to contact me for 10 years, and I'm supposed to be focused on my work and giving a talk. I couldn't possibly concentrate if I knew I had to spend time going to see him and started worrying about what he would say."

   Helper immediacy: _____

2. *Client:* "You sure haven't been very helpful today. You don't give me any good advice. I don't know why I bother coming here. It's a waste of time."

   Helper immediacy: _____

3. *Client:* (silent for 5 minutes)

   Helper immediacy: _____

4. (Client talks on and on without pausing for 15 minutes.)

   Helper immediacy: _____

Possible Helper Responses

1. "I'm sorry I suggested that you contact your old boyfriend. It obviously was hurtful to you. Maybe we could spend some time talking about what was going on between us, given that I don't usually tell you what to do."
   "I feel concerned that you are blaming me when my memory is that you were the one to suggest that you go to see him."

2. "I also am feeling frustrated that we don't seem to be getting anywhere."
   "I feel upset right now because I put a lot of time and energy into our relationship and yet it doesn't seem to be enough for you."

3. "You seem angry with me. Can you talk about what's going on?"
   "I am worried about you right now because you seem so distant."

4. "I'm feeling bored right now. I wonder if you're aware that you've been talking nonstop for 15 minutes? What do you suppose is going on inside you?"
   "I'm feeling a little irritated that we're not getting anywhere. You seem like you're more interested in telling stories than working today. How do you feel?"

---

i LAB 10. Immediacy

A downloadable PDF of this Lab is available in the student resources area of the Helping Skills, *3rd ed. Web site:http://www.apa.org/books/resources/Hill3.*

Exercise 1

Goal: To help students learn about immediacy from their personal experience.

Instructions: In a large group, the lab leader asks the group members to reflect on their experiences in the here and now in the group. Group members might talk about things such as their comfort level in the group and who talks the most in the group. The lab leader should monitor to make sure that everyone has a chance to talk (e.g., going around the circle can be a useful way to make sure that everyone talks) and that the tone is kept positive.

Review: Go around the circle and have group members talk about how it felt to reveal immediate feelings.

Exercise 2

Goal: For helpers to practice immediacy in the context of the other helping skills.
This lab is meant for advanced students who are seeing "real" clients. In this lab, I recommend forming groups of four to six people. I suggest that a helper who is currently seeing a client present a case. The helper plays the part of the client so the helper can portray how the client behaves (and also gain more empathy for the client by playing the client). A second group

member plays the role of the helper. Other group members can provide ideas to the helper about other possible ways of intervening or take over the role of helper if the helper gets stuck. Each group should have a designated lab leader (other than the helper) to organize and coordinate the session.

Helper's and Client's Tasks During the Helping Exchange

1. The client (played by the actual helper) role-plays how the actual client presents him- or herself, trying to portray the client's behavior that makes it particularly difficult for the actual helper to respond therapeutically. The actual helper should not provide any introductory material, talk about the actual client, or the history of the helping interaction prior to the role-play, because the idea is for group members to respond naturally, without receiving potentially biasing information.
2. The helper should respond for several speaking turns using the exploration skills (open question, restatement, reflection) until she or he has formed some rapport and has experienced an inner reaction to the client.
3. When the interactional patterns are at least somewhat clear, the lab leader should ask the helper to pause for a moment.
4. Everyone (except the client) can write down an immediacy statement. Helpers can each ask themselves, "What am I feeling right now?" "What is going on in the relationship?" "How much of this is due to my own personal issues?"
5. Each helper should give an immediacy statement and allow the client time to respond.

Observers' Tasks During the Helping Exchange

Everyone should observe all the interactions and note which ones seemed particularly helpful or unhelpful and why. How does the helper present the immediacy statement? Does the helper take responsibility for her or his feelings? How does the client respond to the immediacy statement? How does the relationship between the helper and client appear? How would you feel in each role?

After the Helping Exchange

The client can talk about reactions to hearing the immediacy intervention. The helper can talk about how it felt to use immediacy. Observers can provide feedback about their observations and perceptions of the interaction.

Switch Roles

Exercise 3

Goal: To integrate the exploration and insight skills. Students should pair up. One person will be the helper and one the client.

Helper's and Client's Tasks During the Helping Exchange

1. Clients should talk about something that they do but they don't know why they do it, or about something that confuses or puzzles them.
2. Helpers should use exploration skills (open questions, restatement, and reflection of feelings) for 5 to 10 minutes to help the client explore.
3. Once they have established some rapport, helpers should begin using insight skills (challenge, interpretation, self-disclosure, and immediacy) when appropriate, interspersed with exploration skills.

After the Helping Exchange

Clients can talk about their reactions. Helpers can talk about their intentions and their perceptions of the client reactions.

Switch Roles

Personal Reflections

- How do you feel about dealing with interpersonal conflict?
- For the helpers who played the roles of their clients: What did you learn about your clients? How did your feelings change toward the clients? Describe any new ideas you learned for dealing with your clients.
- How would you respond to a client who wanted to give you feedback?

Integrating the Skills of the Insight Stage | 13

He who has a *why* to live can bear with almost any *how*.

—Nietzsche

Benjamin, who has been unable to choose a career, comes to realize that he is afraid to compete with his father, a businessman who is extremely successful but distant from his family. Yvonne comes to understand that her feelings of inadequacy are based on other children making fun of her for having a slight speech impediment. Nigel gains the insight that he avoids all risks because of his fear of dying at a young age as his father did. These are examples of new understandings that clients come to with the aid of helpers in the insight stage.

I n the insight stage, helpers assist clients in developing new perspectives about themselves, their feelings, and their behaviors. Helpers choose which skills to use depending on their intentions, what the client is presenting at the moment, what the client can tolerate, and their overall plan for the session. They maintain an empathic connection with clients and continue using the exploration skills, but they also challenge clients' discrepancies, irrational ideas, or defenses to raise awareness; ask open questions to encourage clients to think about the reasons for their behaviors; use interpretations and disclosures of insight to facilitate new understandings of the underlying reasons or motivations for thoughts and behaviors; and use immediacy to help clients become aware of how they come across to others and to deal with tensions or misunderstandings in the therapeutic relationship. These interventions help clients achieve greater depths of self-understanding and insight about who they are, how they got to be the way they are, and how they are perceived by others.

From the clients' side, it is hoped they gain some new understandings of themselves at a deep, emotional level by the end of the insight stage. They see things in new ways or from different perspectives, are able to identify patterns or make connections, have ideas about why they do what they do, and have a deeper understanding of themselves. These insights usually have an "aha" quality to them, and clients feel relieved that they have explanations for their behaviors and thoughts. Clients "own" their new understandings because they have been instrumental in helping to construct them.

Steps for Interpretive Interventions

There are six steps helpers can follow to help guide clients through the insight stage.

STEP 1: SET THE STAGE

Helpers pave the way for the insight stage through empathy, reflections of feelings, and helping the client explore. There needs to be a good bond between the helper and the client, and the client needs to feel that it is safe to explore reasons behind feelings and thoughts, without fear of judgment.

Another reason for taking adequate time is so the helper can observe the client. Helpers formulate challenges and interpretations from their observations of clients, so they must be alert and trust their observations. Before going into insight interventions, helpers need to collect an adequate amount of evidence to clarify what is going on rather than jumping to conclusions.

The need for empathy remains a key element of the insight stage. When dealing with difficult clinical situations, if helpers can put themselves in the client's shoes and try to understand what is going on with the client, helpers will often be able to avoid being judgmental and will be able to forge an alliance with their client. In a recent study, Vivino, Thompson, Hill, and Ladany (in press) found that experienced therapists who were able to step back and try to understand what was going on for clients were able to rekindle their compassion for difficult clients.

STEP 2: LOOK FOR MARKERS OF CLIENT READINESS FOR INSIGHT

The markers for readiness for challenges, insight work, and immediacy differ somewhat. Hence, they are presented separately in this step.

Markers for Challenging

Helpers look for markers that indicate that clients are ready to gain awareness. These markers include expressions of ambivalence, contradictions, discrepancies, or confusion or feeling stuck or unable to make a decision. Helpers can observe and listen to clients carefully for "sour notes"—things that do not sound right, make sense, fit, or go together, or things that are done out of "shoulds," cause ambivalences, or result in struggles. These sour notes can point the way to issues about which clients feel contradictions and uncertainties. These markers suggest that clients are ready to allow the problem to "come into awareness."

Helpers can try to think about why the client might feel confused or stuck. Rather than blaming or condemning the client, the helper tries to understand the client's dynamics. The empathy generated through this process can help the helper become curious about checking out the hypotheses rather than becoming invested in pointing out a discrepancy or trying to make the client change.

Markers for Insight

Once the relationship is established, helpers watch for markers that clients are ready and eager for insight. Possible markers of readiness are (a) a clear statement of awareness of a problem, (b) a statement of a lack of understanding, (c) a stated eagerness or willingness to understand, and (d) a high level of affective distress that is experienced as a pressure for resolution of the problem. The client might say something like, "I just don't understand why I get so angry at my boyfriend. He usually does nothing wrong. I just suddenly get furious and I can't control my rage. I really wish I understood it because it is making me miserable and is about to destroy the best relationship I have ever had." Possible markers indicating a lack of readiness are clients telling a story, asking for advice, or blaming others for problems. Skills for facilitating exploration or awareness are probably more suited than insight skills when clients are not ready.

Some clients are psychologically minded and value probing into their dynamics and motives. Other clients, however, are not so interested in probing into the underlying dynamics and are more concerned with exploration or fixing problems. It is important, however, to stress that helpers should not assume from stereotypes that certain groups of clients (e.g., clients from a low socioeconomic class) are not suited for interpretations. Furthermore, some clients can be taught to be more introspective.

It is also important to be aware that some cultures may not value interpretive activity as much as the European American culture does. Some cultures (e.g., Asian, Hispanic) value action more than understanding, although sometimes education about why insight is valuable can be persuasive. Because it is important to respect others' values, however, helpers should not force clients to work on insight if they are not amenable after being educated about it.

Markers for Immediacy

One set of markers comes from observing the client. Does the client seem distraught, particularly quiet, unusually talkative, more vague than usual, acting hostile or too friendly toward you? Does the client mention references to other people that might be a reference to you (e.g., "no one understands me," "everyone makes me feel bad"). If so, these behaviors may be signs that something is going on inside the client about the helping relationship.

Another set of markers is feelings that helpers have about clients. Typical markers are feeling bored, sexually attracted, angry, stuck, incompetent, prideful, or brilliant, especially if these feelings are extreme. Another typical marker for helpers is feeling afraid and wanting to avoid certain topics with the client, or not using specific helping skills when they know they would be useful (e.g., not exploring; not using insight skills).

Becoming aware of these feelings is often difficult for helpers, who like to think of themselves as being accepting and nurturing rather than as having negative feelings. To get into these potential feelings, helpers can ask themselves:

- "What am I feeling when I am with this client?"
- "What do I want to do or not do when I am with this client?"
- "What keeps me from using the skills that I know I would like to be using with this client?"

Helpers need to allow themselves to have their feelings without judging themselves as "bad" or incompetent. Rather, helpers can view themselves as instruments and use their feelings to determine how they resonate with or react to clients. Supervision can be useful in facilitating helpers in their struggle with experiencing negative feelings toward clients because supervisors can normalize such feelings. For example, the supervisor might say, "If I were in this situation, I would feel sexually attracted to this client. She is so seductive that I would feel distracted in sessions." When supervisors are able to admit to having "politically incorrect" feelings, helpers often are then able to acknowledge their own feelings. Thus, supervision is invaluable for enabling helpers to become aware of their feelings and also for ensuring that helpers do not act out impulsively on their feelings.

Once the helper becomes aware of the automatic reactions, he or she can stop the reactions and try to understand the reactions. Rather than taking it personally and feeling badly that they had these strong emotions or blaming the client for the reactions, helpers can try to cultivate a sense of curiosity about what contributes to clients acting as they do. Often, clients have developed these behaviors as defenses. For example, if a client is very talkative and does not let anyone else contribute to the discussion, the client could be defending against letting anyone get close for fear of becoming engulfed. Thus, the constant talking may serve a defensive function of keeping others at a safe distance.

By coming to an understanding of what they are feeling with clients, helpers can regain some objectivity, which permits them to distance themselves from their reactions and begin to help their clients. For example, by becoming aware that a client's whining pulls for the helper to be sadistic, the helper can stop trying to silence the client and shift to wondering what causes the client to whine. The helper can then think about how to provide the client with feedback about the effects of her or his whining.

Of course, helpers need to evaluate whether any of their own issues could be implicated in the feelings they have when they are with clients. For example, a helper might be sensitive to a client's talkativeness and aggressiveness because the helper's mother is very dominant and talks incessantly. If helpers find they have similar feelings with several clients (e.g., being sexually attracted to several clients), this could be a clue that it is the helper's rather than the clients' problem.

STEP 3: DETERMINE INTENTIONS

Helpers need to think about their intentions at a particular moment in the helping process. The most appropriate intention here is to promote insight. Inappropriate intentions would be to make oneself look good at the expense of the client, to show off, or to punish clients for being frustrating. If helpers realize that they want to give a challenge or an interpretation to meet their own needs, they can pause, think about themselves and the client, and try to figure out what is going on in the relationship.

STEP 4: IMPLEMENT THE INSIGHT SKILLS

Of overall importance is for the helper to be gentle, tentative, and empathic when using insight skills. The posture should be one of curiosity rather than one of showing off or being judgmental. Furthermore, the helper typically wants to collaborate with the client to discover meaning. Thus, there is a lot of back and forth with both people brainstorming about what might be going on: The helper asks the client an open question and listens intently, and then perhaps the helper offers a tentative interpretation, which the client adds to or modifies, and then the helper perhaps challenges, and perhaps at this point the client has a glimmer of insight, which the helper restates and asks for more elaboration, and so on. The idea here is to help the client get unblocked so that he or she can go out and continue thinking on his or her own.

It is also important for the helper to observe client reactions to these insight interventions and make modifications if needed. Helpers should carefully observe clients' reactions after any insight intervention. And because clients often conceal negative reactions, helpers might need to go beyond observing to asking explicitly about clients' reactions to interpretations. Helpers should also remember to use exploration skills frequently during this stage because clients need the opportunity to process new information in a safe and supportive setting.

STEP 5: FOLLOW UP

Single challenges, interpretations, or immediacy statements rarely trigger new insight immediately. Clients typically require many reiterations before they begin to understand, incorporate, and use the insight. At first, these insight interventions may seem strange and foreign, but as clients hear them numerous times in different ways, they begin to understand them. Helpers thus need to plan enough time in sessions to work through the new insights. They also need to follow up on insight interventions in subsequent sessions. Clients typically continue the interpretative process outside of sessions (which of course is the goal of helping), so following up on what the client has been thinking in between sessions can be fruitful.

STEP 6: ASK CLIENT FOR HIS OR HER CURRENT UNDERSTANDING

Often what the helper thinks at the end of this stage can be quite different from what the client thinks. It is thus really useful for the helper to check out what the client absorbed from the process. I recall one session when I was sure that the client had gained a lot of insight but was surprised when she said that nothing much had changed. Knowing where the client is at can help you plan for future interventions.

Caveats About Using
Insight Skills

Several caveats apply to the use of insight interventions. First, the therapeutic relationship must be solid before insight skills are used. Clients must trust their helpers, and helpers must have a base of knowledge about clients from which to formulate insight interventions. A relationship can sometimes be established quickly, but at other times, a long period of testing is needed before the relationship can withstand insight interventions. One way of determining whether the client is ready for insight is by trying a mild insight intervention to see how the client reacts. If the client rejects it adamantly, it is likely that the client is not ready. If the client, however, responds positively, then the helper can proceed cautiously, always attending to how the client is responding.

In addition, helpers should always be attentive to client reactions to insight interventions. The most superb insight interventions are worthless if clients are not ready for them, and relationships can be damaged by premature insight interventions.

It is best to encourage clients to come to their own insights, if possible, through open questions and interpretations that add just a bit beyond the client's current understanding. If clients are productively working on insight, helpers can stay in the background and encourage and coach clients. The process in the insight stage is thus still as collaborative as it was in the exploration stage. Helpers and clients work together to construct understanding rather than helpers articulating the insights for the clients.

When used, interpretive interventions need to be delivered gently and tentatively, with caring and empathy rather than with judgment or blame. They should be preceded by and interspersed with exploration skills (reflection of feelings, restatement, and open questions). As clients contemplate what they have learned from insight interventions, they are at a new level and need time and support to explore what they have discovered about themselves. Furthermore, helpers continually revise their insight interventions based on emerging information, treating them as working hypotheses rather than as fundamental truths.

In addition, insight interventions may need to be repeated many times, in diverse ways, over long periods of time, so that clients can begin to incorporate them, use them to change their thinking, and apply them to different parts of their lives. Altering ingrained ways of thinking is difficult, and repetition often assists clients in being able to hear and use the new insights. The first time often plants the seed, which starts the client thinking, and then the helper follows up on the idea and elaborates more at a different time.

Cultural Considerations

Given that helpers are relying more on their own reactions and thoughts in the insight stage, they have to be extraordinarily careful about imposing their values on clients from other cultures. For example, a Western helper might challenge a 22-year-old Asian student to be more independent and separate from her parents, but this might contradict the client's cultural value to be dependent on her parents until marriage. As another example, a helper might interpret a client's caring for an aging parent as self-defeating in terms of career advancement, whereas the client may feel a cultural obligation to sacrifice self for others, especially family. Western values promote individualism and self-actualization, whereas Eastern cultures value collectivism and familial obligations (Kim, Atkinson, & Umemoto, 2001; Kim, Atkinson, & Yang, 1999); these differences in values can lead to cultural clashes in terms of understanding dynamics and psychological problems.

Another cultural consideration related to the insight stage is that some cultures teach people to think that authority figures have the ultimate answers. Hence, interpretations may take on greater meaning to such clients as the "right" answer. In such instances, helpers have to be especially careful about what they say. In addition, clients from non-Western cultures might benefit from judicious self-disclosure of insight as a way of building trust (D. W. Sue & Sue, 1999). Disclosure of insight might provide a model for clients to ponder new ideas without dictating what the client should think.

An additional cultural consideration is that immediacy may seem quite rude and intrusive to people from cultures in which open, here-and-now communication is not valued. Again, helpers should be attentive to clients' reactions and ask about any discomfort and adjust their therapeutic interventions accordingly.

Difficulties Helpers Might Experience in the Insight Stage

Becoming competent in the skills used during the insight stage is difficult; these skills often take many years to master. In addition, the skills cannot be applied in a rote, technical fashion to every client, which makes it challenging for instructors to teach and for students to learn these skills. Helpers have to use their intuition and rely on their reactions to clients, so there is more danger of countertransference interfering with the process. Helpers need to proceed slowly and observe clients' reactions to their insight interventions, but helpers should not avoid insight interventions because they might miss opportunities to help clients understand themselves at deeper levels.

MOVING PREMATURELY INTO INSIGHT

Helpers sometimes move into the insight stage before the therapeutic relationship has been firmly established, before the client has adequately explored the problems, or before the helper has a deep understanding of the problems. It is crucial that challenge, open questions for insight, interpretation, disclosure of insight, and immediacy be used within the context of a strong therapeutic relationship and with a strong foundation of understanding. Otherwise, these techniques have the potential for damaging clients. For example, if a helper challenges before the client trusts the helper, the client might doubt the helper's motives and terminate the helping relationship.

TAKING TOO MUCH RESPONSIBILITY FOR DEVELOPING INSIGHT

Some helpers feel that they have to be the ones to "put it all together" and connect all the client's past experiences with the client's present behaviors in a new way. Or, the helper may be impatient because the client cannot see what is blatantly obvious to the helper. To this helper, figuring out clients is more important than helping clients figure out themselves. From my perspective, the more important task is for helpers to empathize with clients, determine what contributes to clients having difficulty putting it all together, ask clients about their thoughts about insight, and work collaboratively with clients to construct insights.

GETTING STUCK IN ONE THEORETICAL PERSPECTIVE

One of the dangers in the insight stage is that helpers may get stuck in using only one theoretical perspective too rigidly. For example, a helper may try to apply psychoanalytic theory, even though the theory might not fit for an individual client. Thus, a helper could be convinced that every client is suffering from an Oedipal/Electra complex because Freud said so, rather than attending to the data that the client presents. Or, as another example, a helper could conceptualize and treat the client from a cognitive viewpoint, assuming that maladaptive thoughts need to be challenged, even though the client is not receptive to cognitive work. It is helpful for helpers to be aware that theories are guidelines rather than cookbooks and that helpers must be judicious in applying them.

TAKING CLIENTS AT FACE VALUE AND NOT DIGGING DEEPER

Sometimes helpers are afraid of upsetting clients and being intrusive, so they fail to search deeper to help their clients. However, clients often value hearing another perspective about their problems because they feel stuck, so helpers need to be willing to help clients construct new understandings.

FORGETTING TO BE EMPATHIC

Some helpers get so excited about figuring out the puzzle of the client's problems that they forget to be empathic. They do not remember the importance of keeping clients involved in the therapeutic experience. It is crucial to be constantly aware of how clients are feeling and reacting and to work at maintaining the collaborative relationship.

FORGETTING THAT NOT ALL CLIENTS NEED OR WANT INSIGHT

No matter how much we as helpers personally value insight, not all of our clients are equally enamored. Some clients (and even some helpers) do not want or need insight. They prefer support without challenge and insight, or they want immediate behavior change without insight. They may want to feel better without understanding why they felt badly. Because the three-stage approach presented in this book is essentially client-centered and values empathy above all, it is important not to impose insight on such clients but to respect their choice not to understand themselves. For such clients, I recommend making an assessment about whether they primarily need support, behavior change, or something helpers cannot offer. If clients need support to make behavior changes, helpers can provide that and reduce the emphasis on the insight stage. If clients need other things (e.g., medication, support groups, welfare), helpers can refer them to other sources.

COUNTERTRANSFERENCE

Finally, countertransference (defined and discussed in chap. 2) can interfere with the helper's ability to deliver insight interventions effectively. For example, a client talking about abortion or divorce might stimulate unresolved feelings about these issues on the part of a helper. Similarly, a helper who has problems dealing with anger might withdraw when a client becomes angry at her. Once again, therapy and supervision can help to ensure that personal issues on the part of the helper do not unduly and negatively influence the helping relationship.

Strategies for Overcoming Difficulties in Implementing the Insight Stage

Helpers can overcome difficulties in the insight stage by focusing on empathy and using exploration skills, dealing with their personal feelings, and dealing with the helping relationship.

FOCUS ON EMPATHY AND USE EXPLORATION SKILLS

When helpers are in doubt or having problems, they can try to get back in touch with basic empathy for the client—How does the client feel? What would it be like to be the client? And, to facilitate empathy, the helper can use the basic skills of attending and listening, open questions, restatement, and reflection of feelings. In effect, helpers need to backtrack, rebuild trust, and make sure they hear the client's real problems. Helpers can keep exploring until an idea for a challenge or interpretation emerges naturally and the client is ready to hear it.

DEAL WITH PERSONAL FEELINGS

It is important for helpers to be as aware as possible of what they are feeling. They need to sort out how much is a reaction to the client and how much is related to their personal issues. Helpers can get personal therapy to deal with strong emotional reactions that arise when they are helpers. In addition, it is helpful to talk to supervisors about feelings that come up when working with clients.

DEAL WITH THE RELATIONSHIP

In one study (Rhodes, Hill, Thompson, & Elliott, 1994), satisfied clients were asked what their helpers had done to resolve major misunderstandings that arose in relationships. The clients reported that their helpers asked them how they were feeling about what was going on in the therapeutic relationship. Helpers listened nondefensively to the clients and were willing to hear what they were doing wrong with clients. They apologized if they made a mistake or hurt the client's feelings. If helpers acknowledge their part in problems in the helping relationship, they serve as models for how to deal with mistakes and how to respond in a human way to another person. In addition, helpers can talk about their feelings about the relationship to let clients know how their behaviors influence others. Providing a place where clients can discuss both positive and negative feelings toward the helper and the sessions is both challenging and critically important. Finally, helpers can thank clients for sharing their feelings. It is often painful and difficult to process the therapeutic relationship, so clients need to be assured that they can bring up both positive and negative feelings.

Example of an Extended Interaction in the Insight Stage

In this example, the helper has already established rapport, and the client has explored her feelings about her relationship with her daughter. The example starts at the beginning of the insight stage:

Helper: So you said your daughter is not doing well in middle school and you're worried that she's going to flunk out of school. (The helper wants to tie together what the client has been talking about and so offers a summary statement.)

Client: Yeah, she just never does her homework. She watches television all the time, talks on the phone to her friends constantly, and eats. She's not even doing any extracurricular activities at school. I just can't get her to do anything. She just got her grades, which she wouldn't even let me see at first. I finally got them from her, and she's flunking two classes.

Helper: Have you considered getting her a tutor? (The helper jumps prematurely to the action stage here to offer suggestions for what to do about the problem.)

Client: We keep trying to get her to a tutor, but she doesn't want one. Last year we made her see a tutor, but it didn't help. She still flunked the course, and we wasted a lot of money.

Helper: You sound really frustrated. (The helper comes back to a focus on the client instead of on the client's daughter.)

Client: Yeah, I really am frustrated. I just don't know what to do. I feel so helpless. School was so important to me, and I feel that if she doesn't get a good education, she won't get anywhere in life. (The client really takes in the reflection and talks in more depth about her feelings about the problem with her daughter.)

Helper: You know, in my experience with my kids, it was really hard to separate myself from them. I wanted so much for them to be perfect to show that I was a perfect parent. (Helper uses disclosure to stimulate client insight.)

Client: Yeah, I get into that. I feel like I'm not a very good parent. Everyone else's kids are doing so well. They're all talking about their kids going to these expensive colleges. I want my kids to have all the things I didn't have and not feel as bad about themselves as adults as I do.

Helper: You really want the best for your children. (Helper shows support through a restatement.)

Client: Yeah. Education wasn't a big thing in my family. My parents pushed me on religion and health food. In fact, they were really pushy; well, at least my mother was pushy about wanting me to be a missionary. We had such incredible fights when I was a teenager. They didn't even notice that I did well in school. So it was something that I could do on my own.

Helper: Interesting—you wanted to be independent from your parents and make your own decisions in life, but you want your daughter to do what you tell her to do. (Helper challenges client with a contradiction of which the client seems to be unaware.)

Client: Wow, you're right! I can't believe that I would be doing the same thing to her that my parents did to me. I guess it seemed like such a different thing. I want her to do well in school, and my parents wanted to control me about religion. But I don't know how to be any different. I really try hard to be a good parent. It's so important to me.

Helper: I wonder if you think I'm judging you and maybe thinking you're bad for your parenting? (Helper picks up on the client's self-blaming and wants to see if she feels negatively toward her, so helper uses an immediacy statement.)

Client: Well, I don't know if you blame me. I blame myself. I just don't know how to quit doing what I'm doing with my daughter. I feel stuck. I don't know any other way to be a parent. I've tried as hard as I can.

Helper: You're feeling very discouraged. (Helper reflects feelings to support client.)

Client: When I was younger, I didn't want to be a parent because I thought I would be rotten at it. I thought people should have to pass tests before they could become parents. There are so many rotten parents out there. But I was in therapy for a lot of years, and I thought I had solved a lot of my problems. But I guess I didn't solve them all. You know it was so much easier when the kids were younger.

Helper: Perhaps you're having problems now that your kids are teenagers because that's when you had your problems with your parents. You didn't get much of a model on how to be a parent of teenagers. (Helper interprets client's current difficulties as related to past experiences.)

Client: Boy, that's really true. I sure didn't. You know, I still haven't forgiven my parents for some of the things they did. You wouldn't believe how controlling my mother was.

Helper: You still have some anger at them. I wonder if you can identify with your daughter's anger? (Helper reflects feelings and interprets a parallel of the client's feelings with her daughter's to help client get some empathy with daughter.)

Client: Yeah, I know she feels angry at me. And you know, I feel good that she can express it. I used to just withdraw and get depressed when I was a kid. She at least can express herself pretty well sometimes. You know she does have a lot of spirit. She's different from me in some ways, yet in some ways she's a lot like me. School really is difficult for her. It's not fun for her to sit down and read a book like it is for me. She's just not academically oriented. But I guess she has to find her own way. She's not 5 years old anymore. Maybe I just have to trust that she will find herself. I have to accept her as she is just as I have to accept myself as I am. Maybe what I need to do is go back and do some more work on myself to see why I'm so controlling.

Helper: You've done a really good job of focusing on yourself. You've gone from blaming your daughter to looking at your part in this whole situation. (Helper wants to reinforce client for all the work she's done.)

Client: Yeah, it's not easy though. It's so much easier to blame her.

Helper: How do you feel about the work we've done today in trying to understand your conflicts with your daughter? (Helper asks how the client is feeling about their interaction.)

Client: I think I have a new understanding of my issues with my daughter. I'm not sure yet that I'll be able to stop having the fights because they happen so quickly, but I do have a better idea what my part in the struggles is all about. I'll need to do a lot more thinking about what kind of relationship I want to have with my daughter.

What Do You Think?

- Several students have noted how difficult it is to learn and use the insight interventions. They have said that the exploration skills seemed easy, whereas now all of a sudden the insight skills seem hard. What is your experience?
- Many students forget to use the exploration skills when trying to use challenge, interpretation, disclosure, and immediacy. They revert to using lots of closed questions. What is your experience? What can you do to remember to integrate the exploration skills into the insight stage?
- How do you think clients from different cultures react to the insight skills as compared with the exploration skills?
- Debate the advantages and disadvantages of the insight stage. Identify the benefits and possible problems with moving clients to deeper awareness.
- Check which of the following obstacles you are most likely to face in your development of insight skills:
  _____ moving prematurely into the insight stage
  _____ taking too much responsibility for developing insight
  _____ applying psychoanalytic theory too rigidly
  _____ forgetting to be empathic
  _____ clients not wanting or needing insight from helper
- Which of the following strategies might help you cope with the potential obstacles you could face in the insight stage?
  _____ rely on the exploration skills
  _____ deal with personal feelings
  _____ deal with the relationship

i LAB 11. Integration of Exploration and Insight Skills

A downloadable PDF of this Lab is available in the student resources area of the Helping Skills, *3rd ed. Web site: http://www.apa.org/books/resources/Hill3.*

You are ready to integrate the exploration and insight skills. In this lab, you will meet with a volunteer client. You will first use exploration skills to help the client explore and use both exploration and insight skills to help the client gain insight.

Goal: For helpers to integrate exploration and insight skills.

Exercise 1. Helping Interchange

Helper's and Client's Tasks During the Helping Exchange

1. Each helper will pair up with a volunteer client whom they do not know.
2. Helpers bring copies of the following forms to the session: the Session Review Form (Web Form A), the Helper Intentions List (Web Form D), and Client Reactions System (Web Form G). The observer brings the Supervisor Rating Form (Web Form B).
3. Helpers bring an audio- or videotape recorder (tested ahead of time to ensure that it works) and a tape. They turn the recorder on at the beginning of the session.
4. Helpers introduce themselves and remind clients that whatever they say is confidential (except if the client intends to harm self or others, or if childhood abuse is revealed). Helpers also indicate exactly who will be observing or listening to the session (e.g., peer, supervisor).
5. Each helper conducts a 40-minute session with a client, being as helpful as possible. Use exploration skills to help the client explore for about 20 minutes, and then move to combining exploration and insight skills to help the client gain insight for about 20 minutes. Watch the client's reactions to each of your interventions and modify subsequent interventions when appropriate.
6. Watch the time carefully. About 5 minutes before the time is up, let the client know that you need to stop soon. Spend the remaining time asking the client about what she or he liked most and least about the session. When the time is up, say something like, "We need to stop now. Thank you for helping me practice my helping skills."

Supervisor's Tasks During Session

Supervisors use the Supervisor Rating Form (Web Form B) to record their observations and evaluations.

Postsession

1. After the session, the helper goes over the tape with the client. (Review of a 40-minute session takes about 90 minutes. Alternatively, helpers might just review 10 minutes of each stage.) Helpers stop the tape after each helper intervention (except minimal acknowledgments such as "um-hmm" and "yeah") and write the key words on the Session Review Form (Web Form A) so the exact spot on the tape can be located later for transcribing the session.
2. Helpers rate the helpfulness of the intervention and write down the numbers (from the Helper Intentions List, Web Form D) of up to three intentions that they had for the intervention, responding according to how they felt during the session rather than when listening to the tape of the session. Use the whole range of the Helpfulness Scale and as many categories as possible on the Helper Intentions List. Do not complete these ratings collaboratively with clients.
3. Clients rate the helpfulness of each intervention and write down the numbers of up to three reactions (from the Client Reactions System, Web Form G). Clients respond according to how

they felt during the session rather than how they feel listening to the tape and use the whole range of the Helpfulness Scale and as many categories as possible on the Reactions System (remember that helpers learn more from honest feedback than from "nice" statements that are not genuine). Clients should not collaborate with helpers in doing the ratings.

4. Helpers and clients write down the most and least helpful event in the session.
5. The supervisor gives feedback to the helper.
6. Helpers type a transcript of their 40-minute session (see Web Form C), skipping minimal utterances such as "okay," "you know," "er," "uh."

   a. Divide the helper speech into response units (see Web Form F).
   b. Using the Helping Skills System (Web Form E), determine which skill was used for each response unit (grammatical sentence) in your transcript.
   c. Indicate on the transcript what you would say differently for each intervention if you could do it again.
   d. Erase the tape. Make sure no identifying information is on the transcript.

Exercise 2. Watching the Insight Stage in the DVD

The leader plays the insight stage portion of the DVD that accompanies this book, *Helping Skills in Practice: A Three-Stage Model*. After all the participants have viewed this portion of the DVD, the leader facilitates a discussion about what was helpful and not helpful. The leader also asks students to think about what they have learned about the client and her dynamics.

Personal Reflections

▪ What are your strengths in the insight stage?
▪ What do you still need to work on?

ACTION STAGE

Overview of the Action Stage 14

It is movement, not just insight, that produces change.

—Waters and Lawrence (1993, p. 40)

Consuela sought help because she was feeling vaguely uninterested in life. During exploration with her helper, she described her situation as being devoid of close friendships. She also indicated that she had not been doing well in her job since she was promoted to a managerial position. She described her childhood as idyllic, with no major problems. After further exploration, Consuela revealed that her parents had been killed in a car accident a year ago. In the insight stage, the helper and Consuela began to piece together that Consuela had not had a chance to grieve the loss of her parents because she felt pressured to perform in her new job. She had moved to a new city to take the job right before her parents' deaths, and so she did not have friends to support her in the aftermath. In addition, Consuela's childhood was not as idyllic as she had initially indicated, in that Consuela had gone through a rough adolescence with many fights with her parents. Through the helping process, she was able to understand that she felt angry at her parents because they had been so strict and had not allowed her to develop friendships outside the home. She was able to grieve her parents and the support they provided. At this point, the helper decided to move into the action stage. Because Consuela indicated that she wanted to make new friends and deal with the stress of her job, they did assertiveness training to help her state more clearly what she wanted and needed from friends, relaxation training for helping her deal with stress, and some behavioral work to help to think about different ways of behaving in the work situation. After several sessions, Consuela started to make some friends and was feeling more calm about her work situation.

After clients have explored and gained insight, they are ready for the action stage, during which helpers collaborate with clients to explore the idea of change, explore options for change, and help them figure out how to make changes. These changes can be in thoughts (e.g., fewer self-defeating statements), feelings (e.g., less hostility), or behaviors (e.g., less overeating). The action stage also involves exploring feelings and examining values, priorities, barriers, and support in relation to change. The emphasis in this stage is on helping clients think about and make decisions about action rather than on dictating action to clients. Helpers are coaches rather than experts dispensing advice.

Rationale for the Action Stage

There are two important reasons for moving beyond insight to action. First, because most clients seek help to feel better or to change specific behaviors, thoughts, or feelings, it is important to help them attain these goals. Clients usually feel better if they not only gain insight but also develop some ideas about how to make needed changes in their lives. For example, Betty sought help because of problems with her roommate. She came to understand that it was hard for her to tell her roommate about her feelings because her family was very covert and indirect and never talked about feelings. This insight was important, but Betty also needed to translate the insight into action and change her behavior with her roommate.

Second, taking action is crucial for consolidating the new thinking patterns learned in the insight stage. Action makes insight more understandable and practical. New understandings can be fleeting unless something is done to help the client consolidate the insights. Old thinking patterns and behaviors easily resurface unless new thinking and behaviors are practiced and incorporated into existing schemas. For example, Miguel's old thinking pattern was that he was worthless unless he was perfect. When the helper challenged his thoughts, Miguel came to realize that he did not have to be perfect to accept himself. Miguel also came to understand that he acted needy and dependent because his parents never accepted him for who he is. His parents idealized his older, brilliant, and successful brother because they had never achieved much in their own lives. They had constantly put Miguel down for being only average in intelligence. Through the insight stage, Miguel came to realize that even though his parents did not accept him fully for who he was, he was still a worthy and lovable person. This insight was fragile and could have eroded, however, unless the helper helped Miguel incorporate the learning into a new pattern of behavior and thinking. Thus, the helper worked with Miguel to think about possible changes. They devised a list of things that Miguel wanted to do (e.g., skydiving, rollerblading, going back to school) and developed a plan for how he could pursue these activities. Beginning to do things he wanted to do and at which he succeeded enabled Miguel to feel better about himself. The helper also worked with Miguel to help him meet friends with shared interests, so that he could receive social support. When he felt better about himself, Miguel began to question the things he had told himself about needing to be perfect. Hence, Miguel cycled back to insight after making changes.

Deterrents to Action

Sometimes newly gained insights lead spontaneously to action. Clients begin to say things such as, "I can see that I've been so angry at the world because it felt unfair that I am not as smart and good-looking as my brother. I don't need to feel so angry now, because I can accept who I am and see that I have things to offer people. I am going to do the things that I want to do with my life," or "It makes sense that I had a hard time in my job if I kept treating my boss like my father. I don't need to do that anymore. I'm going to stand up to him and ask him for a raise." Hence, moving to action comes naturally to some clients as they begin to talk about how they might apply what they have learned about themselves in the insight stage.

At other times, however, insight does not spontaneously lead to action, perhaps because clients feel stuck, understand the situation incompletely or only at an intellectual level, or do not take personal responsibility for their role in the maintenance of the problem. For example, Stefan might realize intellectually that he is upset about being fired, but he might not have allowed himself to feel the humiliation of the loss or experience his anger at his boss. He also might not have understood how he set himself up in self-defeating ways. Expressing, understanding, and accepting his feelings and his role in creating the situation are important tasks before moving to action, so Stefan and his helper might need to spend more time in the insight stage.

Another reason that insight might not lead directly to action is that clients might not have the necessary skills. For example, even though Margarita understood why she was not assertive and wanted to change her behavior, she did not know how to stand up for herself. She could not behave more assertively because she did not have the skills needed for being assertive (e.g., maintaining eye contact, stating needs directly without blaming). Hence, clients may need to be taught these skills and may need to practice and get feedback about their performance to develop the skills adequately.

Even if they understand themselves thoroughly and have the skills to change, clients may lack the motivation to change. They may feel blocked from changing because old habits are hard to alter and they are afraid of trying anything new (e.g., a client learning to be more assertive might be reluctant to confront a friend for fear of losing the friendship). They may feel demoralized and not believe they can change. They may need encouragement to even begin thinking about change.

Finally, clients cannot always make all the changes they may want or need to make because of limited talents and resources. For example, if Andrew has earned poor grades in college, getting into a high-ranking graduate program is an unlikely proposition. Hence, the goal of this stage is to enable clients to learn to make changes within the limits of the possibilities and to expand these possibilities as much as possible. For example, Andrew's helper might help him explore advanced training in a related field so that he can pursue a career related to his goals. Although this view does not fit with the idealistic notion that every person can do whatever he or she wants, it fits with the more realistic idea of realizing one's limits and maximizing one's potentials within those limits.

Philosophical Underpinnings

The major philosophical underpinning of the action stage is that clients are the active agents of their own lives. They know when things are not going well and seek input to help them fix problems, but ultimately they make the decisions about how they want to be. The role of the helper in this stage is to serve as a coach, cheerleader, supporter, information-giver, and consultant, but not to take over and "fix" the client.

This stage, then, is still client-centered, with helpers facilitating clients in thinking about change rather than imposing change on them. Helpers do not have to know the best action plans for clients. In fact, helpers rarely need to form an opinion about what clients "must" or "should" do. The goal for helpers in this stage is to provide a supportive environment and facilitate clients in resolving their problems and making their decisions. Hence, helpers need to be just as empathic and supportive as they were in earlier stages. Mickelson and Stevic (1971) found that behaviorally oriented counselors who were warm, empathic, and genuine were more effective in generating information-seeking responses in their clients than were those who were low in these facilitative conditions.

When clients decide for themselves what to do differently, they are more likely to take responsibility and ownership for their actions than if helpers dictate what they should do. Telling clients what to do, even if clients ask for advice, is often not helpful because clients become dependent on the helpers, especially if the client has a similar pattern in other relationships (see Teyber, 2006). Helpers cannot always be there for clients, so they need to teach clients how to motivate themselves to change and how to implement changes in their lives. Thus, rather than solving clients' problems, helpers seek to enhance clients' problem-solving capacities. With better coping skills, clients can address the problems that led them to seek help and are better equipped to solve problems in the future.

As you can see, helpers need to be supportive of clients and not be invested in whether and how they change. Whether the client chooses to change is the client's choice and responsibility rather than a reflection on the helper's skills and personal qualities. The helper's skills are involved in helping the client explore and make decisions about changes, not in which decision is made. Thus, the helper's goal is to encourage clients to explore whether they want to change, and if so, to assist them in making the changes they have identified as desirable. Although this objective stance is difficult to achieve, it is crucial that helpers not care which direction clients choose, while still caring for the client. Otherwise, it is too easy for clients to replicate childhood patterns (e.g., acting or not acting) to please or defy helpers as they did their parents. Instead, helpers collaborate with clients in making choices, serving as facilitators of the process rather than as experts who provide the answers and tell clients what to do.

Here is an example that illustrates the need for the action stage and shows how it is implemented. Casey acted silly (e.g., giggled uncontrollably) when she went out dancing because she was extremely nervous. Because Casey felt so embarrassed and panicked when she acted silly, she would leave early and then feel badly that she had missed all the fun. Through exploration and insight, she came to realize that her anxiety at dances arose from her fear of being with men. She was afraid no one would like her because her brothers had made fun of her when she was a child. Her brothers had told her that she was ugly and had taunted her about her face and hair. Insight was not enough, however. Casey needed something to help her deal with the anxiety in the situation. The helper taught her relaxation and then strategized with her about how to handle specific situations at dances. When she felt a "silly" attack coming on, she and the helper planned that she would take a time-out in the bathroom, practice deep breathing, and watch what she was saying to herself. After practicing several times in sessions, Casey was able to attend a dance and enjoy it. She was even able to let a man touch her and allow herself to think that she was attractive. Being able to master the situation made Casey feel better about herself. She then began to reevaluate whether she was indeed ugly and wonder what had motivated her brothers to be so mean to her. Hence, insight led to action, which in turn led to more insight.

Markers for Knowing When to Move to Action

It is generally best to wait until the client is ready for action. There are several indicators that a client might be ready to move on to action. The first is when the client has gained insight and starts spontaneously talking about action. This situation is the ideal because the helper is following the client's lead and providing what the client seems to need at the time.

Another situation when action would be called for (sometimes at the very beginning of the first session) is when the client presents with a specific problem and simply wants relief from that problem (e.g., a simple phobia). In such cases, it makes sense for helpers to approach the problem straightforwardly and offer the client what help they know how to give (e.g., relaxation, exposure), after doing just enough exploration to make sure that they are working on the right problem. By giving clients what they ask for, helpers respect clients and acknowledge their right to the type of services they want.

It is important to note that not all clients like the insight process of reflecting and trying to understand themselves. Rather, some clients want specific things to make them feel better. Instead of trying to change their style and preferences, helpers should respect these wishes and move to action. It may be that after making specific behavior changes, such clients will be curious about reasons for their behavior, but it is equally likely that they will just want to feel better.

Another marker for moving to action is when the client is stuck at insight and is not making changes. The classic example is the client who wallows in insight for years in therapy and knows exactly why she or he is dysfunctional (and often blames someone else) but then does nothing to accept the situation, take responsibility for the future, and change. Such clients can be gently encouraged to move to action.

Finally, some clients are in crisis and need to make some changes immediately. With such clients, helpers need to move quickly to action, shortening the exploration and insight stages. Such clients need more direct interventions because they are in crisis, are not psychologically minded, or cannot articulate their concerns. Some clients just want something or someone to make them feel better, and it is important for the helper to meet clients where they are rather than imposing her or his values on them. For example, a person who has been kicked out of his house, has no job or food, and has delusions may need immediate help in terms of housing, food, and medication before he can focus on understanding. To rephrase Maslow's (1970) statement, "people cannot live on bread alone unless they have no bread." These clients, after they have received direct guidance about how to solve a pressing problem, might be willing to go back and understand what contributed to the problem or work on other problems.

Theoretical Background: Behavioral and Cognitive Theories

Behavioral theories lay the foundation for the action stage. In this section, I discuss the underlying assumptions of these theories, the principles of learning, and treatment strategies.

ASSUMPTIONS OF BEHAVIORAL THEORIES

Behavioral theories share several basic assumptions (Gelso & Fretz, 2001; Rimm & Masters, 1979):

- a focus on overt behaviors rather than unconscious motivations
- a focus on what creates and maintains symptoms rather than on what caused them
- an assumption that behaviors are learned;
- an emphasis on the present as opposed to the past;
- an emphasis on the importance of specific, clearly defined goals;
- a valuing of an active, directive, and prescriptive role for helpers;
- a belief that the helper–client relationship is important to establish rapport and gain client collaboration but is not enough to help clients change;
- a focus on determining adaptive behaviors for a situation rather than on personality change; and
- a reliance on empirical data and scientific methods.

One of the defining characteristics of behavioral approaches is that behaviors, emotions, and cognitions (both adaptive and maladaptive) are learned (Gelso & Fretz, 2001); therefore, it is important to talk about how learning takes place. Rather than covering all behavioral theory, I cover those aspects most relevant to helping skills training: operant conditioning, modeling (also called observational learning), and cognitively mediated learning. Although the three types of learning are not as distinct as once thought, it is still useful to be aware of the different types.

OPERANT CONDITIONING

In operant conditioning, behaviors are controlled by their consequences (Kazdin, 2001; Rimm & Masters, 1979; Skinner, 1953). Reinforcement is anything that follows a behavior and increases the probability that the behavior will occur again. An event, behavior, privilege, or material object whose addition increases the likelihood of a behavior occurring again is called a *positive reinforcer*. Primary reinforcers (e.g., food, water, sex) are biological necessities, whereas secondary reinforcers (e.g., praise, money) gain their reinforcing properties through association with primary reinforcers. An example of a positive reinforcer related to helping is an approval–reassurance given after a client talks about feelings. Note that reinforcers are not always reinforcing (e.g., food is typically reinforcing only if a person is hungry) and that reinforcers are not the same for all individuals (e.g., a long bath may be reinforcing for one person but not another). Whether something is a reinforcer can only be determined by looking at whether the target behavior increases when the reinforcer is administered. Thus, a helper can determine whether something is reinforcing by observing the client's response.

To be effective, reinforcement must be contingent on, or linked directly to, the behavior (Rimm & Masters, 1979). An office worker who receives a raise every 3 months regardless of the quality of work is less likely to change his or her behavior than is the office worker whose raise is contingent on good performance.

For a behavior to be reinforced, it must first be performed. Hence, helpers often have to engage in *shaping*, which refers to the gradual training of a complex response by reinforcing closer and closer approximations to the desired behavior. Goldfried and Davison (1994) gave the example of training a developmentally disabled child to make his bed by first reinforcing him for fluffing up his pillow, then for pulling the top sheet forward, and so on. Each of these acts is a successive approximation to the final desired behavior. An example of shaping is how we teach exploration skills. We first ask the trainee to practice listening empathically without saying anything, we then ask the trainee to repeat exactly what the client said, next we ask the trainee to say the main word the client is communicating, and finally we ask the trainee to give restatements and reflections of feelings. Thus, we try to shape the helper's skills by starting with the easier skills and moving on to more difficult ones only after the trainee has mastered the easier ones.

Punishment occurs after a behavior and reduces the probability that the behavior will occur again. Goldfried and Davison (1994) identified three punishment procedures: (a) presenting an aversive event (e.g., a frown when the client reports something undesirable), (b) removing a person from a situation in which she or he would otherwise be able to earn reinforcers (e.g., a time-out in a room separate from the counselor who could provide positive reinforcement), and (c) reducing a person's collection of reinforcers (e.g., taking away candy). The purpose of punishment in clinical situations is to decrease the frequency of maladaptive behaviors (e.g., inappropriate interrupting, nonstop talking).

It is difficult to deliver punishment contingent on the behavior. Often, what gets punished is being discovered rather than the behavior itself. Hence, when punishment is used as the primary mode of behavior management, people often figure out how to avoid getting caught rather than decrease the problematic behavior. For example, a child who steals cookies feels great (is reinforced) when he gets the cookies because they taste good, but he feels lousy several hours later when he gets caught because it does not feel good to get caught and be punished. Because the punishment is contingent on getting caught rather than on eating the cookies, the child figures that he should not get caught again. If he is clever, he figures out a way to get the cookies without getting caught.

Another important behavioral concept is *generalization*, which involves the transfer of learning from one situation to similar situations. For example, if kicking and hitting are punished with time-outs and cooperative behavior is positively reinforced at school, one would expect a decrease in kicking and hitting and an increase in cooperative behavior in the home setting. However, these behaviors are most likely to generalize if they are punished and reinforced in the same manner in the home setting as in the school setting. Another example of generalization is when a person acts frightened of a teacher or helper because she or he was punished by authority figures in the past (a concept similar to transference).

Extinction reduces the probability of a behavior occurring by withholding reinforcers after the behavior is established (Goldfried & Davison, 1994). For example, if a parent's attention seems to reinforce fighting among siblings (when no other problems are apparent), a helper might instruct the parents to ignore the fighting and let the kids work out their problems on their own (unless one child is in danger of getting hurt) in the hopes that it will extinguish. Goldfried and Davison noted that extinction is best facilitated by concurrently reinforcing an incompatible and more adaptive behavior. Thus, in the previous example, the parents might suggest that the siblings play separately and then praise them if they play quietly.

Operant conditioning is often used when working with children because they are not usually amenable to insight-oriented approaches. For example, I used operant methods for several specific behavioral problems with my children (e.g., for fighting between siblings, when one child did not want to sleep in her own bed, to help the children get off to school on time in the morning). It can also be useful for changing bad habits (e.g., nail-biting, procrastination, overeating, underexercising, drinking) for adults. For more detail on self-help methods for dealing with behavioral problems, see Watson and Tharp (2006).

Although the concepts of operant conditioning sound relatively straightforward, helpers often have difficulty applying them because of the complexity of human nature and because helpers often have minimal control over the reinforcers and punishments in the environment. In fact, Goldfried and Davison (1994) noted that helpers typically do not reinforce the actual changes but rather reinforce the client's talking about making specific changes. Clients have to transfer the reinforcement from talking about changing to implementing the changes outside the session. Thus, helpers act more as consultants, whereas clients are the actual change agents.

MODELING

People sometimes learn things even though they have never been reinforced for performing them. The explanation for this learning is through modeling or observational learning, which occurs when a person observes another person (a model) perform a behavior and receive consequences (Bandura, 1977; Kazdin, 2001). For example, children learn how to be parents by watching their parents and experiencing the effects of their child-rearing practices. Students learn how to be teachers by observing effective and ineffective educators. Helpers learn how to help by observing the behaviors of effective and ineffective helpers.

To understand how modeling works, learning and performance must be distinguished. A person can observe a model and thus learn a behavior. Whether the person actually performs the learned behavior, however, depends on the consequences at the time of performance. Bandura (1965) demonstrated this distinction between learning and performance with his classic Bobo doll study. Children observed a film in which an adult hit or kicked a Bobo doll (a life-size, inflatable, plastic doll that is weighted so it pops upright after it is punched down). The adult's behavior was rewarded, punished, or met with no consequences. When the children were put in the room with the Bobo doll, those who had observed the aggression being punished were less aggressive than were those who had observed the aggression being rewarded or ignored. When all children were given an incentive for performing the aggressive behavior, there were no differences among conditions, indicating that the children in all conditions learned the aggressive behaviors equally well. Bandura concluded that the learning occurred through observation but that the performance depended on whether the child perceived that the adult was rewarded or punished.

Kazdin (2001) noted that imitation of models by observers is greater when models are similar to observers, more prestigious, higher in status and expertise than observers, and when several models perform the same behavior. Thus, helpers can learn about helping by watching videotapes of many experts. In addition, clients are probably more willing to listen to and accept suggestions from helpers whom they perceive to be credible and expert.

COGNITIVE THEORY

Early behaviorists such as Skinner believed in a stimulus–response model, meaning that people respond directly to environmental cues (e.g., noise leads to a startle response). Cognitive theorists (e.g., Beck, 1976; Ellis, 1962; Meichenbaum & Turk, 1987) introduced a stimulus–organism–response (S-O-R) model, suggesting that the organism (i.e., person) processes the stimulus before determining how to respond. Thus, people respond not to stimuli but to their interpretation of stimuli. For example, how Estaben reacts to a noise heard in the middle of the night is dependent on whether he thinks it is a benign noise (the house "settling") or whether he thinks the noise was made by a burglar. Thus, it is important to look for and dispute irrational thoughts (e.g., "I must be perfect," "Everyone must love me"). Theorists such as Beck, Ellis, and Meichenbaum suggest that it is not so much events that cause a person to become upset but what the person thinks about the events.

Cognitive processes are of utmost importance to the helping situation. As discussed in chapter 2, much of the helping process takes place at covert levels. Helpers' intentions for their interventions as well as their perceptions of clients' reactions influence their subsequent interventions. In addition, clients have reactions to helpers' interventions as well as intentions for how to influence helpers. Hence, a cognitively mediated model for understanding the helping process makes sense.

HOW BEHAVIORAL AND COGNITIVE THEORIES RELATE TO THE ACTION STAGE

Behavioral and cognitive theories fit well into the action stage of the helping model because they provide specific strategies for helping clients change. When clients have explored thoughts and feelings thoroughly and obtained insight about themselves, action allows them to determine how they would like to change their lives. Thus, helpers need to focus on action to help clients attain their goals. When used in an empathic and collaborative manner at the appropriate time, behavioral and cognitive treatments can facilitate change. Core components of behavioral (e.g., reinforcement, modeling) and cognitive theories (e.g., intentions) are incorporated into the steps for working with the four action goals (see chap. 16).

Goals of the Action Stage

The goals of the action stage are for helpers to encourage clients to explore possible new behaviors, assist clients in deciding on actions, facilitate the development of skills for action, provide feedback about attempted changes, assist clients in evaluating and modifying action plans, and encourage clients in processing feelings about action (see Exhibit 14.1). While in the action stage, helpers need to remember to be empathic and pace themselves according to clients' needs. A stance of exploring, rather than prescribing, action is typically most helpful.

Skills in this stage are combined into discrete steps. Hence, I briefly present the skills that are used in the action stage (see chap. 15) and then discuss how the skills are integrated in a separate chapter (see chap. 16).

SKILLS USED IN THE ACTION STAGE

The skills used in the action stage are open questions for action, information, feedback about the client, process advisement, direct guidance, and disclosure of strategies. The purpose of the most frequently used skill, open questions for action, is to stimulate clients in their thinking about action. Information is important to educate clients about options for action. Feedback about the client allows helpers to let clients know how

---

EXHIBIT 14.1

List of Goals, Skills, and Steps to Facilitate the Action Stage

---

Goals
   Explore possible new behaviors
   Assist clients in deciding on actions
   Facilitate the development of skills for action
   Provide feedback about attempted changes
   Assist clients in evaluating and modifying action plans
   Encourage clients in processing feelings about action
Types of Action
   Relaxation
   Behavior change
   Behavioral rehearsal/assertiveness
   Decision making
Skills
   Open questions for action
   Information
   Feedback about client
   Process advisement
   Direct guidance
   Disclosures of strategies

---

they come across to the helpers. Process advisement is used to direct the process of sessions, particularly in doing therapeutic exercises (e.g., behavioral rehearsal) within sessions. Direct guidance is occasionally useful to give some advice to clients about the best strategies. Disclosure of strategies is another, more tentative, way to suggest action ideas.

Helpers also continue to use exploration skills throughout the action stage. Restatements and reflections of feelings are particularly useful for uncovering feelings related to change, demonstrating support, and ensuring that helpers accurately hear what clients are saying. When clients are stuck, insight skills such as challenge, interpretation, self-disclosure, and immediacy are used to uncover obstacles to action.

STEPS OF THE ACTION STAGE

Helpers are urged to learn the individual skills but to focus most of their attention on putting these skills together into the steps for working with four targets of action: relaxation, behavior change, behavioral rehearsal, and decision making. These four types of action cover most of the types of action that beginning helpers will face.

Concluding Comments

Action is a natural outgrowth of exploration and insight. However, because of difficulties encountered in making changes, clients often need support and guidance to take action. Some helpers are nervous and uncomfortable with pursuing action, so they ignore the action stage. I encourage such helpers to look at their own attitudes about action and to struggle to implement this stage. If clients do not make changes in their lives outside of helping (in thoughts, behaviors, or feelings), helping has not been as successful as it could have been.

What Do You Think?

- Are clients naturally propelled toward action, or do they need help to change?
- What is the role of helpers in assisting clients in changing?
- Brainstorm ideas for how helpers can make the transition from insight to action.
- Do you think a helper's manner of introducing action ideas influences the client's acceptance of the ideas?
- Is the helper or client responsible for client change?

Skills to Implement Action Goals 15

Many seek advice, few profit from it.

—Publius Syrus (42 B.C.)

Through working on a dream, Yelin came to realize that he allowed his mother to dominate him. When Yelin was 16, his father died after asking Yelin to take care of his mother. His mother, although only 45 years old and healthy, depended on Yelin to drive her everywhere and to be her companion. She refused to learn English, make friends, or work. She clung to hopes of returning to her country of origin. Yelin felt like he would never be able to marry or have his own life. Consequently, he was beginning to drink several beers each night and isolate himself from his peers. After thorough exploration and insight that he was withdrawing from his mother and punishing her, Yelin was eager to make changes in his life. He asked for information about alcohol treatment, so the helper told Yelin about Alcoholics Anonymous and suggested he attend meetings. In addition, Yelin and his mother came in for a joint session and worked on their communication.

The skills most suited for accomplishing action goals are open questions for action, giving information, feedback about the client, process advisement, direct guidance, and disclosures about strategies. These skills are the focus of this chapter. Helpers should remember of course that exploration skills such as reflections and restatement are still very useful for helping clients explore action.

These action skills require more input on the part of the helper, so helpers have to be sure that clients are ready for these interventions (i.e., have explored enough). Helpers also need to be attentive to observing client reactions to see how they are responding and to make sure that clients are actively involved in the process.

Unlike other chapters that present skills, I do not provide a lab for this chapter. Instead, after reading about these skills, helpers can move directly to chapter 16, which focuses on putting the skills together into the steps of the action stage for different problem areas.

Open Questions for Action

Open questions for action are questions aimed specifically at helping clients explore action (see Exhibit 15.1). For example,

- What kinds of things have you tried?
- How did it work when you tried that?
- What ideas do you have about what to do in this situation?
- What might happen if you tried that?

RATIONALE FOR USING OPEN QUESTIONS FOR ACTION

Open questions for action are particularly useful for gently guiding clients through the action stage. They are the primary tool by which helpers find out whether clients are ready to change, what they have tried before, what ideas they have for action, what barriers they see to change, and

---

EXHIBIT 15.1

Overview of Open Questions for Action

Definition	*Open questions for action* invite clients to explore action goals.
Example	"What have you tried before?"
	"What would be the benefits of changing?"
Typical intentions	To promote insight (see Web Form D)
Possible client reactions	Clear, feelings (see Web Form G)
Desired client behaviors	Recounting, affective exploration (see Web Form H)
Helpful hints	Convey empathy with your question.
	Make sure your questions are open instead of closed.
	Avoid multiple questions.
	Focus on the client rather than on others.
	Observe client reactions to your questions.

how they respond to action ideas. By asking open questions, the helper implicitly communicates that she or he is guiding or coaching the client to figure out about action rather than providing answers. Thus, helpers encourage clients to solve problems with their support, communicate respect that clients have self-healing capacity, and minimize the likelihood of imposing helpers' values on clients. By using open questions, helpers can also teach clients a process of thinking through problems and possible solutions.

Open questions for action are similar to open questions for exploration and insight. All are open questions but differ in what they inquire about. I refer readers back to chapters 6, 7, and 11 for the rationale for using open questions.

HOW TO USE OPEN QUESTIONS FOR ACTION

As discussed with open questions for exploration and insight, open questions for action should be done gently and with an air of curiosity. The helper is collaboratively inquiring and helping the client figure out about action. Helpers should be careful not to ask too many questions at one time, make sure to give clients time to respond, vary questions with other skills so that they do not sound repetitive, and make sure that questions are open rather than closed.

EXAMPLES OF OPEN QUESTIONS FOR ACTION

The following shows a helper using open questions for action (in italics) in a session:

Helper:	So you've talked quite a bit about these kids bullying you and kicking in your locker. *What are your thoughts about what you might do?*
Client:	I don't know.
Helper:	You sound a little anxious as you say that. What's going on inside?
Client:	I'm scared. There's four of them, and only one of me. They're a lot bigger.
Helper:	Yeah, I would be scared too. *What have they told you at school about this kind of bullying?*
Client:	They said that we should report it to the vice principal.
Helper:	*What would that be like for you?*
Client:	I don't know. I guess it feels like I would be grassing on them. They might get back at me. But the principal made a big thing that bullying is not okay and that we should say something.
Helper:	*Would you like to try that?*
Client:	I think I would like to say something.

Giving Information

Giving information can be defined as providing specific data, facts, resources, answers to questions, or opinions to clients (see Exhibit 15.2). There are several types of information:

- Explaining intentions and goals (e.g., "Let's explore what you've done in the past about this problem, brainstorm some ideas for what you could do differently, make some choices about what you want to do, try out your choices, and then evaluate how you feel about your choices.")
- Educating the client about various types of actions (e.g., "Role-playing involves practicing how you might respond differently when you talk to your mother." "Having a specific place to study allows students to concentrate better on their studies without distractions.")
- Providing information about activities or psychological tests (e.g., "The Strong Interest Inventory measures a person's interests and compares them with interests of people happily employed in a variety of occupations.")
- Educating the client about the world or psychological principles (e.g., "A moderate amount of stress is typically helpful to motivate a person, but too much or too little stress can be counterproductive." "Many women become depressed after giving birth. There's even a term for it—it's called postpartum depression.")

EXHIBIT 15.2

Overview of Giving Information

Definition	*Giving information* refers to supplying data, opinions, facts, resources, answers to questions, or opinions.
Example	"Both the career center and counseling center have information about careers." "The test takes about 2 hours to complete."
Typical intentions	To give information, to promote change (see Web Form D)
Possible client reactions	Educated, new ways to behave, hopeful, no reaction (see Web Form G)
Desired client behaviors	Agreement, therapeutic changes (see Web Form H)
Helpful hints	Make sure the client needs the information. Remember to be empathic, gentle, and not authoritarian. Observe the client's reaction. Do not provide too much information at one time. Put crucial information in writing. Turn the focus back to the client after giving information.

RATIONALE FOR GIVING INFORMATION

In the action stage, helpers sometimes shift into a teacher's role to provide information. Helpers act as educators, which is appropriate if the information is given in a caring manner when clients need information and are ready to listen. For example, a helper might educate a client about his mental condition or about what to expect in different situations. Or, a helper might explain what happens during panic attacks as a way of teaching a client that the physical sensations she experiences (e.g., heart palpitations) are due to anxiety rather than a heart attack. Such information can lead to change when clients are open to learning.

Sometimes, helpers do not have information to give. Rather than assume that one must know everything before becoming a helper (obviously an impossible task), helpers can be aware of some basic information (e.g., referral sources) but then focus on helping clients figure out how to get the needed information themselves.

Information is not always the most appropriate intervention in a situation, however, even when the client requests this type of assistance. Sometimes clients need to explore how they feel about situations without being told what is "normal" or expected. Other clients need to seek out information themselves rather than having the investigative work done for them. Some clients need to be challenged to think about why they do not already have the desired information and to think about what motivates them to rely on others to give them information.

HOW TO GIVE INFORMATION

Before giving information, helpers may find it useful to ask what information or what misinformation clients possess (e.g., "What do you know about getting into graduate school?"). Thus, rather than assuming clients need information, helpers can assess clients' knowledge base. They can also ask clients what strategies they have used to gather information.

Examination of intentions is critical to ensure that information is delivered appropriately. Helpers should think carefully about their intentions. Helpers can ask themselves what is motivating them to want to give information at this particular point, and for whom (the client or helper) this information will be helpful. Helpers can ask themselves the following:

- Do I want to educate the client?
- Do I want to normalize the experience?
- Do I want to explain what is happening in the session?

If the answer to any of these questions is affirmative, giving information is the right skill to use.

If the issue is straightforward and not motivated by inappropriate needs, and if the helper has the requisite information, helpers can provide information. Sometimes helpers do have valuable information and can serve as resources for clients. When giving information, of course, helpers should be empathic, gentle, and sensitive to how clients are reacting. The goal of delivering information is not to lecture clients or act as an expert, but rather to educate clients when they are ready to learn and when it does not undermine clients' independence in searching out their own information.

If helpers determine that giving information is appropriate, they should not provide too much information at one time. In medical relationships, Meichenbaum and Turk (1987) found that patients remember very little of the information that doctors give them. Ironically, the more information given by doctors, the less patients remember. Similarly, when clients are anxious in helping situations, it is easy for them to forget information. Thus, helpers may just give a small amount of information and put crucial information (e.g., referral numbers, homework assignments) in writing to assist clients in accessing the information later.

As with disclosures, helpers turn the focus back to the client after providing information to see the client's reaction. For example, after describing his position on the use of prescription drugs for psychiatric illnesses, a helper might ask the client about her thoughts and reactions to using prescription drugs.

If a client requests information, the helper can try to understand what is motivating the client to ask for information at this particular point in the therapeutic process. Awareness of a client's motives can help the helper decide how to respond. Helpers can ask themselves the following:

- Is the client trying to make you feel needed or like an expert?
- Is the client trying to avoid exploration or insight?
- Is the client resorting to familiar defenses of being dependent on others?
- Does giving information foster further dependency in the client?
- Does the client expect you to be like a medical doctor who asks questions about the problem and then gives a diagnosis and course of treatment?
- Is the client testing you or your credibility?

Helpers may ask clients what is motivating them to ask for information, what they want to do with the information, or what they hope the helper will do for them (e.g., "I'd be happy to answer your question, but first let's talk about why you ask"). If the client is requesting information as a ploy in the interpersonal interaction (e.g., for dependency needs or to make the helper feel needed), the helper can use immediacy skills to address this issue (see chap. 12). It is better to find out what is beneath the request than to ignore it or engage in a power struggle over who controls the information.

Once the helper knows the motives behind the request for information, he or she can address these motives directly. For example, if the client expects the helper to make a diagnosis and dictate the course of treatment, the helper can either educate the client that she or he uses a different treatment strategy or refer the client to someone who is more likely to meet these expectations. Helpers need to think carefully about how to handle these situations (and, as always, talking the situation over with supervisors can aid helpers in dealing with such situations in the future).

On the other hand, there are times when it is good to avoid giving information. When helpers answer "yes" to any of the following questions, they might want to use other skills:

- Do I want to stop exploration?
- Do I want to reduce client anxiety?
- Do I want to show the client how much I know?

EXAMPLES OF GIVING INFORMATION

The following shows a helper giving information (in italics) in a session:

Client: So tell me all about your class. I think I want to take it next year.

Helper: It sounds like you would be interested in learning helping skills.

Client: Yeah, I've always had the idea that maybe I might want to be a social worker. But on the other hand, I'm not sure I would be very good at helping.

Helper: What concerns do you have about learning helping skills?

Client: I'm afraid of getting too involved with the clients. I feel so responsible for my friends when they talk about their problems. I feel like I have to solve all their problems and tell them exactly what to do.

Helper: So maybe you're worried that you won't be able to have any distance from clients in a helping setting.

Client: Yeah, do they talk about how to deal with that in the class?

Helper: Sounds like you really need some help with that.

Client: I do. I had a friend talk to me just yesterday, and I felt totally depressed when we were done because I felt like I had done nothing to help her. I'm afraid that she felt worse when we were done. It reminded me of my mother and father, who both want to talk to me ever since they divorced. Both want me to be on their side. Sometimes I feel split in half.

Helper: I can see why you'd be nervous about the helping situation after having to be a helper with your parents.

Client: Yeah. What was it like for you?

> Helper: *I have had a good experience in the class. The professor has talked a lot about how we have to get personal issues dealt with in our own therapy or else it is difficult to help clients with their issues. I wonder if you have ever explored the idea of getting into therapy?*
>
> Client: Not really. I don't know much about it.
>
> Helper: *There's a counseling center on campus that offers 12 sessions of free therapy for students.*
>
> Client: Really? I'll have to think about that. Maybe I'll check it out.

Feedback About the Client

Giving feedback can be defined as the helper giving information to the client about his or her behaviors or impact on others (see Exhibit 15.3). It is a type of information (see previous section), but it is confined to information about the client specifically. Examples of feedback about the client include the following:

- You expressed yourself very clearly and concisely in the role-play.
- You are smiling a lot and seem more open to making changes.
- I noticed that you were tapping your foot during the relaxation exercise.

EXHIBIT 15.3

Overview of Feedback About the Client

Definition	Giving information to the client about his or her behaviors or impact on others
Example	"You maintained good eye contact during the role-play, but your voice sounded hesitant when you told your partner that you were leaving the relationship."
	"You did a good job of stating what is difficult about making a decision, but I wonder if you could give me an example."
Typical intentions	To give information, to promote change (see Web Form D)
Possible client reactions	New ways to behave, responsibility, misunderstood (see Web Form G)
Desired client behaviors	Cognitive–behavioral exploration, affective exploration, therapeutic changes (see Web Form H)
Helpful hints	Make sure you have a good relationship before you provide feedback.
	Give mostly positive feedback.
	Present positive feedback before negative feedback.
	Make sure to note that the feedback is your personal observation rather than "fact."
	Make the feedback descriptive and behavioral rather than evaluative.
	Observe the client's reactions.

RATIONALE FOR GIVING FEEDBACK ABOUT THE CLIENT

Brammer and MacDonald (1996) suggested that effective feedback can increase clients' self-awareness, which can in turn lead to behavior change. For example, if the helper comments that Jennifer always ends her sentences with a question and thus sounds very tentative when she speaks, this might lead Jennifer to become aware of how she talks and try to change her behavior. When she begins to make definite statements, other people might begin to take Jennifer more seriously.

Research shows that clients prefer positive feedback and think it is more accurate than negative feedback (Claiborn, Goodyear, & Horner, 2002). Positive feedback is good to use early on to establish the relationship and enhance credibility. In addition, if negative feedback must be given, it is best to precede it with positive feedback or to sandwich it between two pieces of positive feedback.

Feedback about the client is similar to immediacy. Both are feedback about the client, except that feedback about the client is only about the client (e.g., "you") individually, whereas immediacy is about the interaction between helper and client in the therapeutic relationship (e.g., "we" or "you and I"). In addition, whereas immediacy is used in the insight stage to promote insight and deal with problems in the therapeutic relationship, feedback about the client is used in the action stage to assist clients in generating, implementing, and maintaining changes in thoughts, feelings, and behaviors.

It can be difficult for beginning helpers to provide feedback to clients because it is a very different behavior than one usually uses in social interactions and can be met with resistance. Beginning helpers often become victims of the *mum effect,* a tendency to withhold bad news even if it is in the best interest of others to hear it (Egan, 1994). In ancient times, bearers of bad news were killed, which not too surprisingly led to some reluctance to be the one to bear bad news or give negative feedback.

HOW TO GIVE FEEDBACK

Feedback about the client must be given cautiously, with the clear understanding that the helper is offering his or her personal observations about the client's behavior. Making the statements descriptive (e.g., "You spoke very softly") rather than evaluative (e.g., "You aren't taking this role-play very seriously") and emphasizing strengths (e.g., "You effectively articulated your feelings") before weaknesses (e.g., "but you didn't sound like you really believed it") can make it easier for clients to hear the feedback. It is also important to give feedback (a) about things clients can change (e.g., nonverbal behaviors, actions) rather than about physical characteristics or life circumstances that cannot be changed (e.g., height, personality), and (b) in close proximity in terms of time to the occurrence of the behavior (e.g., "You spoke with more assurance that time") rather than waiting for a long time and then trying to recreate the situation (e.g., "A while back you looked away from me and didn't say anything").

As with the other action skills, feedback needs to be given with a lot of empathy and support. Negative feedback could damage the helping process if it is perceived as threatening or inaccurate, so helpers need to do it gently and tentatively after a good relationship is established.

EXAMPLE OF FEEDBACK

The following shows a helper giving feedback (in italics) in a session:

Client: I tried the homework you suggested about trying to make more friends.

Helper: Fantastic. How did it go?

Client: Well, I smiled more often and tried to look people in the eye when I was crossing campus.

Helper: That's great. How did that feel?

Client: It was a little strange at first, but then it was nice to see people smiling back at me. No one came up to me, but it felt like a start.

Helper: You were also going to try to initiate a conversation with someone in class. How did that go?

Client: That didn't go so well. I picked Sally because she usually seems friendly. I sat near her as planned, but then I got scared at the last minute and didn't say anything to her.

Helper: Let's role-play that so I can see how you did it. Let's pretend that I'm Sally.

Client: I sat next to her but I didn't say anything, so there's nothing really to role-play.

Helper: Okay, let's try it where I play you and you play Sally and see if we can come up with some ideas about how to do it. Would that be okay?

Client: Sure, that would be great.

Helper: Hi Sally, how's it going?

Client: Oh hi, pretty good, except I'm stressed out about this test.

Helper: Me too. Would you be interested in studying together?

Client: Sure. Want to meet later for coffee and study?

Helper: How did that feel? Do you think you'd be able to do that?

Client: Yeah, I think I could. Let me try . . . Hi Sally. Umm, how's it going? Would you like to study for the exam together?

> *Helper:* Great, you did it, you got it out, and you looked directly at me when you said it. That's a big improvement. Maybe next time you could just slow down a bit when you are talking. Let's practice again, because it can really help to practice until you feel comfortable here.

Process Advisement

With *process advisement,* helpers direct clients to do things within helping sessions (e.g., "Show me how you acted when your roommate asked to borrow your new dress" or "Play the part of the man in your fantasy"). Process advisement is a type of advice or direct guidance (see next section), but it is confined to directing what goes on in the session (see Exhibit 15.4).

RATIONALE FOR GIVING PROCESS ADVISEMENT

Helpers are experts on how to facilitate the helping process and, hence, often have suggestions about what clients can do in sessions to facilitate the change process. Clients, in contrast, are not experts in the helping process and consequently rely (within limits) on helpers for judgments about how to proceed in sessions. The primary use of process advisement in the action stage is through behavioral exercises such as behavioral rehearsal or role-playing (see chap. 16).

EXHIBIT 15.4

Overview of Process Advisement

Definition	*Process advisement* refers to helper directives for what the client should do within the session
Example	"Let's try a role-play to practice a new way of acting in that situation. You be yourself and I'll be your boss. Try to use the assertive behaviors we practiced earlier."
Typical intention	To promote change (see Web Form D)
Possible client reactions	Educated, unstuck, new ways to behave, hopeful, confused, misunderstood, no reaction (see Web Form G)
Desired client behaviors	Agreement, therapeutic changes (see Web Form H)
Helpful hints	Give a credible rationale for suggesting an exercise in the session. Be clear and unapologetic about what you want the client to do. Observe how the client responds to process advisement and modify if needed to fit the client. Do not get involved in a control struggle over what to do—in such a situation, help the client explore the resistance or use immediacy to discuss the relationship.

HOW TO GIVE PROCESS ADVISEMENT

Clients are generally agreeable to trying things in sessions that helpers deem appropriate if they trust the helper and are presented with a credible rationale for why the exercise might be helpful (e.g., "Let's try this role-play to help you learn how to be more assertive. It may feel silly at first, but it can be helpful"). So the idea is to present the idea in a clear, calm manner that transmits confidence that this exercise will help the client.

Helpers must be attentive to signs that clients do not want to follow process advisements. Signs may range from passive resistance (e.g., hesitance, not responding, changing the topic) to more active resistance (saying "Yes, but" or arguing). It may be that the helper has presented the process advisement poorly, and so the client is reluctant to try it. Helpers are sometimes apologetic (e.g., "I don't suppose you'd want to do this exercise that my supervisor suggested?") and defeat the possibility of gaining client cooperation. Or sometimes helpers are not clear about their suggestions or do not provide a clear rationale.

Some clients are resistant to suggestions regardless of how skillfully they are presented. At all times, helpers need to respect the client's decision not to participate in an exercise. Perhaps the worst thing to do with reluctant or resistant clients is to get into a control struggle with them because control struggles tend to escalate, sometimes leading to disastrous consequences, with both people feeling that they will lose "face" if they back down. If a control struggle starts, helpers can step back and use exploration skills to understand why clients are reluctant, or they can use immediacy to work with the therapeutic relationship.

EXAMPLE OF PROCESS ADVISEMENT

The following shows a helper giving process advisement (in italics) in a session:

Helper: You've talked a lot about your indecision about whether to put your mother in an assisted living home. *I wonder if you would be willing to try something here in the session?*

Client: What?

Helper: *What I'd like you to do is to pretend that your mother is over there in that chair and tell her how you're feeling.*

Client: Yikes, that sounds a little scary.

Helper: *Yeah, it might be at first. Would you be willing to try it?*

Client: Sure, why not. So she's in that chair? (helper nods) Mom, I know you don't want to go, but I don't know what to do.

Helper: *Take a deep breath.* (pause while client take a deep breath) *Now think about what you would like to say.*

Client: Okay, let me try again. Mom, I know you're scared of going to the assisted living place, and I am too, but I think it's time. I can't take care of you when I live 1,000 miles away, and it's not safe for you to be alone.

Helper: Good. How did that feel?

Client: It felt a lot better. I felt like I knew what I wanted to say.

Helper: Yeah, you sounded good. *Now let's see how she might respond and how you could handle that . . .*

Direct Guidance

Direct guidance can be defined as making suggestions, giving directives, or providing advice for what helpers think clients should do outside of helping sessions (see Exhibit 15.5). Examples include providing suggestions to parents who are exploring ways of dealing with bedtime for a young

---

EXHIBIT 15.5

Overview of Direct Guidance

Definition	*Direct guidance* refers to helper suggestions, directives, or advice for the client
Example	"When you have the nightmare the next time, wake yourself up and imagine a new ending where you get angry at the intruder and chase him out of the house."
Typical intention	To promote change (see Web Form D)
Possible client reactions	Educated, unstuck, new ways to behave, hopeful, confused, misunderstood, no reaction (see Web Form G)
Desired client behaviors	Agreement, therapeutic changes (see Web Form H)
Helpful hints	Make sure that you have thoroughly explored the problem.
	Collaborate with the client to figure out the best homework assignment.
	Choose a task that fits the problem, is not difficult to implement, and is based on the client's strengths.
	Give a credible rationale for the guidance.
	Be clear about what you want the client to do; write it down if necessary.
	Observe how the client responds to the direct guidance and modify if needed to fit the client.
	Do not get involved in a control struggle over what to do—in such a situation, help the client explore the resistance or use immediacy to discuss the relationship.

child, to a client about coping strategies after a hospitalization, or to a middle-aged person for dealing with an elderly parent with Alzheimer's disease.

One form of direct guidance is homework. Helpers often suggest that clients do homework (e.g., monitor exercise and eating behaviors, read a self-help book, seek information, practice being assertive, record dreams) so that clients can practice what they are learning in helping sessions. Homework can be a particularly useful way to keep clients involved in the change process in between sessions. In addition, homework can speed up the helping process because clients are actively involved in changing and bringing feedback about change efforts back to the session. Homework can also encourage clients to act on their own without the helper's immediate monitoring.

Of course, the manner in which homework is assigned can make a big difference in terms of client receptivity and willingness to implement the homework. Research suggests that clients are more likely to implement homework suggestions if therapists choose tasks that fit the problem, are not difficult to implement, and are based on clients' strengths (Conoley, Padula, Payton, & Daniels, 1994; Scheel, Seaman, Roach, Mullin, & Mahoney, 1999; Wonnell & Hill, 2002). In a study on homework, Conoley et al. (1994) gave an example in which a client was depressed and angry. During the session, the client said that he wished he had written down instances when he felt badly the previous week so that he could remember them to talk about in the sessions. For homework, the helper asked the client to write down instances when he felt badly, recording what he was thinking, doing, and feeling, and what the situation was so they could discuss the problem more specifically in the next session. The client responded favorably, saying he liked to write and that writing had helped him in the past. Thus, the recommendation was judged as not being difficult because it required only a small amount of time, was not anxiety producing, and was clear. In addition, it was based on the client's strengths, given that the client had indicated that he liked to write. Furthermore, it matched his problem because it facilitated the client in remembering situations in which he was depressed and angry. During the next session, the client indicated that he had implemented the recommendation. In contrast, the directive to write would not have been good for other clients who do not like to write.

It is important to note that helpers in some job settings (e.g., rehabilitation counseling, job placement) need to do more direct guidance than helpers do in other settings (e.g., college counseling centers). For example, clients in rehabilitation settings often need specific guidance for how they could handle their major life obstacles, whereas clients in university counseling centers may be able to solve their problems by talking with an interested helper. Similarly, clients from some cultures want more direct guidance. For example, in Asian cultures clients often want their helpers to give them specific advice, and they might think less of helpers who do not provide suggestions. They might not necessarily implement the advice, but advice is expected from experts in that culture.

Direct guidance is different from information giving. When helpers give information, they provide facts or data but do not suggest what clients should do. In contrast, direct guidance indicates what helpers think clients should do. For example, contrast the effects of "The counseling center is in the Shoemaker Building" (information) versus "You should go to the counseling center" (direct guidance). Information often has an implied directive about what the client ought to do (e.g., "In my opinion, students earn better grades when they get a full night of sleep before taking a test"), but it does not state directly that the client should take a particular action (e.g., "You should make sure you get 8 hours of sleep before taking the test").

RATIONALE FOR GIVING DIRECT GUIDANCE

Dear Abby, Ann Landers, Dr. Laura, Dr. Joyce Brothers, Dr. Phil, and others give advice to millions of people. Many people (including me) read the newspaper columns and listen to the radio shows, which have become immensely popular because they are so entertaining. Providing advice is probably as old as human speech, but what are the consequences? Do people follow the advice, and if so, is it helpful or harmful? Unfortunately, no one has the answers to these concerns, except perhaps anecdotally. My main concern about direct guidance given in these entertainment formats is that the advice is not preceded by thorough exploration; the wrong problem might be addressed, and the recipient might think that it is not necessary to explore all the angles of the problem. Furthermore, in such situations people might begin to rely on others to make their decisions rather than coming to trust their own instincts. Moreover, some people seek guidance from many people and then either become confused or consider only the opinions they want to hear. It can be valuable to gain input from many people, but it can then be difficult for people to determine what they want to do. In addition, people may follow direct guidance out of fear of hurting the feelings of the advice giver or out of fear of retribution rather than because of choosing freely.

Direct guidance, however, can occasionally be useful in helping situations, especially when given by a trusted helper whose opinions are based on solid knowledge and experience and are given after extensive client exploration and insight. Helpers can have good ideas about what might be helpful for clients to do. For example, Dorothy asked her helper for advice on negotiating her salary for her first job in an academic setting. This was an area her helper knew something about because she had worked in an academic setting. They talked about the information Dorothy had gathered about the salary range of other recent hires, what her values were, and what she wanted. They then discussed how Dorothy could navigate the negotiation process. The helper suggested that Dorothy not name a specific salary but say that she was dissatisfied with what had been offered. They talked about that possibility, and Dorothy modified it to fit her style. The process was collaborative because the helper respected Dorothy's right and ability to make her own decisions. The helper was not invested in which strategy Dorothy chose but was interested in presenting alternatives for Dorothy to consider so she could develop a plan that worked for her. Although the strategy did not work exactly as planned when Dorothy tried it (which is typical in the real world), Dorothy was able to modify it during the negotiation. She accepted the job at a competitive salary and started her new job soon afterward.

Although most clients are able to make their own decisions, especially if they have input from others, an individual in a crisis situation may need more explicit guidance. When clients are suicidal, for example, they often have "tunnel vision" that prevents them from seeing options other than death. Helpers may need to intervene in such situations and try to ensure that clients do not harm themselves (refer to chap. 18 for discussion about dealing with suicidal clients). It is important to emphasize that other than in extreme cases (e.g., child abuse, suicidal or homicidal risk), helpers typically do not take over and manage what clients do. Offering suggestions is quite different from demanding that clients do what you tell them to do.

HOW TO GIVE DIRECT GUIDANCE

Helpers should think about their intentions before using direct guidance. They should make sure they are using this skill because clients are ready to hear advice. As with information, helpers should not give direct guidance until they have assessed clients' motivation (as well as their own).

When giving direct guidance, helpers also need to remember that it is easier for clients to make small, specific changes than to change many big things all at once. Helpers should be specific about which small steps could be done and when they could be done, and they should reinforce approximations toward the desired behaviors. For example, rather than suggesting that an inactive client try to lose 5 pounds in the next week (which is not under the client's control), the helper might suggest that the client walk for 15 minutes three times in the next week, reinforce herself by taking a hot bath after each walk, and allow herself to read a novel (assuming the helper has discovered that the client enjoys doing these things).

I also suggest that helpers write down homework assignments to help clients remember them given that it is often difficult to remember everything that happens in sessions. Furthermore, clients are more likely to take written assignments seriously. Following up on homework assignments in subsequent sessions (e.g., asking clients about their experience in trying to implement the homework) is also important, otherwise clients might feel that such assignments are frivolous and not to be taken seriously. And, as always, it is important to observe client reactions to see how they respond to such interventions.

When clients ask (or sometimes even beg) for direct guidance, helpers have to be particularly careful to distinguish between the honest and direct request for direct guidance and the expression of dependent feelings. When in doubt, it is probably best to deal first with the feelings involved (e.g., "You seem pretty desperate to get some advice. I wonder what's going on with you?") After such exploration, helpers have additional data to consider how to deal with the request. Helpers also have to assess their own motivation and ensure that their needs to take care of others do not interfere with allowing clients to make their own decisions.

Clients often have negative reactions if helpers ignore their requests for advice. Some clients want direct guidance and are angry when helpers refuse to tell them what to do. An example is a case presented in Hill (1989), in which a woman wanted direct guidance about family issues in the early sessions, and the helper did not give it to her because she wanted to do insight-oriented helping. The client felt disregarded by the helper and became less invested in the therapy thereafter. In cases such as this, it may be better to give advice if the helper genuinely feels he or she has useful advice, and then process with the client later about the origin of the desire for advice. In addition, openly addressing the client's feelings using immediacy skills may help repair breaches in relationships that occur when clients become angry at helpers for not providing any, enough, or the "right" direct guidance.

CAUTIONS WHEN GIVING DIRECT GUIDANCE

Helpers also need to be aware that they can offer help but cannot force clients to take it. Helpers are not taking over for clients but are providing options for clients to consider. Clients have the right to decide for themselves what to do, even in the most desperate of circumstances.

Furthermore, helpers have to know the limits of how much they can offer. Friedman (1990) recounted a fable about a rescuer who holds a rope over the rail of a bridge to save a drowning person. The drowning person grabs the rope but refuses to climb up. After a while, the rescuer holding the rope cannot hang on any longer because the drowning person is so heavy. The rescuer has to make a decision about letting go or falling from the bridge himself, which clearly would not help either the drowning person or the rescuer.

Another problem with direct guidance is that it can foster dependency by shifting the responsibility for solutions from clients to helpers. Clients can become passive and helpless if helpers insinuate that they are not competent enough to solve their problems. In addition, when helpers rather than clients are responsible for the guidance, clients often blame the helpers when things do not go so well. Moreover, when helpers use too much direct guidance, it can lead to tension, resistance, or rebellion if clients choose to ignore helpers who demand that clients pursue their advice. Hence, direct guidance can cause problems in therapeutic relationships if it is not done collaboratively, with helpers and clients together constructing the direct guidance.

EXAMPLE OF DIRECT GUIDANCE

The following shows a helper giving direct guidance (in italics) in a session:

> *Client:* Our 3-year-old daughter has gotten into the habit of coming into our bedroom in the middle of the night and climbing in bed with us and wanting to stay until morning. At first it seemed okay because she seemed to need comforting, but it has gotten out of hand. We only have a double bed, and my husband takes up more than his half, so I end up being unable to sleep because I can't move. When I try to move her, she doesn't want to leave. So we've got to do something.
>
> *Helper:* You sound frustrated.
>
> *Client:* I am. We can't figure out what to do. I don't want to traumatize her if she needs comforting. She seems to really like sleeping with us.
>
> *Helper:* What have you tried so far?
>
> *Client:* Nothing really. It just started getting intolerable. So now I know we have to do something. Plus I think she's getting a little too old to be doing this.
>
> *Helper:* What is your goal?
>
> *Client:* When she wakes up and is upset, I'd like to comfort her and then have her go back to her bed. I don't want her to get into our bed. Once she gets in, it's hard to get her out.
>
> *Helper:* What are your usual strategies for dealing with problems with kids?
>
> *Client:* We talk things out ahead of time so the kids are prepared and are in on it.
>
> *Helper:* *Maybe that would work here if you talked with her ahead of time about what you are planning to do.* How would you do it?
>
> *Client:* Before bedtime, I could tell her that during the night when she wakes up, she can't come into our bed anymore. But I'm afraid there's nothing positive to replace it with.

> *Helper:* That's a good point. *What if you were to lie down next to her on her bed until she went back to sleep. Then you could go back to your own bed.*
>
> *Client:* That sounds like a good idea. So when she comes into our room, I would just take her back to her room, lay down with her for awhile until she's asleep, and then go back to my bed. I think that would work, especially if I tell her about it ahead of time. I might miss some sleep but not as much as I am now.
>
> *Helper:* Sounds good. Do you see any problems?
>
> *Client:* Well, I might fall asleep on her bed, but probably not for long because it would be uncomfortable there too. I might also be groggy in the middle of the night and just let her in out of habit.
>
> *Helper:* *Well, it probably would only take three to five nights, so you could tell yourself that if you can just do it for that long, the habit will be broken.*
>
> *Client:* Good point. I'm going to do it. It fits with the way I like to do things, so I know it will work.

Disclosure of Strategies

Helpers make suggestions through disclosing strategies that they personally have tried in the past (another form of disclosure). In effect, rather than telling clients what to do, helpers provide suggestions through disclosing what has worked for them previously if they think their strategy might work for the client (see Exhibit 15.6). Helpers then turn the focus back to the clients and ask for their reaction (e.g., "When I feel angry, I take a deep breath and count to 10. I wonder if that would work for you?").

RATIONALE FOR DISCLOSING STRATEGIES

It is important to disclose only those strategies that seem like they might work for the client. The object is not to show off strategies that work for you but rather to help clients expand their possibilities.

Hearing what another person has done can provide specific ideas for new behaviors (e.g., "I brush my teeth as soon as I have finished eating so I don't forget to do it or am too tired to do it") and can also encourage clients to think of novel action plans (e.g., "I treat myself to a cruise each year as a reward for working hard all year. I wonder what you could do?"). Disclosing what has worked for the helper is also somewhat disarming—rather than telling clients what to do, helpers

---

EXHIBIT 15.6

Overview of Disclosure of Strategies

Definition	*Disclosure of strategies* refers to the helper's presentation of actions that he or she has used in the past to cope with problems
Example	"When I have been in similar situations with my mother, I call her and ask to talk. I try to be as honest as possible and let her know that I messed up. Usually she is pretty understanding."
Typical intention	To promote change (see Web Form D)
Typical client reactions	Educated, unstuck, new ways to behave, hopeful, confused, misunderstood, no reaction (see Web Form G)
Desired client behaviors	Agreement, therapeutic changes (see Web Form H)
Helpful hints	Make sure that you have thoroughly explored the problem.
	Imagine a strategy you used that might benefit the client.
	Choose a strategy that fits the problem, is not difficult to implement, and is based on the client's strengths.
	Make the disclosure short; do not go into detail about what your problem was.
	Observe how the client responds to the disclosure.
	Shift the focus back to the client after the disclosure.

---

communicate that they do not have the answers but are willing to share what has worked for them. By disclosing strategies, helpers provide ideas for clients without imposing the type of demands that may result from directives. Disclosing strategies is a more tentative way of giving information or direct guidance.

HOW TO DISCLOSE STRATEGIES

As with self-disclosures of insight, helpers need to give the disclosure but then turn the focus back to the client. For example, the helper might say, "When I'm reading a textbook, I make myself read a chapter and then I reward myself by doing something I like—I might get a soda, make a phone call, or play a video game, although I limit any of those activities to 10 minutes. Would that work for you?"

CAUTIONS RELATED TO DISCLOSING STRATEGIES

Helpers should be aware that a client might be unduly influenced by the helper's disclosure to adopt a similar action plan. For this reason, the helpers might provide the option tentatively, indicate that it might or might not work for the client, and then turn the focus back to the client for her or his reaction. In addition, helpers need to be careful not to slip into disclosures to relieve their own feelings because then the focus shifts from the client to the helper (e.g., "Let me tell you all about what I did because it's so fascinating and interesting").

EXAMPLE OF DISCLOSING STRATEGIES

The following shows a helper disclosing strategies (in italics) in a session:

Client: I know that I need to exercise, but I just can never seem to find anything I like to do.

Helper: *One thing that works for me is to go for a half-hour walk every morning with my husband. I get exercise and get to spend some time with my husband at the beginning of the day.* I wonder if something like that would work for you?

Client: Well, that kind of appeals to me, but I'm really out of shape.

Helper: *I started out walking 10 minutes a day and worked my way up over several years. Now I hate to miss my morning walk.* Would 10 minutes be easier for you?

Client: Yeah, but how would I get my husband involved?

Helper: What thoughts do you have about that?

What Do You Think?

- Clients often ask for information. How would you decide when to give clients the requested information and when to probe them for their ideas?
- How can you determine whether clients really want or need direct guidance?
- Argue for or against the opinion that direct guidance should generally be given tentatively and only after thorough exploration and insight.
- Describe what it might be like for you to tell clients that you do not know the answer to their questions. How might not knowing an answer influence the client's perception of the helper?
- How do you feel about receiving information from other people? What feelings do you have when you seek information or when people ask you for information?
- Debate the pros and cons related to radio talk show psychologists giving direct guidance after having spoken only briefly with callers.
- What difficulties might you experience when using a self-disclosing strategy?

Steps for Working With Four Types of Action

16

Vision without action is a daydream. Action without vision is a nightmare.

—Japanese proverb

A helper at a homeless shelter listened to Debi talk about her rage, feelings of powerlessness, and sense of humiliation at being evicted from her home. The helper challenged Debi's irrational thoughts that she was worthless and a social outcast. The helper disclosed about her own experiences with poverty and losing her job and how she had been forced to figure out what she wanted to do with her life. Debi felt better after expressing her feelings and gaining insights about how she had gotten to this situation, but she also wanted to learn skills so she would never be homeless again. The helper asked for more details about how she had come to lose her job and home. Debi said that she had been fired because of downsizing and had become discouraged about getting another job after being turned down by 15 employers. The helper gave Debi some tests to figure out her interests, helped her write a resume, and then did role-playing with her about how to do a job interview. Debi applied for several jobs while living at the shelter and was offered one that she liked. The helper then worked with Debi about skills she would need to do the job well (being on time, dressing appropriately, not using the telephone for personal calls). Debi was still in her job at a 6-month follow-up.

T he action skills can be integrated in a series of steps for four different types of action: (a) relaxation, (b) behavior change, (c) behavior rehearsal, and (d) decision making. Helpers serve as coaches or guides to help clients move through these steps so that they can make changes in their lives.

These steps are not presented in this chapter as rigid requirements for how to do the action stage. Rather, they are presented as guidelines to give helpers an idea of how the action stage might look. Helpers can start with these steps and modify them in creative ways to be responsive to the needs of the particular client (e.g., some clients might be ready to start changing and will not need to spend as much time exploring action; other clients might not have tried to change their behavior in the past, so the step about assessing past change attempts can be skipped). When clients have strong reactions to any of the steps, helpers can step back, help clients process their reactions, and possibly alter their strategies. Exhibit 16.1 presents an overview of the steps and the skills used to implement the steps.

Relaxation

Relaxation is particularly important for clients who have problems with stress and anxiety. An extensive amount of data shows that relaxing one's muscles reduces anxiety (Jacobson, 1929; Lang, Melamed, & Hart, 1970; Paul, 1969) and that it is useful to teach certain (especially anxious) clients to relax (Bernstein & Borkovec, 1973; Goldfried & Trier, 1974). When people are relaxed, they are more open and able to handle information, so relaxation is a good thing for helpers to teach prior to trying to implement other behavioral interventions.

Particularly good times for helpers to do relaxation are when clients have a fear of flying, are extremely anxious about taking tests or speaking in public, have anxiety in social situations, or seem especially tense during the session. In contrast, helpers should be cautious about offering to do relaxation with clients who are paranoid, fear losing control, or have delusions.

STEP 1: IDENTIFY STRESS/ANXIETY AS A SPECIFIC PROBLEM

Through exploration, clients often identify stress and anxiety as a major problem. Helpers can also observe when clients seem particularly tense (e.g., they might speak rapidly, act fidgety, or panic). Helpers may then ask whether the client would like to learn relaxation techniques to calm

EXHIBIT 16.1

Steps for Each of the Types of Action

Goal	Step	Skills to use (and examples)
Relaxation	1. Identify stress/anxiety as a specific problem	Open questions ("How are you feeling?") Process advisement ("Let's try a relaxation exercise.")
	2. Teach relaxation	Process advisement (get comfortable, relax, repeat a phrase when breathing out, let all thoughts go/return to phrase)
Behavior change	1. Identify a specific problem	Open questions ("What would you like to change in your life?")
	2. Explore idea of action	Open questions ("What would be the benefits of changing?" "What would be the benefits of not changing?")
	3. Assess previous change attempts and resources	Open questions ("What have you tried before?" "What worked?" "What didn't work?" "What kind of social support do you have for working on this problem?")
	4. Generate options together	Open questions ("Tell me all the different possible ideas you have for how you could fix this problem.") Direct guidance ("What about trying ___?") Disclosure of strategies ("When I was in that situation, I tried ___.")
	5. Evaluate options	Open questions ("Which options seem most appealing?" "Which options seem least appealing?") Information ("Let me tell you about ___.")
	6. Choose an option	Open questions ("Which one would you like to commit yourself to trying?") Direct guidance ("I wonder if you might try ___.")
	7. Assign homework	Direct guidance ("Given what you've said, maybe you could try ___." "Go slow.") Open questions ("What would help you do ____?" "What would keep you from doing ____?")
	8. Check progress/ modify	Open questions ("How did it go when you tried to do the homework?") Direct guidance ("Given what you've said, it seems like we tried to do too much last week. Perhaps you should try less of ___.") Approval–reassurance ("I'm impressed with how well you did with a difficult task.")

(continued)

EXHIBIT 16.1 (*Continued*)

Steps for Each of the Types of Action

Goal	Step	Skills to use (and examples)
Behavioral rehearsal	1. Assess behavior	Open questions ("What happens when you try ___?") Process advisement ("Role-play what you do in that situation.")
	2. Determine goals (based on values and rights)	Open questions ("What would you like to have happen?" "What values influence this issue?" "What are your rights?")
	3. Provide a model	Process advisement ("You play the other person, and I'll be you.") Open questions ("What would that be like for you to do that?")
	4. Role-play with feedback	Process advisement ("Let's try it again where you play your part." "Say it again like you really mean it this time.") Approval–reassurance ("You really sounded convincing.")
	5. Assign homework	Direct guidance ("Perhaps this week you could try ___.")
	6. Check progress/modify	Open questions ("How did it go when you tried it out?")
Decision making	1. Articulate the options	Open questions ("What are the different options?")
	2. Clarify values	Open questions ("What are your values related to this?")
	3. Rate options/values	Process advisement ("Rate the options given your values.")
	4. Evaluate results	Open questions ("How do you feel about the results of this exercise?" "Would you like to modify any of your options, your values, or your ratings?")

down in the immediate moment and to be able to calm themselves down outside of sessions in times of stress. The explanation is that if a person is physiologically relaxed, this state is incompatible with anxiety, and relaxation is a good coping strategy.

STEP 2: TEACH RELAXATION

Although many methods of relaxation training exist (e.g., meditation, deep muscle relaxation), Benson's (1975) extensive research has found two main components: (a) the repetition of any word, sound, prayer, thought, phrase, or muscular activity; and (b) the passive return to repeating when other thoughts intrude. Following Benson's suggestions, helpers can teach clients to relax by going through the following steps, using a calm, slow voice:

1. "Get as comfortable as possible in your seat. Remove everything from your lap and put your feet firmly on the floor. Close your eyes."
2. "Relax your body starting from your toes up through your head. Shrug your shoulders and release the tension. Breathe deeply."
3. "Pick a word (e.g., one, peace), sound (e.g., om), prayer (e.g., the Lord's Prayer), thought, or phrase (e.g., the river runs through it). Pick something that fits with your beliefs and feels comfortable to you. Repeat that phrase each time you breathe out."
4. "Let all your other thoughts go. When you find yourself thinking about something else, don't worry, just passively let it go and return to repeating."
5. "Do this for 3 to 5 minutes and then sit quietly for a minute."

Because doing a relaxation exercise during a session could be difficult or scary for some clients (e.g., they might feel worried about whether they are doing it "right," they might feel vulnerable sitting with their eyes closed), helpers may want to ask clients about thoughts and feelings before, during, and after the exercise. Helpers may also want to check with clients about how much they liked doing the relaxation. If clients feel that it would be useful, helpers can suggest that they practice relaxing 10 to 20 minutes, twice a day (e.g., in morning before breakfast and in the late afternoon) in a quiet place where they will not be distracted. A good explanation for practicing is that the client will then be able to induce relaxation in new situations more quickly. If clients like relaxation and have a tendency to become panicked in sessions, helpers can also suggest that they use it within sessions.

Other relaxation methods can also be helpful for some clients. The most basic one is deep breathing, which I particularly recommend for helpers when they are first doing sessions. The idea here is to remember to take a deep breath, which gives you time to reflect and gather yourself. It is also often helpful to ask clients to take a deep breath, which gives them a chance to step back, clear their heads, relax, and refocus attention on the task.

Another relaxation method is mindfulness, which Kabat-Zinn (2003) defined as the awareness that comes from attending nonjudgmentally to one's experience in the moment. The idea behind mindfulness is to become aware of (i.e., mindful) about emotions and reactions, take them out and observe them, and then let them go (Segal, Williams, & Teasdale, 2002). A good example of mindfulness involves eating. When eating mindfully, one pays full attention to eating, savoring every bite, tasting each flavor, and smelling each aroma rather than gobbling down the food while doing something else.

Yet another possible method is deep muscle relaxation (Jacobson, 1929), wherein the helper teaches the client to systematically concentrate on each muscle in the body and tense it for 30 seconds and then relax; after practicing relaxation systematically, one can begin to induce it when needed. Alternatively, it is often helpful to induce relaxation using visual imagery, such as sand filling the body or being a marionette and feeling limp with relaxation being "poured in."

Behavior Change

Many clients (and indeed every person) have specific behaviors that need to be changed. Clients do too much of some behaviors (e.g., eating too much, drinking too much, nail-biting), not enough of other behaviors (e.g., exercise, teeth-brushing), and use inappropriate behaviors (e.g., poor social skills, poor study skills, procrastination). Behavior therapy is ideal in such situations because it involves helping clients make specific behavior changes.

STEP 1: IDENTIFY A SPECIFIC PROBLEM

If a clear, specific problem was not identified earlier, the helper can now work with the client to choose one. This step is particularly important for clients whose concerns are more global or vague (e.g., general feelings of dissatisfaction). This work often requires helping the client explore the problem, think about values, and develop more understanding and motivation for change (in other words, going back to do more exploration and insight about the problem and the client's life situation).

To help the client identify a specific problem on which to focus in the action stage, the helper can use open questions for action such as the following:

- "What is the first thing that you would like to be different?"
- "What do you specifically want to change in your life?"
- "Describe your dreams for the future. What would you need to change to make those dreams become a reality?"

The helper may also want to use approval–reassurance to support the client:

- "That sounds like a good problem to start with given what we have talked about."

If the client has identified a specific problem (e.g., becoming violently angry), the helper may ask for a specific example (along with details) of when the behavior last occurred:

- "Tell me about the last time you got angry. Describe the situation to me as fully as possible."

Helpers should focus on one problem at a time because dealing with several problems simultaneously can be confusing and diffuse change efforts. If the client has multiple problems, the helper could work with the client to list all the problems, order them, and then choose which one to start with. It is better to focus initially on easier (but still meaningful) problems, so clients can gain a sense of accomplishment when they change. Furthermore, accomplishing small changes can provide clients with the confidence to pursue additional challenges.

Some clients might want to change things that seem inappropriate to the helper. Oscar Wilde said that "the only thing worse than not getting what you want is getting what you want" (from *Lady Windemere's Fan*, Act 3; Murray, 1989). Some clients might want to stay in abusive relationships, assume that they can finish a degree program when they have been terminated from it, or have aspirations of getting a job that may be out of their reach. By exploring these issues without judgment, helpers can work with clients to think about what they want and why.

By the end of this step, the client should have a well-articulated, specific problem that she or he wants to address. It could be a behavior (e.g., wanting to be more assertive) or a thought (e.g., not wanting to think that everyone should love me). The helper should also know details of what happened during a specific instance (e.g., details of the last argument with a partner), because it is easier to do behavior change with a specific event rather than with a vague description.

STEP 2: EXPLORE THE IDEA OF ACTION FOR THIS PROBLEM

Rather than assume clients are eager to change, it is important to allow them to explore the idea of changing. Most of us are ambivalent about changing. Although we might be unhappy with the way things are, we are often scared by what things might be like if we change. Rather than rushing to change, clients need an opportunity to explore the pros and cons of changing and make good choices about whether to change.

Furthermore, not every client is ready to change. In chapter 2, five stages of clients' readiness for change were presented: precontemplation, contemplation, preparation, action, and maintenance (Prochaska, DiClemente, & Norcross, 1992). Assessing the client's current stage is important before proceeding to the action stage. In the precontemplation and contemplation stages, clients typically require much time to explore their feelings and develop insights before making a commitment to change; homework might involve listing the benefits of change and obstacles to change. Clients in the preparation and action stages often are more ready to move directly to action; they might be ready to tackle the actual change exercises. Clients in the maintenance stage probably are more interested in stabilizing the changes they already have made.

If helpers plunge too quickly into action with clients who are not ready, they typically hear "Yes, but. . . ." These clients will have all kinds of reasons why action is not possible. Alternatively, some clients may simply withdraw and act compliant but have no intention of following through on the action. Helpers need to respect clients' choices about whether to change.

Helpers should not be invested in whether or not clients choose to change. Rather than perceiving that their success as a helper is based on clients making radical changes, helpers need to view their success as based on helping clients decide what is best for them. After all, how can helpers possibly know what is ultimately best for clients?

The key is to provide a good-enough climate so that clients feel comfortable talking about and then making decisions about changing. Helpers can encourage clients to express their thoughts and feelings about action and examine the benefits and drawbacks of changing or not changing. Helpers can maintain an attitude of curiosity and ask open questions to assess client readiness to change and encourage client exploration of feelings:

- "What are the benefits of changing?"
- "What are the benefits of not changing?"
- "How would changing make you feel?"
- "What keeps you from changing?"
- "What goes through your mind as we talk about changing?"
- "What feelings are you having when you contemplate making changes in your life?"
- "How would others react to your changing?"

The helper also can support clients and facilitate exploration of change through restatements and reflection of feelings, such as,

- "You haven't thought much about whether you want to change."
- "It's exciting for you to think about doing something new."

Hence, the primary skills used in this step are open questions and reflection of feelings. Open questions are often used to begin the discussion, which helpers can then facilitate by reflecting feelings and drawing clients into a discussion of values, needs, and problems related to change.

If the client is clearly conflicted about changing, it might be helpful to use a two-chair technique (see Elliott, Watson, Goldman, & Greenberg,

2004; Greenberg, Rice, & Elliott, 1993) to allow the client to experience and express both sides of the conflict. Resolution of the conflict is typically easier after both sides of the conflict are brought into awareness. For this technique, the helper uses process advisement. For example,

Helper: Be the side of you that says you should quit biting your fingernails. You can pretend that you're talking to that part of you sitting in the chair over there.

Client: (to empty chair) It's disgusting when you do that. Look how awful you look. Just stop it.

Helper: Can you say it a little louder, like your father might have said it to you when you were 12 years old?

Client: [to empty chair] Yeah, (louder) just stop it. You look ugly when you chew your fingernails. What's wrong with you, anyway? Stop it right now.

Helper: Now go over to the other chair and be the 12-year-old side of you who wants to chew her fingernails. What would you have wanted to say back to your father?

Client: (from other chair to empty chair) I'll chew my fingernails if I want. You can't stop me. I don't care what you think. All you want is for me to be perfect, so I'll look good for you. (role play continues for a while)

Helper: How did that feel to you going through that? Did you learn something new about why you might chew your fingernails?

Client: I sure did. I can see that I wanted to get back at my father. It was a small way that I could have some control over my life.

Helper: When you think about it that way, what do you think about being ready to change your fingernail biting now?

Client: I think I'm ready to change biting my fingernails. I'm pretty disgusted by it too at this point. But I want to come back after that to try to understand more about my relationship with my father.

Helper: OK, then. Let's spend some time working on the fingernails first and then go back to the issue with your father.

After weighing all the options, some clients might choose not to change. They might decide that the costs of changing are not worth the benefits. Sometimes change is too painful, and sometimes clients discover that their current life is not so bad. Choosing not to change can be just as valid a choice as deciding to change. For example, after having tried for years to be assertive with her boss, only to be punished and ridiculed in front of her coworkers, Sandra decided not to fight back any longer against her boss's inappropriate behaviors. The helper (who was initially overly invested in the client being assertive) had to respect this decision and assist Sandra in developing coping skills to help manage her reactions at work. Thus, the goal changed from being assertive to coping.

By the end of this step, the client should have made some commitment about changing. Note that clients are rarely 100% in favor of change, but the advantages should clearly outweigh the disadvantages, or else it is not a good idea to go forward with the next step; helpers can instead return to exploration and insight to determine the resistance to change.

STEP 3: ASSESS PREVIOUS CHANGE ATTEMPTS AND RESOURCES

When the helper has established that the client wants to change, the helper can assess what attempts, if any, the client has already made. Finding out about previous attempts can avoid encouraging actions that have not worked in the past, indicate that the helper respects the client's change efforts, and let the client know the helper is aware that the client has been attempting to solve problems. After all, clients have usually had lengthy experiences with their problems and have undoubtedly tried, and have many feelings about, various alternatives. Helpers act as consultants with clients, collaboratively working to learn what they have tried and how these strategies have worked.

The following are examples of open questions helpers can use to assess previous efforts:

- ▪ "What have you tried before?"
- ▪ "Describe the strategies you have used in trying to change."

In this step, helpers also need to assess what worked and what did not work in the previous attempts. In effect, the helper is assessing the forces facilitating change as well as the forces inhibiting change. Helpers can focus on both internal (e.g., motivation, anxiety, insecurity, self-confidence) and external factors (resources that clients have available in their environment to support them when they make changes, obstacles such as discrimination and social injustice). It is better to know as much as possible about the factors influencing the change process from the outset so that the same problems are not repeated. It is important to realize that clients may not be aware of all the influencing factors, but it is good to get as many as possible out in the open.

Helpers use open questions to assess the facilitating and restraining influences:

- ▪ "What parts of what you tried worked?"
- ▪ "What parts didn't work?"

- "What problems did you encounter that made it difficult the last time?"
- "When you tried the last time, what things made it easier for you?"
- "What was going on in your environment when you tried last time?"
- "What thoughts and feelings were you having?"

It is important for helpers to remember to support client exploration of change attempts because it can sometimes be quite threatening to discuss. Using restatements and reflections of feelings can demonstrate to clients that helpers are listening.

- "Sounds like you've tried lots of things to help you overcome your depression."
- "You sound frustrated that after all your efforts, nothing happened."

Using approval–reassurance can let clients know that helpers are aware of their hard work in exploring and that helpers value what clients are saying.

- "You've done a great job working so hard to get information about services available in the community. You've been very resourceful."

Finally, helpers can assess social support, given that it is very important in terms of change efforts (Sarason, Sarason, & Pierce, 1990). Breier and Strauss (1984) noted that the benefits of a social support system include a forum for ventilation, reality testing, support and approval, integration into the community, problem solving, and constancy. Positive support can provide encouragement and reinforcement (e.g., having a supportive, nonjudgmental partner can enable one to stick to a diet). In contrast, negative support can undermine the person's resolve (e.g., if a woman decides to go on a diet and her partner says that she was more attractive before or can't stay on a diet, it will be very difficult for that woman to continue the diet). In addition, helpers can discuss with clients how change will influence their social network.

- "How much can you rely on other people to help you with this problem?"
- "How do others respond to you about this problem?"
- "How would others react if you change?"

By the end of this step, the helper should have a fairly good idea of what the client has tried before and how much social support the client has in his or her environment. In addition, the helper should have some ideas of what has worked and what has not worked in terms of previous change attempts. The helper puts the data together with data gathered during the exploration and insight stage to begin to conceptualize the strengths and obstacles the client will have in terms of making changes (e.g., resistance to an authority figure telling client to change).

STEP 4: GENERATE OPTIONS TOGETHER

One of the biggest benefits for clients of working with helpers is that they can come up with options together. Through collaboration, more ideas can usually be produced by two people (or even better by a group of people) than can be generated by one person alone or two or more people working independently. The goal in this step is to generate as many ideas as possible, without judgment, to enable clients to see that there are many alternatives. Reality can come later when deciding among the possibilities, but the ideas must first be generated. One strategy is to set a specific time limit, such as 2 minutes, for this thought-showering process. It is important for clients to lift restrictions on themselves while generating ideas and to suspend judgment about what is possible so they do not censor any possibilities. Although I do not usually recommend that helpers take notes, it can be helpful during this step for helpers to write down the ideas so they can refer back to them in the next step.

To aid in the thought-showering process, helpers can use open questions to ask clients to think of whatever action comes to mind, no matter how unlikely or silly it might initially sound to them.

- "If money or time were not an issue, how would you try to change this problem behavior?"
- "What would you suggest to someone else in this situation?"

Helpers can add ideas of their own using direct guidance. It is fine for helpers to make suggestions here because it can open clients up to new ideas they might not have considered. Of course, it is important for helpers not to get invested in their ideas but just to offer possibilities to give clients more options.

- "What about talking to your boss?"
- "Maybe you could . . ."

Helpers can also disclose about strategies they have tried in similar situations. By disclosing, helpers not only admit that they too have had problems but also make clear that this option worked for them but might not work for the client.

- "When I have trouble remembering all the things I have to do, I make a list."
- "I try to keep a routine and brush my teeth right after my shower."

Helpers can also think about Grandma's rule ("Eat vegetables before dessert.") in thinking of strategies. So they could suggest to do the new behavior (e.g., studying) before something fun (e.g., watching television). Or helpers could use Premack's principle, which involves pairing a low-frequency behavior (e.g., teeth brushing) with a high-frequency behavior (e.g., surfing the Internet).

By the end of this step, the helper and client should have a list of possibilities that the client might try. No order of preference is expected at this point, but it is hoped a lot of ideas have been generated.

STEP 5: EVALUATE THE OPTIONS

Once a number of options have been generated, the task for the helper is to help the client think through the options systematically and evaluate them. Clients need to select ideas that are specific, realistic, within the realm of possibility, and consistent with their values. Helpers can ask which options seem appealing and why. Helpers can also ask about clients' values to determine whether any of the options violate these values. For example, even though a quick way to obtain money might be to rob a bank, clients (one hopes) have values against theft.

The following are examples of open questions that helpers might use to help a client choose the best idea:

- "Which options seem most appealing?"
- "Which options seem least appealing?"
- "What are your values about the different alternatives that you might try?"
- "What options go against your values or beliefs?"

Helpers also might want to use information to educate clients about the various possibilities. For example,

- "One way to work with anxiety is by doing relaxation exercises to help you learn how to cope with the anxiety. In relaxation training, we go through the various muscles and teach you to tense them and then relax them. We go through the training in the session and then you practice it on your own several times. After practicing several times, most people are able to relax by just thinking about relaxing. Then you can do deep breathing to get you right into a state of relaxation."

Helpers can also ask clients to list the advantages and disadvantages to different options. If the disadvantages of the option outweigh the advantages, it is unlikely that the client will want to implement the option. By looking at the barriers, it may be possible to figure out how to overcome difficulties:

- "What are the advantages of practicing relaxation each night?"
- "What are the disadvantages of practicing relaxation each night?"
- "What would make it difficult to practice relaxation?"

I typically encourage helpers to work with clients to choose options that involve changing themselves rather than trying to change other people (except for behavior change with children). It is difficult to change others, and it presents ethical problems. For example, a woman may want help in getting her husband to exercise more, or a man may want to stop his friend from drinking so much.

By the end of this step, the helper should have an idea of the rankings of the client's preference for options. This step may be quite short if the client immediately jumps into the problem solving that takes place in Step 6. The client may be quite reluctant, however, which can alert the helper to problems in the relationship that must be addressed by cycling back to the exploration and insight stages. Finally, some clients may have gotten enough out of action at this stage and not need to go further (e.g., the client may have a clear idea about what to change and not need further help).

STEP 6: CHOOSE AN OPTION

After thinking through the various possibilities, the client comes to the point of choosing which option to implement. Although several options may be appealing, it is typically helpful to choose one to allow plenty of time to think through issues of implementation.

Once the client chooses an option, it can be useful to assess his or her current level of functioning on the problem in terms of the ABCs of it (i.e., the antecedents, behaviors, and consequences). The assessment may involve interviewing the client about the target behavior. If the client is vague or unsure or not a good observer of the process, the helper may ask the client to monitor his or her behavior over the course of 1 to 2 weeks to gather specific information about the antecedents, behaviors, and consequences. For example, a client who wants to reduce his overeating may be asked to write down all the food he eats, where he eats it, who he is with when he eats, and how he feels before and after eating. Clients often learn that their behavior differs dramatically from what they reported earlier to helpers. For example, an overweight man who claims that he never snacks might learn that he consistently nibbles on something while working or while watching television in the evenings. A person who feels lonely might discover that she never looks people in the eye and never says hello when passing others.

When helpers have an idea of the baseline (typical) behavior, they can help clients determine realistic goals for change. For example, if an overweight person wants to lose 50 pounds in 1 month, the helper can work with the client to choose a more realistic goal. Often the goals have to be modified to be more attainable. For example, instead of encouraging the overweight client to begin a severely restricted diet of 800 calories per day, the helper might encourage the client to walk

20 minutes a day in addition to eating more moderately (e.g., 1,500 calories per day) to facilitate gradual weight loss, which is most likely to be maintained.

Helpers can also work with clients to identify realistic reinforcers. For example, one client might find it reinforcing to look forward to going on a vacation to a Caribbean island if she can get all As on her report card. Another client might need the more immediate reinforcement of being able to call a friend after he studies for 1 hour.

Once the target behavior is identified, baseline information has been gathered, realistic goals set, and reinforcers identified, the helper works with the client to figure out how to modify the behavior. This process is very creative because each client is different.

- It is generally preferable to look for ways to increase positive behavior than to decrease negative behaviors because it is easier to change in the positive direction. For example, for a problem with social anxiety, the helper might identify that the client needs to make more overtures to others.
- The chosen behaviors must be observable, behavioral, and specific (e.g., smiling at strangers) rather than broad and vague (e.g., becoming more friendly) because specific behaviors are easier to work on and monitor for changes.
- Helpers target specific behaviors to change (e.g., a certain amount of homework) rather than trying to change the outcome (e.g., the final grade) because the specific behaviors are within one's control, whereas the outcome is not (e.g., one never knows how instructors will curve the grades).
- The principle of "baby steps" is also important here. Rather than expecting the client to make huge changes immediately, small changes are more likely to be attainable.

By the end of this step, the helper and client should have a good idea of steps the client can take to work on the problem. If the client is eager and cooperative and seems to enjoy doing the behavioral work, the helper can proceed to Step 7. If the client has not gotten engaged in this step, the helper could work with the client to understand the resistance, whether it relates to issues in the therapeutic relationship (e.g., not liking the helper telling the client what to do) or whether it relates more to dynamic issues within the client (e.g., not being ready to give up anger at a parent).

STEP 7: ASSIGN HOMEWORK

Helpers often assign homework so that the client can implement tasks that they have developed in the session. For example, after discussing study skills, a helper might make a contract with a client to study at least

30 minutes a night at his desk, after which he can reinforce himself by getting a soda and calling his girlfriend. In choosing tasks, helpers need to be attentive to choosing tasks that (a) fit the problem, (b) are not difficult to implement, and (c) are based on the client's strengths.

Helpers might also warn clients to "go slow" to prevent too much enthusiastic initial behavior that often results in not being able to sustain the change. Many people enthusiastically say they will make an extreme change (e.g., exercise 3 hours a day) but then get discouraged when they discover how difficult it is to carry out this change. It is better to take too small a step but do it than to overestimate what one can do. To assign tasks, helpers use direct guidance or disclosure of strategies:

- "Based on what we've talked about in the session, I'd like to suggest a couple of things. First, keep a journal for the next week. When you catch yourself chewing your nails, write down what you are feeling so we can try to figure out what's going on there. Also, put a quarter in a jar for each time you're able to stop biting your fingernails and save up for something special that you'd like. What do you think of those two suggestions?"
- "What worked for me when I used to bite my nails was to keep a nail clipper and file close by. When I felt those ragged edges and felt the compulsion to chew, I immediately smoothed the edges. Then I rewarded myself with a quarter. I wonder how that would be with you to try those two things next week?"

In addition to being aware of the types of tasks assigned, it is important for helpers not to be too "bossy." Several studies have shown that clients become resistant and uncooperative if helpers become too directive (Bischoff & Tracey, 1995; Gillespie, 1951; Mahalik, 1994; Patterson & Forgatch, 1985), so helpers need to remember to be collaborative in developing homework assignments with clients. One way to do this is to follow up direct guidance with open questions to see how the client reacts to the direct guidance.

- "What I'd like you to try over the next week is to say hello to one new person each day when you're walking on campus. How would that be for you?"
- "How about doing some more thinking over the week about what you really want to do in the future. You could keep a journal and write in it at least 5 minutes a night. Would that work for you?"

Helpers also need to work with clients to identify potential facilitating and restraining forces in implementing the tasks to avoid failure to complete the assignment. For example, a man thinking about beginning an exercise program in which he walks for 15 minutes each day might identify the restraining forces as the time commitment and weather and the facilitating forces as eventual weight loss and increased self-efficacy.

Furthermore, if the client does not discuss social support as a facilitating or restraining force, it is a good idea to ask specifically about this because other people can be powerful helping and hindering forces. The idea here is to play out the behavior change and see what the roadblocks are to successfully implementing it. To assess the facilitating and restraining forces, the helper can ask open questions:

- "What things would help you in doing the homework?"
- "What things would prevent you from doing the homework?"
- "What kind of social support do you have to help you do the homework?"

Then, helpers can work with the client to figure out ways to manage the restraining forces. For example, the helper can work with the client to help him figure out how to get 15 minutes for exercise and what to do when the weather is bad.

An example of how this step might be implemented involves Charlene, a 30-year-old homemaker, who was depressed, overweight, and out of shape. Through the exploration and insight stages, the helper discovered that Charlene was frustrated about staying home but felt that it was her duty to take care of the children full time. She came to the insight that she thought she should be a stay-at-home mom because she believed that was the only way her husband would love her. She recounted memories of her parents having an awful relationship and her dad resenting her mom for having a successful career. Through helping, she came to understand that she could achieve in a career without destroying her husband. At this point, however, she realized that she had been unemployed outside the home for so long that she did not know how to cope with the world of work. The helper worked with Charlene to devise a plan to get her back in shape physically to gain some confidence. Her homework for the first week was to take a 30-minute walk at least three times with her husband (to lose weight and have some private time with her husband) and to monitor her caloric intake. Once there was some resolution on this problem, the helper and client tackled other problems.

By the end of this step, the client should have chosen some task that he or she can practice outside the session. Of course, some clients might not need outside tasks because it is not appropriate for their problems or because they are not ready to take this step.

STEP 8: CHECK ON PROGRESS AND MODIFY ASSIGNMENTS

Problems almost always arise when clients try to implement actions on their own outside sessions. Changing is often more difficult than anticipated and may include obstacles that were not anticipated. On the basis of experiences clients have had trying out homework in the real world, helpers can work with clients in subsequent sessions to modify homework assignments.

Helpers need to determine what did and did not work for the client in trying to implement the tasks, without judging clients for their efforts, so that modifications can be made to the tasks. If helpers think of themselves as uninvested observers or scientists, they can help clients modify the plans to make them more effective. Rather than becoming angry with clients for not implementing the homework perfectly, helpers might try to view modifications as a natural part of the process. Often clients are not aware of all the barriers in their environment until they try to change, so it is rare to come up with "perfect" assignments right away; most require some modification. Helpers can use open questions to ask about the experience:

- "How did it go last week when you tried to talk to your mother? Tell me exactly what happened."
- "What was it like for you to try to exercise 15 minutes a day?"

Developing effective homework is a process of trial and error because the helper has to figure out what does and does not work for the individual client.

- "Last week we suggested that you study 30 minutes before you took a break, but that seemed like it was too long. What would you think about trying to study for 15 minutes and stopping as soon as you have a hard time concentrating?"
- "So it seems that it did not work so well when you tried to confront your roommate about leaving the dishes unwashed when you were really angry. I wonder if it would be a little easier to talk with her at a time that you're not angry and maybe just say that you want to talk about how to keep the apartment clean?"

Clients can become discouraged with relapses. Brownell, Marlatt, Lichenstein, and Wilson (1986) advocated that a slip or lapse need not lead to a relapse. Helpers can work with clients to help them adopt an attitude of forgiving themselves for lapses and learning from them. For example, when Frank drinks too much at a party after having been sober for 6 months, he might learn that he cannot drink even in moderation. This learning might lead him to take steps to determine how to handle parties in the future. In contrast, if Frank beats himself up too much for the relapse, he will probably feel worse about himself and will not be able to cope productively with the problem, which might lead him right back to the problematic drinking.

Throughout this step, helpers can also give clients feedback about their progress. Reinforcement for what they are doing well provides support and encouragement for clients. Given how hard it is to make changes, it helps to get support. All feedback should be given in a caring manner, be brief and to the point, focus on client behavior rather than personality characteristics, be given in moderate doses so as not to overwhelm the client, and have a balance between positive and negative feedback (Egan, 1994).

- ▪ "You did a really good job recording how many times you yell at your daughter and what provokes you to do it. Now you can start to try to figure out other ways to behave when you get angry."
- ▪ "Congratulations on being able to keep organized this week."
- ▪ "It seems that you had some trouble keeping up your end of the bargain about getting home before curfew several times this week."

By the end of this step (which may take some time), the client should have had some success implementing the change process for one particular problem. The helper and client will then have to decide if helping is over or if they want to go back and tackle another problem. In either event, it is a good time for the helper and client to evaluate how they feel about what has gone on so far.

EXAMPLE OF STEPS FOR BEHAVIOR CHANGE

In this example, the helper has already explored with Sam his feelings about his recent diagnosis of terminal cancer. They have come to the insight that his depression over the diagnosis is due to feelings that he has not yet lived fully. They have traced his passivity back to his having controlling parents who told him how to live his life. Sam now recognizes that no matter what his childhood was like, he is the one responsible for the rest of his life and he cannot blame anyone else.

Readers should note that this example is meant to illustrate how the steps can work. Of course, each situation is different, and it will not always go so smoothly for each helper who tries this out. In addition, sometimes there is not enough time to go through all the steps in one session, so this process gets divided into several sessions.

Helper: So what specifically would you like to work on changing? (Step 1)

Client: I want to change my lifestyle, but I am not certain how to do that.

Helper: What do you mean by that?

Client: I want to change my priorities in terms of how I spend my time.

Helper: You've been talking about how you would like the remainder of your life to be different. What would it mean for you to make changes at this time? (Step 2)

Client: It would be scary because I've been resistant and angry and blaming my parents for so long, but I want to try.

Helper: You sound sure about wanting to change.

Client: Yeah, I am, even though it's going to be tough. Maybe if I take it slowly, it will be easier. But I don't have much time left, so I want to get started.

Helper: Okay, well, let's take the issues one at a time. First, you indicated that you want to have more meaningful relationships. What have you tried in the past? (Step 3)

Client: Well, I'm pretty shy. It's not easy for me to make friends. I never joined groups or clubs or anything. I guess I hoped that people would come to me. My parents always pushed people on me, so I never took an active role in making friends. I don't need a lot of friends. I would be more interested in having two or three close friends—people I could really count on.

Helper: You sound like you know yourself pretty well.

Client: Yeah, I've thought a lot about myself and these issues.

Helper: Okay, let's brainstorm how you might go about making some new friends. What ideas do you have? (Step 4)

Client: I thought about joining a cancer support group. There would be people there who are going through the same thing I am and would understand me. Also, my neighbor suggested that there's a poker game starting with a bunch of guys in the building. It's only once a month, but I like playing poker. I always wanted to do something like that, but I thought I should be working. Oh, I just remembered that a person who I used to be friends with in college moved back to town. Maybe I could get together with him.

Helper: Those sound like terrific ideas. Which ones are most appealing? (Step 5)

Client: Actually, I think I could easily do all of them. The cancer support group is once a week, and it's not far away. The poker game is only once a month. And I've been meaning to call my friend anyway. So that doesn't seem like too much at all. I definitely want to do those things.

Helper: Terrific. I like your enthusiasm. Let's just pick one right now to talk about it in more depth. (Step 6)

Client: Okay, we can focus on the cancer support group first.

Helper: So tell me about it.

Client: The group is at a local hospital. I think there are 8 to 10 people in it, and all of them have had cancer and are recovering.

Helper: What would be the most difficult part about going?

Client: I won't know anyone.

Helper: What might you say to yourself to help you with that?

Client: I might say that they don't have to become my best friends. I just need to talk to some people who are experiencing the same things as I am.

Helper: Would that help?

Client: A little bit, but I think I might still have some trouble making myself go to it.

Helper: Can you think of what you might do to reinforce yourself for going?

Client: Maybe if I go to the group, I could stop afterward and get a coffee.

Helper: Would that be a good motivator?

Client: Yeah, I think it would.

Helper: Could we then set up a deal where you go to the cancer support group this next week? (Step 7)

Client: I think this would be reasonable. I'm kind of looking forward to it.

[Next session]

Helper: How did it go when you went to the cancer support group? (Step 8)

Client: I went, and it was okay, but I didn't really feel comfortable. Everyone was a lot younger than me.

Helper: That's too bad because you were looking forward to it.

Client: Yeah, I'm a little disappointed. But I heard about a different group that's supposed to have more older people. I think I might try that.

Helper: How did it work with telling yourself that the people don't have to become your best friends?

Client: That worked pretty well. I also told myself that I didn't have to go back if I didn't like it, and that helped. But what really helped was getting myself the coffee afterward. In fact, I went into the coffee shop and met up with a person I had gone to college with and we had a good talk. So that turned out really well.

> Helper: Okay, so what can you take out of this with you?
> Client: I think I've just got to get out there and try different things. I'm definitely going to try this other support group. And maybe I'll hang out at the coffeeshop too—they have Internet connections so maybe I could just spend some time there and see what happens.

Behavioral Rehearsal

Behavioral rehearsal (also called *role-playing*) is used to help clients learn new ways of responding to specific life situations (Goldfried & Davison, 1994). Rather than talking about behavior changes in the helping setting, helpers teach clients new behaviors through acting-out situations in which the behaviors could be used. Because problems with assertiveness are common, I illustrate interventions designed to increase assertive behaviors. Note of course that behavioral rehearsal can be used for other concerns (e.g., rehearsing for a job interview).

According to Alberti and Emmons (2001), the goal of assertiveness training is to teach clients to stand up for their rights without infringing on the rights of others. Unassertive people let others walk all over them, whereas aggressive people walk all over other people. Both unassertive and aggressive people can be taught to express positive and negative feelings more appropriately, although one cannot guarantee that clients get their way when they assert themselves. In fact, aggressive people who are used to getting their way are not likely to respond favorably to a previously unassertive person acting assertively. Hence, helpers also have to assist clients in thinking not only of how to present an initial, empathic, assertive statement but also then of how to respond assertively to escalated aggressiveness.

Do not rush through these steps. It is usually helpful to encourage the client to explore a lot in each step.

STEP 1: ASSESS THE ACTUAL BEHAVIOR IN A SPECIFIC SITUATION

After more general exploration in which a problem with assertiveness is revealed, the helper asks the client to describe a specific example of when the problem occurred and then role-play exactly how she or he behaved (with the helper playing the role of the other person). It is a good idea to choose a specific example (e.g., the last time it happened) so that the client can relate specifically what went on in that instance. For example, a client might present with extreme awkwardness and unassertiveness in interactions with interesting men. The helper can role-play a specific situation in which the client recently met an attractive man at a party. The helper should observe the client's behavior (e.g., eye contact, voice volume, statement of needs, attitude), although the helper should not comment on these behaviors at this point. Helpers can ask clients for self-evaluations of how assertive they were and how they felt in the situation to help clients begin to look inward and evaluate their behavior. The helper can also ask the client to describe various things he or she has tried in similar situations.

STEP 2: DETERMINE GOALS

Helpers work with clients to determine specific goals of how they would like to behave differently (e.g., make one comment during class discussion) given that clients are much more likely to make changes when they have specific, clear goals than if goals are vague. To construct goals, helpers and clients can generate different possible behaviors and determine which behaviors would feel comfortable to clients. There is no "right" way to be assertive, so this step is crucial in devising goals that clients can embrace. For example, one female client might want to learn how to ask an interesting man for a date, whereas another would not find this action desirable.

During this step, it is helpful to talk about the client's values because values influence goals (e.g., a woman may not feel comfortable approaching a man for a date). It also can be helpful to talk about rights (e.g., to privacy, to self-determination), which are of course influenced by values and culture. In addition, it is important to help clients explore the possible consequences of their goals (e.g., they might get their way but lose a friend). It may be helpful here to do thought-showering to think about various possible goals and helper disclosure may be useful to provide goals if the client is stuck.

STEP 3: PROVIDE A MODEL

Once the target behavior is determined, helpers can reverse roles with clients and provide a model of how clients could implement the new behaviors (e.g., the helper could show how she would ask an instructor for an extension of a deadline because of a documented illness). Once the role-play is done, the helper can ask the client how it would be for him or her to try to do it that way. In the basis of the feedback, the helper can try role-playing it again to get it closer to the way that the client would feel comfortable trying to do the behavior.

Helpers should start with relatively easy behaviors first (e.g., questioning a clerk in a store) rather than major behaviors (e.g., asking for a raise) to maximize the possibility of success. In the previous example, the client might first work on initiating a conversation with a man in class and work up to asking him out on a date.

STEP 4: DO ANOTHER ROLE-PLAY AND PROVIDE FEEDBACK/COACHING

Helpers then can ask clients to try the chosen behavior in a role-play, again observing the client's behavior carefully. After the role-play, helpers should provide honest positive feedback ("You did a really good job of using eye contact and of stating your needs"). Even if the positive feedback is about something minor, clients need to feel that they are doing something well and making some progress. Helpers then can give corrective feedback about one or two specific things, remembering the behavioral principle of working on small, manageable steps.

Helpers may also provide some coaching about what clients could try differently in the next role-play (e.g., "Okay, say it louder and with more conviction this time"). Using videotape feedback, if available, can be invaluable because clients may be unaware of how they are perceived. Role-plays may need to be done several times until the client feels confident that she or he can perform the desired behaviors. During the role-plays, helpers may also discover that they need to do relaxation training or cognitive restructuring with clients to overcome obstacles to change.

One major principle that helpers can think about in providing feedback is to encourage clients to be empathic with the other person. By thinking about the other person's feelings, clients are more likely to present themselves more compellingly (e.g., "I know you would really like to talk with me right now, but I can't do it now. Can we set up a time to talk tomorrow?").

Another principle is that it is often better not to apologize a lot because apologies invite the other person to find solutions. Hence, rather than saying, "I'm so sorry that I can't go to lunch right now because I've got to run errands and do a million things but maybe another time," the person might say, "I'm sorry that I won't be able to go to lunch right now."

Another helpful technique is to be a "broken record" and keep repeating yourself when the other person doesn't listen. For example, if you are saving a seat for someone in a theater and another person tries to take the seat, you might say, "I'm sorry, but this seat is saved." When they try to debate with you, you continue saying, "I'm sorry, this seat is saved."

STEPS 5 AND 6: ASSIGN HOMEWORK AND MODIFY ON THE BASIS OF EXPERIENCES

These steps are the same as in the previous section in this chapter on behavior change.

EXAMPLE OF STEPS FOR BEHAVIORAL REHEARSAL

This example is a continuation of the helping session with Sam, the client we met in the last section on behavior change. After the helper and Sam talked about his progress with joining the cancer support group, Sam said:

Client: One other thing, though. I would like to have a good relationship with a woman before I die. I wonder, you know, I've been thinking a lot about my ex-wife lately. I think that a lot of the problems in our marriage were due to my passivity and never having resolved things with my parents. Now that I have some understanding of my relationship with my parents, I think I could be different with my ex-wife. I realize now that she is not my mother. She does have some quirks, but I do still care for her.

Helper: How would you feel about checking whether she's still available and interested? (Step 1)

Client: I know that she's not with anybody because of what my daughter says. If I got back together with my ex-wife, I could also spend more time with my daughter, which is something I really want to do.

Helper: It sounds like that might work. But I need to caution you that things might not be so smooth given all the past history that you and she had. You were very passive and might still have a tendency to fall into those behaviors. Perhaps we could work on some assertiveness training to help you stand up to her better and say what's on your mind.

Client: That would be helpful. Could we begin today?

Helper: Sure, give me an example of a recent situation with your ex-wife in which you were passive and you wished that you had behaved differently.

Client: She might say something like she thinks I ought to be spending more time with our daughter. She gets mad that I don't take more responsibility. She has her ideas of exactly what I should be doing and doesn't mince words. Yesterday she called and wanted to know exactly what I planned to do about the babysitting situation. I just said I didn't know, I hadn't really thought about it, and I was really busy right then. I felt irritated that she was bringing it up and was so bossy that I shut down and wouldn't give her any satisfaction.

Helper: Okay, let's role-play to get a clear idea of what happened. I'll be your ex-wife, and you be you. I want you first to role-play exactly what you did in the situation. So, I'm your ex-wife. [as ex-wife] Sam, I want you to take more responsibility for our daughter. I just can't handle it all. I'm working full time, and I can't be the one to take off for everything. I'm going to lose my job if I keep taking off every time she gets sick or needs to go to the doctor. You know that the day-care center won't let her come if she has even the slightest sniffle. Plus, she needs to see her father more. She needs to have you around.

Client: (whines) Well, I just can't do more right now. I'm so busy at school.

Helper: OK, let's stop there. What are you aware of feeling?

Client: I felt resentful. She's bossing me around again, and I don't like it. She's right, of course, that I ought to spend more time taking my share of the burden, but as soon as she starts up, I just don't want to do anything. I hear my mother's voice nagging me, and I shut down.

Helper: That's great, you can really identify what's going on inside you. And did you notice your tone of voice?

Client: Not really. I didn't notice anything.

Helper: You sounded totally different from before. You actually started whining. Before, in talking with me, you were talking like an adult, but as soon as you role-played talking with your ex-wife, you sounded like a whiny child (illustrates).

Client: Wow, that's incredible. That's exactly what I do with my mother. I can't believe that it came out so quickly without my awareness. And you played it exactly the way my ex-wife does—so bossy and controlling. I hate it when we get into these power struggles. Neither of us wins. But I can see how she feels that she has no choice but to get bossy and controlling when I get so passive and withdrawn.

Helper: Now what would you like to say to her instead? (Step 2)

Client: I would like to say that she's right and that we need to work out a schedule because I really want to do my part. I want to spend more time with my daughter— that's really not a chore. But I wish she wouldn't treat me like a child. Perhaps if we could work on this like two equal adults, we could resolve this problem. I recognize my side of it, but she's got to see what she's doing too.

Helper: That sounds great. Let's try it out here. Say this to her. (Step 4—note that Step 3 was skipped because the client did not seem to need a model)

Client: [to ex-wife] I really want to make this work. Could we set up a schedule?

Helper: [as ex-wife] Well, I don't know if I trust you.

Client: [to ex-wife] I've done a lot of work, and I'm beginning to see my side of the problem. I can't promise that I will be perfect, but I do want to try.

Helper: [as ex-wife] OK, let's try, but I'm cautious about how this is going to work.

Client: [to ex-wife] I'm cautious too, but I think it's worth it to try. Perhaps we could go for some couples counseling to get some help?

Helper: [as ex-wife] Sounds like a really good idea. [as helper] How was that for you?

Client: Good. I liked how it went. Thank you.

Helper: You were terrific. You sounded firm but not nasty. You weren't whiny. You sounded more in control of the situation, and I believed that you wanted to work it out with her. I think if I were your ex-wife, I would be willing to talk with you rationally. Do you think that you could do this with her?

Client: I think I could. I would have to overcome a lot of past experiences with her. But I think I could do that. I want to because I want things to change.

Helper: Well, you were able to do it here, so I have confidence that you could be assertive with her. One thing that might help is if you took a deep breath before you say anything to her. Think about what you want to say, what you want to accomplish. Remind yourself that you are an adult and that she's not your mother.

Client: Yeah, I think that would work. If I told her ahead of time what I was trying to do, she would be very understanding. She often has said that we get tangled up in these situations that we can't seem to resolve. I think she knows that she gets bossy and doesn't want to but just feels really frustrated with the situation.

Helper: Let's role-play it one more time to make sure you have it down. Again, I'm your ex-wife. [as ex-wife] Sam, I want you to take more responsibility for our daughter. I want you to spend more time with her and help me out more when she needs to go to the doctor. I can't keep taking off work every time she needs to be taken out of day care (pause). Now remember to take a deep breath, Sam, and think about what you want to say to her.

Client: You know, you're absolutely right to be angry at me. I haven't done my share in the past, and I want to start doing my share now. But we need to step back and talk about how you and I are going to handle this situation. I want to quit acting like the bad child and forcing you to play the nagging mother to increase my involvement with our daughter. I'd like us to work on this like equal adults because I want us to have a better relationship.

Helper: That's great. You didn't have any whine in your voice. You assertively told her what you would like to happen rather than blaming her.

Client: Thanks, it felt good. I might have to practice it a couple more times, but I liked how it felt. I think it would work with her too.

Helper: Unfortunately, we are almost out of time for today. But I wanted to check in with you about how you felt about the ideas we came up with for you to make some changes.

Client: I am really excited because I think this is something I can try. I feel hopeful about being able to have a better relationship with her.

Helper: So you think you'll be able to try this out with your wife? (Step 5)

Client: Yes, I definitely will.

Helper: Great. Try it out and let's talk next week about how it went. We can see if we need to make any changes in the plan then after we see how it goes.

[Next session]

Helper: So how did it go this last week when you tried to talk with your ex-wife? (Step 6)

Client: Well, some good, some bad. The part that worked was I did say what we practiced.

Helper: Terrific. Way to go.

Client: But the part that didn't go so good was that she didn't respond positively, and then I slipped back into the same old patterns.

Helper: That often happens. So let's do some problem solving. What might you do make that better? (continues)

Decision Making

Clients often have major life decisions to make: which job to take, whether to go to graduate school, whether it is best to buy a house or rent an apartment, whether to get married, or how to care for an ailing parent. In decision making, helpers work with clients to help them articulate their options, explore their values, and evaluate the options according to their values (Carkhuff, 1973).

STEP 1: ARTICULATE THE OPTIONS

The helper first asks the client to explore the issue and the background and then to articulate the various options. As an example, let us consider that the helper is working with a middle-aged teacher, Bess, who is trying to plan her future. Bess states that she has several options she has been considering: She and her husband could retire at 55, sell their house, and travel around the country in a recreational vehicle; she could wait until 65 to retire and then get involved in volunteer activities; she could keep teaching indefinitely since there is no mandatory retirement age in her job. As Bess is talking, the helper makes a grid and records the options along the top with one option in each column (see Exhibit 16.2). Note that sometimes it takes a fair amount of exploration

---

EXHIBIT 16.2

Example of Bess's Decision-Making Chart

	Option		
	---	---	---
Value	**Retire at 55 and tour country**	**Retire at 65 and volunteer**	**Stay at same job indefinitely**
Travel (5)	+3 (15)	+1 (5)	−2 (−10)
Intellectual stimulation (9)	−3 (−27)	+1 (9)	+3 (27)
Time with spouse (7)	2 (14)	+1 (7)	−2 (−14)
Friends (2)	+1 (2)	+1 (2)	−1 (−2)
Money (5)	−3 (−15)	+1 (5)	+3 (15)
Being near children (1)	−2 (−20)	+2 (20)	+2 (20)
Meaning of life (8)	0 (0)	+1 (8)	+2 (16)
Total	−29	54	52

Note. The number in parentheses after each of the values is the weighting of that value (range is 1 to 10, where 10 = the greatest weighting). The numbers in the columns are the ratings of each option on the particular value (range from −3 to +3, where +3 = the highest rating). The number in the parentheses after the rating for each option is the multiplicative value of the rating by the weighting of the value (e.g., +3 × 5 for the option of retiring at 55 for the value of traveling).

for all these options to emerge, and clients sometimes add or modify options as they go through the steps.

STEP 2: VALUES CLARIFICATION

Next, the helper asks the client to generate no more than 10 relevant values, desires, or needs related to this topic. Through considerable exploration, Bess says that the important considerations for her are that she wants to travel, she likes to be intellectually stimulated, she wants to spend time with her husband, she wants more time to be with friends, she wants to have enough money to be comfortable, she wants to feel that she is doing something meaningful with her life, and she wants to be near her children, especially when they have grandchildren. The helper writes values in rows of the grid.

The helper then asks the client to weight the importance of each consideration (1 = *not important,* 10 = *extremely important*). Bess says that intellectual stimulation is her most important value and gives it a weight of 9, whereas she ranks having time to spend with friends at the bottom of her list and gives it a weight of 2. Each weight can be used only once so that the client is forced to figure out priorities.

STEP 3: RATE THE OPTIONS BASED ON THE VALUES

The goal in this step is to evaluate all the options based on the values. Using a scale of −3 to +3 (−3, −2, −1, 0, +1, +2, +3), the helper asks the client to rate the various options on each of the values and also to discuss the reasons for the ratings. For example, Bess says that retiring at 55 would get a +3 on travel because they would be touring the country, but she rates retirement at 55 a −3 on intellectual stimulation because she would not be teaching any longer and probably would not be doing as much reading and talking with others about ideas.

The next step is to multiply the rating for the option by the weight for the value and then add up the scores for each option. For Bess, the options of retiring at 65 and working indefinitely both received the highest total scores, indicating that she preferred these two options to the other option. The process of putting numbers on feelings was valuable because it helped Bess be more concrete and sort through her feelings.

STEP 4: EVALUATE THE RESULTS AND REVISE THE WEIGHTINGS

The goal here is to look at the results and see how they fit for the client. Thus, the helper asked Bess what she thought about these results. When Bess looked at the total scores for each option, she realized that the scores were not reflective of what she truly wanted. In fact, she realized that traveling and having free time were indeed more important than she had thought, so she changed her ratings. Sometimes people change their options and their values at this point because they have a clearer idea of these. At this point, it might also be helpful to do some problem solving to figure out how to make the options more appealing. It might also be helpful to use behavioral rehearsal or a two-chair technique to help the client think through the various options.

STEP 5: FOLLOW UP

It is important for helpers to come back and check in with clients about their feelings. In the case of Bess, the helper asked her reactions during the next session. Bess replied that she had gone home and talked with her husband. Together they began to make some plans for retirement. They also decided to they needed to do some financial planning to ensure that they had enough money for retirement.

Some clients really like this systematic method of decision making, whereas others get annoyed by all the numbers and prefer a more intuitive approach. Obviously, helpers will want to use decision making only if the client seems to like this type of structured approach.

What Do You Think?

- How do the action steps fit for you?
- How do you know when to move from one action step to another? How do you know when you have spent enough time in each of the steps?
- How should helpers decide which action possibilities to pursue for clients?
- What do you think is going on when clients say "Yes, but . . ." frequently?
- How can you tell the difference between client resistance to change and the helper's lack of competence in progressing through the action steps?
- In what instances and with what clients do you think specific interventions (e.g., relaxation training, systematic desensitization) would be useful?

i LAB 12. Steps of the Action Stage

A downloadable PDF of this Lab is available in the student resources area of the Helping Skills, *3rd ed. Web site: http://www.apa.org/books/resources/Hill3.*

Goal: To teach helpers about how to do the steps of the action stage for two types of action.

Exercise 1: Behavior Change

Divide into groups of four to six people, with one person taking the role of the client. The other people will alternate in the role of helper. A lab leader should direct the flow of the session. Helpers are encouraged to bring in a sheet outlining the steps (Exhibit 16.1) so that they remember what to do in each step.

Helper's and Client's Tasks During the Helping Exchange

1. Clients should talk about something that they understand at least somewhat and that they want to change (e.g., increasing amount of study or exercise).
2. Helper 1 should ask the client to explore (using primarily open questions, restatements, and reflections of feelings) for about 5 to 10 minutes.
3. Helper 2 should then take over and do the insight stage for 5 to 10 minutes. The helper should intersperse challenges, interpretations, disclosures, and immediacy with open questions, restatements, and reflections of feelings (thinking carefully first about his or her intentions).
4. When the client has gained some insight, Helper 3 should take over and do Step 1 (identifying the problem) with the client.
5. Helper 4 should do Step 2 (exploring action) with the client.
6. Helper 5 should do Step 3 (assessing situation) with the client.
7. Helper 6 should do Step 4 (generating options) with the client.
8. Helper 7 should do Step 5 (evaluating options) with the client.
9. Helper 8 should do Step 6 (choosing an option) with the client. Remember to explore values related to the different options and to examine the restraining and facilitating forces for each action.
10. Helper 9 should do Step 7 (assigning homework) with the client. When helpers have trouble with this step, the lab leader can prompt them about what to do or another helper can take over.
11. Helper 10 should do Step 8 (checking progress) with the client.

Processing the Helping Exchange

The client can talk about what the experience was like and which steps were most helpful. The helpers can talk about how they felt trying to do the different steps. The lab leader can give specific behavioral feedback about the helpers' skills during the different steps.

Exercise 2: Decision Making

Using the same format as in Exercise 1, the group does decision making.

Personal Reflections

- What are your strengths and areas that need improvement in terms of doing the action steps?
- Were you able to maintain empathy with the client while going through the steps?
- How comfortable are you with implementing the four types of action (relaxation training, behavior change, behavioral rehearsal, decision making)?
- How could you apply the behavioral principles to improve your skills as a helper?
- Which skills (e.g., probes for action, direct guidance) of the action stage were easier or more difficult for you to use?

Integrating the Skills of the Action Stage   17

Ideal teachers are those who use themselves as bridges over which they invite their students to cross, then having facilitated their crossing, joyfully collapse, encouraging them to create bridges of their own.

—Leo Buscaglia

Tako came into therapy feeling vague dissatisfaction in his marriage and work. He worked long hours and felt that he was not very connected with his wife. Working with his helper, he explored his desire to change his lifestyle. In the insight stage, he came to understand that he worked too much because of cultural demands about providing for his family and achieving. In the action stage, Tako decided that he wanted to have a better relationship with his wife. He and his helper brainstormed several ways that Tako could make changes.

In initial sessions, helpers may focus completely on exploration and insight, with only minimal attention to action (depending on client needs). If action is approached in initial sessions, it is usually brief and focused on exploring the possibility of changing, helping clients think about whether and what they want to change, or if they want to return for another session. In later sessions, the focus of the action stage moves to discussing and choosing specific action plans, evaluating the positive and negative consequences of changes the client has tried to make, making modifications in action plans, and planning for termination of the helping relationship.

The action stage is often challenging for beginning helpers, who tend either to avoid action in favor of being empathic and insightful or become overly directive and authoritarian while neglecting their empathic skills. Leaving enough time for action can also be difficult for beginning helpers who have trouble with time management in managing sessions.

Action is also difficult for many clients. Demoralization and hopelessness are major hurdles that clients must overcome before they can change (Frank & Frank, 1991). Clients often feel discouraged or defeated about their ability to change because of negative experiences with past attempts. Accordingly, helpers might encourage clients to take "baby steps" (i.e., make small changes such as 15 minutes of walking) and explore the idea of change first, while recognizing how hard it is to change.

Although the action stage presents many challenges for both helpers and clients, helpers should not neglect helping clients make changes in their lives. They do, however, need to approach the action stage with appropriate caution, self-awareness, and empathy for their clients.

Integrating the Action Skills

It is difficult to make changes, so clients need empathy, support, and encouragement from helpers throughout the entire action stage, even if they decide not to change or have only accomplished one small step toward their goals. Clients need to feel that helpers are on their side. In addition, clients appreciate knowing that their helpers are benevolent coaches or guides rather than harsh parents or dictators.

NEED FOR FLEXIBILITY

Flexibility and creativity are critical in the action stage. I presented the steps for the four types of action in a clear-cut linear manner in the previous chapter so students can learn them easily. But in practice, these steps are rarely implemented in such a straightforward manner, and the four types are not so easily distinguished. Helpers need to learn the steps for all four types and then modify them to fit the needs of the client.

If one intervention does not work, helpers need to try something else. If several interventions are unsuccessful or the client continually says, "Yes, but . . ." in response to interventions, helpers might explore how clients feel about the therapeutic relationship or the process of change. Helpers also can use insight skills to help clients understand their resistance to change.

Furthermore, when clients implement changes in the real world, things rarely go as planned. Clients need to be prepared for disappointment or for others not responding well to their changes. It can be useful for helpers to prepare clients for such disappointment.

NEED TO REMAIN HUMBLE ABOUT THE DIFFICULTIES IN CHANGING

Changing is hard, and people are very complicated. Helpers need to remember that carrying out action ideas is not easy. If it were easy, clients would have already implemented the ideas. All of us sometimes have a fantasy about the wizard who will be able to tell us what to do. But taking over for clients has the potential of undermining their efficacy and self-healing potential.

It can also be useful for helpers to recall that the problems clients bring in are real and that their suggestions can have major consequences. For example, if a client is asking for help about whether she should tell her father about dating someone of another race, the helper needs to be sensitive that advice to be open and honest might have adverse consequences (e.g., the client being disowned). This concern speaks to the helper being cautious about exploring carefully the full context before rushing to action.

Remembering how difficult it is to make changes in our own lives can assist helpers in being empathic with clients who are struggling with changing. Helpers also need to remember that clients developed their problems over many years; changing ingrained patterns is difficult.

MULTICULTURAL CONSIDERATIONS

Some clients want and expect a lot of action and direction from their helpers, whom they perceive as authorities or wise people (Pedersen, Draguns, Lonner, & Trimble, 2002). If helpers do not focus on action, these clients might lose respect for the helper and the helping process. Such clients may get frustrated if helpers do not tell them what to do.

Another multicultural consideration is that helpers may need to incorporate spirituality into the action stage (e.g., using prayer as an action strategy) for clients for whom spirituality and religion are important issues (Fukuyama & Sevig, 2002). If helpers are not responsive to such needs, clients may feel disrespected and may devalue the helping process. But because spirituality is a sensitive topic, helpers might wait to pick up clues from clients whether they would like a focus on spirituality. And of course helpers should only work with spirituality if they feel that they can do so authentically.

Finally, helpers need to be aware of barriers to action faced by clients from other cultures. For example, clients who are poor may not have transportation, child care, or access to public services. Clients who are immigrants often face discrimination and language problems. Clients who are elderly and infirm may not be able to leave their houses. Asian clients may not want to go outside the family for help or may not know how to change in a way that respects and incorporates the family's needs. Helpers need to be aware of such cultural considerations, ask clients about possible barriers, and be sensitive to different needs.

Difficulties Helpers Might Experience in the Action Stage

There are a number of difficulties that helpers experience in the action stage.

MOVING TOO QUICKLY TO ACTION

Some helpers rush to action before they have established a firm enough foundation of exploration and insight. They might feel impatient with the long process of exploration and insight; they might feel that they "know" what the client should do; they might feel compelled to "do" something for the client. Unfortunately, when helpers move too quickly to action, clients often are resistant, not attuned with the helper, unable to take responsibility for their changes, or unmotivated to make changes. Helpers need to remember to spend the majority of their time in exploration to establish the foundation for insight and action.

If information or advice is provided before clients are ready for it, clients might not be able to use it. For example, some volunteers in battered women's shelters provide information to the women about how to make it on their own when the women first come in. At this point, the women more often need to explore their feelings about being in an abusive relationship. They are not ready yet to use information, no matter how helpful or well intentioned it is.

Some helpers move to action before they know enough about the client's situation. They might jump quickly to a solution before exploring the complexity of the situation. It can appear disparaging to clients for helpers to jump to quick solutions and imply that they were inept for not knowing how to solve such simple problems. If problems were so simple, clients would have solved them on their own.

NEEDING TO BE THE EXPERT

Providing information and giving advice gratify some helpers' needs to be viewed as the expert. Some helpers like being perceived as "knowing it all" and enjoy having clients admire them. These helpers might be trying to look like the experts at the expense of encouraging clients to seek out their own information and make their own decisions. Other helpers might embrace the role of expert because they want to assist clients, and they believe that helpers should provide all the answers and give lots of helpful information to clients. Both types of helpers do a disservice in neglecting the client's role in the information-generating process. Although helpers might know more about helping than their clients do, they do not know more than clients about clients' inner experiences or what actions clients should implement.

TOO MUCH INVESTMENT IN THE CLIENT CHANGING

Perhaps the major clinical issue that arises in the action stage is the helper becoming too invested in the client changing. Some helpers feel so responsible for developing action plans that they try to make decisions for the client. They feel that things would be much easier if clients just did what they were told to do. However, taking over for clients is typically counterproductive (except in extreme cases of suicidal or homicidal ideation or intent) because clients become dependent and do not develop the skills needed to make changes in the future. In addition, what might work for the helper might not work for the client. Furthermore, if helpers become too invested in what they think clients should do, it is difficult for helpers to listen supportively and objectively to clients. Hence, helpers generally need to be uninvested (but not uncaring) in what action the client chooses (or does not choose). Helpers must allow clients to make their own decisions and should serve as guides and supporters rather than as bosses.

IMPOSING ONE'S VALUES ON CLIENTS

Sometimes helpers lose sight of trying to help clients uncover their values and instead impose their own beliefs and values on clients. It can be difficult for helpers to accept that clients have different values, especially when the values differ significantly from the helper's cherished beliefs. For example, a client dying of a terminal illness might want to talk about the possibility of suicide. If helpers are rigid about the value of life, they might not allow clients to explore the possibility of suicide, thus limiting the client's ability to contemplate all the options thoroughly and make an informed decision. In another example, a helper might tell a client to smile more because he wants all women to appear happy. Helpers always need to be attentive to their own issues and needs and try to minimize their effect on clients.

NOT BEING BOLD ENOUGH IN ENCOURAGING CLIENTS TO MAKE CHANGES

Helpers may not challenge clients enough to make changes. Some helpers are worried about intruding on their clients and, thus, do not encourage them to change. They believe it is not their place to challenge. Although clients need to be the ones who choose to change, helpers can encourage and challenge clients when they are stuck and struggling.

In addition, helpers are sometimes nervous about challenging clients because they are not sure what to do to help clients. In this case, I suggest that these helpers study the action skills carefully and practice (use the exercises in the book and practice with peers).

NOT BEING SUPPORTIVE ENOUGH

Sometimes helpers become so involved in developing the action plan during this stage that they forget to be supportive. Encouragement and reinforcement are crucial both for actual change and for efforts to change. I suspect that when helpers remember aspects of their lives that are difficult to change, they may be more sympathetic to clients who have difficulty changing.

GETTING STUCK ON ONE ACTION IDEA

Helpers often remain committed to action ideas that they have developed, even when it is clear that these ideas are inappropriate and clients cannot or will not follow them. Perhaps these helpers have spent a lot of time thinking about what their clients should do and have become very invested in the action plans. However, helpers need to realize that helping requires flexibility, and that action ideas often require adjustment because helpers and clients are not aware of all the problems that can arise. They need to select and keep the parts of the action plans that work and revise the parts that do not.

ADHERING TOO RIGIDLY TO THE STEPS

Helpers who follow the action steps in chapter 16 precisely will probably feel frustrated because the exact sequence of steps will not apply to every client. These steps are provided so that students can see a structure of how to proceed through the action stage. Helpers will need to learn and practice the steps as presented but then use their creativity and flexibility to modify the procedures for themselves and the individual client. This stage allows for incredible flexibility as helpers try to creatively work with individual clients to help them.

Strategies for Overcoming the Difficulties

There are a number of strategies that helpers can use to manage the difficulties.

SELF-REFLECTION

When helpers get trapped in any of the pitfalls (moving too quickly to action, becoming too invested in clients' changing, imposing their values on clients, not being challenging enough, not being supportive enough, or getting stuck on one plan), they might spend some time reflecting and hypothesizing about what caused them to have problems. If helpers discover that they get overly invested or use a lot of direct guidance across several clients and clients are reacting with resistance, helpers need to look inward to understand themselves so they do not harm clients. Consulting with peers, seeking personal therapy, and receiving supervision are all helpful methods for learning more about oneself. In addition, helpers can go back and use the management strategies suggested in chapter 8 for dealing with anxiety (e.g., relaxation, imagery, positive self-talk, focus on the client).

USE EXPLORATION SKILLS

When an impasse or problem arises in the action stage, it is often helpful to return to cultivating an empathic attitude and using the exploration skills (open questions, restatement, and reflection). The helper needs to try to understand what is going on with the client at this particular time. When clients feel misunderstood, helpers also need to rebuild trust and reassure clients that helpers can listen to and collaborate with them.

DEAL WITH PROBLEMS IN THE THERAPEUTIC RELATIONSHIP

Helpers can ask clients how they are feeling about what is going on in the helping relationship, particularly when they have reached an impasse, defined by Elkind (1992) as a deadlock or stalemate that causes helping to become so difficult that progress is not possible. Using immediacy to deal with the relationship and resolve problems is particularly crucial (see chap. 12). Helpers need to listen for feedback from clients and be willing to hear how they might improve their work with their clients. If appropriate for the helping situation, helpers can talk about their own immediate feelings (without burdening clients with their personal problems). Acknowledging their part in the problems in helping relationships (e.g., apologizing if they have made a mistake) can be therapeutically beneficial. Helpers also can thank clients for sharing their feelings and working hard to make positive changes in their lives.

What Do You Think?

- Which of the following obstacles do you anticipate that you are most likely to experience in using the action skills?
  _____ moving too quickly to action
  _____ needing to be the expert
  _____ being too invested in clients' changes
  _____ imposing one's values on clients
  _____ not encouraging enough change
  _____ not being supportive
  _____ getting stuck on one action idea
  _____ adhering too rigidly to the steps
- Which strategies would work to help you cope with the obstacles in the action stage?
  _____ self-reflection
  _____ address issues related to the therapeutic relationship
  _____ consultation with supervisors, peers, or teachers
  _____ return to exploration skills

INTEGRATION | V

Integrating the Three Stages 18

*And the time came when the risk to remain tight in a bud was
more painful than the risk it took to blossom.*

—*Anaïs Nin*

In this final chapter, I discuss putting all the skills together to
work in a session with a client. Once again, I would note that
it is important to learn the individual skills to make sure you
have the ability to use each one, and then you can put these
components together.

Session Management

There is no "right" way to implement the helping model.
Each helper has a different style, and each client has different
needs and unique reactions. It is not possible to provide an
exact road map or cookbook for helpers. Thus, once helpers
have learned how to deliver the specific skills, they need to
develop their own style and integrate helping skills into their
way of being. Helpers also need to apply the scientific method
to each helping interaction (e.g., observe what does and does
not work in each situation and modify behaviors accordingly). Being open to feedback from clients, teachers, and
supervisors is an excellent way to improve one's skills.

FIRST SESSIONS

There are a number of things to think about in the first session. Helpers need to start the session, establish goals, clarify expectations, develop a focus, and end the session.

Beginning

Helpers begin the initial session by providing information about the helping process. First, the helper explains the process (e.g., "We are going to be spending 30 minutes together, and our goal is to help you explore whatever topic you would like to address"). Helpers can also briefly self-disclose about facts or credentials to educate clients about their background as helpers (e.g., "I am a beginning helper"), especially if clients ask for such information. Helpers should also inform clients at the beginning of the session if they will be recorded, observed live, or supervised (e.g., "I will be recording this session, and my supervisor is watching through that one-way mirror"), and the disposition of any tape recordings ("All recordings will be erased as soon as my supervisor listens to them").

Helpers often tell clients about some of the rules (e.g., length of sessions, cost) at the beginning of the initial session. They inform clients about other rules as the need arises (e.g., when clients ask for information that is too personal, the helper might explain why he or she chooses not to divulge such information; when a client repeatedly asks for hugs, the helper might explain why that is not a good idea). Providing information about the process of helping can educate clients about what to expect. If clients know what to expect, they are more likely to be full partners in the helping process.

Helpers also clarify issues of confidentiality. They say something like, "Everything you say will be kept in strict confidence, with a couple of exceptions: If you reveal anything about abuse or intent to harm yourself or others, or if a child or older person is suspected of being abused in some way, I will need to break confidentiality." Note that such statements about the limits of confidentiality are not just good therapeutic practice, they are also legally required. Although it is crucial to provide relevant information about confidentiality, clients do not usually need a lot of detail because they are more interested in moving on to talk about what brought them to helping. Hence, helpers must find a way to provide relevant information to clients in such a way that clients do not get bored, become passive, or tune out. Once again, helpers need to gauge client reactions and be responsive to client needs.

Helpers then ask clients whether they have any questions about what to expect from the process (e.g., "Is there anything you want to know about me or about the process?"). Rather than talking more, helpers then turn the focus onto clients by asking an open question, such as "What would you like to talk about?" or "What's on your mind?" to encourage clients to share their concerns.

If a client does not respond right away to the opening probe, or if she or he responds by saying "I don't have anything to talk about," the helper might pause (empathically of course) to give the client a chance to think and talk. It is important not to rush clients but to give them the message that it is their turn to talk. If the client still does not talk, the helper might reflect possible feelings (e.g., discomfort, uncertainty) to allow the client to focus on feelings. When helpers listen patiently and empathically, clients often begin talking within a few minutes. Some clients are anxious about whether what they have to say is important enough to be discussed in helping and need reassurance that the helper is listening and thinks what they are talking about is important. The most important thing helpers do at this point in the session is to listen empathically to encourage the client to begin talking and exploring.

Throughout the exploration stage, helpers should use appropriate attending behaviors because these enable helpers to encourage clients to explore and to listen carefully to what clients are saying. Helpers should also observe clients' responses and modify attending behaviors accordingly (e.g., if clients draw away from eye contact, helpers should not look at them intensely). In addition, helpers offer approval and reassurance (e.g., "That's tough," "You're doing a good job talking about the problem") if the client seems to need encouragement. Most important, when clients are talking productively about their concerns, helpers can sit quietly and listen attentively and empathically.

Establish Goals and Clarify Expectations

An important task of the first session is to determine why the client sought out a helping experience at this particular time and what the client's goals are for counseling. It is helpful to know what motivated the client to seek help at the particular time because this tells the helper something about what is going on with the client. Many people have experienced distress for a long period, but something tips them over the edge to seek help at a particular time.

In addition, it is important to learn about what the client expects and wants from the helping experience. If expectations are unrealistic, the helper can clarify what helping can realistically provide. If the number of sessions is limited, helpers and clients need to have realistic expectations for what can be accomplished. If there are only a few sessions, helpers can help clients explore and work through some problems. With more sessions, helpers can help clients with more deeply rooted personality problems (e.g., working through childhood sexual abuse, engrained interpersonal deficits, or personality change). The helper and the client must agree that the goals are reasonable and possible to attain.

Throughout this process of establishing goals, the helper may come to realize that the client is not ready for helping or that he or she is not the best helper for this client (e.g., the client has an active eating disorder, the client needs medication, the clients wants a cognitive–behavioral approach and the helper does not have expertise in this approach; the helper has strong negative countertransference reactions). The most ethical thing to do in this situation is to refer the client to a more qualified service provider, but of course to do so in a gentle, nonjudgmental way.

Develop a Focus

A crucial task of the first (and every) session is developing a focus for that particular session. It is best for helpers to focus on one problem at a time; otherwise, there is a danger of becoming so diffuse that nothing gets accomplished. A clear focus typically involves a specific incident or behavior, such as a fight with a roommate, procrastination over completing assignments, or concern over how to communicate with a partner. The focus should be neither too vague nor too diffuse. To develop a focus, helpers typically ask clients what is troubling them *now*. It may take a few minutes to determine what the most pressing issue is, because clients often start with one concern whereas another issue is actually more critical. For example, Michael initially said that he was concerned about his grandmother's imminent death. After talking for a few minutes, it emerged that Michael was far more concerned about the end of a relationship with a woman whom he had been dating for 4 years. Thus, the helper focused on Michael's feelings about the breakup for the rest of the session. If it is not possible to get the client to focus, the lack of focus in itself becomes the important issue for the session that the helper needs to talk about with the client.

Helpers must respect the client's decisions about the focus of the sessions. For example, Judy wanted to work on existential issues such as the meaning of life, whereas the helper was much more concerned with the high likelihood that Judy was about to flunk out of school and lose her job. Although the helper needs to keep the holistic picture of the client in mind (and perhaps later challenge the client about the discrepancies), it is important that the helper not impose his or her wishes on the client.

At all times, however, helpers need to remember to keep the focus on the client, even when the client talks primarily about others. For example, if a client says, "My mother is really awful," the helper can say, "You are really irritated with your mother," thereby changing the focus from the mother to the client's reaction to her or his mother. The guiding principle is that it is easier and more efficient (and more ethical) to help a client change than to attempt to help the client change another person.

Helpers also need to maintain the focus on a specific concern (although each specific concern has many parts). Many beginning helpers let clients jump from topic to topic (e.g., academic concerns, interpersonal relationships, spirituality), so that by the end of a session, clients have covered a lot of things superficially but have not explored anything in depth. Focusing on a specific issue is important to making progress, especially in brief treatments. Helpers can use a combination of skills to assist clients in focusing on one issue in depth. Specifically, they can observe clients to determine which issue has the most salience for them (e.g., where is the most intense affect?). After identifying the most important issue, helpers can reflect the feelings clients are experiencing about that issue. Helpers can branch off to explore aspects of the central focus. Although the focus stays on the problem, helpers also facilitate client exploration of how the concern is affected by, and influences, other parts of the person's past, current, and future life. For example, if the helper determines that academic concerns are the central focus for Sam, the helper might ask Sam to explore parental expectations for academic performance, ask Sam to explore thoughts about his future occupational preferences, and encourage Sam to talk about study skills. In this way, the helper is sticking to the central topic of academic concerns but is helping Sam explore many aspects of it.

Ending the First Session

Helpers need to be aware of the time in sessions. Five to 10 minutes before the end of the session, helpers might advise clients that the session is almost over. Mentioning the approaching end of the session gives clients time to prepare for leaving the session and to reflect on what they have accomplished in the session. Some clients wait until a couple of minutes before the end of session to bring up important feelings. They could be ambivalent about discussing the topic, anxious about the helper's reaction, or trying to manipulate the helper into extending the session.

As a way to start to close the session, helpers might ask clients how they felt about the session and the work that was done. This processing of sessions is important so that helpers can become aware of how clients reacted to various interventions. For helpers to be able to plan the next sessions, they need to know what worked and what was not effective. As discussed in chapter 2, clients often do not reveal their feelings about the helper and the helping process unless asked explicitly. Helpers should not, however, ask only for clients' reactions to elicit platitudes about their skills. In fact, they should be suspicious if clients only talk about how wonderful helpers were. Instead, they should be genuinely interested in hearing both the positive and negative reactions from clients. Helpers might also want to reinforce clients for what they have accomplished in sessions and encourage them to think about carrying these changes over to their lives outside sessions.

In closing, helpers sometimes shake hands or engage in a small amount of social pleasantries (e.g., "Have a good week," "Enjoy the holiday"). These rituals can serve as a transition for clients in returning to their everyday life.

INTAKES

Many mental health clinics use initial intake sessions with potential clients to formulate a diagnosis, assess for risk, and determine the best treatment (I am grateful to Dr. Barbara Thompson for her clinical wisdom about this section). The actual intake protocol will depend on the agency, but it is usually based on a clinical interview. Whiston (2005) noted that a good intake usually involves gathering information about the following:

- Demographics (e.g., name, age, sex, address, ethnicity, education and work history, presenting problems, previous counseling, urgency of request): Often this information is collected prior to the intake interview, and the helper reviews it at the start of the intake interview.
- Presenting concerns: Although this information is often also on the screening form, the helper goes over the presenting complaints in more detail with the client during the intake.
- Client background information or psychosocial history: Obtain a brief overview of the client's background as it relates to the presenting problem (e.g., family of origin, current family and relationships, employment and school status, living situation).
- Health and medical history: This information is needed to understand the client holistically and usually includes current health issues, medications, substance use/abuse, caffeine intake, sleep, eating patterns, and exercise patterns.
- Defining the client's problem: Gather information about each problem from affective, cognitive, and relational perspectives; gather details about each problem (when problem began, history of problem, what was going on in the client's life at the time of the problem, how others contribute to the problem, intensity of the problem, changeability of the problem, methods used to solve the problem).
- Risk factors: Assess for danger to self, danger to others, and alcohol and substance abuse.

Although the purpose of the intake is to gather information and thus calls for the helper being more directive and using more probes and closed questions than she or he normally would in helping sessions, it is important for helpers to continue using attending and exploration skills (e.g., reflections of feelings, restatements, summaries) to help the client feel at ease and explore. Without good attending and helping skills, helpers will not get much information from clients.

SUBSEQUENT SESSIONS

In subsequent sessions, helpers need to begin the session and establish a focus.

Beginning

At the beginning of subsequent sessions, helpers might sit quietly and wait for clients to talk about what is on their minds (if they have educated clients to expect this); they might summarize what took place in the former session; they might start by asking how the client felt about the previous session; or they might simply ask what the client would like to talk about during the session. All are appropriate, but which one should helpers use? It depends on the client and the helper. The helper might personally like more or less structure or assess that the client needs more or less structure.

Establishing a Focus

As with the first session, helpers need to establish a focus for the discussion in each session. Helpers cannot assume that clients will continue talking about what they discussed the previous session or that clients have the same feelings that they had during the previous session. Many beginning helpers spend a great deal of time debriefing after sessions and approach subsequent sessions with an agenda about what to do to help clients with problems raised in the previous session. Helpers are often surprised, however, when clients are not concerned with or interested in talking about the same issues. When clients leave the therapy setting, many things happen that change the way they feel. They may have spent time thinking about the issues and resolved them, or other issues might have become more salient in the interim that clients are concerned about and want to discuss. Thus, helpers have to be prepared to respond to clients in the moment. Being prepared, yet flexible, is one of the biggest challenges for beginning helpers.

HELPERS' WORK BETWEEN SESSIONS

Helpers need to think about their clients between sessions to try to conceptualize their problems. Specifically, they need to think about origins of clients' problems, the underlying themes in the problems, and appropriate interventions to help clients.

One way to facilitate this conceptualization process is for helpers to listen to the audiotapes or, even better, to watch the videotapes of their sessions. Observing sessions enables helpers to recreate what they were thinking and feeling and to observe clients' reactions to their interventions. It also can provide a powerful self-confrontation about one's use of attending and helping skills.

Helpers can write extensive process notes (see Web Form F for an example form) after each session to facilitate their recall of the salient issues that were covered during the session. In the process notes, which are best done as soon as possible after sessions and observing the session, helpers can use their experience and perceptions to write about the following areas (M. A. Hoffman, personal communication, January 9, 1998):

- manifest content (what the client talked about)
- underlying content (unspoken meanings in what the client said)
- defenses and barriers to change (how the client avoids anxiety)
- client distortions (ways in which the client responds to you as she or he has to other significant persons in her or his life, i.e., transference)
- countertransference (ways in which your emotional, attitudinal, and behavioral responses may have been stimulated by the process)
- personal assessment (your evaluation of your interventions; what would you do differently and why)

Helpers should look for underlying themes and recurring patterns across all the problems that clients raise. For example, is the client always the passive victim in every encounter, does the client idealize everyone, or is the client always angry? These themes provide important clues for the underlying personality problems that need attention in therapy.

Thorough exploration allows helpers to develop hypotheses about clients that lay the foundation for choosing interventions. They should pay close attention to each client's personality and verbal and nonverbal behaviors. How does the client respond to interventions? How does the client's way of interacting influence the helping process?

Helpers can make observations about clients and develop hypotheses about what factors led clients to come to where they are. After thinking about a client, helpers should be able to answer several questions:

- How serious is the problem?
- How is the client behaving?
- How much does the client disclose or withhold about the problem?
- Are there discrepancies in what the client is saying?
- What is the client's role in the creation and maintenance of the problem?

Ideally, beginning helpers should meet with supervisors after each session for assistance in conceptualizing clients. Supervisors can aid helpers in thinking about various hypotheses about what caused and maintained problems as well as possible interventions to help clients. They can also provide a different perspective to aid helpers when they become stuck in their perceptions and countertransferences. Helpers also need to educate themselves about theories and research to obtain a framework with which to understand client dynamics (i.e., what causes and maintains problems). Helpers need to select a theoretical framework and read current research so they can think carefully about their interventions with clients. Furthermore, if clients are from a different culture or have a problem with which the helper is not familiar, the helper should read about the issue and consult with supervisors between sessions to ensure that she or he can give the best available services to the client.

TERMINATION

Because therapy sessions do not continue forever (even in long-term psychoanalytic therapy), separation is inevitable. After helpers and clients have accomplished as much as they can within the confines of their contracted relationship, the time comes to terminate the therapy relationship. The helper and client might have gone through several cycles of exploration–insight–action, dealing with several different problems, with the client gradually taking more responsibility until he or she feels ready to manage his or her life independently. One goal of therapy is to prepare clients to leave therapy and become self-reliant. Just as parents raise children to grow up, leave home, and function on their own, helpers teach and encourage clients to cope on their own.

When to Terminate

How can helpers determine when to terminate the therapy relationship? Sometimes the end is imposed by external time limits (e.g., beginning helpers often are only allowed to provide 1 to 3 sessions with volunteer clients; some counseling centers on university campuses allow only 6 sessions, although others allow 12 sessions). In such cases, helpers may have to be ready to refer clients (to be covered shortly) if they still need help.

In contrast, in open-ended, long-term therapy, helpers and clients decide when they are ready to terminate the relationship. Rarely is there such a thing as a "cure," because cure implies a static state rather than the continual changes and challenges involved in living. Most often, clients decide they are tired, have reached a plateau and are ready for a break, do not have anything else pressing to talk about, or have accomplished as much as they can with a particular helper. Sometimes clients directly tell helpers that they are ready to terminate. At other times, helpers have to tell clients that they think they are ready to terminate.

According to the "Ethical Principles of Psychologists and Code of Conduct" (American Psychological Association, 2002), helpers should terminate with clients when they feel they are no longer working productively. Sometimes therapy goes on interminably because neither helper nor client knows when and how to end it. Helpers need to be mindful of continuing therapy sessions only when clients are benefiting and making changes.

Budman and Gurman (1988) proposed that helpers adopt a model such as that of family doctors. Just as one would never expect that antibiotics would inoculate patients against the flu for the rest of their lives, they argued that helpers should not assume that one course of therapy could cure a client for life. It makes more sense for helpers to see clients until the current issues or crises are resolved and then see them again when other crises or life transitions arise. With such a model, termination is not typically as difficult because clients know that they can return to their helpers when they need further help (if that helper is still available).

How to Terminate

Mann (1973) considered termination of therapy to be an important task because loss is an existential fact of life; everyone must cope with loss. He recommended that helpers spend considerable time in planning and preparing for termination in both short- and long-term therapy. He suggested that helpers discuss termination in every session to remind clients where they are in the process (e.g., "This is our eighth session; we have four more sessions. How do you feel about being almost through with therapy?").

Clients sometimes think that helpers are exaggerating the concerns about termination because they cannot anticipate how they will feel when they leave the therapy relationship. Once they have terminated, they have an understanding of the feelings involved, but then it is too late for helpers to process the feelings of abandonment and loss with clients. Hence, before termination, helpers must assess whether clients might have strong feelings about ending the relationship so that these feelings can be addressed adequately.

There are three main steps to effective termination of therapy relationships: (a) looking back, (b) looking forward, and (c) saying goodbye (Dewald, 1971; Marx & Gelso, 1987; Ward, 1984). In looking back, helpers review with clients what they have learned and how they have changed. Clients also can provide feedback about the most helpful and least helpful aspects of the therapy process. Reviewing the process can help clients consolidate their changes and feel a sense of accomplishment; it can facilitate helpers too in giving them a sense of what skills they need to work on for future clients. In looking forward, helpers and clients set an ending date, discuss future plans, and consider the need for possible additional counseling. Helpers review with clients the issues they still want to address. No therapy process is ever complete. We keep changing (for better or worse) for the rest of our lives. The task for helpers is to assist clients in identifying the ongoing issues, determining how they will address these issues, and clarifying how they can find support in their lives for making changes. If such plans are not realistic, helpers need to confront clients so they do not set themselves up for failure. Finally, in saying goodbye, clients express their thanks to helpers and both share their feelings about ending and say their farewells.

Termination is often challenging for both helpers and clients. Once two people have spoken about many deep and personal issues, it is frequently difficult for them to think about not seeing each other again. Termination thus often brings up issues of loss for both helpers and clients. Some evidence shows that helpers and clients who have the most trouble with termination are those who have a history of painful losses (Boyer & Hoffman, 1993; Marx & Gelso, 1987). If loss has been painful in the past, it is difficult to go through another loss. Other clients may not experience intense sadness but may struggle with how to thank the helper and show appreciation for the helper's role in their process of change. Other clients may be disappointed about not having received the "magic cure" and feel upset that they still have unresolved problems. Helpers need to talk openly with clients about the separation. Furthermore, they need to anticipate the separation well ahead of time, so they have time to deal with the clients' feelings that arise from ending the relationship (and deal with their own loss issues in therapy or supervision).

Making Referrals

Clients' needs are sometimes beyond what helpers are qualified to address or capable of delivering. For example, a client might have an eating disorder, substance abuse problem, or serious mental illness, and the helper might lack expertise in that area. Sometimes the helper and client have accomplished as much as they can together, and the client needs a different kind of help. For example, a referral may be needed because a client needs marital or family therapy, but the helper is trained only in individual therapy (note that family treatment is typically more beneficial than individual treatment if clients are having difficulties with family members; Haley, 1987; Minuchin, 1974; Nichols & Schwartz, 1991; Satir, 1988). In addition, clients might need referrals for medication, long-term therapy, assessment of learning disabilities, financial assistance, housing information, spiritual guidance, or legal advice.

The helper needs to explain the reason for the referral to the client. Otherwise, clients could easily feel that they are hopeless, need endless treatment, or are "bad clients." If helpers do a thorough job of the three steps of termination discussed earlier, clients are less likely to have negative feelings about being referred.

Dealing With Difficult Clients and Clinical Situations

RELUCTANT AND RESISTANT CLIENTS

Most clients (and indeed most people) have at least some reluctance to change. Some possible roots of reluctance are fear of intensity, lack of trust, fear of falling apart, shame, fear of change, and lack of motivation to change (Egan, 1994; Young, 2001). For many clients, it is easier to stick with known misery than to face the unknown of what life might be like after changing. Signs of reluctance are varied and often covert. Reluctant clients might talk only about safe subjects, seem unsure of what they want from therapy, act overly cooperative, set unrealistic goals and then give up on them, not work very hard at changing, blame others for their problems, criticize the helper, come late to sessions, fail to keep appointments, forget to pay fees, intellectualize, terminate prematurely, use humor, ask for personal favors, present irrelevant material, engage in small talk, or disclose important things on the way out the door.

Whereas reluctance is relatively passive, resistance (i.e., feeling coerced and wanting to fight back) is more active (Egan, 1994). Resistant clients often present themselves as not needing help and as feeling misused. They show minimal willingness to form a relationship and often try to manipulate the helper. They might be resentful, try to sabotage the therapy process, terminate as quickly as possible, and act abusively or belligerently to the helper. Clients who come to therapy because they are forced to do so (e.g., are ordered by the court to participate in therapy) are often resistant. For example, one male client who was ordered by a judge to participate in 12 therapy sessions because he had urinated on public property was resistant about being there and got very little out of the experience (he even asked the helper for a date!).

Egan (1994) suggested that resistance can come from seeing no reason for therapy, resenting being referred for help, feeling awkward about participating in therapy, or having a history of rebelliousness. Other reasons for resistance are having values or expectations that are inconsistent with the help being offered, having negative attitudes about therapy, feeling that going for therapy is admitting weakness and inadequacy, feeling a lack of trust, or disliking the helper. Reluctant and resistant clients are typically at the precontemplation stage in terms of readiness to change (refer back to chap. 2).

When faced with clients who are reluctant or resistant, helpers often become confused, panicked, angry, guilty, or depressed (Egan, 1994). They might try to placate the client, become impatient or hostile to the client, become passive, or lower their expectations and do a half-hearted job. Alternatively, helpers might become warmer and more accepting to win over the client, engage in a power struggle with the client, allow themselves to be abused or bullied by the client, or try to terminate the therapy process. The source of the stress is not only the client's behavior but also the helper's self-defeating attitudes and assumptions. Helpers might be saying things to themselves like, "All clients should be committed to change," "Every client must like and trust me," "Every client can be helped," "No unwilling client can be helped," "I am responsible for what happens to the client," "I must succeed with every client," or "I am a rotten helper if I cannot help this client." Helpers need to become aware of these self-defeating attitudes and assumptions to reduce their influence on the therapy process.

Helpers should not avoid dealing with reluctance and resistance, but they also should avoid reinforcing these processes in clients (Egan, 1994). Goldfried and Davison (1994) suggested that the role of the helper is to make the reluctant or resistant client ready for change; hence, the challenge for helpers is to find creative ways to deal with reluctance and resistance. Here are several suggestions for dealing with reluctance and resistance (Egan, 1994; Pipes & Davenport, 1999; van Wormer, 1996; Young, 2001):

- Learn to see reluctance and resistance as normal.
- Recognize that reluctance and resistance are sometimes a form of avoidance and are not necessarily due to ill will toward the helper.
- Explore your own reluctance and resistance to changing problematic aspects of your life. Once helpers figure out how they cope with their own reluctance and resistance, they probably are more able to help clients with theirs. An awareness of their own foibles can make helpers more empathic and less impatient.
- Examine the quality of your interventions. Helpers might be provoking resistance by being too directive or too passive or by disliking the client.
- Consider whether you would be willing to do what you're asking the client to do.
- Be empathic; try to understand what it is like to be the client. It is hard to fight with someone who is being empathic, accepting, not threatening, and not wanting to fight. In effect, you join with the client rather than resisting the client.
- Do not use labels, jargon, or bureaucratic language with hostile clients.

- Work directly with the client's reluctance and resistance rather than ignoring it, being intimidated by it, or being angry at the clients for his or her behaviors.
- Help the client explore feelings about the reluctance or resistance to therapy.
- Be realistic about what you can accomplish with a client.
- Establish a relationship on the basis of mutual trust and shared planning rather than trying to assume all the power.
- Work with the client to search for incentives for changing.
- Draw attention to the behavior and invite the client to explore it.
- Listen carefully to what the client says and agree with part of it but then show that you are doing something different; this can provide some reassurance and enhance your credibility.
- Don't give up.

OVERLY TALKATIVE CLIENTS

Some clients talk nonstop about things that are not related to therapeutic goals (although helpers have to be careful about making judgments about what is worth discussing in therapy). In the Client Behavior System (see chap. 2 and Web Form H), this type of client behavior is considered recounting rather than affective or cognitive–behavioral exploration. Talkativeness is often a defense on the part of clients, in that it is an attempt to keep others at a distance. In situations in which the client's talking is not productive, the helper needs to intervene cautiously after several minutes and interrupt the talking, saying something like, "Sorry to interrupt, but I'm not going to be able to help you unless I can add a few things here and there. Let me see if I understand what you're saying right now . . ." Subsequently, helpers could hold up a hand, or make a T-sign to indicate a time-out, and say, "Excuse me again, but I want to make sure I am hearing you correctly." Thus, helpers let clients know that they are interrupting to assist (not because of boredom or irritation).

Interruptions done in a hostile manner ("Whoa, hold on there, you're talking too much") could hinder the therapeutic relationship and make the client feel that she or he had done something bad. If interruptions are done appropriately, gently, and respectfully, however, clients could feel relieved that their helpers interrupted them to help them overcome their defenses and learn how to interact more appropriately.

Rather than getting angry at clients for monopolizing the conversation, the helper can empathize with the client's difficulty in communicating. The helper can also hypothesize about why the client uses talking as a defense, recognizing that it keeps the client from forming close relationships. Such conceptualization can lead to the development of better interventions.

Helpers can also use their immediacy skills with overly talkative clients if helpers judge that the client can handle the interpersonal challenge. Helpers can talk about how they feel when clients do not let them have a chance to talk and ask about clients' experiences when talking.

OVERLY QUIET CLIENTS

Overly quiet clients are sometimes shy and do not talk much anywhere. Other times clients are very quiet because they are anxious or have difficulty expressing themselves; they may fear being in interpersonal situations because of poor interactions with significant others in the past. And yet other times overly quiet clients are resistant and hostile, and may defiantly challenge the helper to break through and get them to talk. It is important for the helper to try to assess why the client is being quiet. Being aware of the likely reason for the quietness can enable the helper to think about what to do. Helpers will want to use a different strategy with the client who is introverted and shy than with the hostile, defiantly silent client.

First and foremost, try to step back to the client's pace. Let the client come out at his or her own time. Open questions can be quite helpful with quiet clients because they clearly specify what you would like the client to do.

Another direction to take is to encourage the withdrawn client to open up by a positive reframing (van Wormer, 1996). You could say something like, "I think you are actually a much more feeling person than you seem on the surface." With this type of intervention, the client may feel deeply understood and thus be willing to try to open up and start talking.

CLIENTS WITH SUICIDAL IDEATION

As a beginning helper, you must be prepared to deal with clients with suicidal ideation. When a client mentions suicide or appears to be depressed and perhaps considering suicide, the helper needs to take the suicide gestures seriously. Suicide is a leading cause of death (the 11th leading cause of death across all age groups, the 3rd leading cause of death among youths from the ages of 15 to 24), and is often viewed by clients as the only way out of problems. The helper needs to actively and directly assess the seriousness of the suicidal risk rather than ignoring or minimizing it (Berman, Jobes, & Silverman, 2006; Rudd, Joiner, Jobes, & King, 1999). Helpers can assume clients are asking for help when they bring up the topic of suicide.

There are a series of steps that helpers can follow with suicidal clients. First, a general assessment of suicidal risk usually involves asking directly about suicidal potential. Helpers might ask the following questions:

- "Are you thinking about suicide?"
- "Do you have a plan for attempting suicide?"
- "Do you have the means to carry out the plan?"
- "Have you attempted suicide in the past?"
- "Do you use (or plan on using) alcohol or drugs?"
- "Have you been withdrawn and isolated lately?"
- "Have you been focused on death (e.g., giving away prized possessions or planning your funeral)?"
- "Are you feeling helpless or worthless?"
- "Do you have plans for the future?"
- "Who knows about your suicidal feelings?"
- "How would others feel if they knew you committed suicide?"

If a client indicates a clear intent to commit suicide, has a clear viable plan, and has the means to carry out the plan (e.g., a client plans on killing himself or herself in the immediate future and has obtained the means necessary to accomplish this plan), the client is at a high risk of suicide. In such a case, helper needs to take steps to ensure the client's safety (Frankish, 1994). The beginning helper should first consult with a colleague or supervisor to determine the best steps to take (the client should not be left alone during the consultation because he or she might leave to carry out the plan or implement the plan in the helper's office).

In some cases, helpers (in consultation with supervisors) might decide that suicidal clients should be hospitalized to protect themselves from self-injury. In some cases, clients realize the danger and agree to be hospitalized to receive intensive psychiatric and psychological treatment. In other cases, helpers may have to admit clients to the hospital against their will. In yet other cases, helpers (in consultation with supervisors) may ascertain that hospitalization is not necessary and instead can develop a written behavioral contract with the client that involves the client agreeing not to hurt him- or herself and promising to contact the helper or a crisis line for assistance if thoughts of suicide occur (this should done only if there is a good relationship with the client and the helper has help from a supervisor). In these cases, it may be useful for helpers to notify the client's family, close friends, or significant others about the client's suicidal ideation. Note that when clients threaten to harm themselves, confidentiality no longer applies. Hence, helpers can perform the necessary steps to ensure the safety of suicidal clients (still, of course, being empathic rather than authoritarian and demanding).

Helpers can provide the numbers of 24-hour crisis lines and assist the client in identifying a support system given that social support is very important. Additional sessions can be suggested, or the helper can offer to call the client between sessions to provide extra support. Helpers can also refer clients for additional treatment (e.g., group therapy). If a suicidal client does not show up for treatment, the helper might consider (after consultation with the supervisor) calling the client. For legal purposes, helpers should document in writing the procedures that were followed to assess and assist suicidal clients, including the questions that were asked, consultations that occurred, the decision-making process, and interventions that were made.

As helpers who have provided crisis counseling know, dealing with someone who is contemplating suicide can be challenging. Beginning helpers often fear that asking about suicidal feelings encourages clients to think about or commit suicide. In fact, the opposite is typically true— by talking about suicidal feelings, clients can bring their worst fears into the open and feel like someone listens and understands them. Clients often appreciate that helpers view their problems as serious. If helpers are not willing to discuss suicidal feelings, clients often feel even more alone, ashamed, strange, or "crazy." Perhaps the *worst* thing to do is to diminish or negate the feelings (e.g., "You'll feel better tomorrow"), point out positive aspects of their lives (e.g., "You have so much to live for"), or give false reassurance (e.g., "Everything will be okay"). These responses often result in clients not only feeling depressed and suicidal but also feeling desperate because they cannot get help, hopeless that they are beyond help, misunderstood, and worried that their suicidal feelings are unacceptable or too frightening to others. But it is also important that helpers not feel that they have to become the only lifeline for the suicidal client, or else the helper will burn out and not be of help to anyone; mobilizing other resources is crucial.

One of the most difficult issues any mental health professional can face is dealing with the aftermath of a client who committed suicide. Many helpers agonize, feel guilty, and spend a lot of time second-guessing whether there was something else they could have done to prevent the suicide. A certain amount of introspection is important and may enable helpers to handle similar situations better in the future, but helpers should not unnecessarily take on too much responsibility. It is often wise for helpers to seek supervision and therapy after such a difficult situation to help them cope and understand their feelings (Knox, Burkhard, Jackson, Schaak, & Hess, 2006).

SEXUAL ATTRACTION

Helper sexual attraction toward clients is a common occurrence in therapy relationships. Approximately 87% of surveyed helpers reported that they have been sexually attracted to clients at some point in their careers; many felt guilty, anxious, and confused about the attraction (Pope, Keith-

Spiegel, & Tabachnick, 1986; Pope & Tabachnick, 1993). Feeling attracted is not unethical, but acting on the attraction (e.g., socializing with the client, having a sexual relationship) is considered unethical because it can harm clients.

As a beginning helper, you may find yourself sexually attracted to someone you are trying to help. Although discussing this attraction with a supervisor could be uncomfortable (some helpers might feel ashamed or guilty for having these feelings), a supervisor can assist you in working through these feelings in a healthy, rather than a destructive, manner (Ladany et al., 1997; Pope, Sonne, & Holroyd, 1993). For example, Sally found herself attracted to a client who communicated admiration, respect, and even awe for the assistance she provided for him. Although Sally had a good relationship with her partner, she enjoyed the positive feedback from the client and began thinking about him in a romantic way. Fortunately, she talked with her supervisor, who helped her sort out her feelings and come to understand that they related at least partially to the intimacy of the helping situation. Sally benefited from coming to understand how these feelings developed and how they could negatively influence the therapy process. The supervisor also normalized her feelings by letting her know that many helpers (including the supervisor) become attracted to clients during their career.

CLIENTS WHO ARE ANGRY

For most helpers, it is extremely stressful when clients are directly and hostilely angry at them (Deutsch, 1984; Farber, 1983; Hill, Kellems, et al., 2003; Matsakis, 1998; Plutchik, Conte, & Karasu, 1994). In fact, in one study, more than 80% of helpers said that they felt afraid or angry when clients were verbally abusive toward them (Pope & Tabachnick, 1993). Matsakis (1998) noted that client anger often disrupts the therapy process, especially when helpers feel angry, confused, hurt, guilty, anxious, or incompetent, instead of being able to remain empathic and objective and talk about the client anger.

To avert the negative consequences associated with inappropriately managing client anger, several authors have suggested that helpers respond to client anger as they would to any other emotion by encouraging clients to talk openly about it (Adler, 1984; Burns & Auerbach, 1996; Cahill, 1981; Hill, Kellems, et al., 2003; Joines, 1995; Kaplan, Brooks, McComb, Shapiro, & Sodano, 1983; Lynch, 1975; Matsakis, 1998; Newman, 1997; Ormont, 1984). These authors also recommended that helpers work with clients to help them uncover underlying feelings, express anger verbally instead of acting it out physically, and decide what to do about the anger. To achieve these goals, they suggested that helpers need to listen nonjudgmentally and nondefinsively when clients are angry and try to understand the anger. Furthermore, if clients are justified in their anger at the helpers, helpers need to alter their inappropriate behaviors.

Example of an Extended Interaction

An example is presented to illustrate working through all three stages (exploration, insight, and action). For ease of presentation, this example presents all three stages in a single session, although working through all three stages for a given problem often requires more than a single session.

The example involves a session with a young woman, Maria, who sought assistance because she could not decide on a major. Career concerns are common issues that many people struggle with throughout the life cycle (Brown & Brooks, 1991; Zunker, 1994). However, career difficulties are not as simplistic as psychologists once thought. It is not simply a matter of deciding on one's talents, interests, and skills. Our career identities are intertwined with our personal lives (Blustein, 1987; Brown, 1985; Hackett, 1993; Herr, 1989; Richardson, 1993; Savickas, 1994; Spokane, 1989), and hence both must be addressed in the helping process.

EXPLORATION STAGE

Helper: Tell me a little about yourself and why you came for helping today. (The helper uses an open question to start the interaction and to allow Maria to communicate her most pressing concerns.)

Client: I'm a junior at the university. I should have declared a major already, but I just cannot decide what I want to do. I feel stuck, and they're trying to force me to declare something in the next couple of weeks. I don't want to just put something down and then have to shift after a semester or two. But I just don't have anything that I'm particularly good at. You know, in high school when everyone else was in plays or orchestra or dancing or sports, I wasn't really doing anything. I just don't have any major talents. I seem to be mediocre in everything.

Helper: You sound anxious about having to declare a major so quickly. (The helper wants to focus Maria on her feelings about the urgency of the situation.)

Client: I am really anxious. You wouldn't believe how anxious I am. I haven't been able to sleep at night. I just keep trying to figure out what I want to do with my life. I guess I have never had any major ambitions.

Helper: I wonder if you have feelings about trying to figure out who you are? (The helper wants to determine how much of Maria's life is influenced by this issue.)

Client: I have been feeling out of sorts. But I guess it's really hard to tell how much of it is because of trying to choose a major and not knowing who I am or where I'm going, and how much of it is due to feeling badly that I have never had a boyfriend and also feeling under stress that my parents are going through a divorce.

Helper: Wow! Sounds like you have a lot of difficult things going on right now. (The helper wants to support Maria.)

Client: Yeah, it's been a rough semester. I just found out my parents were going to get a divorce over the holidays. They said that they stayed together until my younger sister went to college. I'm not sure that their staying together was actually so good for us because they were always fighting. Each of my parents has always talked to me about how horrible the other one was. I feel like I've always been the mediator, trying to help each of them understand the other.

Helper: How was it for you being the one in the middle? (The helper wants to allow Maria to explore her feelings more deeply.)

Client: Part of me liked it because they both needed me. But it was also pretty bad because I felt like they both depended on me too much and I couldn't live my own life. I was glad to get away to college, but then I felt guilty about leaving. I go home a lot. I also feel like I have to take care of my little sister and shield her from the pain. I don't want her to end up feeling as badly about herself as I do about myself.

Helper: It sounds like you feel pretty overwhelmed right now. (The helper wants to help Maria become aware of her feelings.)

Client: I do. I feel about 20 years older than the other kids here. They are always talking about parties and drinking. It all seems so trivial.

Helper: You mentioned that you have to choose a major soon. You also said that there's nothing you're particularly good in. Tell me more about that. (The helper wants to guide Maria back to exploring her problem in choosing a major.)

Client: Well, I think I'm an average student. I get Bs in most of my courses. I probably don't put as much time in as I could, but I just can't get into studying.

Helper: Tell me something about the courses that you have enjoyed. (The helper wants to help Maria explore specific interests.)

Client: Well, I'm rotten at math and science. I almost flunked biology last semester. I guess the classes I have enjoyed most are my psychology courses. I like trying to figure people out. You know, I'm always the person whom people talk to about their problems. I'm taking this class in helping skills and am excited about it. I think I'm pretty good at helping. At least I enjoy being a helper.

INSIGHT STAGE

Helper: What do you think got you so excited about learning helping skills? (The helper wants to assist Maria in thinking about her motives.)

Client: Everyone has always come to me with their problems, and I feel like I'm good at listening. And I was able to help my sister when she got so upset.

Helper: I wonder if operating as a helper in your family helped you become interested in the helping field? (The helper tries an interpretation to see whether Maria can engage in the interpretive process.)

Client: You know, you may be right. Maybe helping my sister and mediating my parents' arguments helped me develop effective helping skills. It's funny that I've never really thought about majoring in psychology before. I guess my parents have always looked down on psychology. They would never go to a helper because they have always said people should solve their own problems. Well, they didn't do too good a job on their own. But I don't know, what do you think I should do? Why did you choose psychology?

Helper: I really liked to help other people with their problems. I also found that all my friends turned to me to talk about their problems. (The helper uses disclosure to reassure Maria that her feelings are normal.)

Client: That's interesting. Do you like the field?

Helper: Yes, I like it a lot. Tell me more about your thoughts about psychology. (The helper wants to turn the focus back to Maria.)

Client: Well, I think I might like to do it, but I don't know if I'm smart enough for it. I've heard an awful lot about how you have to be really smart to get into graduate school in psychology. I might not be able to make it.

Helper: You know, you say you're not really smart, but I haven't heard much evidence for that. (The helper challenges Maria about her lack of self-efficacy.)

Client: Well, I haven't gotten very good grades in college. I did get pretty good grades in high school though, and my SAT scores were pretty high. In fact, I was close to the top of my class.

Helper: So something has happened during college to make you lose your confidence and not do as well in your classes. What might have contributed to your inability to study? (The helper wants to facilitate Maria to think about insight and so restates and then asks an open question.)

Client: Well, I'm not sure. Perhaps it has to do with my family, but I'm not sure how.

Helper: Perhaps your concern about your parents and leaving home has distracted you from your ability to study. (The helper works with Maria to stimulate insight. Maria had a glimmer that her difficulties were related to her family, so the helper gives an interpretation that goes just beyond what Maria has stated.)

Client: Hmm, I had never thought about that, but you're probably right. I've been so concerned about everyone else that I haven't had time to take care of myself. It's not really fair that my parents messed up my life just because they cannot get their act together.

Helper: Yeah, you seem angry at them. (Maria has responded well to the interpretation, so the helper wants to help her explore her feelings about her discoveries.)

Client: I am. I have been so worried about leaving my sister at home and not being able to calm my parents during their horrible arguments. These are supposed to be the best years of my life. And all I'm concerned about is them. When do I get my chance?

Helper: I wonder if your parents really need you as much as you think they do? (The helper challenges Maria about her assumed need to be in the middle.)

Client: Maybe they don't. In fact, maybe if I quit interfering, they would be able to make a decision about what they need to do. And you know my sister is not a kid anymore. She's 18 years old. I mean, I love them, but maybe I've just been doing too much, going home all the time.

ACTION STAGE

Helper: So what would you like to do differently? (The helper wants to move Maria into thinking about how to make changes in her life.)

Client: Well, I think I'm going to tell my parents that I am going to stop listening to each of their problems. I am going to suggest that they go to a helper. It's been so helpful talking to you. That's what I think they need to do. If they don't do it, that's their problem, but I've got to get out from the middle.

Helper: What feelings might come up for you in telling your parents your decision not to be in the middle? (The helper wants to have Maria explore her feelings about this change.)

Client: I'm pretty fed up right now, so I think I could do it. The difficult part will come when my mom calls late at night crying and says I'm the only one who really understands her. You wouldn't believe how many times she's done that right before a major exam.

Helper: What could you do when that happens? (The helper wants to guide Maria into problem solving what to do in the specific situation.)

Client: Well, I could go to the library to study when I really need to focus on my work. Then my mom couldn't reach me. I really study better at the library anyway because the residence hall is so noisy.

Helper: That's a great idea. (The helper reinforces Maria's feelings.)

Client: Yeah, I don't know why I didn't think of that sooner. I guess I was just stuck in thinking I was the only one who could help my mom. You know, maybe I even kept her from going to a helper because she could always talk to me. In fact, maybe I wanted her to talk to me because it made me feel so important and helpful.

Helper: Yeah, that might be hard to give up. You feel pretty special when you believe that you're the one who can make everyone feel better. (The helper wants to warn Maria that it might be hard to change.)

Client: Yeah, it could be hard. But I think it's time to start living my own life instead of living in their world.

Helper: What could you do to make the transition easier? (Again, the helper wants to prepare Maria for the difficulties involved in changing.)

Client: Well, I would like to continue to talk with you. Would that be possible? I think if I had your support, it would be easier to change.

Helper: Sure, we could arrange for eight sessions. That's the limit of the number of sessions I can offer to you through the counseling center. (The helper wants to let Maria know the limits of her availability.)

Client: That would be great. Thanks.

Helper: Now back to the major. What are your thoughts about what you would like to do about that at this point? (The helper wants to bring some closure to the topic about the major since that was Maria's presenting concern.)

Client: I'm leaning toward psychology. I get excited about some of the psychology courses I've had, particularly the ones that involve personality and helping people. But I'm also interested in English. I've always liked to write. I've kept a journal for years. I have a fantasy of some day writing a novel or working on a newspaper.

Helper: Perhaps you can do some more thinking about your likes and dislikes before the next session. It would also be a good idea to gather some information about majors and careers. There's some excellent information in the career center on campus. Perhaps you could go there before our next session. I'd also like you to take some vocational interest tests so we can determine more about your interests. What do you think? (The helper wants to give Maria specific guidance about how to proceed with this issue, but does not want to be seen as being too pushy.)

Client: Terrific. Sounds like a great idea. Where do I take the tests?

Helper: I'll take you down and show you where to sign up after the session. How are you feeling about what we've done today? (The helper wants to give Maria specific information about how to find the tests and also wants to assess how Maria felt about the session.)

Client: I feel better than I've felt for so long. I actually have energy. I can't wait to take the tests. I can't wait to talk to my parents. I think they are going to understand that I need to do this for myself. They've been worried about me. It's not like me to be as upset as I've been. I can see some light at the end of the tunnel. It's very exciting.

Helper: Good for you. So let's plan on meeting next week at the same time?

Concluding Comments

I hope this book has provided you with the essential tools to begin your journey toward becoming a helper. I would encourage you to complete the Counselor Self-Efficacy Measure (Web Form K), so you can make a self-assessment of your therapy skills, your skills in managing sessions, and your skills in terms of handling difficult clinical situations. You can complete the measure for how you feel right now, as well as retrospectively for how you think you were before reading this book and practicing the skills. This assessment might give you some ideas about what you have learned as well as about areas that still need work.

As a result of learning about helping skills, many of you may have decided that you would like to pursue a career that involves extensive use of these skills; others may have decided not to pursue such a career. Regardless of the career you have chosen, these helping skills can be used to enhance your personal and professional functioning. I encourage each of you to set specific goals on how to continue to develop these skills, given that this text and these practice exercises provide only a foundation on which your skills can be cultivated. Many sites are available for advanced training in therapy skills (e.g., graduate programs in counseling and clinical psychology, social work, counseling, psychiatry, psychiatric nursing). Volunteering at nonprofit agencies also provides a useful setting for obtaining additional practice for your skills while assisting people with pressing concerns. Whatever your path, I hope that it involves continued exploration of your feelings, increased self-awareness and insight, and positive changes that enable you to fulfill your potential and succeed in your interpersonal relationships and in your career.

I would appreciate any feedback (on the form at the end of the book) that you might have about this text. I will continue to revise this book to make it responsive to student needs.

Thank you for joining me on this journey of learning helping skills. I wish you the best in continued endeavors.

What Do You Think?

- What do you think would be the effects of discussing confidentiality for the therapeutic relationship?
- How would you know when you have explored enough?
- Discuss other possible ways that helpers could manage sessions (e.g., begin sessions, develop a focus, end sessions).
- Debate whether clients should ever be forced to go for helping.
- Describe the personality characteristics a helper could have that might influence her or his ability to respond effectively to reluctant or resistant clients, overly talkative clients, suicidal clients, or angry clients.
- What would you do if you felt sexual attraction for a client?
- Identify what steps you might take if you were a helper dealing with the following suicidal clients:

  A. *Ilya is a 23-year-old man who mentions that he feels really depressed because his girlfriend broke up with him last week. He states that he does not think he can live without her. He does not have a plan and has never attempted suicide before. He drinks occasionally and recently has been drinking more.*

  B. *Jackie is a 45-year-old woman who recently lost her job as a manager for a public relations firm. She was divorced 5 years ago, and her husband has custody of their two children. At the time of the divorce, she attempted suicide by ingesting 50 aspirins. She was hospitalized at that time. She recently returned to counseling because of a general dissatisfaction with her life. She plans on taking 100 aspirins and has a bottle in her purse. She has written notes to both of her children.*

  C. *Omar is a 17-year-old boy who was suspended from school for fighting with another student. His parents are angry with him and have insisted that he attend counseling. He states that maybe he should try to hurt himself because then they would really think he had a problem. He does not have a plan and has never attempted suicide before. He says, "I'd never really hurt myself. I want to go to college and get away from my parents and have fun."*

- What do you think about the suggestions regarding termination?
- Who should decide that it is an appropriate time to terminate, and what marker should help them decide that termination is appropriate?
- What do you think the ideal length of a therapy relationship is?
- Debate the issue of whether time limits are beneficial for the therapeutic process.

■ What theoretical orientation is emerging for you? Describe your goals for learning more about this theoretical orientation.

■ What goals do you have for the continued development of your therapy skills?

i LAB 13. Integrating the Skills

A downloadable PDF of this Lab is available in the student resources area of the Helping Skills, 3rd ed. Web site: http://www.apa.org/books/resources/Hill3.

Exercise 1: Integration of Exploration, Insight, and Action Skills

Goal: For helpers to participate in a 50-minute helping session using all of the helping skills.
    You are ready to integrate the skills that you have learned so far. In this lab, you meet with a client and first use exploration skills to help the client explore. Next, you use exploration and insight skills to facilitate the client gaining insight. Then you use exploration and action skills to assist the client in deciding what type of action to take.

Helper's and Client's Tasks During the Helping Exchange

1. Each helper should be paired with a volunteer client whom they do not know.
2. Helpers should bring the following forms with them to the session: the Session Review Form (Web Form A), Helper Intentions List (Web Form D), Client Reactions System (Web Form G), Session Process and Outcome Measures (Web Form I), and Self-Awareness and Management Strategies Survey (Web Form J). Supervisors bring the Supervisor Rating Form (Web Form B).
3. Helpers should bring an audio- or videotape recorder (tested ahead of time to ensure that it works) and a tape. They should turn the recorder on at the beginning of the session.
4. Helpers should introduce themselves and remind clients that everything they say will be kept confidential. Helpers should indicate exactly who will be listening to the session (e.g., peer, supervisor).
5. Each helper should conduct a 50-minute session (about 20 minutes of exploration, 15 minutes of insight, 15 minutes of action) with the client. Be as helpful to your client as possible. Watch for the client's reactions to each of your interventions and modify subsequent interventions when appropriate.
6. Watch your time carefully. About 2 minutes before the end of the session, let the client know you need to stop soon (e.g., "We need to stop soon. Did you have any reactions to the session?")

Supervisor's Tasks During Session

Supervisors should use the Supervisor Rating Form (Web Form B) to record their observations and evaluations.

Postsession

1. Both the helper and client complete the Session Process and Outcome Measures (Web Form I); the helper also completes the Self-Awareness and Management Strategies Survey (Web Form J).
2. After the session, each helper reviews the tape with his or her client (review of a 50-minute session takes about 90–120 minutes); alternatively, helpers might just

review 10 minutes of each stage. Helpers should stop the tape after each helper intervention (except minimal acknowledgments such as "um-hmm," and "yeah"). Helpers should write down the key words on the Session Review Form (Web Form A) to enable locating the exact spot on the tape later.

3. Helpers rate the helpfulness of each intervention and write down the numbers of up to three intentions for that intervention (responding according to how they felt during the session rather than when listening to the tape of the session). Use the whole range of the Helpfulness Scale and as many intentions as possible. Do not collaborate with the client in completing ratings.

4. Clients rate the helpfulness of each intervention and write down the numbers of up to three reactions, circling any reactions that they hid from helpers during the session. Clients should respond according to how they felt during session rather than how they feel listening to the tape of the session. Use the whole range of the Helpfulness Scale and as many categories as possible on the reactions system. Do not collaborate with helpers in doing the ratings.

5. Helpers and clients write down the most and least helpful event.

6. Supervisors give feedback to helpers based on the Supervisor Rating Form (Web Form B).

7. Helpers should type a transcript of their session. Skip minimal utterances such as "okay," "you know," "er," and "uh."

   a. Divide the helper speech into response units.
   b. Using the Helping Skills System (Web Form E), determine which skill was used for each response unit in your transcript.
   c. Indicate what you would say if you could do each intervention again.
   d. Erase the tape. Make sure the transcript has no identifying information.

Exercise 2: Conceptualizing Clients

Goal: To teach helpers about how to conceptualize clients and to think more about the timing of interventions.

This lab is meant for advanced students who are seeing "real" clients. Within a classroom setting of 5 to 10 students, one student should role-play a client that he or she is seeing. The student who is doing the role-playing should provide a brief description of the client (age, gender, occupation, involvement in relationship with significant other, presenting problem); the rest will be learned through the role-play. Another student should begin taking the role of the helper doing the exploration stage. Other students can take over the role of helper whenever necessary to continue the exploration.

When the leader determines that enough exploration has occurred (about 10–15 minutes), he or she can stop the process and ask the students to conceptualize the client's problems. They can talk about what they have learned so far about the client and what they do not know.

All of the students can take turns being helpers and try using challenge, interpretation, self-disclosure, or immediacy. Each helper can interact with the client for two or three exchanges to see how the interaction works. The "client" should stay in the role and refrain from talking about interventions that he or she used with the real client or providing more information about the real client.

When the leader determines that an adequate amount of time has been spent in the insight stage, she or he can stop the process and ask the students to conceptualize the client's problems again. Helpers can discuss what they have learned through the insight stage. Helpers can talk about the theories that they think best explain how the client developed and maintains his or her problems. Furthermore, the leader can ask helpers to share what feelings and reactions were evoked in them by the client (e.g., boredom, anger, irritation, sexual attraction, deep empathy). Helpers can then turn their attention to discussing the action stage. Do they think the client is ready for action? If not, why not? What else needs to be done? If yes, what actions might be appropriate? How could the helper implement the desired interventions?

Again, one helper can begin the action stage with the "client," going through the steps outlined in chapter 16 for one of the types of action. Other helpers can take over when the helper needs assistance.

Processing the Exchange

The "client" can talk about what the experience was like and about what he or she learned that will help in working with the real client.

Exercise 3. Watching the Action Stage in the DVD

The leader plays the action stage portion of the DVD that accompanies this book, *Helping Skills in Practice: A Three-Stage Model*. After all the participants have viewed this portion of the DVD, the leader facilitates a discussion about what was helpful and not helpful. The leader also asks about client dynamics and the possibility of other action strategies.

Personal Reflections

- What did you learn about yourself in this session as compared with the other sessions you did during the course?
- What problems did you have getting the client to think about action?
- Were you able to move smoothly from exploration to insight to action?
- What are your strengths and weaknesses in terms of conceptualizing clients?
- What specific issues tend to "hook" you most and make it difficult for you to respond objectively to clients (e.g., hostility, sexuality, passivity, dependency)?

References

Adler, G. (1984). Special problems for the therapist. *International Journal of Psychiatry in Medicine, 14,* 91–98.

Ainsworth, M. D. S. (1989). Attachments beyond infancy. *American Psychologist, 44,* 709–716.

Ainsworth, M. D. S., Blehar, M. C., Waters, E., & Wall, S. (1978). *Patterns of attachment: A psychological study of the Strange Situation.* Hillsdale, NJ: Erlbaum.

Alberti, R. E., & Emmons, M. L. (2001). *Your perfect right: Assertiveness and equality in your life and relationships* (8th ed.). Atascadero, CA: Impact.

American Association for Marriage and Family Therapy. (2002). *AAMFT code of ethics.* Alexandria, VA: Author.

American Counseling Association. (1995). *Code of ethics and standards of practice.* Alexandria, VA: Author.

American Psychological Association. (2002). Ethical principles of psychologists and code of conduct. *American Psychologist, 57,* 1060–1073.

American Psychological Association. (2003). Guidelines for multicultural education, training, research, practice, and organizational change for psychologists. *American Psychologist, 58,* 377–402.

American School Counselor Association. (1998). *Ethical standards for school counselors.* Alexandria, VA: Author.

Andersen, B., & Anderson, W. (1985). Client perceptions of counselors using positive and negative self-involving statements. *Journal of Counseling Psychology, 32,* 462–465.

Archer, D., & Akert, R. M. (1977). Words and everything else: Verbal and nonverbal cues in social interpretation. *Journal of Personality and Social Psychology, 35,* 443–449.

Arlow, J. A. (1995). Psychoanalysis. In R. J. Corsini & D. Wedding (Eds.), *Current psychotherapies* (5th ed., pp. 15–50). Itasca, IL: R. E. Peacock.

Arredondo, P., Toporek, R., Brown, S. P., Jones, J., Locke, D. C., Sanchez, J., & Stadler, H. (1996). Operationalization of the multicultural competencies. *Journal of Multicultural Counseling and Development, 24,* 42–78.

Atkinson, A. P., Dittrick, W. H., Gemmell, A. J., & Young, A. W. (2004). Emotion perception from dynamic and static body expressions in point-light and full-light displays. *Perception, 33,* 717–746.

Atkinson, D. R., & Hackett, G. (1998). *Counseling diverse populations* (2nd ed.). Boston: McGraw-Hill.

Atkinson, D. R., Morten, G., & Sue, D. W. (Eds.). (1993). *Counseling American minorities* (4th ed.). Madison, WI: Brown & Benchmark.

Atkinson, D. R., Morten, G., & Sue, D. W. (1998). *Counseling American minorities: A cross-cultural perspective* (5th ed.). Boston: McGraw-Hill.

Axelson, J. A. (1999). *Counseling and development in a multicultural society* (3rd ed.). Pacific Grove, CA: Brooks/Cole.

Ayoko, O. B., & Hartel, C. E. J. (2003). The role of space as both a conflict trigger and a conflict control mechanism in heterogeneous workgroups. *International Review of Applied Psychology, 52,* 383–412.

Bachelor, A. (1995). Clients' perception of the therapeutic alliance: A qualitative analysis. *Journal of Counseling Psychology, 42,* 323–327.

Bandura, A. (1965). Influence of models' reinforcement contingencies on the acquisition of imitative responses. *Journal of Personality and Social Psychology, 1,* 589–595.

Bandura, A. (1969). *Principles of behavior modification.* New York: Holt, Rinehart & Winston.

Bandura, A. (1977). *Social learning theory.* Englewood Cliffs, NJ: Prentice Hall.

Barkham, M., & Shapiro, D. A. (1986). Counselor verbal response modes and experienced empathy. *Journal of Counseling Psychology, 33,* 3–10.

Basch, M. F. (1980). *Doing psychotherapy.* New York: Basic Books.

Basescu, S. (1990). Tools of the trade: The use of self in psychotherapy. *Group, 14,* 157–165.

Beattie, G., & Shovelton, H. (2005). Why the spontaneous images created by the hands during talk can help make TV advertisements more effective. *British Journal of Psychology, 96,* 21–37.

Beauchamp, T. L., & Childress, J. F. (1994). *Principles of biomedical ethics,* (4th ed.). New York: Oxford University Press.

Beck, A. T. (1976). *Cognitive therapy and the emotional disorders.* New York: International Universities Press.

Beck, A. T., & Emery, G. (1985). *Anxiety disorders and phobias: A cognitive perspective.* New York: Basic Books.

Beck, A. T., & Freeman, A. (1990). *Cognitive therapy of the personality disorders.* New York: Guilford Press.

Beck, A. T., Rush, A. J., Shaw, B. R., & Emery, G. (1979). *Cognitive therapy of depression.* New York: Guilford Press.

Beck, A. T., & Weishaar, M. (1995). Cognitive therapy. In R. Corsini & D. Wedding (Eds.), *Current psychotherapies* (5th ed., pp. 229–261). Itasca, IL: F. E. Peacock.

Benson, H. (1975). *The relaxation response.* New York: Morrow.

Berman, A. L., Jobes, D. A., & Silverman, M. M. (2006). *Adolescent suicide: Assessment and intervention* (2nd ed.). Washington, DC: American Psychological Association.

Bernstein, D. A., & Borkovec, T. D. (1973). *Progressive relaxation training.* Champaign, IL: Research Press.

Beutler, L. E., & Bergan, J. (1991). Value change in counseling and psychotherapy: A search for scientific credibility. *Journal of Counseling Psychology, 38,* 16–24.

Bibring, E. (1954). Psychoanalysis and the dynamic psychotherapies. *Journal of the American Psychoanalytic Association, 2,* 745–770.

Bischoff, M. M., & Tracey, T. J. G. (1995). Client resistance as predicted by therapist behavior: A study of sequential dependence. *Journal of Counseling Psychology, 42,* 487–495.

Blanck, G. (1966). Some technical implications of ego psychology. *International Journal of Psychoanalysis, 47,* 6–13.

Blustein, D. L. (1987). Integrating career counseling and psychotherapy: A comprehensive treatment strategy. *Psychotherapy, 24,* 794–799.

Bohart, A. C., Elliott, R., Greenberg, L. S., & Watson, J. C. (2002). Empathy. In J. C. Norcross (Ed.), *Psychotherapy relationships that work: Therapist contributions and responsiveness to patients* (pp. 89–108). New York: Oxford University Press.

Bohart, A. C., & Tallman, K. (1999). *How clients make therapy work: The process of active self-healing.* Washington, DC: American Psychological Association.

Bonanno, G., Keltner, D., Noll, J., Putnam, F., Trickett, P., Lejeune, J., & Anderson, C. (2002). When the face reveals what words do not: Facial expressions of emotion, smiling, and the willingness to disclose childhood sexual abuse. *Journal of Personality and Social Psychology, 83,* 94–110.

Book, H. E. (1998). *How to practice brief psychodynamic psychotherapy: The core conflictual relationship theme method.* Washington, DC: American Psychological Association.

Borys, D. S., & Pope, K. S. (1989). Dual relationships between therapist and client: A national survey of psychologists, psychiatrists, and social workers. *Professional Psychology: Research and Practice, 20,* 283–293.

Bowlby, J. (1969). *Attachment and loss: Vol. 1. Attachment.* New York: Basic Books.

Bowlby, J. (1988). *A secure base.* New York: Basic Books.

Boyer, S. P., & Hoffman, M. A. (1993). Counselor affective reactions to termination: Impact of counselor loss history and perceived client sensitivity to loss. *Journal of Counseling Psychology, 40,* 271–277.

Brainerd, C. J., & Reyna, V. F. (1998). When things that never happened are easier to "remember" than things that did. *Psychological Science, 9,* 484–489.

Brammer, L. M., & MacDonald, G. (1996). *The helping relationship: Process and skills* (6th ed.). Boston: Allyn & Bacon.

Breier, A., & Strauss, J. S. (1984). The role of social relationships in the recovery from psychotic disorders. *American Journal of Psychiatry, 141,* 949–955.

Brown, D. (1985). Career counseling: Before, after, or instead of personal counseling. *Vocational Guidance Quarterly, 33,* 197–201.

Brown, D., & Brooks, L. (1991). *Career counseling techniques.* Boston: Allyn & Bacon.

Brownell, K. D., Marlatt, G. A., Lichenstein, E., & Wilson, G. T. (1986). Understanding and preventing relapse. *American Psychologist, 41,* 765–782.

Budman, S. H., & Gurman, A. S. (1988). *Theory and practice of brief therapy.* New York: Guilford Press.

Bugental, J. T. (1965). *The search for authenticity.* New York: Holt, Rinehart & Winston.

Burns, D. D. (1999). *The feeling good handbook* (Rev. ed.). New York: Plume/Penguin Books.

Burns, D. D., & Auerbach, A. (1996). Therapeutic empathy in cognitive–behavioral therapy: Does it really make a difference? In P. M. Salkovskis (Ed.), *Frontiers of cognitive therapy* (pp. 135–164). New York: Guilford Press.

Burton, M. V., Parker, R. W., & Wollner, J. M. (1991). The psychotherapeutic value of a "chat": A verbal response modes study of a placebo attention control with breast cancer patients. *Psychotherapy Research, 1,* 39–61.

Cahill, A. J. (1981). Aggression revisited: The value of anger in therapy and other close relationships. *Adolescent Psychiatry, 9,* 539–549.

Carkhuff, R. R. (1969). *Human and helping relations* (Vols. 1 & 2). New York: Holt, Rinehart & Winston.

Carkhuff, R. R. (1973). *The art of problem-solving.* Amherst, MA: Human Resource Development.

Carkhuff, R. R., & Anthony, W. A. (1979). *The skills of helping: An introduction to counseling skills.* Amherst, MA: Human Resources Development.

Carkhuff, R. R., & Berenson, B. G. (1967). *Beyond counseling and psychotherapy.* New York: Holt, Rinehart & Winston.

Carroll, L. (1962). *Alice's adventures in wonderland.* Harmondsworth, Middlesex, England: Penguin Books. (Original work published 1865)

Cashdan, S. (1988). *Object relations therapy.* New York: Norton.

Cassidy, J., & Shaver, P. R. (Eds.). (2008). *Handbook of attachment: Theory, research, and clinical application* (2nd ed.). New York: Guilford Press.

Claiborn, C. D., Goodyear, R. K., & Horner, P. A. (2002). Feedback. In J. C. Norcross (Ed.), *Psychotherapy relationships that work: Therapist contributions and responsiveness to patients* (pp. 217–233). New York: Oxford University Press.

Cobb, S. (1976). Social support as a moderator of life stress. *Psychosomatic Medicine, 38,* 300–314.

Colby, K. M. (1961). On the greater amplifying power of causal-correlative over interrogative inputs on free association in an experimental psychoanalytic situation. *Behavioral Science, 10,* 233–239.

Conoley, C. W., Padula, M. A., Payton, D. S., & Daniels, J. A. (1994). Predictors of client implementation of counselor recommendations: Match with problem, difficulty level, and building on client strengths. *Journal of Counseling Psychology, 41,* 3–7.

Conte, H. R., Plutchik, R., Picard, S., & Karasu, T. B. (1989). Ethics in the practice of psychotherapy: A survey. *American Journal of Psychotherapy, 43,* 32–42.

Cornett, C. (1991). The "risky" intervention: Twinship self-object impasses and therapist self-disclosure in psychodynamic psychotherapy. *Clinical Social Work Journal, 19,* 49–61.

Cournoyer, R. J., & Mahalik, J. R. (1995). Cross-sectional study of gender role conflict examining college-aged and middle-aged men. *Journal of Counseling Psychology, 42,* 11–19.

Crits-Christoph, P., Barber, J. P., & Kurcias, J. S. (1991). Introduction and historical background. In P. Crits-Christoph & J. P. Barber (Eds.), *Handbook of short-term dynamic psychotherapy* (pp. 1–16). New York: Basic Books.

Crits-Christoph, P., Cooper, A., & Luborsky, L. (1988). The accuracy of therapists' interpretations and the outcome of dynamic psychotherapy. *Journal of Consulting and Clinical Psychology, 56,* 490–495.

Crits-Christoph, P., & Gibbons, B. B. C. (2002). Relational interpretations. In J. C. Norcross (Ed.), *Psychotherapy relationships that work: Therapist contributions and responsiveness to patients* (pp. 285–300). New York: Oxford University Press.

Curtis, J. M. (1981). Indications and contraindications in the use of therapist's self-disclosure. *Psychological Reports, 49,* 499–507.

Curtis, J. M. (1982). Principles and techniques of non-disclosure by the therapist during psychotherapy. *Psychological Reports, 51,* 907–914.

Darwin, C. R. (1872). *The expression of the emotions in man and animals* (1st ed.). London: John Murray.

Delaney, D. J., & Heimann, R. A. (1966). Effectiveness of sensitivity training on the perception of non-verbal communications. *Journal of Counseling Psychology, 4,* 436–440.

Deutsch, C. J. (1984). Self-reported sources of stress among psychotherapists. *Professional Psychology: Research and Practice, 15,* 833–845.

Dewald, P. A. (1971). *Psychotherapy: A dynamic approach.* New York: Basic Books.

Duan, C., & Hill, C. E. (1996). Theoretical confusions in the construct of empathy: A review of the literature. *Journal of Counseling Psychology, 43,* 261–274.

Egan, G. (1994). *The skilled helper* (5th ed.). Monterey, CA: Brooks/Cole.

Eibl-Eibesfeldt, I. (1971). *Love and hate: The natural history of behavior patterns.* New York: Holt, Rinehart & Winston.

Ekman, P. (1993). Facial expression and emotion. *American Psychologist, 48,* 384–392.

Ekman, P., & Friesen, W. V. (1969). Non-verbal leakage and clues to deception. *Psychiatry, 32,* 88–106.

Ekman, P., & Friesen, W. V. (1984). *Unmasking the face* (Reprint ed.). Palo Alto, CA: Consulting Psychologists Press.

Elkind, S. N. (1992). *Resolving impasses in therapeutic relationships.* New York: Guilford Press.

Elliott, R. (1985). Helpful and nonhelpful events in brief counseling interviews: An empirical taxonomy. *Journal of Counseling Psychology, 32,* 307–322.

Elliott, R., Barker, C. B., Caskey, N., & Pistrang, N. (1982). Differential helpfulness of counselor verbal response modes. *Journal of Counseling Psychology, 29,* 354–361.

Elliott, R., Greenberg, L. S., & Lietaer, G. (2004). Research on experiential psychotherapies. In M. J. Lambert (Ed.), *Bergin and Garfield's handbook of psychotherapy and behavior change* (5th ed., pp. 493–539). New York: Wiley.

Elliott, R., Shapiro, D. A., Firth-Cozens, J., Stiles, W. B., Hardy, G. E., Llewelyn, S. P., & Margison, F. R. (1994). Comprehensive process analysis of insight events in cognitive–behavioral and psychodynamic–interpersonal psychotherapies. *Journal of Counseling Psychology, 41,* 449–463.

Elliott, R., Watson, J. C., Goldman, R. N., & Greenberg, L. S. (2004). *Learning emotion-focused therapy: The process–experiential approach to change.* Washington, DC: American Psychological Association.

Ellis, A. (1962). *Reason and emotion in psychotherapy.* New York: Lyle Stuart.

Ellis, A. (1995). Rational emotive behavior therapy. In R. Corsini & D. Wedding (Eds.), *Current psychotherapies* (5th ed., pp. 161–196). Itasca, IL: F. E. Peacock.

Epstein, R. S., Simon, R. I., & Kay, G. G. (1992). Assessing boundary violations in psychotherapy: Survey results with the exploitation index. *Bulletin of the Menninger Clinic, 54,* 150–166.

Erikson, E. H. (1963). *Childhood and society* (2nd ed.). New York: Norton.

Falk, D., & Hill, C. E. (1992). Counselor interventions preceding client laughter in brief therapy. *Journal of Counseling Psychology, 39,* 39–45.

Farber, B. A. (1983). Psychotherapists' perceptions of stressful patient behavior. *Professional Psychology: Research and Practice, 14,* 697–705.

Farber, B. A., & Geller, J. D. (1994). Gender and representation in psychotherapy. *Psychotherapy, 31,* 318–326.

Farber, B. A., & Lane, J. S. (2002). Positive regard. In J. C. Norcross (Ed.), *Psychotherapy relationships that work: Therapist contributions and responsiveness to patients* (pp. 175–194). New York: Oxford University Press.

Ferenczi, S., & Rank, O. (1956). *The development of psycho-analysis* (C. Newton, Trans.). New York: Dover. (Original work published 1925)

Fitzpatrick, M. R., Stalikas, A., & Iwakabe, S. (2001). Examining counselor interventions and client progress in the context of the therapeutic alliance. *Psychotherapy: Theory, Research, Practice, and Training, 38,* 160–170.

Fouad, N. A., & Brown, M. T. (2000). Role of race and social class in development: Implications for counseling psychology. In S. D. Brown & R. W. Lent (Eds.), *Handbook of counseling psychology* (3rd ed., pp. 379–408). New York: Wiley.

Frank, J. D., & Frank, J. B. (1991). *Persuasion and healing: A comparative study of psychotherapy* (3rd ed.). Baltimore: Johns Hopkins University Press.

Frankish, J. (1994). Crisis centers and their role in treatment: Suicide prevention versus health promotion. *Death Studies, 18,* 327–340.

Frankl, V. (1959). *Man's search for meaning.* New York: Simon & Schuster.

Freud, S. (1933). *New introductory lectures on psychoanalysis* (J. H. Sprott, Trans.). New York: Norton.

Freud, S. (1943). *A general introduction to psychoanalysis* (J. Riviere, Trans.). New York: Garden City. (Original work published 1920)

Freud, S. (1949). *An outline of psychoanalysis* (J. Strachey, Trans.). New York: Norton. (Original work published 1940)

Freud, S. (1953a). Fragment of an analysis of a case of hysteria. In J. Strachey (Ed.), *Standard edition of the complete psychological works of Sigmund Freud* (Vol. 7, pp. 15–122). London: Hogarth. (Original work published 1905)

Freud, S. (1953b). Remembering, repeating, and working through. In J. Strachey (Ed.), *Standard edition of the complete psychological works of*

Sigmund Freud (Vol. 12, pp. 147–156). London: Hogarth. (Original work published 1914)

Freud, S. (1959). The dynamics of transference. In E. Jones (Ed.) & J. Riviere (Trans.), *Collected papers* (pp. 312–322). New York: Basic Books. (Original work published 1912)

Freud, S. (1961). The ego and the id. In J. Strachey (Ed. & Trans.), *The standard edition of the complete psychological works of Sigmund Freud* (Vol. 19, pp. 3–66). London: Hogarth. (Original work published 1923)

Freud, S. (1963). *Character and culture*. Oxford, England: Crowell-Collier. (Original work published 1923)

Friedman, E. H. (1990). *Friedman's fables*. New York: Guilford Press.

Fromm-Reichmann, F. (1950). *Principles of intensive psychotherapy*. Chicago: University of Chicago Press.

Fukuyama, M. A., & Sevig, T. D. (2002). Spirituality in counseling across cultures: Many rivers to the sea. In P. B. Pedersen, J. G. Draguns, W. J. Lonner, & J. E. Trimble (Eds.), *Counseling across cultures* (5th ed., pp. 273–296). Thousand Oaks, CA: Sage.

Fuller, F., & Hill, C. E. (1985). Counselor and helpee perceptions of counselor intentions in relationship to outcome in a single counseling session. *Journal of Counseling Psychology, 32,* 329–338.

Geller, J. D. (2003). Self-disclosure in psychoanalytic and existential therapy. *Journal of Clinical Psychology, 59,* 541–554.

Geller, J. D., Cooley, R. S., & Hartley, D. (1981). Images of the psychotherapist: A theoretical and methodological perspective. *Imagination, Cognition, and Personality, 1,* 123–146.

Geller, J. D., & Farber, B. A. (1993). Factors influencing the process of internalization in psychotherapy. *Psychotherapy Research, 3,* 166–180.

Gelso, C. J., & Carter, J. A. (1985). The relationship in counseling and psychotherapy. *Counseling Psychologist, 13,* 155–243.

Gelso, C. J., & Carter, J. A. (1994). Components of the psychotherapy relationship: Their interaction and unfolding during treatment. *Journal of Counseling Psychology, 41,* 296–306.

Gelso, C. J., & Fretz, B. R. (2001). *Counseling psychology* (2nd ed.). Belmont, CA: Thomson-Wadsworth.

Gelso, C. J., & Hayes, J. A. (1998). *The psychotherapy relationship: Theory, research, and practice*. New York: Wiley.

Gelso, C. J., & Hayes, J. A. (2007). *Countertransference and the therapist's inner experience: Perils and possibilities*. Mahwah, NJ: Erlbaum.

Gelso, C. J., Hill, C. E., Mohr, J., Rochlen, A., & Zack, J. (1999). Describing the face of transference: Psychodynamic therapists' recollections about transference in cases of successful long-term therapy. *Journal of Counseling Psychology, 46,* 257–267.

Gillespie, J. F., Jr. (1951). Verbal signs of resistance in client-centered therapy. *Dissertation Abstracts International, 5*(01), 454B. (University Microfilms No. AAI000305)

Glass, A. L., & Holyoak, L. J. (1986). *Cognition* (2nd ed.). New York: Random House.

Goates-Jones, M. K., Hill, C. E., Stahl, J., & Doschek, E. (in press). Therapist response modes in the exploration stage: Timing and effectiveness. *Counseling Psychology Quarterly.*

Goldfried, M. R., Burckell, L. A., & Eubanks-Carter, C. (2003). Therapist self-disclosure in cognitive–behavior therapy. *Journal of Clinical Psychology, 59,* 555–568.

Goldfried, M. R., & Davison, G. C. (1994). *Clinical behavior therapy* (Expanded ed.). Oxford, England: Wiley.

Goldfried, M. R., & Trier, C. S. (1974). Effectiveness of relaxation as an active coping skill. *Journal of Abnormal Psychology, 83,* 348–355.

Good, G. E., Robertson, J. M., O'Neil, J. M., Fitzgerald, L. E., Stevens, M., DeBrod, K. A., et al. (1995). Male gender role conflict: Psychometric issues and relations to psychological distress. *Journal of Counseling Psychology, 42,* 3–10.

Gourash, N. (1978). Help-seeking: A review of the literature. *American Journal of Community Psychology, 6,* 413–423.

Grace, M., Kivlighan, D. M., & Kunce, J. (1995). The effect of nonverbal skills training on counselor trainee nonverbal sensitivity and responsiveness and on session impact and working alliance ratings. *Journal of Counseling and Development, 73,* 547–552.

Greenberg, L. S. (2002). *Emotion-focused therapy.* New York: Guilford Press.

Greenberg, L. S., Rice, L. N., & Elliott, R. (1993). *Facilitating emotional change.* New York: Guilford Press.

Greenson, R. R. (1967). *The technique and practice of psychoanalysis* (Vol. 1). Madison, CT: International Universities Press.

Grissom, G. R., Lyons, J. S., & Lutz, W. (2002). Standing on the shoulders of a giant: Development of an outcome management system based on the dose model and phase model of psychotherapy. *Psychotherapy Research, 12,* 397–412.

Gross, A. E., & McMullen, P. A. (1983). Models of the help-seeking process. In B. DePaulo, A. Nadler, & J. D. Fisher (Eds.), *New directions in helping* (Vol. 2. pp. 45–70). New York: Academic Press.

Haase, R. F., & Tepper, D. T., Jr. (1972). Nonverbal components of empathic communication. *Journal of Counseling Psychology, 19,* 417–426.

Hackett, G. (1993). Career counseling and psychotherapy: False dichotomies and recommended remedies. *Journal of Career Assessment, I,* 105–117.

Haldeman, D. C. (2002). Gay rights, patient rights: The implications of sexual orientation conversion therapy. *Professional Psychology: Research and Practice, 33,* 260–264.

Haley, J. (1987). *Problem-solving therapy.* San Francisco: Jossey-Bass.

Hall, E. T. (1963). A system for the notation of proxemic behavior. *American Anthropologist, 63,* 1003–1026.

Hall, E. T. (1968). Proxemics. *Current Anthropology, 9,* 83–108.

Hanna, F. J., & Ritchie, M. H. (1995). Seeking the active ingredients of psychotherapeutic change: Within and outside the context of therapy. *Professional Psychology: Research and Practice, 26,* 176–183.

Harper, R. G., Wiens, A. N., & Matarazzo, J. D. (1978). *Nonverbal communication: The state of the art.* New York: Wiley.

Helms, J. E. (1990). *Black and White racial identity: Theory, research, and practice.* Westport, CT: Greenwood.

Helms, J. E., & Cook, D. A. (1999). *Using race and culture in counseling and psychotherapy: Theory and practice.* Needham, MA: Allyn & Bacon.

Herr, E. L. (1989). Career development and mental health. *Journal of Career Development, 16,* 5–18.

Highlen, P. S., & Hill, C. E. (1984). Factors affecting client change in individual counseling: Current status and theoretical speculations. In S. D. Brown & R. W. Lent (Eds.), *Handbook of counseling psychology* (pp. 334–398). New York: Wiley.

Hill, C. E. (1978). Development of a counselor verbal response category system. *Journal of Counseling Psychology, 25,* 461–468.

Hill, C. E. (1989). *Therapist techniques and client outcomes: Eight cases of brief psychotherapy.* Newbury Park, CA: Sage.

Hill, C. E. (1992). An overview of four measures developed to test the Hill process model: Therapist intentions, therapist response modes, client reactions, and client behaviors. *Journal of Counseling and Development, 70,* 729–737.

Hill, C. E. (Ed.). (2001). *Helping skills: The empirical foundation.* Washington, DC: American Psychological Association.

Hill, C. E. (Ed.). (2004). *Dream work in therapy: Facilitating exploration, insight, and action.* Washington, DC: American Psychological Association.

Hill, C. E. (2005a). The role of individual and marital therapy in my development. In J. D. Geller, J. C. Norcross, & D. E. Orlinsky (Eds.), *The psychotherapist's own psychotherapy: Patient and clinician perspectives* (pp. 129–144). New York: Oxford University Press.

Hill, C. E. (2005b). Therapist techniques, client involvement, and the therapeutic relationship: Inextricably intertwined in the therapy process. *Psychotherapy: Theory, Research, Practice, Training,* 431–442.

Hill, C. E. (2007). My personal reactions to Rogers (1957): The facilitative but neither necessary nor sufficient conditions of therapeutic personality change. *Psychotherapy: Theory, Research, Practice, Training, 44,* 260–264.

Hill, C. E., Carter, J. A., & O'Farrell, M. K. (1983). A case study of the process and outcome of time-limited counseling. *Journal of Counseling Psychology, 30,* 3–18.

Hill, C. E., & Gormally, J. (1977). Effect of reflection, restatement, probe, and nonverbal behavior on client affect. *Journal of Counseling Psychology, 24,* 92–97.

Hill, C. E., Helms, J. E., Spiegel, S. B., & Tichenor, V. (1988). Development of a system for categorizing client reactions to therapist interventions. *Journal of Counseling Psychology, 35,* 27–36.

Hill, C. E., Helms, J. E., Tichenor, V., Spiegel, S. B., O'Grady, K. E., & Perry, E. S. (1988). The effects of therapist response modes in brief psychotherapy. *Journal of Counseling Psychology, 35,* 222–233.

Hill, C. E., Kellems, I. S., Kolchakian, M. R., Wonnell, T. L., Davis, T. L., & Nakayama, E. Y. (2003). The therapist experience of being the target of hostile versus suspected-unasserted client anger: Factors associated with resolution. *Psychotherapy Research, 13,* 475–491.

Hill, C. E., & Knox, S. (2002). Therapist self-disclosure. In J. C. Norcross (Ed.), *Psychotherapy relationships that work: Therapist contributions and responsiveness to patients* (pp. 255–265). Oxford, England: Oxford University Press.

Hill, C. E., & Knox, S. (2008). Facilitating insight in counseling and psychotherapy. In S. D. Brown & R. W. Lent (Eds.), *Handbook of counseling psychology* (4th ed., pp. 284–302). New York: Wiley.

Hill, C. E., & Knox, S. (in press). Processing the therapeutic relationship. *Psychotherapy Research.*

Hill, C. E., Knox, S., Hess, S., Crook-Lyon, R., Goates-Jones, M., & Sim, W. (2007). The attainment of insight in the Hill dream model: A single case study. In L. G. Castonguay & C. E. Hill (Eds.), *Insight in psychotherapy* (pp. 207–230). Washington, DC: American Psychological Association.

Hill, C. E., & Lent, R. W. (2006). A narrative and meta-analytic review of helping skills training: Time to revive a dormant area of inquiry. *Psychotherapy: Theory, Research, Practice, Training, 43,* 154–172.

Hill, C. E., Nutt-Williams, E., Heaton, K. J., Thompson, B. J., & Rhodes, R. H. (1996). Therapist retrospective recall of impasses in long-term psychotherapy: A qualitative analysis. *Journal of Counseling Psychology, 43,* 207–217.

Hill, C. E., & O'Grady, K. E. (1985). List of therapist intentions illustrated in a case study and with therapists of varying theoretical orientations. *Journal of Counseling Psychology, 32,* 3–22.

Hill, C. E., Roffman, M., Stahl, J., Friedman, S., Hummel, A., & Wallace, C. (2008). Helping skills training for undergraduates: Outcomes and predictors of outcomes. *Journal of Counseling Psychology, 55,* 359–370.

Hill, C. E., Siegelman, L., Gronsky, B., Sturniolo, R., & Fretz, B. R. (1981). Nonverbal communication and counseling outcome. *Journal of Counseling Psychology, 28,* 203–212.

Hill, C. E., Sim, W., Spangler, P., Stahl, J., Sullivan, C., & Teyber, E. (2008). Therapist immediacy in brief psychotherapy therapy: Case Study II. *Psychotherapy: Theory, Research, Practice, Training, 45,* 298–315.

Hill, C. E., Sullivan, C., Knox, S., & Schlosser, L. (2007). Becoming psychotherapists: Experiences of novice therapists in a beginning graduate class. *Psychotherapy: Theory, Research, Practice, Training, 44,* 434–449.

Hill, C. E., Thompson, B. J., Cogar, M. M., & Denman, D. W. (1993). Beneath the surface of long-term therapy: Client and therapist report of their own and each other's covert processes. *Journal of Counseling Psychology, 40,* 278–288.

Hill, C. E., Thompson, B. J., & Corbett, M. M. (1992). The impact of therapist ability to perceive displayed and hidden client reactions on immediate outcome in first sessions of brief therapy. *Psychotherapy Research, 2,* 143–155.

Hill, C. E., Thompson, B. J., & Ladany, N. (2003). Therapist use of silence in therapy: A survey. *Journal of Clinical Psychology, 59,* 513–524.

Hill, C. E., Thompson, B. J., & Mahalik, J. R. (1989). Therapist interpretation. In C. E. Hill (Ed.), *Therapist techniques and client outcomes: Eight cases of brief psychotherapy* (pp. 284–310). Newbury Park, CA: Sage.

Holroyd, J. C., & Brodsky, A. (1977). Psychologists' attitudes and practices regarding erotic and nonerotic physical contact with patients. *American Psychologist, 32,* 843–849.

Horvath, A. O., & Bedi, R. P. (2002). The alliance. In J. C. Norcross (Ed.), *Psychotherapy relationships that work: Therapist contributions and responsiveness to patients* (pp. 37–70). New York: Oxford University Press.

Howard, K. I., Lueger, R. J., Maling, M. S., & Martinovich, Z. (1993). A phase model of psychotherapy outcome: Causal mediation of change. *Journal of Consulting and Clinical Psychology, 59,* 12–19.

Hunter, M., & Struve, J. (1998). *The ethical use of touch in psychotherapy.* Thousand Oaks, CA: Sage.

Ivey, A. E. (1994). *Intentional interviewing and counseling: Facilitating client development in a multicultural society* (3rd ed.). Pacific Grove, CA: Brooks/Cole.

Izard, C. E. (1977). *Human emotions.* New York: Plenum.

Jacobson, E. (1929). *Progressive relaxation.* Chicago: University of Chicago Press.

Joines, V. S. (1995). A developmental approach to anger. *Transactional Analysis Journal, 25,* 112–118.

Jourard, S. M. (1971). *The transparent self.* New York: Van Nostrand Reinhold.

Jung, C. G. (1984). *Dream analysis.* Princeton, NJ: Princeton University Press.

Kabat-Zinn, J. (2003). Mindfulness-based interventions in context: Past, present, and future. *Clinical Psychology: Science and Practice, 10,* 144–156.

Kaplan, A., Brooks, B., McComb, A. L., Shapiro, E. R., & Sodano, A. (1983). Women and anger in psychotherapy. *Women and Therapy, 2,* 29–40.

Kasper, L., Hill, C. E., & Kivlighan, D. (2008). Therapist immediacy in brief psychotherapy therapy: Case Study I. *Psychotherapy: Theory, Research, Practice, Training, 45,* 281–287.

Kazdin, A. E. (2001). *Behavior modification in applied settings* (6th ed.). Pacific Grove, CA: Brooks/Cole.

Kelly, A. E. (1998). Clients' secret keeping in outpatient therapy. *Journal of Counseling Psychology, 45,* 50–57.

Kendon, A. (1967). Some functions of gaze-direction in social interaction. *Acta Psychologica, 26,* 22–63.

Kertay, L., & Reviere, S. L. (1998). Touch in context. In E. W. Smith, P. R. Clance, & S. Imes (Eds.), *Touch in psychotherapy: Theory, research, and practice* (pp. 16–35). New York: Guilford Press.

Kestenbaum, R. (1992). Feeling happy versus feeling good: The processing of discrete and global categories of emotional expressions by children and adults. *Developmental Psychology, 28,* 1132–1142.

Kiesler, D. J. (1988). *Therapeutic metacommunication: Therapist impact disclosure as feedback in psychotherapy.* Palo Alto, CA: Consulting Psychologists Press.

Kiesler, D. J. (1996). *Contemporary interpersonal theory and research: Personality, psychopathology, and psychotherapy.* Oxford, England: Wiley.

Kim, B. S. K., & Abreu, J. M. (2001). Acculturation measurement: Theory, current instruments, and future directions. In J. G. Ponterotto, J. M. Casas, L. A. Suzuki, & C. M. Alexander (Eds.), *Handbook of multicultural counseling* (2nd ed., pp. 394–424). Thousand Oaks, CA: Sage.

Kim, B. S. K., Atkinson, D. R., & Umemoto, D. (2001). Asian cultural values and the counseling process: Current knowledge and directions for future research. *Counseling Psychologist, 29,* 570–603.

Kim, B. S. K., Atkinson, D. R., & Yang, P. H. (1999). The Asian Values Scale: Development, factor analysis, validation, and reliability. *Journal of Counseling Psychology, 46,* 342–352.

Kitchener, K. S. (1984). Intuition, critical evaluation and ethical principles: The foundation for ethical decisions for counseling psychology. *The Counseling Psychologist, 12,* 43–55.

Klein, M. H., Kolden, G. G., Michels, J. L., & Chisholm-Stockard, S. (2002). Congruence. In J. C. Norcross (Ed.), *Psychotherapy relationships that work: Therapist contributions and responsiveness to patients* (pp. 195–215). New York: Oxford University Press.

Kleinke, C. L. (1986). Gaze and eye contact: A research review. *Psychological Bulletin, 100,* 78–100.

Knox, S., Burkhard, A. W., Jackson, J. A., Schaak, A. M., & Hess, S. (2006). Therapists-in-training who experience a client suicide: Implications for supervision. *Professional Psychology: Research and Practice, 37,* 547–557.

Knox, S., Goldberg, J. L., Woodhouse, S., & Hill, C. E. (1999). Clients' internal representations of their therapists. *Journal of Counseling Psychology, 46,* 244–256.

Knox, S., Hill, C. E., Hess, S., & Crook-Lyon, R. (2008). The attainment of insight in the Hill dream model: Replication and extension. *Psychotherapy Research, 18,* 200–215.

Kohut, H. (1971). *The analysis of the self.* New York: International Universities Press.

Kohut, H. (1977). *The restoration of the self.* New York: International Universities Press.

Kohut, H. (1984). *How does analysis cure?* Chicago: University of Chicago Press.

Kopta, S. M., Howard, K. I., Lowry, J. L., & Beutler, L. E. (1994). Patterns of symptomatic recovery in psychotherapy. *Journal of Consulting and Clinical Psychology, 62,* 1009–1016.

Kraft, H. S. (2007). *Rule number two: Lessons I learned in a combat hospital.* New York: Little, Brown.

Ladany, N., Hill, C. E., Thompson, B. J., & O'Brien, K. M. (2004). Therapist perspectives on using silence in therapy: A qualitative study. *Counselling and Psychotherapy Research, 4,* 80–89.

Ladany, N., O'Brien, K. M., Hill, C. E., Melincoff, D. S., Knox, S., & Petersen, D. A. (1997). Sexual attraction toward clients, use of supervision, and prior training: A qualitative study of psychotherapy predoctoral interns. *Journal of Counseling Psychology, 44,* 413–424.

Ladany, N., Walker, J. A., Pate-Carolan, L. M., & Gray Evans, L. (2008). *Practicing counseling and psychotherapy: Insights from trainees, supervisors, and clients.* New York: Routledge.

LaFrance, M., & Mayo, C. (1976). Racial differences in gaze behavior during conversations: Two systematic observational studies. *Journal of Personality and Social Psychology, 33,* 547–552.

Laing, R. D., & Esterson, A. (1970). *Sanity, madness, and the family.* Middlesex, England: Penguin.

Lambert, M. J., & Hill, C. E. (1994). Assessing psychotherapy outcomes and processes. In A. E. Bergin & S. L. Garfield (Eds.), *Handbook of psychotherapy and behavior change* (4th ed., pp. 72–113). New York: Wiley.

Lang, P. J., Melamed, B. G., & Hart, J. (1970). A psychophysiological analysis of fear modification using an automated desensitization procedure. *Journal of Abnormal Psychology, 76,* 220–234.

Lauver, P., & Harvey, D. R. (1997). *The practical counselor: Elements of effective helping.* Pacific Grove, CA: Brooks/Cole.

Levy, L. H. (1963). *Psychological interpretation.* New York: Holt, Rinehart & Winston.

Loftus, E. (1988). *Memory.* New York: Ardsley House.

Luborsky, L., & Crits-Christoph, P. (1990). *Understanding transference: The CCRT method.* New York: Basic Books.

Lynch, C. (1975). The freedom to get mad: Impediments to expressing anger and how to deal with them. *Family Therapy, 2,* 101–122.

Mahalik, J. R. (1994). Development of the Client Resistance Scale. *Journal of Counseling Psychology, 41,* 58–68.

Mahler, M. S. (1968). *On human symbiosis of the vicissitudes of individuation.* New York: International Universities Press.

Maki, M. T., & Kitano, H. H. L. (2002). Counseling Asian Americans. In P. B. Pedersen, J. G. Draguns, W. J. Lonner, & J. E. Trimble (Eds.), *Counseling across cultures* (5th ed., pp. 109–131). Thousand Oaks, CA: Sage.

Malan, D. H. (1976a). *The frontier of brief psychotherapy.* New York: Plenum.

Malan, D. H. (1976b). *Toward a validation of dynamic psychotherapy: A replication.* New York: Plenum.

Mallinckrodt, B. (2000). Attachment, social competencies, social support, and interpersonal process in psychotherapy. *Psychotherapy Research, 10,* 239–266.

Mallinckrodt, B., Gantt, D. L., & Coble, H. M. (1995). Attachment patterns in the psychotherapy relationship: Development of the Client Attachment to Therapist Scale. *Journal of Counseling Psychology, 42,* 307–317.

Mann, J. (1973). *Time-limited psychotherapy.* Cambridge, MA: Harvard University Press.

Markus, H., & Kitayama, S. (1991). Culture and the self: Implications for cognition, emotion, and motivation. *Psychological Review, 98,* 224–253.

Martin, J., Martin, W., & Slemon, A. G. (1989). Cognitive–mediational models of action–act sequences in counseling. *Journal of Counseling Psychology, 36,* 8–16.

Marx, J. A., & Gelso, C. J. (1987). Termination of individual counseling in a university counseling center. *Journal of Counseling Psychology, 34,* 3–9.

Maslow, A. (1970). *Motivation and personality* (Rev. ed.). New York: Harper & Row.

Matarazzo, R. G., Phillips, J. S., Wiens, A. N., & Saslow, G. (1965). Learning the art of interviewing: A study of what beginning students do and their pattern of change. *Psychotherapy: Theory, Research, and Practice, 2,* 49–60.

Matsakis, A. (1998). *Managing client anger: What to do when a client is angry at you.* Oakland, CA: New Harbinger.

Matsumoto, D., Kudoh, T., Sherer, K., & Wallbott, H. (1988). Antecedents of and reactions to emotions in the United States and Japan. *Journal of Cross-Cultural Psychology, 19,* 267–286.

McGoldrick, M. (Ed.). (1998). *Re-visioning family therapy: Race, culture, and gender in clinical practice.* New York: Guilford Press.

McGoldrick, M. (2005). Irish families. In M. McGoldrick, J. Giordano, & N. Garcia-Preto (Eds.), *Ethnicity and family therapy* (3rd ed., pp. 595–615). New York: Guilford Press.

McGoldrick, M., Giordano, J., & Garcia-Preto, N. (Eds.). (2005a). *Ethnicity and family therapy* (3rd ed.). New York: Guilford Press.

McGoldrick, M., Giordano, J., & Garcia-Preto, N. (2005b). Overview: Ethnicity and family therapy. In M. McGoldrick, J. Giordano, & N. Garcia-Preto (Eds.), *Ethnicity and family therapy* (3rd ed., pp. 1–42). New York: Guilford Press.

McGoldrick, M., Giordano, J., & Pearce, J. K. (Eds.). (1996). *Ethnicity and family therapy*. New York: Guilford Press.

McGough, E. (1975). *Understanding body talk*. New York: Scholastic Book Service.

McWhirter, E. H. (1994). *Counseling for empowerment*. Alexandria, VA: American Counseling Association.

McWilliams, N. (2004). *Psychoanalytic psychotherapy: A practitioner's guide*. New York: Guilford Press.

Meador, B. D., & Rogers, C. R. (1973). Client-centered therapy. In R. Corsini (Ed.), *Current psychotherapies* (pp. 119–166). Itasca, IL: R. E. Peacock.

Meara, N. M., Schmidt, L. D., & Day, J. D. (1996). Principles and virtues: A foundation for ethical decisions, policies, and character. *The Counseling Psychologist, 24*, 4–77.

Medin, D. L., & Ross, B. H. (1992). *Cognitive psychology*. New York: Harcourt Brace Jovanovich.

Meichenbaum, D., & Turk, D. C. (1987). *Facilitating treatment adherence: A practitioner's handbook*. New York: Plenum.

Mendel, W. M. (1964). The phenomenon of interpretation. *American Journal of Psychoanalysis, 24*, 184–189.

Meyer, B., & Pilkonis, P. A. (2002). Attachment style. In J. C. Norcross (Ed.), *Psychotherapy relationships that work: Therapist contributions and responsiveness to patients* (pp. 367–382). Oxford, England: Oxford University Press.

Mickelson, D., & Stevic, R. (1971). Differential effects of facilitative and nonfacilitative behavioral counselors. *Journal of Counseling Psychology, 18*, 314–319.

Miller, J. B. (1976). *Toward a new psychology of women*. Boston: Beacon.

Miller, W. R., Benefield, R. G., & Tonigan, J. S. (1993). Enhancing motivation for change in problem drinking: A controlled comparison of two therapist styles. *Journal of Consulting and Clinical Psychology, 61*, 455–461.

Minuchin, S. (1974). *Families and family therapy*. Cambridge, MA: Harvard University Press.

Mitchell, S. A. (1993). *Hope and dread in psychoanalysis*. New York: Basic Books.

Montagu, A. (Ed.). (1971). *Touching: The significance of the human skin*. New York: Columbia University Press.

Muran, J. C. (Ed.). (2007). *Dialogues on difference: Studies of diversity in the therapeutic relationship*. Washington, DC: American Psychological Association.

Murray, I. (Ed.). (1989). *Oscar Wilde*. Oxford, England: Oxford University Press.

National Association for Social Workers. (1996). *NASW code of ethics.* Washington, DC: Author.

Natterson, J. M. (1993). Dreams: The gateway to consciousness. In G. Delaney (Ed.), *New directions in dream interpretation* (pp. 41–76). Albany: State University of New York Press.

Newman, C. R. (1997). Maintaining professionalism in the face of emotional abuse from clients. *Cognitive and Behavioral Practice, 4,* 1–29.

Nichols, M., & Schwartz, R. (1991). *Family therapy: Concepts and methods* (2nd ed.). Boston: Allyn & Bacon.

Nirenberg, G. I., & Calero, H. H. (1971). *How to read a person like a book.* New York: Hawthorn Books.

Nisbett, R. E., & Wilson, T. D. (1977). Telling more than we can know. *Psychological Review, 83,* 231–259.

Norman S. L. (1982). Nonverbal communication: Implications for and use by counselors. *American Journal of Individual Psychology, 38,* 353–359.

Nutt-Williams, E., & Hill, C. E. (1996). The relationship between therapist self-talk and counseling process variables for novice therapists. *Journal of Counseling Psychology, 43,* 170–177.

Olson, D. H., & Claiborn, C. D. (1990). Interpretation and arousal in the counseling process. *Journal of Counseling Psychology, 37,* 131–137.

O'Neil, J. M. (1981). Male sex-role conflicts, sexism, and masculinity: Psychological implications for men, women, and the counseling psychologist. *The Counseling Psychologist, 9,* 61–81.

Orlinsky, D. E., & Geller, J. D. (1993). Patients' representations of their therapists and therapy: New measures. In N. E. Miller, L. Luborsky, J. P. Barber, & J. P. Docherty (Eds.), *Psychodynamic treatment research: A handbook for psychodynamic research* (pp. 423–466). New York: Basic Books.

Orlinsky, D. E., & Ronnestad, M. H. (2005). *How psychotherapists develop: A study of therapeutic work and professional growth.* Washington, DC: American Psychological Association.

Ormont, L. R. (1984). The leader's role in dealing with aggression in groups. *International Journal of Group Psychotherapy, 34,* 553–572.

Patterson, G. R., & Forgatch, M. S. (1985). Therapist behavior as a determinant for client noncompliance: A paradox for the behavior modifier. *Journal of Consulting and Clinical Psychology, 53,* 846–851.

Patton, M. J., & Meara, N. M. (1992). *Psychoanalytic counseling.* New York: Wiley.

Paul, G. L. (1969). Outcome of systematic desensitization: II. Controlled investigations of individual treatment, technique variations, and current status. In C. M. Franks (Ed.), *Behavior therapy: Appraisal and status* (pp. 105–159). New York: McGraw-Hill.

Pedersen, P. B. (1991). Multiculturalism as a generic approach to counseling. *Journal of Counseling and Development, 70,* 6–12.

Pedersen, P. B. (1997). *Culture-centered counseling interventions: Striving for accuracy.* Thousand Oaks, CA: Sage.

Pedersen, P. B., Draguns, J. G., Lonner, W. J., & Trimble, J. E. (Eds.). (2002). *Counseling across cultures* (5th ed.). Thousand Oaks, CA: Sage.

Pedersen, P. B., & Ivey, A. (1993). *Culture-centered counseling and interviewing skills: A practical guide.* Westport, CT: Praeger.

Piper, W. E. (2008). Underutilization of short-term group therapy: Enigmatic or understandable? *Psychotherapy Research, 18,* 127–138.

Pipes, R., & Davenport, D. (1999). *Introduction to psychotherapy: Common clinical wisdom* (2nd ed.). Needham Heights, MA: Allyn & Bacon.

Plutchik, R., Conte, H. R., & Karasu, T. B. (1994). Critical incidents in psychotherapy. *American Journal of Psychotherapy, 48,* 75–84.

Ponterotto, J. G., Casas, J. M., Suzuki, L. A., & Alexander, C. M. (Eds.). (1995). *Handbook of multicultural counseling.* Thousand Oaks, CA: Sage.

Poortinga, Y. H. (1990). Toward a conceptualization of culture for psychology. *Cross-Cultural Psychology Bulletin, 24,* 2–10.

Pope, K. S. (1994). *Sexual involvement with therapists: Patient assessment, subsequent therapy, forensics.* Washington, DC: American Psychological Association.

Pope, K. S., Keith-Spiegel, P., & Tabachnick, B. (1986). Sexual attraction to clients: The human therapist and the (sometimes) inhuman training system. *American Psychologist, 41,* 147–158.

Pope, K. S., Sonne, J. L., & Holyroyd, J. (1993). *Sexual feelings in psychotherapy: Explorations for therapists and therapists-in-training.* Washington, DC: American Psychological Association.

Pope, K. S., & Tabachnick, B. (1993). Therapists' anger, hate, fear, and sexual feelings: National survey of therapists' responses, client characteristics, critical events, formal complaints, and training. *Professional Psychology: Research and Practice, 24,* 142–152.

Prochaska, J. O., DiClemente, C. C., & Norcross, J. C. (1992). In search of how people change: Applications to addictive behavior. *American Psychologist, 47,* 1102–1114.

Prochaska, J. O., Norcross, J. C., & DiClemente, C. C. (1994). *Changing for good.* New York: Guilford Press.

Prochaska, J. O., Norcross, J. C., & DiClemente, C. C. (2005). Stages of change: Prescriptive guidelines. In G. P. Koocher, J. C. Norcross, & S. S. Hill (Eds.), *Psychologists' desk reference* (2nd ed., pp. 226–231). New York: Oxford University Press.

Regan, A. M., & Hill, C. E. (1992). Investigation of what clients and counselors do not say in brief therapy. *Journal of Counseling Psychology, 39,* 168–174.

Reid, J. R., & Finesinger, J. E. (1952). The role of insight in psychotherapy. *American Journal of Psychiatry, 108,* 726–734.

Reik, T. (1935). *Surprise and the psychoanalyst.* London: Routledge.

Reik, T. (1948). *Listening with the third ear.* New York: Grove.

Rennie, D. L. (1994). Clients' deference in psychotherapy. *Journal of Counseling Psychology, 41,* 427–437.

Rhodes, R. H., Hill, C. E., Thompson, B. J., & Elliott, R. (1994). Client retrospective recall of resolved and unresolved misunderstanding events. *Journal of Counseling Psychology, 41,* 473–483.

Richardson, M. S. (1993). Work in people's lives: A location for counseling psychologists. *Journal of Counseling Psychology, 40,* 425–433.

Rimm, D. C., & Masters, J. C. (1979). *Behavior therapy: Techniques and empirical findings.* New York: Academic Press.

Robitschek, C. G., & McCarthy, P. R. (1991). Prevalence of counselor self-reference in the therapeutic dyad. *Journal of Counseling and Development, 69,* 218–221.

Rogers, C. R. (1942). *Counseling and psychotherapy.* Boston: Houghton Mifflin.

Rogers, C. R. (1951). *Client-centered therapy: Its current practice, implications, and theory.* Boston: Houghton Mifflin.

Rogers, C. R. (1957). The necessary and sufficient conditions of therapeutic personality change. *Journal of Consulting Psychology, 21,* 95–103.

Rogers, C. R. (1959). A theory of therapy, personality, and interpersonal relationships, as developed in the client-centered framework. In S. Koch (Ed.), *Psychology: A study of a science: Vol. 3. Formulations of the person and the social context* (pp. 184–256). New York: McGraw-Hill.

Rogers, C. R. (Ed.). (1967). *The therapeutic relationship and its impact: A study of psychotherapy with schizophrenics.* Madison: University of Wisconsin Press.

Rogers, C. R. (1980). *A way of being.* Boston: Houghton Mifflin.

Rogers, C. R., & Dymond, R. (1954). *Psychotherapy and personality change.* Chicago: University of Chicago Press.

Rose, A. J., Carlson, W., & Waller, E. M. (2007). Prospective associations of co-rumination with friendship and emotional adjustment: Considering the socio-emotional trade-offs of co-rumination. *Developmental Psychology, 43,* 1019–1031.

Rosenthal, R., Hall, J. A., DiMatteo, M. R., Rogers, P. L., & Archer, D. (1979). *Sensitivity to nonverbal communication: The PONS test.* Baltimore: Johns Hopkins University Press.

Rudd, M. D., Joiner, T. E., Jobes, D. A., & King, C. A. (1999). The outpatient treatment of suicidality: An integration of science and recognition of its limitations. *Professional Psychology: Research and Practice, 30,* 437–444.

Safran, J. D., & Muran, J. C. (2000). *Negotiating the therapeutic alliance: A relational treatment guide.* New York: Guilford Press.

Safran, J. D., Muran, J. C., Samstag, L. W., & Stevens, C. (2002). Repairing alliance ruptures. In J. C. Norcross (Ed.), *Psychotherapy relationships that work: Therapist contributions and responsiveness to patients* (pp. 235–254). Oxford, England: Oxford University Press.

Salerno, M., Farber, B. A., McCullough, L., Winston, A., & Trujillo, M. (1992). The effects of confrontation and clarification on patient affective and defensive responding. *Psychotherapy Research, 2,* 181–192.

Sarason, I. G., Sarason, B. R., & Pierce, G. R. (1990). Social support: The search for theory. *Journal of Social and Clinical Psychology, 9,* 133–147.

Satir, V. M. (1988). *The new peoplemaking.* Palo Alto, CA: Science and Behavior Books.

Savickas, M. L. (1994). Vocational psychology in the postmodern era: Comment on Richardson (1993). *Journal of Counseling Psychology, 41,* 105–107.

Scheel, M. J., Seaman, S., Roach, K., Mullin, T., & Mahoney, K. B. (1999). Client implementation of therapist recommendations predicted by client perception of fit, difficulty of implementation, and therapist influence. *Journal of Counseling Psychology, 46,* 308–316.

Segal, Z. V., Williams, J. M. G., & Teasdale, J. D. (2002). *Mindfulness-based cognitive therapy for depression.* New York: Guilford Press.

Segall, M. H. (1979). *Cross-cultural psychology.* Monterey, CA: Brooks-Cole.

Shakespeare, W. (1980). *Macbeth* [Play]. New York: Bantam. (Original work published 1603)

Shapiro, E. G. (1984). Help-seeking: Why people don't. *Research in the Sociology of Organizations, 3,* 213–236.

Sileo, R. J., & Kopala, M. (1993). An A-B-C-D-E worksheet for promoting beneficence when considering ethical values. *Counseling and Values, 37,* 89–95.

Simon, J. C. (1988). Criteria for therapist self-disclosure. *American Journal of Psychotherapy, 42,* 404–415.

Singer, E. (1970). *New concepts in psychotherapy.* New York: Basic Books.

Skinner, B. F. (1953). *Science and human behavior.* New York: Macmillan.

Skovholt, T. M., & Jennings, L. (2004). *Master therapists: Exploring expertise in therapy and counseling.* New York: Pearson/Allyn & Bacon.

Skovholt, T. M., & Rivers, D. A. (2003). *Skills and procedures of helping.* Denver, CO: Love.

Smith, E. W. L. (1998). A taxonomy and ethics of touch. In E. W. Smith, P. R. Clance, & S. Imes (Eds.), *Touch in psychotherapy: Theory, research, and practice* (pp. 36–51). New York: Guilford Press.

Smith, M. L., Glass, G. V., & Miller, T. J. (1980). *The benefits of psychotherapy.* Baltimore: Johns Hopkins University Press.

Snyder, J. F., Hill, C. E., & Derksen, T. P. (1972). Why some students do not use university counseling facilities. *Journal of Counseling Psychology, 19,* 263–368.

Sommers-Flanagan, R., & Sommers-Flanagan, J. (1999). *Clinical interviewing* (2nd ed.). New York: Wiley.

Spangler, P. T., & Hill, C. E. (in press). Therapist dreams about clients: A qualitative investigation. *Psychotherapy Research.*

Speisman, J. C. (1959). Depth of interpretation and verbal resistance in psychotherapy. *Journal of Consulting Psychology, 23,* 93–99.

Spence, D. P., Dahl, H., & Jones, E. E. (1993). Impact of interpretation on associative freedom. *Journal of Consulting and Clinical Psychology, 61,* 395–402.

Spokane, A. R. (1989). Are there psychological and mental health consequences of difficult career decisions? *Journal of Career Development, 16,* 19–23.

Stadter, M. (1996). *Object relations brief therapy: The therapeutic relationship in short-term work.* Northvale, NJ: Jason Aronson.

Stahl, J., & Hill, C. E. (2008). A comparison of four methods for assessing natural helpers. *Journal of Community Psychology, 64,* 289–298.

Stenzel, C. L., & Rupert, P. A. (2004). Psychologists' use of touch in individual psychotherapy. *Psychotherapy: Theory, Research, Practice, Training, 41,* 332–345.

Strong, S. R., & Claiborn, C. D. (1982). *Change through interaction: Social psychological processes of counseling and psychotherapy.* New York: Wiley.

Strupp, H. H., & Binder, J. L. (1984). *Psychotherapy in a new key: A guide to time-limited dynamic psychotherapy.* New York: Basic Books.

Strupp, H. H., & Hadley, S. W. (1977). A tripartite model of mental health and therapeutic outcomes: With special reference to negative effects in psychotherapy. *American Psychologist, 32,* 187–196.

Sue, D., Sue, D. W., & Sue, S. (1994). *Understanding abnormal behavior* (4th ed.). Princeton, NJ: Houghton Mifflin.

Sue, D. W., & Sue, D. (1999). *Counseling the culturally different: Theory and practice* (3rd ed.). New York: Wiley.

Suinn, R. M. (1988). Imagery rehearsal applications to performance enhancement. *Behavior Therapist, 8,* 155–159.

Sweeney, M. A., & Cottle, W. C. (1976). Nonverbal acuity: A comparison of counselors and noncounselors. *Journal of Counseling Psychology, 23,* 394–397.

Teyber, E. (2006). *Interpersonal process in psychotherapy: A relational approach* (5th ed.). Pacific Grove, CA: Brooks/Cole.

Tinsley, H. E. A., de St. Aubin, T. M., & Brown, M. T. (1982). College students' help-seeking preferences. *Journal of Counseling Psychology, 29,* 523–533.

Truax, C. B. (1966). Reinforcement and nonreinforcement in Rogerian psychotherapy. *Journal of Abnormal Psychology, 71,* 1–9.

Truax, C. B., & Carkhuff, R. R. (1967). *Toward effective counseling and psychotherapy.* Chicago: Aldine.

Van den Stock, J., Righart, R., & de Gelder, B. (2007). Body expressions influence recognition of emotions in the face and voice. *Emotion, 7,* 487–494.

van Wormer, L. (1996). Teaching/learning the language of therapy: Guidelines for teacher and student. *Issues in Social Work Education, 16,* 28–45.

Vivino, B., Thompson, B., Hill, C. E., & Ladany, N. (in press). Compassion in psychotherapy: The perspective of psychotherapists nominated as compassionate. *Psychotherapy Research.*

Wachtel, P. L. (2008). *Relational theory and the practice of psychotherapy.* New York: Guilford Press.

Wampold, B. E. (2001). *The great psychotherapy debate: Models, methods, and findings.* Mahwah, NJ: Erlbaum.

Wampold, B. E., Mondin, G. W., Moody, M., Stich, P., Benson, K., & Ann, H. (1997). A metaanalysis of outcome studies comparing bona fide psychotherapies: Empirically "all must have prizes." *Psychological Bulletin, 122,* 203–215.

Ward, D. E. (1984). Termination of individual counseling: Concepts and strategies. *Journal of Counseling and Development, 63,* 21–25.

Waters, D. B., & Lawrence, E. C. (1993). *Competence, courage, and change: An approach to family therapy.* New York: Norton.

Watson, D. L., & Tharp, R. G. (2006). *Self-directed behavior: Self-modification for personal adjustment* (9th ed.). Florence, KY: Cengage Learning.

Watzlawick, P., Weakland, J. H., & Fisch, R. (1974). *Change: Principles of problem formation and problem resolution.* New York: Norton.

Webster, D. W., & Fretz, B. R. (1978). Asian-American, Black and White college students' preference for help-giving sources. *Journal of Counseling Psychology, 25,* 124–130.

Weiss, J., Sampson, H., & the Mount Zion Psychotherapy Research Group. (1986). *The psychoanalytic process: Theory, clinical observations, and empirical research.* New York: Guilford Press.

Whiston, S. C. (2005). *Principles and applications of assessment in counseling.* Belmont CA: Thomson, Brooks/Cole.

Williams, E. N., Hurley, K., O'Brien, K., & DeGregorio, A. (2003). Development and validation of the Self-Awareness and Management Strategies (SAMS) Scales for therapists. *Psychotherapy, 40,* 278–288.

Williams, E. N., Judge, A., Hill, C. E., & Hoffman, M. A. (1997). Experiences of novice therapists in prepracticum: Trainees', clients', and supervisees' perceptions of therapists' personal reactions and management strategies. *Journal of Counseling Psychology, 44,* 390–399.

Wonnell, T. L., & Hill, C. E. (2002, June). *The action stage and predictors of action in dream interpretation.* Paper presented at the annual meeting of the Society for Psychotherapy Research, Santa Barbara, CA.

Yalom, I. D. (1980). *Existential psychotherapy.* New York: Basic Books.

Yalom, I. D. (1995). *Theory and practice of group psychotherapy* (4th ed.). New York: Basic Books.

Young, M. E. (2001). *Learning the art of helping: Building blocks and techniques.* Upper Saddle River, NJ: Prentice-Hall.

Zunker, V. G. (1994). *Career counseling: Applied concepts and life planning* (4th ed.). Pacific Grove, CA: Brooks/Cole.

Index

About the Author

Clara E. Hill, PhD, earned her doctorate at Southern Illinois University in 1974. She also began her career that year as an assistant professor in the Department of Psychology at the University of Maryland, College Park, and is still there as a professor and codirector of the Counseling Psychology Program. She has been the president of the Society for Psychotherapy Research and the North American Society for Psychotherapy Research; the editor of the *Journal of Counseling Psychology;* and the editor of *Psychotherapy Research,* the journal of the Society for Psychotherapy Research. She was awarded the Leona Tyler Award from the American Psychological Association's (APA's) Division 17 (Society of Counseling Psychology) and the Distinguished Psychologist Award from APA's Division 29 (Psychotherapy), the Distinguished Research Career Award from the Society for Psychotherapy Research, and the Outstanding Lifetime Achievement Award from the Section on Counseling and Psychotherapy Process and Outcome Research of the Society for Counseling Psychology. Her major research interests are helping skills, psychotherapy process and outcome, training therapists, dream work, and qualitative research. She has published 165 journal articles; 34 chapters in books; and 7 books, including *Therapist Techniques and Client Outcomes: Eight Cases of Brief Psychotherapy* (1989); *Working With Dreams in Psychotherapy* (1996); *Helping*

Skills: Facilitating Exploration, Insight, and Action (1st ed., with Karen M. O'Brien, 1999); *Helping Skills: The Empirical Foundation* (2001); *Dream Work in Therapy: Facilitating Exploration, Insight, and Action* (APA, 2004); *Helping Skills: Facilitating Exploration, Insight, and Action* (2nd ed., APA, 2004); and, with Louis G. Castonguay, *Insight in Psychotherapy* (APA, 2007).

Feedback Form

To the reader of this book:

I hope that *Helping Skills: Facilitating Exploration, Insight, and Action, 3rd Edition,* has been useful to you in learning the helping skills. I would like to hear your feedback so that we can improve future editions of the book. Please complete this sheet and send it to the American Psychological Association. Thank you for your help.

Name (optional): _____

School and address: _____

_____

Department: _____

Instructor's name: _____

Name of course for which this book was used: _____

_____

1. What did you like most about this book?

2. What did you like least about this book?

3. In the space below or on a separate sheet of paper, please write specific suggestions for improving this book and anything else that you would like to write about your experience using this book and trying to learn the helping skills.

4. What is the most important or surprising thing you learned about helping skills from reading this book?

Please return this form to APA Books, 750 First Street NE, Washington, DC 20002-4242.